EDITED BY LYNNE DAVIS

Alliances

Re/Envisioning Indigenous-Non-Indigenous Relationships

UNIVERSITY OF TORONTO PRESS
Toronto Buffalo London

© University of Toronto Press Incorporated 2010
Toronto Buffalo London
www.utppublishing.com
Printed in Canada
Reprinted 2010

ISBN 978-1-4426-4023-8 (cloth)
ISBN 978-1-4426-0997-6 (paper)

Library and Archives Canada Cataloguing in Publication

Alliances: re/envisioning Indigenous-non-Indigenous relationships/edited by
Lynne Davis

Includes bibliographical references and index.
ISBN 978-1-4426-4023-8 (bound).   ISBN 978-1-4426-0997-6 (pbk.)

1. Indigenous peoples.   2. Native peoples – Canada.   3. Indians of North
America.   4. Cooperation.   I. Davis, Lynne, 1951–

PE77.A55 2010   305.8   C2009-906663-7

University of Toronto Press acknowledges the financial assistance to its
publishing program of the Canada Council for the Arts and the Ontario
Arts Council.

 Canada Council   Conseil des Arts
for the Arts   du Canada
 ONTARIO ARTS COUNCIL
CONSEIL DES ARTS DE L'ONTARIO

University of Toronto Press acknowledges the financial support for its
publishing activities of the Government of Canada through the Book
Publishing Industry Development Program (BPIDP).

ALLIANCES
Re/Envisioning Indigenous-Non-Indigenous Relationships

Edited by Lynne Davis

When Indigenous and non-Indigenous activists work together, what are the ends that they seek, and how do they negotiate their relationships while pursuing social change? *Alliances* brings together Indigenous and non-Indigenous leaders, activsts, and scholars to share their experiences of alliance-building for Indigenous rights and self-determination and for social and environmental justice.

The contributors, both Indigenous and non-Indigenous, come from diverse backgrounds as community activists and academics. They write from the front lines of political and personal struggle, from spaces of reflection rooted in past experiences and from emerging theoretical perspectives, to shed light on contemporary meanings of alliance. Some contributors explore methods of mental decolonization while others use Indigenous concepts of respectful relationships to analyse present-day interactions. Most important, *Alliances* delves into the complex political and personal relationships inherent in both Indigenous and non-Indigenous struggles for social justice to provide insights into the tensions and possibilities of Indigenous-non-Indigenous alliance and coalition-building in the early twenty-first century.

LYNNE DAVIS is an associate professor in the Department of Indigenous Studies at Trent University.

This work is dedicated to the memory of Sam George, whose steadfast pursuit of justice after the killing of his brother, Dudley George, set a very high bar for all who strive for a world of justice and peace. May our work benefit future generations and all life.

Contents

Gchi Miigwech – Thank You!!

First, I acknowledge and offer thanks to the Mississaugas in whose territories I reside. Here on the shores of Pigeon Lake and on the Otonobee River at Trent University, this book has unfolded through their generous sharing of beautiful waters, rolling hills, forested landscapes, and valued friendships.

I am immensely grateful to the authors of this volume. They responded promptly to numerous editorial requests with unfailing good humour and diligent attention to detail. Their enthusiasm for this project and their messages of encouragement made the editing process a true honour. *Gchi miigwech* to them, to Anishnaabe scholar Leanne Simpson for writing the book's first words, and to Anishnaabe-kwe artist and scholar Renée Bedard for offering the photo of the twig bundle for its cover.

This collection would not have come about without a Standard Research Grant (410-2004-1404) from the Social Sciences and Humanities Research Council, which enabled the launch of the Alliances Project and the 2006 Re/Envisioning Relationships conference, from which many of the chapters in this volume derive. The conference was organized through the efforts of an extraordinary group of individuals, who combined vision and depth of experience in designing a gathering that could bring together the diversity of Indigenous/non-Indigenous leaders, activists, and scholars engaged in working together and thinking through the complexities of Indigenous/non-Indigenous relationships in the areas of Indigenous self-determination and social and environmental justice. The members of this organizing working group included Marilyn Buffalo McDonald, Victoria Freeman, Joan Kyek, Ann Pohl, Dan Smoke, Merran Smith, and Rick Wallace. An army of graduate and undergraduate students brought the conference to fruition under the superb leadership of Mara Heiber. Sincere thanks to Heather Sphuniarsky, Karyn

Drane, Frost Centre MA students, and wonderfully enthusiastic students in the Indigenous Studies 305 class of 2006–2007.

The seed for the Alliances Project was first planted when Trent colleagues Kiera Ladner, Leanne Simpson, and I received a small internal research grant from Trent University. After their departure from Trent, the project grew with the assistance of a number of doctoral research associates and assistants. Vivian O'Donnell and Heather Shpuniarsky provided significant contributions at the conceptual stage, and Heather continued with the project over a number of years. Karyn Drane helped with community research, and Adrian Edgar worked on transcription and analysis. Mara Heiber, Chantal Fiola, and Eliza Tru attentively assisted with the preparation of the manuscript over three years. Their efforts have been exemplary.

Colleagues in Indigenous Studies at Trent, including Joeann Argue, Marlene Brant Castellano, Mark Dockstator, Vern Douglas, Chris Furgal, Rosalie Jones, Dan Longboat, Edna Manitowabi, Don McCaskill, Neal McLeod, Marrie Mumford, David Newhouse, Brenda Maracle O'Toole, Barb Rivett, Paula Sherman, Skahendowaneh Swamp, Christine Welter, Doug Williams, and Shirley Williams, have offered an encouraging and inspiring environment in support of this work.

Virgil Duff at University of Toronto Press understood the vision that inspired this work from the outset, and encouraged its realization. Anne Laughlin of UTP and copy editor Patricia Thorvaldson offered excellent advice and infinite patience in polishing the text. I also acknowledge the contributions of several anonymous reviewers whose comments have helped to strengthen the collection as a whole.

This volume was born out of an immense collective effort that stretches through a number of decades. Mentors, teachers, colleagues, fellow activists, and friends, both Indigenous and non-Indigenous, have profoundly shaped the conceptual world that I have brought to the editing of this work. My first attempt to list all of your names, from the Atlantic to the Pacific to the Arctic, was simply overwhelming, so I can only say, simply, you know who you are and you have my profound gratitude.

I owe a great debt to my husband, Cameron Brown, and his family (Bev Brown, Pam Brown, Bess Brown, and Chuck Brown, and their partners), and to my own immediate family (Evelyn Moraff Davis, Harold Davis, Beverley Davis, Patrick Taylor, Shira Taylor, and David Taylor). They have supported me in all that I have undertaken.

And so, thank you seems hardly enough to extend to the many people whose efforts, directly and indirectly, are represented here. This volume is a modest offering for your teaching and friendship. To you all, *Gchi Miigwech – Nia:wen – Giáxsix̌a - Kinanâskomitiniwâw*!

First Words

LEANNE SIMPSON

Indigenous Peoples have been engaged in a movement for justice, freedom, and political change for over 500 years on Turtle Island. Our collective and individual acts of resistance have been expressed in our daily lives and in our lives together as communities, nations, and confederacies. Yet little has been written about our political traditions of dissent and mobilization, our individual and collective acts of resistance, and the strategies we have used in creating and maintaining the longest running social movement in Canadian history. Little has been written about how large, international coalitions have supported our community-based stances, or how we have nurtured relationships of solidarity with our friends and allies.

Those of us involved in the movement for Indigenous self-determination and social and environmental justice are well aware that every hard-fought victory has been a direct result of the alliances and relationships of solidarity we have forged, maintained, and nurtured with supporting Indigenous nations, environmental networks, and social justice organizations. From Haida Gwaii, to Eeyou Istchee, from Grassy Narrows to Burnt Church, from Caledonia to Ardoch Algonquin First Nation, and from Kitchenuhmaykoosib Inninuwug to the Lubicon, to name just a recent few, we have sought out supporters in Canadian society to assist us in our work. These church groups, environmental networks, and social justice organizations have stood alongside us as allies and as friends, often juggling a variety of roles and responsibilities, always under very challenging circumstances.

Building relationships with our supporters has been a key strategy in our movement for change. But these relationships do not always come easily. Too often they have been wrought with cross-cultural misunderstandings, poor communication, stereotypes, and racism. Too often, we have forged these relationships without taking the proper time to clearly discuss our different roles and responsibilities. Too often, tensions and misunderstanding plague even the very best of intentions.

And herein lies the very importance of this book. It is most critical for Indigenous Peoples and our allies to discuss good relationships in terms of alliances and solidarity in times of relative peace, when we all have time to retreat, re-evaluate, challenge, reflect, and envision. When we have the space to consider how to interact with each other in a respectful, responsible way – in a way that promotes the kind of justice we are seeking on a grander scale, one that honours the very best of our traditions.

My Nishinaabeg Elders tell me that good relationships are the foundation of *mno bimaadiziwin*, the good life. They are the foundation of creating healthy relationships within our families, communities, and nations. They are the foundation of creating just relations with other Indigenous nations, nation states, and with the natural world that sustains us.

My Nishinaabeg Elders also tell me that creating good relations takes commitment, patience, and perseverance. This book is an important part of that journey. It is part of our collective responsibility to consider how we interact with our allies, how we build movements of solidarity, and how we maintain strong alliances and coalitions that are impermeable to colonialism's mantra of divide and conquer. It is our collective responsibility to share and consider each other's stories, and in doing so, to pick up our perspective ends of the Friendship Wampum and forge a new journey based on peace, justice, respect, and righteousness.

Introduction

LYNNE DAVIS

The July skies were threatening rain as we drove north up the Vancouver Island highway to Port Hardy to take a flight to Bella Bella on the central coast of British Columbia. We had made an early morning rush to catch the ferry from Vancouver to Nanaimo, after an inauspicious start. In loading up the car in Vancouver, I had locked the car keys in the trunk. Blessed is the faithful British Columbia Automobile Association for its quick house call, as light was barely dawning.

First Nations from up and down the West Coast were due to gather at Bella Bella the next morning. The 1993 'Qátuwas Festival promised to be an historic event that would bring together coastal First Nations' ocean-going canoes, which had almost disappeared from the West Coast for nearly a century.[1] For several years, First Nations communities had been preparing for this gathering: relearning to carve the great canoes from those who still remembered the traditional skills; training intensely to paddle these large vessels; planning a route to Bella Bella with appropriate support vessels and supplies; learning meticulously the songs and protocols that define respectful relationships with other First Nations into whose territories they would enter. The stage was set for an extraordinary historical moment.

In Port Hardy, we organized our luggage strategically for air travel knowing that the small plane would have limited space for excess baggage. Nevertheless, we were loaded down with flats of strawberries and raspberries, which are traditionally traded with my husband's family in Bella Bella for fish. Ensuring that the berries arrive in pristine condition is one of the enduring concerns of our annual summer travel. But this day was not to be in any way routine. As we checked in at the air counter, we were advised that the flight was overbooked and that some members of our party would be unable to travel until a later flight. As we glanced around the airport, we realized that we were being bumped to accommodate a more illustrious traveller, the renowned environmentalist David Suzuki. The next day, we would hear him deliver an inspiring speech at the opening ceremonies of 'Qátuwas. But, for now, we could only fret about the berries sitting on an airport cart on the tarmac in the rain.

This single encounter was the genesis of several years of observing the growing number of partnerships and alliances between First Nations and environmental groups on the West Coast. Environmental organizations were funding local community projects, and new partnerships and alliances were being formed with First Nations. These emerging relationships were intriguing to me as a non-Indigenous researcher and activist, and led to a pilot project to determine whether research into the nature of these relationships would be a fruitful area of inquiry.[2] Based on a number of initial interviews with First Nations leaders and environmentalists, a full research project was developed to explore contemporary relationships between Aboriginal peoples and social movements more generally, particularly alliances and coalitions.

The motivation for this research was one of trying to understand in minute detail how non-Indigenous people, who define their work in the social and environmental justice fields, can work in solidarity with Indigenous peoples without replicating the continuing colonial relations that characterize the broader frame of Indigenous/non-Indigenous relationships in Canada today. Is it even possible to imagine relationships of mutual respect while looking squarely at the bald truth of Indigenous trauma and dispossession that flowed from colonization historically, and is perpetuated in ongoing colonial processes of violence in the present day? Is 'respect' enough? What are the ethical responsibilities of non-Indigenous people collectively and individually in supporting the self-determination of Indigenous peoples? Can relationships be re/envisioned, based on a shared future on Indigenous lands and embracing the self-determination of Indigenous peoples?

These questions run along well-worn trails that others have tread through centuries of Indigenous/non-Indigenous relationships. Historically and today, individuals and Canadian society have tried to make sense of Indigenous/non-Indigenous relationships, all in terms reflective of the ontological, epistemological, and ideological framings of their times (Haig-Brown and Nock, 2006). Indigenous paradigms of relationship such as the Gus-wen-tah (also Kas-wen-tah), or Two Row Wampum,[3] and practices of kinship have been used to communicate how respectful relationships between Indigenous and settler society should operate. Indigenous paradigms of relationship are less known to Western scholars than their own Western theories and ideologies. Theories of colonization, postcolonialism, decolonization, anti-colonization, and a host of other social, cultural, spatial, economic, and political theories have been used to frame, justify, influence, and challenge state policies, and to guide analysis and plan strategic action.

At the time, the 1990 confrontation at Kanasatake (Oka) appeared to be a watershed in Aboriginal/non-Aboriginal relations in Canada. Television images of Mohawk people at Kanasatake protecting sacred burial grounds from being turned into a golf course, and the reactive use of force by the Québec police and Canadian military to repress their resistance, galvanized the Canadian public. The Royal Commission on Aboriginal Peoples (RCAP) was established soon afterwards by federal politicians from all political parties, to thoroughly review the relationship between Canadians and Aboriginal peoples in Canada. The Commission's final report (1996), which distilled 60,000 pages of testimony and countless specialist reports, concluded that Indigenous/non-Indigenous relations would only change by making a bold break with the past to ensure a relationship built on a foundation of recognition, respect, sharing, and responsibility. Governments, not prone to embrace fundamental change without a groundswell of electoral support, promptly ignored the most far-reaching impulses of this recommendation.

Contemporaneously with the RCAP report, and since its publication, Indigenous and non-Indigenous scholars have continued to critically consider how relationships can be transformed. Indigenous theorists such as Taiaiake Alfred (1999; 2005), Dale Turner (2006), Kiera Ladner (2007), and Leanne Simpson (2008) represent a generation of Indigenous academics who are seriously analysing the options for Indigenous survival and resurgence in the twenty-first century. Leading non-Indigenous scholars such as Alain Cairns (2000), Will Kymlicka (1995), and James Tully (1999) have also been theorizing Indigenous/non-Indigenous relationship possibilities within the Canadian state. Cree scholar Willie Ermine (2005, 2007) has initiated a very promising direction of theoretical exploration through the concept of 'ethical space,' which articulates the possibilities of potential relationship that lie at the confluence of two disparate ontological and epistemological worlds. While Ermine first elaborated his theory in the realm on research relationships, it has profound implications for any relationship context between Indigenous and non-Indigenous peoples.

Historically and today, Indigenous communities and organizations engage in many relationships with non-Indigenous parties, including governments, industries, and non-governmental organizations. These may form under coercive conditions because conflicting or overlapping interests make some form of co-operation or consultation unavoidable, or they may arise because there are mutual benefits in working together. Sometimes, relationships are a mixture of both. There has been considerable writing on Indigenous/non-Indigenous relationships in general, as well as numerous historical analyses (e.g., Miller, 2000) and a number of guides on forming partnerships between Indigenous communities and the corporate sector (Hill and Sloan, 1995; Joseph and Joseph, 2007; Government of Ontario, 2001). One of the under-explored areas of research remains relationships between Indigenous peoples and social movement organizations such as social justice groups, the women's movement, environmental organizations, and organized labour.

The Alliances Project, a research project funded by the Social Sciences and Humanities Research Council, was initiated as one stream of research activity to fill this gap. The purpose is to examine contemporary relationships of alliance and coalition that had formed and to understand the micro-dynamics of power relationships between Indigenous peoples and the social movement organizations and actors. As Indigenous, critical, and post-colonial theorists such as Smith (1999), Foucault (1980), and Said (1979) have incisively demonstrated, power relations saturate not only the broad stories that societies formulate about themselves and Others, but also constitute the DNA of day-to-day interactions. By examining a number of social and environmental justice case studies, and by conducting interviews with Indigenous and non-Indigenous activists and leaders who have long experience in engaging in relationships together, it has been possible to distil some important understandings of the way these relationships function (Davis, O'Donnell, and Shpuniarsky, 2007).

The literature in this area is small but beginning to grow. In her seminal book, *Becoming an Ally* (2002), Anne Bishop uses an anti-racism, anti-oppression analysis to provide practical advice on alliance-building. Activist Kevin Thomas (2002) has written about his experiences in organizing the Friends of the Lubicon, and David Long (2000) has analysed the same organization from a theoretical perspective. Fishing disputes have spawned some scholarship (Grossman, 2001a, b; 2002; Koening, 2005) related to local tensions and alliances. There is also an emerging literature related to environmental relationships with First

Nations (e.g., Bobiwash, 2003; Cheechoo, in Simpson, 2008), and, particularly, Clayoquot Sound (e.g., Magnusson and Shaw, 2003; Braun, 2002) and the Great Bear Rainforest (e.g., Rossiter, 2004; Smith, Sterritt, and Armstrong, n.d).

One of the important dimensions of understanding alliances and coalitions as observed in the Alliances research is that individuals and organizations may interact from very different concepts of relationship which embody varying power configurations. These are not necessarily articulated or made explicit and can have an important impact on forming and maintaining relationships. Sometimes alliances are understood as partners walking side-by-side; indeed, Gus-wen-tah, or the Two Row Wampum, describes such a relationship, the symbolic ship of settler society and the canoe of Indigenous society each following its own path, with its own laws, customs, and culture, neither interfering in the business of the other. In this kind of relationship, Indigenous and non-Indigenous partners may come together around a specific agenda to accomplish a particular set of goals over a period of time. Or, as Wallace, Struthers, and Bauman (Chapter 7, this volume) suggest, the partners may have different roles to play or tasks to fulfill, depending upon the circumstances, creating clear divisions of responsibilities.

A second type of relationship is one of paternalism, the long legacy of colonization. In paternalistic relationships, non-Indigenous 'partners' may adopt a position of superiority by assuming they know what is best for Indigenous people; unfortunately, these attitudes may be communicated in subtle, conditioned behaviours and words, often unknowingly. A third stance is one where Indigenous partners provide the leadership, and non-Indigenous people take action in support of the direction that Indigenous people have determined. This is a model that is often found where the assertion of Indigenous self-determination is critical to the Indigenous peoples involved. There can be considerable debate about how Indigenous/non-Indigenous alliances should be structured. Even when the parties aim to work through leadership and decision-making issues, paternalism can creep in, resulting in acrimonious relationship tensions. In practice, relationships may have elements of all three types and may transmute in the process. From the beginning, then, defining the nature of the alliance is a first step in negotiating the power relations that will ensue. Case study research has been helpful in identifying some of the dynamic tensions of relationship (Davis, O'Donnell, and Shpuniarsky, 2007; Davis, 2009; Davis and Shpuniarsky, Chapter 20, this volume).

The Re/Envisioning Relationships Conference

In addition to the exploration of relationships through case study research, an important mandate of the Alliances Project was to bring together various parties who have been engaged in Indigenous/non-Indigenous alliances and coalitions. The Re/Envisioning Relationships Conference was convened at Trent University, Peterborough, Ontario, in early November 2006. A national steering committee of very experienced Indigenous and non-Indigenous leaders and activists created a vision for the conference, guided its planning, and facilitated its processes. Marilyn Buffalo McDonald (Cree, former president of the Native Women's Association of Canada), Victoria Freeman (University of Toronto historian), Dan Smoke (Seneca, broadcaster and activist in London, Ontario), Joan Kuyek (national coordinator, Mining Watch Canada), Rick Wallace (doctoral student in peace studies at Bradford University), Merran Smith (forest campaigner, Forest Ethics), and Ann Pohl (founder of the Turtle Island Support Group) deserve medals of honour for planning this event with so much attention to the quality of learning and exchange among participants.

Trent University was an appropriate setting for such a gathering. The first president of Trent University, Tom Symons, actively supported the establishment of Canada's first Indigenous Studies program at Trent in the university's earliest years. Those who attended the Re/Envisioning Relationships Conference represented people and organizations across the spectrum of alliance-building activities that are going on throughout Canada. Keynote speakers included Mohawk Elder Jake Swamp, who emphasized the importance of bringing about an age of global peace for all life on this planet; Native Women Association of Canada's then-president Bev Jacobs, who spoke about missing or murdered Aboriginal women whose disappearances have not been properly investigated; community leader Judy Da Silva, who talked about the ongoing blockade at Grassy Narrows; and the late Sam George, who related his arduous journey to justice after the killing of his brother, Dudley George, at Ipperwash Provincial Park on 6 September 1995. There were representatives from church and human rights organizations (e.g., Mennonite Central Committee, Quakers, KAIROS, Amnesty International, Rights and Democracy) who shared their work and experiences in standing in solidarity with Indigenous peoples. Representatives from Treaty 3 and the city of Kenora in northwestern Ontario talked about their own imaginative work to create 'Common

Ground' as a basis for transforming antagonistic local relationships to ones based on common history and identity formation.

At the conference, we also heard about the work of Indigenous and non-Indigenous individuals of conscience who have initiated projects that have led to ongoing relationships between Indigenous and non-Indigenous peoples. Some of these relationships are institutionally based, as between a university or research institute and Indigenous communities or community organizations. Others operate on the sheer energy and commitment of the parties involved, with minimal financial or institutional resources. Some conference participants discussed how they have taken on the task of trying to uncover and analyse both the macro- and micro-dynamics of relationship, and their own path of struggle in understanding the complex interplay of Indigenous/non-Indigenous relationships in Canada and in their own lives. They shared richly of their triumphs, but also their missteps, difficulties, and failures. Some of the papers presented at the conference, together with other solicited papers, have been brought together in this volume.

Multiplicity of Sites and Discourses

What we learned from the conference, and what we can understand from this collection, is that many Indigenous and non-Indigenous peoples are concerned about issues of alliances, coalitions, and partnerships. They work from different sites, including Indigenous communities, organizations, governments, businesses, the academy, social justice organizations, and environmental groups. They have their own theories and languages for talking about these relationships. For example, when I asked one West Coast First Nations leader about 'alliances and coalitions' with environmentalists, he responded that he doesn't use those words. He said that his Nation has 'partnerships' with environmentalists, as well as partnerships with government and industry, pointedly not making any special distinctions among outside parties. Similarly, authors in this volume speak from their own action or theoretical grounding. Academic-based activists and theorists in this volume come from Indigenous/Native Studies, peace studies, political science, environmental studies, resource management, sociology, education, and law. They come from concrete struggles where language is fluid and is continually being defined and contested.

This diversity has led to the presentation of this collection in four parts, each with its own introduction. Part 1, 'Visionaries,' points out possibilities of alliance-building when conceived within Indigenous ontological and epistemological understandings of relationship that pre-date the colonial presence in the Americas. Part 2, 'From the Front Lines,' documents concrete examples of alliance-building, with many experiences of the successes, tensions, and complexities that arise in efforts of collaboration. Part 3, 'Linking Theory and Practice,' draws upon theoretical understandings from different disciplines while linking to practice in different alliance-building contexts. Part 4, 'The Personal Is Political,' looks at relationship-building at a personal level, where people try to make sense of their positionality at the confluence of social identities and action.

There are many points of connectivity and interrelationship among the four parts. For example, Keefer (Chapter 6), Wallace, Struthers, and Bauman (Chapter 7), and Struthers (Chapter 22) all discuss how non-Indigenous people can become the target of abuse for supporting Indigenous rights when conflict erupts in small communities. Throughout the book, authors struggle not only with large questions of societal dynamics, but also with finely grained questions of positionality and identity.

Haig-Brown and Nock, in their edited book *With Good Intentions* (2006), reach back into the history of colonial society to examine the actions of specific individuals who broke with the prevailing views of their day to challenge how colonial Canada was unjustly and dishonourably oppressive in its relations with Indigenous peoples. The editors offer cautions that despite good intentions, non-Indigenous people still carry the markings of their society: '[This book] tries never to lose sight of the fact that those acknowledged herein are fully implicated in the process of colonization despite their sensitivities. While the book concentrates on non-Aboriginal people working with First Nations peoples of this land, often in resistance to injustices, it also gestures to our current situation of continued participation in a vast web of colonial relations' (2).

This vast web of colonial relations continues to come into play in the works of the authors in this volume. That is why it is useful to undertake analysis that looks at both Indigenous and non-Indigenous perspectives and experiences; macro- and micro-analysis of relationships; the global and the local; the social and the personal. Acts of colonizing and decolonizing relationships inhabit the interstices of social interaction and find expression at all these levels. The authors in this volume provide a rich, layered discussion of how multiple forces converge in

Indigenous and non-Indigenous relationships. There are lessons to be learned at all levels: in planning strategic action to promote social justice; in developing and nurturing relationships based on mutual respect; and in reflecting critically with a face turned towards the truths of injustice, complicities, and contradictions at the level of individual actors and Canadian society as a whole.

Picking Up Our Responsibilities

The cover of this book, designed from a photo by Anishnaabe-kwe artist Renée Bedard, was inspired by the following words: 'A single twig breaks, but the bundle of twigs is strong ...' This well-known phrase has been attributed to Shawnee leader Tecumseh, who exhorted Indigenous Nations to join together to protect their homelands from the occupation of white colonizers. The spirit of this message of unity echoes powerfully through this collection's theme: alliances.

Although we can conclude that the challenges of alliance-building defy simple solutions, the authors of 'Visionaries' point us towards Indigenous understandings of relationship that are rooted in basic values of thanksgiving, honesty, friendship, and justice. Other authors indicate that there are principles and signposts of possibility. While the complexities and 'messiness' of relationship-building in a colonial context may deter some, Mohawk Elder Jake Swamp (Chapter 1) reminds us that there is so much more at stake than individual desire to engage with others:

> We are many people in this world who are coming together, forming all kinds of different groups: peace groups, environmental groups, all kinds of groups. The only thing missing are those who are going to organize it so that it would become a great force, a force that will be able to change our world as it is run now. For the commodities and the resources are going to be running out very shortly. And so we the people have to get together to solve these problems. We have to look institutions in the face.

Jake Swamp's message is directed towards both Indigenous and non-Indigenous peoples in an urgent appeal for all to pick up our responsibilities as human beings for the sake of survival of all life. To effect change, he suggests, there is need for strong, united, respectful leadership if the just world of our imaginations is to become a reality. The starting point is to re/envision relationships in the present. The sites of

10 Lynne Davis

confronting institutions and staging actions are multiple, as the authors in this book indicate. Jake Swamp challenges everyone to find ways of working in solidarity, bringing to bear all that has been learned through the insights of theory, practice, and reflection. If there is a sense of yearning that threads its way through this work, it is the desire to see longstanding injustices resolved and a mutual, respectful future realized, whatever the complexities of getting there.

NOTES

1 The 'Qátuwas Festival was documented by filmmaker Barbara Cramner (1997) in *'Qátuwas: People Gathering Together*.
2 In its earliest stage, this research was initiated with Anishnaabe scholar Leanne Simpson and Cree scholar Kiera Ladner. Both were faculty members at Trent University in 2000, and we applied for an internal grant from the Social Sciences and Humanities Research Council to undertake a literature review and some preliminary investigative research. After they left Trent, I continued with this project and applied for a SSHRC Standard Grant.
3 Final Report of the Royal Commission on Aboriginal People (1996), vol.1 , chap. 5, p. 103. See also Paula Sherman's discussion of wampum in Chapter 8, this volume. Please note that the spelling Kas-Wen-Tah is also used.

REFERENCES

Alfred, Taiaiake. 1999. *Peace, Power, and Righteousness: An Indigenous Manifesto*. Don Mills, ON: Oxford University Press.
– 2005. *Wasáse*. Peterborough, ON: Broadview Publishing.
Bishop, Anne. 2002. *Becoming an Ally: Breaking the Cycle of Oppression*. 2d ed. Halifax: Fernwood Publishing.
Bobiwash, Rodney. 2003. 'Native People and Environmental Crusaders: Racism, Re-Colonization and Do-Gooders.' *Aboriginal Rights Resource Tool Kit*. Ottawa: Canadian Labour Congress.
Braun, Bruce. 2002. *The Intemperate Rainforest: Nature, Culture and Power on Canada's West Coast*. Minneapolis: University of Minnesota Press.
Cairns, Alan. *Citizens Plus: Aboriginal Peoples and the Canadian State*. Vancouver: University of British Columbia Press, 2000.
Cramner, Barbara. Prod., Dir. 1997. *'Qátuwas: People Gathering Together*. National Film Board of Canada.

Davis, Lynne. 2009. 'The High Stakes of Protecting Indigenous Homelands: Coastal First Nations' Turning Point Initiative and Environmental Groups on the B.C. West Coast.' *International Journal of Canadian Studies*, 39: 137–59.

Davis, Lynne, O'Donnell, Vivian, and Shpuniarsky, Heather. 2007. 'Aboriginal-Social Justice Alliances: Understanding the Landscape of Relationships through the Coalition for a Public Inquiry into Ipperwash.' *International Journal of Canadian Studies*, 36 (fall): 95–119.

Ermine, Willie. 2005. 'Ethical Space: Transforming Relations.' Discussion paper. Government of Canada. Canadian Heritage. National Gatherings on Indigenous Knowledge. Wanuskewin, SK, 25–7 May.

– 2007. 'The Ethical Space of Engagement.' *Indigenous Law Journal*, 6(1): 193–203.

Foucault, Michel. 1980. *Power/Knowledge: Selected Interviews and Other Writings 1972–1977*. New York: Pantheon Books.

Government of Ontario. 2001. *The Power of Partnerships: New Opportunities for Aboriginal Peoples and Ontario Businesses*. Toronto: Queen's Printer for Ontario.

Grossman, Zoltán. 2001a.'"Place Membership" in Ethnic Conflict Management: The Case of Native American and White Framers/Ranchers.' Talk at annual meeting of the Association of American Geographers (AAG), New York.

– 2001b. 'Let's Not Create Evilness for This River: Interethnic Environmental Alliances of Native Americans and Rural Whites in Northern Wisconsin.' In *Forging Radical Alliances across Difference: Coalition Politics for the New Millennium*. J. Bystydzienski and S. Schacht. Eds. London: Rowman and Littlefield.

– 2002. 'Effects of White Racial Advantages in Environmental Alliances.' http://www.uwec.edu/grossmzc/zoltangrossmanaag2002.doc.

Haig-Brown, Celia, and Nock, David A. Eds. 2006. *Good Intentions: Euro-Canadian and Aboriginal Relations in Colonial Canada*. Vancouver: University of British Columbia Press.

Hill, Roger, and Sloan, Patricia. 1995. *Corporate Aboriginal Relations: Best Practice Case Studies*. Toronto: Hill Sloan Associates.

Joseph, R., and Joseph, C. 2007. *Working Effectively with Aboriginal Peoples*. 2d ed. North Vancouver, BC: Indigenous Corporate Training.

Koening, Edwin C. 2005. *Cultures and Ecologies: A Native Fishing Conflict on the Saugeen-Bruce Peninsula*. Toronto: University of Toronto Press.

Kymlicka, Will. 1995. *Multicultural Citizenship: A Liberal Theory of Minority Rights*. New York: Oxford University Press.

Ladner, Kiera. 2008. '*Aysaka paykinit*: Contesting the Rope around the Nations' Neck.' In *Group Politics and Social Movements in Canada*. M. Smith. Ed. Peterborough, ON: Broadview Press.

Long, David Alan. 2000. 'The Precarious Pursuit of Justice: Counter-Hegemony in the Lubicon First Nations Coalition.' In *Organizing Dissent: Contemporary Social Movements in Theory and Practice,* 2d ed. William K. Carroll. Ed. Toronto: Garamond Press.

Magnusson, Warren, and Shaw, Karena. Eds. 2003. *A Political Space: Reading the Global through Clayoquot Sound.* Montreal and Kingston: McGill-Queen's University Press.

Miller, J.R. 2000. *Skyscrapers Hide the Heavens: A History of Indian-White Relations in Canada.* Toronto: University of Toronto Press.

Rossiter, David. 2004. 'The Nature of Protest: Constructing the Spaces of the Great Bear Rainforest.' *Cultural Geographies,* 11(2): 139-64.

Royal Commission on Aboriginal Peoples. 1996. *Final Report.* Ottawa: Government of Canada Communications Group.

Said, Edward. 1979. *Orientalism.* New York: Vintage Press.

Simpson, Leanne. Ed. 2008. *Lighting the Eighth Fire: The Liberation, Resurgence, and Protection of Indigenous Nations.* Winnipeg, MB: Arbeiter Ring Publishers.

Smith, Linda Tuhiwai. 1999. *Decolonizing Methodologies: Research and Indigenous Peoples.* New York: Zed Books.

Smith, Merran, Sterrit, Art, and Armstrong, Patrick. n.d. 'From Conflict to Collaboration: The Story of the Great Bear Rainforest.' http://www.forestethics.org/downloads/WWFpaper.pdf.

Thomas, Kevin. 2002. 'Friends of the Lubicon: How a Small Group of People Can Change the World.' http://www.turning-point.ca/?q=node/99.

Tully, James. 1999. 'Aboriginal Peoples: Negotiating Reconciliation.' In *Canadian Politics,* 3d ed., 413–41. J. Bickerton and A.G. Gagnon. Eds. Peterborough: Broadview Press.

Turner, Dale. 2006. *This Is Not a Peace Pipe: Towards a Critical Indigenous Philosophy.* Toronto: University of Toronto Press.

PART 1

Visionaries

As we begin the journey of 're/envisioning relationships,' we are reminded that models and principles of respectful coexistence were already well established in the Americas when the European visitors arrived, and that these understandings guided the earliest interactions with the newcomers. Such models and principles are grounded in the ontologies and epistemologies of the peoples of Turtle Island. The three authors in this section give concrete examples of how Indigenous principles and values can form the foundation of Indigenous/non-Indigenous relations today.

'Visionaries' is about transcendence and responsibility. The authors speak from a place of Indigenous vision, reconciliation, and possibility. Each presents an understanding of relationship that rises above the many indignities that Indigenous peoples experience on a daily basis. Instead, they push towards a vision of what it means to be human in Creation, in a world where respect for human and non-human diversity prevails first and foremost. Each in his own way – Mohawk Elder Jake Swamp, Hotinonshon:ni architect Bill Woodworth, and Wampanoag activist gkisedtanamoogk – expresses a future of peace to which human society can aspire, where the dignity of all life is respected. Jake Swamp speaks to the responsibilities that flow out of the Haudenosaunee Thanksgiving Address, to organize among diverse groups and peoples to stand for Mother Earth and the dignity of all life. Bill Woodworth explains his ambitious project, 'Beacon to the Ancestors,' to restore harmony between the Indigenous hosts and newcomers in Toronto, based on the Hotinonshon:ni Condolence Ceremony. gkisedtanamoogk talks about the educational and reconciliation work underway in the Maritimes to engage communities and citizens (and not just governments) to commit to the mutual responsibilities of the Peace and Friendship Treaties with the Mi'kmaq, Maliseet, and Passamaquoddy peoples – treaties that pre-date the founding of Canada.

In all three chapters, which are strongly grounded in Indigenous oral traditions, there has been an attempt to preserve the orality of the narrative as it is transformed into written text, a well-recognized tension in Indigenous and language studies. Bill Woodworth and gkisedtan-amoogk use upper- and lower-case type and bold type, breaking the rules of written English, to insert the oral into the written text. Spelling is also a site of negotiation, particularly when oral languages are being standardized in Roman orthographies. Examples are the use of 'Haudenosaunee' in the chapter by Jake Swamp, and Hotinonshon:ni (following the practice of the late Cayuga Chief Jake Thomas) in the chapter by Bill Woodworth.

In their visions of positive possibilities, the authors collectively point to the failure of imagination in Euro-Canadian society to move beyond its colonial past. In these writings, we are offered models and principles of relationship that embody peace and respect. The contribution of the 'visionaries' is to shift the ground of imagination and to consider what such relationships would look like if built upon the worldviews that grow in the very soil of Turtle Island.

1 *Kanikonriio*: 'Power of a Good Mind'

JAKE SWAMP

Jake Swamp (Tekaronianeken), a keynote speaker at the Re/Envisioning Relationships Conference, is a Mohawk Elder from Akwesasne, and a former sub-chief of the Wolf Clan of the Haudenosaunee (Iroquois) Confederacy. He has devoted his life to fighting for the rights of Haudenosaunee people and Indigenous peoples throughout the world. Jake has been recognized internationally as a peace and environmental activist. He was involved in the 1968 International Seaway Bridge Blockade, the reclamation of the Mohawk lands in the Adirondack Mountains, and he attended the 4th Russell Tribunal in Rotterdam, The Netherlands, 28 November 1980. He is a past director of the Akwesasne Freedom School, a culture-based Mohawk language immersion school. In the mid 1980s he started the Tree of Peace Society, which promotes cultural preservation, peace and peace studies, and environmental education. Jake has been working to plant trees in just about every part of the world. His work has inspired the planting of over 200 million trees. Jake is a cultural authority, teacher, author, and ceremonialist. He and his wife, Elder Judy Swamp, reside in Akwesasne. Jake Swamp opened his presentation with the Haudenosaunee 'Thanksgiving Address' in the Mohawk language. He began his talk by explaining his opening words and their significance.

At this time I would like to give you a brief translation of the words that I have spoken. And, as I have explained before, that's our relationship to our birthright, our environment, and everything that's on our planet. And we the people are the ones that have been given the responsibility to be caretakers of the earth, because we are the ones who have the ability to do so and to change things around. And that is why we have to make this expression of thanksgiving. Because that is what teaches us, the people, how to be in life, that human relationships differ. I started this talk by collecting our minds together as if we became one people.

And we gave expressions of thanksgiving to one another for arriving safely, as a human family, to be with one another. And for that we are thankful. And I kept saying, 'So be it our minds, when our minds are brought together in that way.' This causes us to travel throughout our world. In other words, we go directly to our Mother Earth and realize the importance of where all life forms are coming from, and she is still performing her original duty and instruction. So we give her thanks.

We also have many beautiful gifts of life. We mention the grasses that grow in this world when we see the greenery of the grass. It gives us hope that everything still lives. And so we say thank you to all the grasses that grow in this world.

We also give thanks to all the waters of this world and all the living things in it. The fish, the insects, everything that contributes to the wellness of that water. And for that we are thankful.

We are thankful to all the foods that come from the ground that nourishes us each and every day. We are thankful to all the berries and the fruits. We are thankful to the medicinal herbs that have been planted on this planet so that we can depend upon them at various times, when sickness comes to visit us.

We are very thankful to all the animals that have been put here on earth. They, too, have been given special responsibilities to give forth life. And in our world the deer is the one who is leader of all the animals. And so with the collectiveness in our minds, we collect all the animals of the world and we say thank you to them for what they do.

We give thanksgiving also to the forest and trees which grow in our world. And we can take a lesson from those trees. There are so many types of trees and they are able to work together, never complaining about who they are and what they do. They just do what they are supposed to do. And so collecting all the trees in our hearts and minds, and also the maple tree, which is the leader in our area, we give them thanks.

We give thanks to the birds who sing above our heads, singing their beautiful songs to take loneliness away from us, especially their leader, the eagle. So we send them our thanksgiving for giving us those beautiful songs that we hear every day.

We give thanks to the four winds who come to us to comfort our minds and renew the air that we breathe. We give thanks to the thunder beings. Sometimes we hear them coming, rumbling across the sky; we know they are to deliver refreshment to the waters of the world, and also to withhold all the monstrous beings that were assigned beneath the surface of the earth. They are the ones who are the caretakers. And so we thank them for that and what they do.

We give thanks to the sun, our oldest brother. He is our example for the steadiness in fulfilling our responsibility. He is like a protector giving his light and his warmth. And so we men imitate the sun, our oldest brother. And we say thank you to the sun, our oldest brother.

And now we give a special thanksgiving and greeting to the moon, whom we see at night-time. She is the one that directs all life, and she is the one that measures the time when new life will come into this world. She is the one that works with the earth, the movement of the water, and works with our female people to bring new life into this world. So we send a special thanksgiving and greeting to our oldest grandmother, the moon.

And now we direct our thoughts of thanksgiving to the stars in the universe. Our ancestors knew many things about the stars. They could make new predictions. They did many things related to how the stars were scattered around the sky. But today, because of the interference that we went through as a cultural people, we have lost a lot of that knowledge. But today we look up into the sky and we marvel at the beauty that we see in the sky, and this sends a message to our minds and our hearts that we must continue to give them thanks for what they do. And so today, this morning, we have done that.

We give a special thanksgiving and greeting to the four protectors that were assigned over the human family – that they are there to protect us from evil and our destructive things, and we rely upon them each and every day of our lives. Sometimes we ignore them when they come into our minds and they say, 'Don't go any further, there's danger ahead.' We say thank you to the four sacred protectors that have been assigned by the Great Spirit to watch over us.

And we have arrived at a special place. Somewhere beyond the heavens lives a Great Spirit. And that spirit's face has been hidden from our view. In other words, no one has ever seen it. We are told that a piece of that spirit is inside every living thing, including us, including the trees and the grass. A piece of that spirit is inside of all living things. And so we say thank you to the Great Spirit of us all. And also we ask the spirit to give us ideas to our challenges in life that we may find solutions to benefit our future children and grandchildren to come. So we send a special thanksgiving and greeting for that to happen.

That was roughly the translation of what I spoke for our gathering today.

Sometimes I get emotional when I look back at all the activities that I've been involved with over the years. And normally I don't go back through them too often. But when it's mentioned again, I realize I've been in touch with many, many, things in my life. I could almost call myself a very nosy person. But what happens is that when we live our lives, wherever we may be, I think it's important that we try to work together as a human family, especially because of what we face. And if you listen to the news lately, there are lots of things that are coming to the forefront that need our attention, and that's part of our relationship-building, to bring cooperation between all cultures of the world.

At the same time, we can't forget that we have a lot of work to do in mending some fences. We have to have a real good understanding of where we're at and where we came from in order to formulate a new future in the people. There are many people in the world that I meet that feel guilty about what their ancestors did. And I also see people who have experienced the atrocities which have been committed against them over time in history. And I always believe that we need to go back to re-visit what happened back then and to investigate the attitudes and reasons that it happened, to get an understanding. And then, from there, we can rebuild something that's global. Global respect. Because we cannot survive by isolating ourselves in different parts of the world. Because we, the people, all possess gifts that were given originally from the Creator. We are all each special people with special gifts, and these gifts are meant to come together by sharing thoughts and ideas. And, sometimes, this is what causes our lives to become free again.

To give an example, I was in Holland at The Hague recently. I was invited to plant a tree of peace at a school in The Hague, and when people found out that I was coming there, at the same time there was another conference going on. The conference was on behalf of the un-represented peoples' organizations of the world. I realized then how many different nations there are who are not represented as being part of the nations that we know. In other words, the UN only recognizes certain peoples to be nations. And so I felt real good to be with these peoples who were not represented, because we had a commonality. We had a commonality in struggle and also in survival.

I learned that, today, there are people running here and there to survive in the mountains of Vietnam. And coming together with these people gave me a new hope, because everyone is trying to survive somehow in their own local regions. So the importance of people learning about one another is why we are here today. Because especially in learning institutions, people have the opportunity for their minds to expand and to have that gift to be able to bridge love and respect between two peoples. And that is the kind of people who are needed today in our world.

When I spoke at the peoples' organization, the unrepresented ones, the first thing that came to mind was in 1980 when we visited Holland and attended the 4th Russell Tribunal, and at that time I myself and my family were behind barricades. We were surrounded by the police force. And we were indicted and we were facing 25 years. And so our people protected us from being arrested. And I remember, it was like yesterday, that the helicopters would come over and say, 'Get your women and children out; we're coming in after you.' And I remember the women getting together and saying, 'No way, we're not going to come out.' And so for almost a year and a half we were in that kind of situation. I was able to cross the St Lawrence River into Canada and fly to Rotterdam as a delegate to the 4th Russell Tribunal. And attending the tribunal gave us the opportunity to link up with other countries of the world. We had Mario Cappana, who was a member of the European Parliament, and he came to Akwesasne and he understood our situation. And he made it known in Europe that we did need help. And we were very grateful for that. So in our world there are people who really understand what needs to be done. And that's why we need all this information.

When I started working as a counsellor with the men, our men who are so angry and so abusive towards their families, I realized there must be a history of why our men behave this way. And the history lesson I gave myself was to first look at myself, where I came from, and what kinds of feelings I had when I was young. I remember that I was a very angry person when I was young. And so protesting against injustice became a part of my family's life at that time. I had to overcome my own anger, not knowing where it had come from. But years later, now I understand. That hate had come from our older history where our people were massacred. A lot of genocide was practised. And the stories that we heard from our families caused us to become angry and to live in that way. And so most of our people, not knowing where it's coming from, experience that pain, so they will find the brown bottle. And that seems to take the pain away momentarily. But it stays there. And so, to work for peace, people have to overcome their own prejudices, their own anger, and recognize that we are individual human beings, and that deep inside of us there's a thing called love and under-standing. And so we have to learn how to tap into that again. It was not permitted before. So everything has a history. Working with men, that's where I found out where it was coming from.

In medieval Europe, there was a law that said if a woman spoke back against her husband, he had the right, by law, to take a brick and smash her mouth. Now when I learned about that, I applied it to what's hap-pening with our people in our culture. We are taught that the most im-portant thing in our lives is the women. It is because it's they who bring forth new life, the new babies, and why should we, the men, be abusive of that. And then time continues and I learned that in the fifteenth cen-tury, there were laws passed by the Christian Church called the Papal Bulls of 1452 and 1493.[1] The world view of the Christians was that they had to take over the whole world and all its peoples. And what that law said was that if they ever came across a land inhabited by what they called non-Christians, they would not be recognized as humans. And they made a law to have the right to take over lands. They would look at it as empty lands. And so you can imagine what went on across South America and North America.

That kind of doctrine, the 'Doctrine of Discovery,' is what they still use today in the court system. And so it is up to the people and the churches to revisit where their belief system came from and to straight-en that out. It was the leadership who were in charge who formed these ideas about how to subjugate and take over lots of land and peoples. Millions of our people were destroyed in the process. And so we have to learn as a people and as a culture what made it happen. And when we go back to it, we will say it's not going to happen anymore because we are not going to permit it to happen anymore. Then, as people, we can accept each other the way we are supposed to be.

Just like our thanksgiving prayer, which talks about the relationship between ourselves and nature. For we are not better than a blade of grass or a leaf on a tree. We are all life forms. If nature goes down, we go down with it, because we are only one part of that life form. But we have been given the responsibility at the beginning of the world to be grateful for what we have, and for the earth. We have the understand-ing and we have the attitude, but it's hard to practise the way we live today. We cannot go to the river to drink from it anymore; therefore, our relationship with the river is now changed. Our relationship to every-thing in the world is now changed. And we have to teach our children to invent new ways of looking at life.

We have to blend that in with our thoughts of survival. Because all the prophecies that were given to our people are now upon us. And I'm one, when I hear prophecy, I do not take it as a time when we should give up. Because people will say, 'Oh, it's going to happen anyway, so why worry about it?' But I do worry about it because I have grandchildren. And I know they're going to have the same feeling that I have, for that's what we are teaching them.

And so we are going to keep trying to plant trees and to train our children to be inventive with something to bring healing to the world. The teaching of when you arrive at the water's edge, do not ever dip for your water unless you have determined which direction that water flows. And so that is a great teaching, but the elders who taught us would not give us the answer. Well, why would you do that? If you dip against the current your cup is going to fill up right away. But it was an environmental teaching that is in everything we do, in everything we invent; it must go with the force of nature in its cycle. And we will never get into trouble if we do that. But when we look back on our record, how many times have the people dipped against the current? And that current of nature is so strong, we cannot hold it back. Eventually it will come back upon us, as we've seen recently. We cannot hold back nature forever.

And there are many things that we must investigate in order to rebuild a new life for our future children, our future global world. And it involves so much forgiveness; it involves so much humanity. And the hardest thing to overcome is the prejudice that we have. I was told by an elder one time, and I believe this to be true, that there is a prophecy that people rarely speak about. He said all the people started together in one place in this world. And he said that we are of different colours and that we started together. But at that time, already we couldn't get along. And so the Creator decided to send the people to different parts of the world to live and to learn. The day would come when all of the people would come back together to share their experiences. Then they would put these experiences together inside a great bundle, and then it will be tied.

Another important event is the founding of the Confederacy by the Peacemaker.[2] He reasoned that it would be very important to have a visible symbol that would serve as a reminder of the peace they established. He chose the white pine tree because of its great height, as it would be noticeable from far distances. He told the people that the needles tied together in bunches of five would represent the five united nations into one body, one heart, and one mind. Then he said the greenery of the tree stays green all year-round; therefore, it will be representative of the peace being continuous. Then he said, 'Now we shall uproot this tree from the earth and into the depths of the earth; we will cast all weapons of war and feelings of hatred, greed, and jealousy.' Then they replanted the tree on top of the weapons.

When all the weapons were buried beneath the Tree of Peace and the Five Nations of that time decided not to have war between each other anymore, the Peacemaker told those first leaders to stand in a circle around this tree that they had planted. And then he gave them a prediction. He said, 'There is a time coming in the future, and as leaders you must remain strong. In fact, you should hold hands together, lock your arms together. For when that time comes, this tree is going to fall, it will land on your joined hands, and it will rest there for a long time. For people will come from some directions, and will see the roots of peace, which are extended from this tree, that go into the four directions. When they see this root, they are going to take offence to it and they're going to take sharp objects and they are going to start chopping at this root. And that's what is going to happen; the tree is going to weaken. It will start to fall and it will land on your joined hands. It will rest there for a long time. You will be burdened with its weight, its heaviness, for a long period of time. And just about when you cannot hold on any longer and you are about to let it go, that's when the children will be born. And when they look in your direction, they are going to say, "Look how burdened they are; let's go help them." And many of them are going to come running. And they are going to get under that tree and put their shoulders against it. And they are going to raise it up again.' And the Peacemaker told them that it would rise again, that tree, but it would be for the last time.

We are many people in this world who are coming together, forming all kinds of different groups: peace groups, environmental groups, all kinds of groups. The only thing missing are those who are going to organize it so that it would become a great force, a force that will be able to change our world as it is run now. For the commodities and the resources are going to be running out very shortly. And so we the people have to get together to solve these problems. We have to look institutions in the face. What are their intentions geared towards? Are they geared towards more extraction of our natural resources with no regard for future generations? Or will we take a step back and look at the whole picture and take the teachings which have been given – the teachings of sharing.

In our life, there are many people who are suffering, wanting of food. Sometimes you see pictures, especially on a Sunday. They show pictures of people starving, and when I eat my lunch or dinner I feel really guilty. How could we send part of our food to those places? And there are small efforts. There are groups who really care. They go around collecting cans and canned stuff and everything and they send it over there. There has got to be another way. And that's the challenge for our young people who have the bright minds: how to bring a new formula to our world so that we can have a new and renewed hope for the future. Because that is our responsibility. When you come to know about these problems, I guarantee that you are never going to sleep again. I sat in the traditional council for 37 years. And they don't work 8 to 5; it's a 24-hour job, every day. There's no monetary payment. But where that payment comes from is when you see development for the next generation of people. I see that it's not that we're giving up everything; it's just that we are coming closer to learning about our home, the earth, and really what it's supposed to be. That's what we are looking for.

The Peacemaker brought three principles of peace. The first principle is that peace comes inside of us as an individual. And if we accept that peace within us, then we become a human being that loves themselves, and is confident about themselves. That's the first principle, to maintain the peace within. The second principle arrives when the peace is put to work, and how that peace emits from the human individual, and how it will affect the other people around them. Because that's what happens when you come next to a peaceful person. It kind of rubs off on you. And you will say to yourself, 'Gee, I want to be that way, too.'

So the Peacemaker had a very brilliant way of doing it. There were five warring nations that were murdering one another, and in the end they were able to come together and accept the three principles. And that's how they obtained the power of a good mind, which is the third principle. And the power of a good mind was experienced this morning when we did the opening and we said, 'Let us put our minds together,' and we created a great power. That special spirit came among us to give us the strength to carry on our day and whatever we are going to be accomplishing today, that whatever comes to us will be beneficial to our future generations. So the more work we do today, the more beneficial it will be to our young people in the future.

And I'm very proud of the young people, because now they have open minds. When I was young and was just starting out I went to a university one time, and was talking about Mother Earth. 'What are you talking about Mother Earth for now? That doesn't make sense. Why don't you get yourself an education and live the way we do?' But I don't mean it that way. We have to pay attention to the Earth. Well, it was hard, but years later it became a household word: 'Mother Earth.' Everyone's talking about it: 'Seven Generations.' We hear those things. You read the United Nations documents, and we're in there, if you read between the lines. So that's how slow the movement is, real slow, but that's the way I like it. Because it's so slow that nobody notices the change. Thank you.

NOTES

1 The Papal Bulls, the concept of 'terra nullius,' and the 'Doctrine of Discovery' were instrumental in shaping Christian approaches to Indigenous peoples and their lands globally, particularly the assertion of European sovereignty over Indigenous territories and the conversion of Indigenous peoples by missionaries. Readers might consult James (Sa'ke'j) Youngblood Henderson, *The Mi'kmaw Concordat*, Halifax: Fernwood Publishing, 1997; Robert J. Miller, *Native America, Discovered and Conquered*, Westport, CT: Praeger, 2006; and Paula Sherman (Chapter 8, this volume).
2 The founding of the Confederacy and the Great Law of Peace have been described in a number of publications. Readers who want more detail might consult Paul Wallace, *The White Roots of Peace*, reprint, Saranac Lake, NY: Chauncy Press, 1986; and North American Indian Travelling College, *Traditional Teachings*, Cornwall Island, ON: NAITC, 1984.

2 Iroquoian Condolence Practised on a Civic Scale

WILLIAM WOODWORTH *RAWENO:KWAS*

The Hotinonshon:ni[1] prophecy of the gathering of peoples from the four directions under the great White Pine Tree of Peace appears to be coming to fruition. The time has come for Indigenous peoples to share their ancient responsibilities to welcome and host visitors to their homelands.

The theme of an envisioned First Nations Grove within Toronto's proposed Lake Ontario Park represents the empowerment of Indigenous peoples through the rekindling of their ancient duties to greet, address, and give comfort to people who are found wandering on their lands – namely the overwhelming number of immigrants who have and are now visiting their lives on this place over the past several hundred years. Many of these people have either forgotten or have never understood the nature of the land which they now call home, and the ways of the First Nations who have been their hosts. Drawing on the wisdom and values of traditional Indigenous knowledge, the focus of this effort is reconciliation and healing among peoples, with the ancestors, and with the created world itself.

Condolence

A central concept in Hotinonshon:ni culture is the custom of 'condolence' – physical and spiritual comfort offered by members of one clan to another, because of loss which has left them dispirited. The origins of the Iroquoian practices of condolence go back to the teachings and practices of the great spiritual messenger, the Peacemaker, the Wendat-Huron Deganawedah.[2] When he began assuming his vision to integrate the five nations which would become the great Iroquoian Confederacy

(Mohawk, Oneida, Onondaga, Cayuga, and Seneca), the Peacemaker found our territories deeply in social trauma. While the men practised forms of warrior-based cannibalism, the women bore and raised their children in the safe retreat of the isolated places and crevices of the land. Deganawedah with the assistance of Hiawatha undertook a healing journey which evolved a psycho-spiritual democratic structure.

A fundamental understanding of these practices is that a good life (peace, power, righteousness) can only take place among the 'clear minded.' This is a fact which is continually recognized in the practice of condolence even today at Six Nations of the Grand River Territory – the modern sanctuary of Hotinonshon:ni traditional knowledge and practices.

In the stories told in the Great Law of Peace, Deganawedah seeks companionship and assistance in his work. He chooses a man who would become the first chief of a new confederacy of nations: Hiawatha. Unconvinced of the Peacemaker's efficacy, and unwilling to leave his family for a cultural duty, Hiawatha refuses. In the intervening time he loses his wife and his three daughters, each in separate incidents. Following each time of loss the Peacemaker renews his request, and each time Hiawatha declines. The Peacemaker finds him wandering aimlessly in the bush, disheartened and distraught. In his compassion he gives Hiawatha comfort and healing in his grief in what was to become the first condolence ceremony – the precursor of modern practices. The wampum shell beads of the condolence strings – 15 distinctive lines of white and purple – guide the order and words of the ceremony used when a member of the community passes into the sky world.

The condolence evolved in several forms out of the needs of the people, including a condensed form of the 'three bare words' of the 'At the Woods Edge' greeting offered to strangers found wandering in our territories. In this simplest of condolences, a small group of 'brothers' is dispatched to meet those found wandering 'on the path.' They approach strangers crying to demonstrate their compassion. They build a fire directly in the trail. There they begin burning tobacco while they carry out a condolence. First they wipe away the tears with a soft doeskin, so that they may look about the place in peace and with clarity. Next, they are assumed to have obstructions in their ears, so they are cleaned that they may more easily listen to the good words spoken. Finally, they are offered fresh spring water to clear the obstructions of their throats so that words of mutual greeting can be spoken freely. Only after the acceptance and participation in this ceremony are the 'strangers' offered a place in the village, where they can eat of the food and sleep in the longhouse if they find these things and practices agreeable. Finally, the fire is extinguished, and they are escorted, if willing, into their adopted 'home.'

The sweet compassion of this respectful, comforting, and consoling ceremony of welcome struck me in a form of 'vision' as a deep and meaningful response to the ennui and disconnection of immigrants to our homeland – past, present, and future. These practices might also recover and reconstruct our traditional identities as Indigenous peoples hosting those wanting to adopt our homeland as their own. In this reconstructed and renewed relationship we might all correct and model a way to address the destructive patterns of colonization which have contaminated relationships among peoples all over the planet over the past several hundred years.

Receiving a 'Vision'

In the crisp clear air of the northern hemisphere as the winter solstice approaches this Turtle Island, I wander in the dreams of the ancestors all around me, supported and informed under their revolving sky field. I live now on the northern shore of Lake Ontario (*kaniatari:io*: beautiful waters which carry a good message), at a place named Toronto (*dolon:do*: the place of the damp fallen torso of a great tree), in the province of Ontario (*kaniatari:io*: place of the beautiful water), in the political nation/state Canada (*kana:da*: a gathering place of the people – a great village) – names anglicized from the Hotinonshon:ni speaking of my ancestors. I am in a good place. In my doctoral work in the Traditional Knowledge Program at the California Institute of Integral Studies in San Francisco, I experienced a localized, knowledge-conveying encounter at Toronto. A very powerful series of earth/sky architectonic conjunctions, deeply rooted in the Indigenous way of being/knowing, began to show themselves to me, starting at the autumn equinox, 20 September 1997.

Urban Toronto is settled on the traditional lands of the Wendat-Huron, the Neutral, and Seneca-Iroquois peoples, succeeded by the southerly migration of the Anishnaabek-Mississaugas, who reside near us today at Six Nations of the Grand River. In their gentle, ephemeral movement patterns, and sometimes conflicted encounters with the Mohawk, they shared the land base on which this modern city is founded. During the course of a mutually beneficial fur trading coexistence with the French, this site remained largely untouched by Eurocentric development even though it was at the confluence of several rivers, notably the Don, the Humber, the Rouge, and the Credit. The site is adjacent to a spacious natural harbour refuge formed by an island spit still providing a natural healing haven and vantage point in a place of mediation with the lake. These benevolent conditions are replicated in many other places along the shores of Lake Ontario, but none are as conspicuous to the Indigenous and Western minds as Toronto. Consequently, first the French, and later the British, began aggressive land claims on this site starting in the early seventeenth century, inspired by its location as a defensible outpost of trade and conquest.[3]

Pre-Roman Anglo-Saxon culture was firmly anchored in the earth, sky, and ancestry-based indigenous roots of the Celtic and Druid traditions. The migrators out of these civilizations were ancestrally nurtured in the relative isolation of the North Atlantic islands off the European continent. Great Britain's own historic struggles with Roman and Gallic colonizations bear a microcosmic analogy to the Eurocentric visitation and appropriation of the Indigenous lands and cultures of Turtle Island. The sympathetic diplomatic and romantic relationships among the Hotinonshon:ni and the British peoples have continually attested to the synergy between their distinct cultural and spiritual ancestries.

This meeting of two cultures and their subsequent consolidation informs the modern urban settlement we experience today at Toronto. The contemporary city has an urban culture which demonstrates and conveys a subtle respect and sensitivity to the land and sky fields showing in the benevolent diversity and democratic protocols which are maintained in vital practice throughout all of the civic endeavours in this place. As a settlement, it thrives as a uniquely vital example of North American clarified urbanity.

This premise is very important to the validity of the synchronous knowledge alignments which I observed here in the fall of 1997. The regularity of my daily walk brought me to an auspicious observation site where I witnessed some powerful conjunctions of the built skyline of the city and Our Brother the Sun, which triggered insight and a vision among *all our relations*[4] here.

Following the trauma of mass desolation which characterized the twentieth century, the subsequent rise of widespread intolerance for injustice and a general yearning for individual respect have found a particularly robust refuge in Toronto. I want to suggest that this special consciousness is expressed in seven recent architectural constructions which are gathered in the built core of the city and now stand aloft of the Earth's surface in a form of communication with the sky.

Since 1969, four potent banking archi-skylons have been erected near the intersection of King and Bay Streets. Their altitudes and the significant colours of their claddings betray a beautiful confirmation of the relationship among the four races and the resonance of the six directions of Aboriginal cosmology:

1 In the west (place of the ancestors and the black race), Mies van der Rohe's Toronto-Dominion Centre of 1969 is a noble addressing of twentieth-century suffering and loss;
2 In the north (place of wisdom and the white race), Edward Durell Stone designed the tallest of these buildings for the Bank of Montreal, and chose white marble for its primary surfaces;
3 In the south (place of trust and the yellow race), the Royal Bank rises in a double tier in intricately folded planes of glass tinted with actual gold, rendering the crystalline facades yellow in the moving sun; and, finally,
4 In the east (the place of return of the 'coming faces' and the red race), the Bank of Nova Scotia, surmounted by an inverted triangular pictogram cast into its peak, is faced in indigenous Quebec red granite.

More recently Skidmore, Owings, and Merrill designed the Brookfield Place, linked by the woodland longhouse evocation – a great white steel ceremonial concourse by the Spanish architect Santiago Calatrava – to join the forces of gender paired towers. The taller of these rises as a great phallic lingam attenuated in a beacon light, bathed in the white ether condensate generated in the building's cleansing cycles. The feminine addressing is an adjacent broad-hipped tower terminating in a double pinnacle. The *men* and the *women* thereby occupy their traditional places on either side of this great east-west longhouse. These towers surround a fifth element the Canadian Imperial Bank of Commerce tower, by I.M. Pei, which personifies the silver covenant chain of agreement, exchanged for the Two Row Wampum, between the Iroquois-Hotinonshon:ni and their allies, the British, who founded the modern city as an outpost of empire.

The sixth element in this spontaneously sacred heptad is nearer the water and to the west: the tallest free-standing construction on the planet until 2007, the CN Tower, erected in 1976 as a great sending and receiving device, an ancestral beckoning shamanic staff rising an aspiring 553.33 metres. Its pinnacle is poignant within the limits of its diaphanous reach. At its base is the great circular Rogers Centre, a great mothering lodge with a retractable roof opening to the star fields over the gathered peoples.

Each of these seven architectures reaches deeply into the Mother Earth, raised in shrill elicitation to the sky and gazing outward into the spirits of the four directions evoking the ancestors of the four great races: red, yellow, black, and white. This urban assembly, which is the Toronto skyline, has been unconsciously streaming ancestral memory, inherent in the Indigenous understanding of the time, form, and space of its first inhabitants. This profound remembrance is being nurtured in the enclave of the Toronto urban community, manifested and conveyed in a prophetic architectonic distillation!

In the fall of 1997 I observed the conjunction of the sky field and the assembly of these elements along the horizon. I began a long habit of visiting a natural viewing place at the western tip of the peninsular parkland which protrudes into Ashbridge's Bay on the city's east side. First, I would visit a place on the southern shore to leave tobacco and offer thanksgiving to the Creator. Sometimes I would look back from these shores of my Hotinonshon:ni ancestors at the dense and spiky architectural assemblage of the core district and think to myself, 'Look what they did!' knowing that this is what 'they' (referring to the non-Indigenous migration) want, and wondering what it now says about this civilization so wilfully imposed on Turtle Island. Was it simply 'their' will? I yearned for something good.

Our ancestors taught us to share with visitors and in the spirit of the Two Row Wampum, showing that our distinct cultures each travel in separate but equal ways. However, we are now linked in the shared waters of their paths. I stand there at the fulcrum of the two ways – I carry, equally, Mohawk and British ancestry – wondering now where I stand.[5] So I go regularly to this earth-sky-water-wind place to commune with the spirits for reassurance and guidance.

A response came to me one afternoon just before sunset on 14 October 1997. As I watched the sun falling into dusk, the glowing sphere came to rest for a moment exactly at the tip of the CN Tower. And then, in succession, its continuing path came onto the phallic tip and finally precisely over the peaks of the double-breasted tower. This ancestral, masculine and feminine conjunction confirmed for me the experience of the ritual prediction, ceremony, and feasting which accompany sky events and architectonic resonances in Indigenous cultures all over the world.

As I stand alone and apart on the shores of my Hotinonshon:ni ancestors, they have been giving me information in the language which I can understand as the architect that I am, to expect the return to balance among *all our relations* – healing everything caught almost helplessly in the dissociated trauma we humans have invented as the modern, Western life way. This is what I can share with you now. In the native language of my Mohawk Ancestors, I was taught: *Tekwanonweraton akionkwetaokoha tsinikaien sewatonhehtstonh tanonsewaianehson ohnahoten skwanatoni. Akewkon nohoten nisewaiere naionkwario? Tonhake.*[6] (We are extending our greetings to be compassionate to our people who have gone on before us, those who are our leaders, and for what they have shown us. The way that you led your lives shows us how we should lead our lives.)

An Indigenous Auto-History of Toronto, Ontario, Canada

In order for Indigenous peoples to participate with any authentic self-respect in the modern cultural conversation, without abandoning our own ways of knowing and history, all people will require a renewed vision of our place in the world. We need now to look back on our shared histories, Native and non-Native, and re-contextualize them in terms which will help Indigenous peoples to recover our cultural intimacy and mutual self-respect in the modern world.

The 'history' of Eurocentric settlements like Toronto has been defined in the short period of colonization; in the case of Toronto, post-1791, when Upper Canada became a distinct province under the British Crown. Indeed, Toronto is an urban development sprung from the minds, hopes, and dreams of principally British settlers. Yet in the brief time of 200 years, it has become a destination of comfort, opportunity, and refuge to people from all over the world, from the 'four directions' referenced by our ancestors. The initial respect and wonder with which these two worlds met in the seventeenth century dissolved into forms of fear-driven colonization where suppression and assimilation, reconditioning and indoctrination drove most Indigenous people away from their own cultures.

The Hotinonshon:ni life way is based in matrilineal extended clan families, spiritual practices in the psycho-spiritual realm of deep, shared relationship with the natural world in a kind of benevolent participation in the environmental 'nest' given to us by the Creator, constantly invoked and appreciated in their ceremonies of Thanksgiving. These ways were nurtured over a long time, resulting in the founding of the Iroquois Confederacy. The contemporary Toronto land base is part of the extensive migratory routes of Indigenous peoples, and was over time shared as a hunting, fishing, and agricultural ground, principally by Hotinonshon:ni people, Wendat-Huron, Neutral, Seneca, Cayuga, and later the Anishnaabek.

The wisdom and values of traditional indigenous knowledge are again being appreciated and invoked from the depths of the sacred and protective silence and seclusion which have conserved it for this time. Now the older story of this place can be told, because the people are ready to listen, and we remember our ways. The psycho-spiritual-cultural event and exhibition series envisioned for the First Nations Grove will examine the setting and settlement of Toronto from the enlarged being/knowing space/time of the Indigenous Hotinonshon:ni and Anishnaabek peoples.

Several premises underlie the credibility of this Indigenous re-contextualization of the urban place:

The first assumption is that *all things revolve in great cycles of return.* The circle is the obvious order of our own planet, the seasons, and the solar system of which it is an integral part, and indeed the rise and fall of civilizations, cities, and individual lives. This is what is seen as 'progress,' when only a small part of this cycle, vector-like, is perceived and lived. Deep memory (the past) is actually what is called creative imagination (the future).

The second assumption is that *the Ancestors, those who came before us and who come after us, look over the people* in all their activities, guiding, informing, and inspiring in their compassionate, equanimous ways, unseen and unheard by aggressive forces but nonetheless touched and directed. Everything is living; everything has meaning; everything makes sense – nothing is accidental or without meaning.

A third assumption is that in these ancestrally protected realms, *spirits of place* are defined as those who embrace the knowing held in the earth, winds, and sky, and who trans-generationally inhabit the land. The physical substance of these 'relations' is, in actuality, returned to the earth (Our Mother, the Earth) – the veritable substance of the soil, clay, and rock of the ground we cultivate and excavate to sustain and accommodate the 'development' of our communities. There is much ancestrally inspired cultural, political, architectural, and planning evidence in Toronto which has been informed by these Indigenous realities:

1 The *location of Toronto* on the shores of waters held sacred by the Hotinonshon:ni ancestors *Kaniadari:io*, Lake Ontario, addresses directly a field of view, a space of release, and a realm of shifting connection, uncontaminated by recent development – the open waters themselves.
2 This 'city/state' has become a literal *compassionate refuge* for a conversation among all the races of the Earth, the 'meeting place' foretold in its naming in the ancestral way. For a short time it was called York, but an ancestrally compelled initiative recovered the name in the Hotinonshon:ni – *Toron:to.*
3 The *city-state politics* parallel the teachings of The Great Law, and the adoption of those seeking a better home is a reflection of the direct instruction of the Peacemaker.
4 The principle *archi-skylons* of the modern city replicate and are informed by an Indigenous perception of the world, addressing the earth, winds, and sky field in powerful evocations of traditional knowledge.
5 The dense emplacement of *thanksgiving and ceremonial observation grounds* (named parks or open spaces) along the shores and heights of the city, centred and to the east and west of the architectural core, the Toronto waterfront, is preparation to begin receiving the people in their balanced relationship with, and honouring of, *all our relations* (all living things).

In the great cycles of return, understood so profoundly in Indigenous life ways, *Toron:to-Ontar:io-Cana:da* has been, and continues to be, unconsciously and subtly reinvigorated and re-contextualized in the spirit of the Ancestors, in 'duty' to Creation at this time. The activities envisioned for the Grove will attempt to demonstrate the deep meaning conveyed in the modern development of the city of Toronto through the use of traditional Indigenous ceremonial events and speeches, reimagined for our present needs, a culturally diverse celebration in an architectural emplacement along a brief stretch of the original shoreline of Ontario. This is 'history' redefined on a grander and more inclusive scale, where there is always an 'uncovering' process, turning and returning in grand cycles. Perhaps in this Grove, we can find a place of healing, gratitude, hope, and vision.

A Proposed Format for the Ceremonial Site Emplacement

The installation of the exhibition will be anchored around five detailed geographical/architectural reconstructions of the Toronto landscape addressing Lake Ontario at seminal periods in the fuller grandeur of its life cycle. The models will be highly detailed, 60 inches (1.5 metres) square, and suspended over a reconstructed sky field above and an earth energy field below.

These models will be placed in the central lodge, a circular space constructed in the Indigenous way like a great inverted basket woven into the upward reaches of an isolated poplar tree. This circular structure will be designed to replicate the standing bent log constructions of the ancestors – bound in strips of bark and deer sinew, clad in elm or basswood bark and moss, and sealed with pine sap. Embracing the central lodge will be two modern 'longhouses' designed in the respectful way of the dominant culture, the organic expression inspired by the work of Frank Lloyd Wright. These longhouses will be the setting for a series of reciprocal gifts, including a series of Hotinonshon:ni and Anishnaabek offerings conveying stories, teachings, music, arts, and ceremonies 'conversing' with reciprocated gifts. Twin apartments will be appended to the outside ends of these longhouses, to accommodate guardianship and continual occupation of the site from both sides. This architectural assemblage will be a ceremonial village for the convening of a great cultural conversation between Indigenous peoples of this land and the cultures visited upon them on and near this site of the modern settlement. It will face the 'beautiful waters,' the sacred Lake Ontario, intercepted by the great, continuously burning fire on the beach sands of the original shoreline.

The whole will have a profound ceremonial arrangement and progression, with a recitation of the Hotinonshon:ni Great Law of Peace and Creation being spoken among the many folds and recesses of the installation in the setting of the modern longhouse constructions.

The opening of the exhibition will be a sunrise Burning Tobacco Ceremony, followed by the greetings and 'cleaning up' of the visitors enacted in the 'At the Woods Edge' Condolence, followed by a traditional early morning Feast. A year-long series of ceremonies reflecting the 15 events of the longhouse Cycle of Ceremonies will follow in a sequence linked to the seasonal changes. A Sacred Fire will be kept burning for the duration of the exhibition and events. The actual events will be structured around the sequence and themes of the 15 longhouse ceremonial events, and will include the recitations of the Good Message of Handsome Lake and the Great Law of Peace, culminating in the extended nine-day ceremonial celebration of the return and recovery, named Mid-Winter. Briefly, I will describe the events, the timing, and the vision which surrounds each:

Constructing the Ceremonial Ground

The preparation of the grounds and the construction of the architectonic interventions into the micro-Indigenous eco-realm of the site, participating with *all our relations*, will be carried out in ritual. These will begin with offerings to the ancestors and spirits of the place and continue with ritual instruction and the receiving of duties by the participants. The actual process will be carried out as quietly and gently as possible, in repentance for the rapacious processes which have accompanied twentieth-century destruction and development. The participants will be drawn from men and women of all ages, from the community of the Hotinonshon:ni and Anishnaabek relations who are the keepers of this land, and from the British and French as the principal first European visitors to this place. Each day will open and close with a Thanksgiving Burning Tobacco, with feasts served throughout the day. Construction will be accompanied by songs, ceremonial speaking, and dances. These rituals are offered to all those things which are informing us, and are giving up their lives and natural place in Creation to afford us the privilege of these sheltering places dedicated to ceremonial duties.

Ceremonial Order Based on the Cycle
of the Hotinonshon:ni Ceremonies

BUSH CEREMONY

Following the dark winter-long process of constructing the emplacement comes the cleaning up and clearing of the site embodied in the Bush Ceremony. Led by volunteer groups of young people from the diverse Hotinonshon:ni and Anishnaabek communities around Lake Ontario, members of the diverse Toronto community led by the British descendants will clear the grounds of all extraneous debris left in the abandonment of duties inherent in colonization. The clearing of the bush of dead wood and fallen trees will be accompanied by the speeches, dances, and songs of the longhouse.

MAPLE SAP CEREMONY

The running of the sap, the first sweet gift of Creation after the long dark winter, is the real beginning of the ceremonial round. In this time, this springtime of receiving, the principal European visitors and allies, the British, will be hosted with a renewing of the cleansing "At the Woods Edge" ritual. This first place will recognize the significant encounters which led to the profound British colonization of the place, and offer these visitors their opportunity to request forgiveness, and make offers of repentance, atonement, and reconciliation, and to renew the original Two Row and Silver Covenant Chain agreements.[7] A member of the British monarchy will be invited to participate.

THUNDER CEREMONY

This is the time when the Grandfathers, our Ancestors, speak to us in the reassuring return of the Thunder Beings. This will provide the spontaneous setting (since the Thunders will come in a time which cannot be predicted) for their approval, that these ceremonies have their blessings and can proceed.

SPRING FEAST FOR THE DEAD

The spirits and remains of *all our relations* who have preceded us and the matter of all those who will be coming after us, and for whom we take care of this place, will be honoured with ceremonies at selected Native and non-Native burial sites around the Greater Toronto Area.

SPRING HADOUI CEREMONY

Members of the Hadoui Society will greet and cleanse descendants of the French settlers, to assist them in remembering the exploits of their relations, and to assist them in reconciliation and compassionate comforting.

SUN CEREMONY/MOON CEREMONY

These great celebrations will respect the place of the diverse sexual expressions which are given to us in Creation. Specifically, the spirits of the Moon, Our Grandmother, which informs the feminine, and Our Elder Brother, the Sun, whose movement reflects the masculine, will be addressed in relation to the sexuality of each individual, whatever balance of these inherent synergistic energies is held individually.

BLESSING SEEDS CEREMONY

The seeds of the corn, beans, and squash, Our Sustenance, the Three

Sisters,[8] are gathered and offered in games of chance – communications from the spirit world, among the men and women, to see who will lead the planting. This will be the setting for the greeting ceremonies for the Scots, Irish, and Welsh. These tribal peoples of the British Isles who suffered under the ebb and flow of British rule were given the choice of exile to these native lands. We respect and honour their journeys, and ask them to see the parallels with our own native encounter with the British.

STRAWBERRY CEREMONY

Strawberries are the particularly special gift to the Hotinonshon:ni – sweet, colourful, pulpy, and beautifully vulnerable as they grow in their delicate setting. These berries are made into the most honoured of the ceremonial drinks, the strawberry juice. The arrival of these berries perhaps even among the growing things on the site, will mark the greetings to the northern European visitors: from Scandinavia, Germany, and the lowlands of Holland and Belgium.

BEAN CEREMONY

The initiation of the first harvest in the growing season is celebrated with the gusto and spirit which might be seen to exemplify the visitors from southern Europe: the Spanish, Portuguese, Italian, and Greek communities. This will provide the general setting for the reconciliation of some of the saddest, most destructive, and cruel forms of colonization inflicted by Spain and Portugal. The Pope of the Catholic Church of Rome will be invited to participate.

SMALL GREEN CORN CEREMONY

The most sacred and leader of the sisters of sustenance is the corn, and so it is watched very carefully and celebrated even for its early sprouting. This spirit we hold out for some of our most distant relations in Russia, China, and Southeast Asia who are settling here once again in a kind of renewal of the ancient spirits of their ancestral migrations. The Dalai Lama of Tibet will be invited to participate.

BIG GREEN CORN CEREMONY

This celebration of the fully matured corn in all its uses and symbolism will be celebrated by all peoples, for whom their cultural ways have been based on corn, including the first peoples of the American southwest, and the Mayans, Incas, Aztecs, and Peruvians of the Middle and South Americas who now find refuge in Toronto.

GAIWI:IO

This important message from the native prophet Handsome Lake *Skanadari:io* about how Native people must live among the settler culture will be taught by prominent ceremonialists from Six Nations of the Grand River, including the rituals of repentance, held in an enlarged community which will include all Indigenous peoples and settlers on this land.

GREAT LAW

A re-creation and evocation of the nine-day recitation of the Great Law of Peace will be carried out by traditional elders. This will be complemented by an important World Conference on Peace based on the Great Law. A great White Pine Tree will be planted and consecrated in a culmination of this event. Heads of state of principal democratic nations, members of the United Nations General Assembly, the prime minister of Canada, the prime minister of the United Kingdom, and the president of the United States will be invited to participate in a gathering of Indigenous traditional leaders and wise Elders from around the world.

HARVEST CEREMONY

This time will provide the setting for an inclusive and large celebration coinciding with the Canadian Thanksgiving to recognize the deep ancestral sources of this tobacco offering and feast.

FALL HADOUI CEREMONY

This will be the setting for the compassionate reception of our relations from Africa to honour their diasporas. Their many forms of masked ceremonial dancing will express the diverse nations of their continent.

FALL FEAST FOR THE DEAD

In recognition of the wandering and persecuted spirits of the Jewish Nation and their articulate, spirited, compassionate, and persevering responses to racial cleansing and cultural diasporas, this feast will be held at Jewish monuments throughout the greater Toronto region.

MID-WINTER

This general and extended celebration will include all peoples, and most especially those for whom a distinct ceremonial opportunity was not offered in the earlier times of the cycle – importantly, those transcendent and harmonizing persons who are of blended ancestry. In the spirit of closing out these duties, the passing of the dark times, the winter solstice, and the return of the light of peace, reconciliation, and diversity will be celebrated.

The more recent migrants from the Muslim world will be accommodated in their own unique way, as we begin to understand their place in the visitations.

Dismantling the Ceremonial Ground

All of the remains of these respectful rituals will be dismantled, gathered together, and rearranged in burning, burial, and earth surface offerings, accompanied by closing speeches, dancing, and a general feast of completion. These ceremonial structures can be rebuilt as permanent structures to house the periodic renewal protocols arising from the event series.

A Sacred Fire kept burning for the duration of the ceremonies, exhibitions, and events will be extinguished by allowing it to burn completely. The ashes will be distributed and scattered among particular places and waters of Toronto to assist the continuing work of the spirits and ancestors in the manifestation of Toronto as their beacon of hope.

Epilogue

In the ensuing years since the formation of an independent foundation to support this vision, the relentless psycho-social and political processes and circumstances for its realization have been unfolding. Many presentations have been made before local authorities who have jurisdiction over possible sites for the emplacement. Local political and professional figures who might be key to its implementation have come forward with offers of support, including primarily the creation of a non-profit foundation and the acceptance of seats on its board. Close collaboration with the development of the Toronto waterfront has now ensured a place for the constructive and meaningful participation of Indigenous peoples in the cosmopolitan conversation which is the contemporary city.

A First Nations Grove has been designated and defined in the Waterfront Toronto Master Plan for the proposed Lake Ontario Park. Most importantly, key figures in the Native community are once again understanding the profound destiny carried in the Hotinonshon:ni Great Law of Peace delivered so many years ago on the very soil of the Province of Ontario. Deganawedah was, in fact, born and did his first teachings at the Bay of Quinte on the north shore of Lake Ontario. All peoples in this compassionate place of refuge named Toronto are beginning to listen to their hearts, and to provide a model for relationships among the peoples of the entire planet.

The Indigenous Ancestors who have nurtured the sublime qualities of this land for thousands of years and whose magisterial visions are their potent legacy may now in our time be unconsciously streaming to us, awaiting our growing consciousness.

NOTES

1 Iroquoian languages have been expressed in a number of linguistic traditions evolved from speech. Out of respect for my teacher, Jacob Ezra Thomas , I will use the Cayuga, which he preferred. *Hotinonshon:ni* is translated 'people who build a long house.' This is the traditional name for the people who are better known as the Iroquoian Confederacy.
2 The Great Law of Peace was most clearly and accurately conveyed in his generation from the recitations and recordings of the great Hotinonshon:ni Cayuga orator and teacher, Jacob Ezra Thomas (1922–1998). Jake used Gibson, *Concerning the League*.
3 See Arthur, *Toronto: No Mean City*.
4 The phrase 'all our relations,' or *akwe:gon,* refers to all the things in Creation to whom we are related: the earth, all that grows and lives in and on her body, all that is held in the sky realm, and the spirits of all those things coming before and after us. It is a 'big' word which shows ultimate respect and gratitude.
5 Jake Thomas spoke about this predicament of some of our people, including myself, who are trying to live in two worlds, one foot in the canoe and the other in the great masted sailing ship of the migrators. He simply asks what we will do if they are in a storm and have to separate. Where will we leap, or will we fall fatefully onto the waters to be rescued or drowned? See Thomas, *Kaianerekowa Hotinonsionne*.
6 Jean Isabel Maracle, *Kahnekotionhta* ['she is walking at the water's edge'], Clan Mother, Ball Deer Clan, Cayuga Nation, Six Nations, Grand River Territory, Ontario, Canada.
7 For some explanation of the complex series of agreements over time, see Jennings, *History and Culture*.
8 In the Hotinonshon:ni teachings these were given to the people as our primary foods.

REFERENCES

Arthur, Eric. *Toronto: No Mean City*. Toronto: University of Toronto Press, 1986.

Gibson, John Arthur. *Concerning the League: The Iroquois League Tradition as Dictated in Onondaga*. Memoir 9. Ed. and Trans. Hanna Woodbury. Winnipeg, MB: Algonquian and Iroquois Linguistics, 1992.

Jennings, Francis. Ed. *The History and Culture of Iroquoian Diplomacy*. Syracuse, NY: Syracuse University Press, 1985.

Thomas, Jake. *Kaianerekowa Hotinonsionne. The Great Law: A Talking Book*. [Video]. Brantford, ON: Iroquois Institute, 1992.

3   Finding Our Way despite Modernity

GKISEDTANAMOOGK

Introduction: Thanksgiving Prayer as Protocol

i greet and give *thanksgivings* to You who help me, and guide me; i greet and give thanksgivings to You, who keep all of life in the Original Purpose; You, who make it possible for us to Be and for us to find our way;

i greet and give *thanksgivings* to You, who are our *Relatives* in the Great Family, our people are Your Relatives, your *life* is our life, and we are *all one*;

i greet You and give *thanksgivings*, for *Those Who Are Yet Coming*; that we who are here will remember their counsel as we live our life, that we see their faces everywhere where we are;

and to You, who *keep* our home life and families, i give *thanksgivings*;

i greet and give You *thanksgivings, Great Mother*, for all Womanlife, for our Clan Mothers, and Great Mothers, for the mothers and sisters, for the daughters, and for the one who gives life to me and to our young ones, and who guides and nurtures me, i give *thanksgivings* for her relatives, for her community, and for her people;

i greet and give You *thanksgivings, Great Father*, for helping me and the Manlife *understand* what is love and the power it provides us to do what is necessary for life; in *thanksgivings* to help me and the fathers, brothers, and sons in our *obligations* to our families, the people, and creation;

i greet and give *thanksgivings* to You who sustain us and give of Your Selves so that we may yet live, that we remember Your sacrifice, that we may too, give such sacrifice so that All will Live;

i greet and give You *thanksgivings*, You who give life to all, that all has a *purpose* and all is connected to one another as family; i honour You with my life, that You will continue to *keep* this great *purpose* so that all life will live; i give You *thanksgivings* so that my life will become *You;* hear me, that these words are true.

Now it is, that i come before *You* in this way, that crosses my *Path of Life,* let my words be true and full of Your *wisdom* and *guidance,* You who are with me; *so be it Your way.*

Autobiographical Background and Wampanoag Teachings

My name is gkisedtanamoogk. i come from the Wampanoag People. We've been in our Homelands since the times of the giants, the *Twins.* Most people do not know about the Wampanoag, so i'll offer you two important historical 'claims to fame.' The first claim to fame is *we* were the ones who had 'Thanksgiving dinner' with the English pilgrims of the *Mayflower.* The other claim to fame is having the bloodiest war in United States history with the very same pilgrims 50 years later.

The unfortunate reality is that this relationship has not progressed much further from those conflicts and wars. For the Wampanoag/ Wabanaki People, we live and work outside of our selves and do not work with the *legacy of the Sacred.* The Wampanoag/Wabanaki people have not been raised by our Longhouses, so the normal social expectations of Western education, for example, represent a colonial, culturally biased, and racially prejudiced design on Indigenous peoples' ways of learning and *Ways of Being.* Western North America views its own social, economic, political, and religious matters as the pinnacle of human-world civilization. Any departure from this construct is an operative of the *alternative,* the *proverbial 'Other'* who is unsubstantiated, unqualified, and undeveloped, judged accordingly, solely from Western standards of worth and legitimacy. The *'Other'* is always lesser and unequal. This defines Indigenous people in North America.

Wampanoag/Wabanaki Nations continue to be in a struggle for survival against rampant North American colonialism. This experience has been an incredibly long and continuous fight for our right to *Be* as we wish to be. At this moment, there is no reason for the Wampanoag to become something other than our selves. Our life and place on this Earth is the intention of *Ki'E'Tan*, the Great Creator. Until such time as *Ki'E'Tan* wills it, we are obliged, as Wampanoag People, to continue our *Original Instructions* and *Purpose for Being and Living*. These inform the basis of Wampanoag Life.

Almost 90 per cent of Wampanoag/Wabanaki people take Christianity and the ideologies of the church to heart, despite the legacy of residential schools, public education, and federal-state-provincial Indian policies deeply and negatively impacting our lives. Our context is that of genocide; whether we speak of 'integration,' 'assimilation,' 'disappearances,' 'imprisonment,' 'land claims,' or 'residential schools,' it all means the end of our consent, self-determination, and our right to remain who we are, in our own territories, in our self-defined context.

Those of us who embraced the church, society, and governance of North America, struggle for simple acceptance and respect from North America, which, on the whole, is never forthcoming. Those who are respectful of their 'progress' as Canadian or American citizens have the dubious status of being second-rate human beings and second-class citizens, or citizens minus. Any person of colour throughout North America is, in reality, *treated* as a second-class citizen.

We no longer understand nor appreciate the true essence of our selves because our cultures have suffered drastic North American punitive repercussions for being and *choosing to remain* Wampanoag/Wabanaki. This perverse cycle continues.

i have chosen to walk another way. i am not a citizen of North America, nor do i embrace any faith tradition other than Wampanoag, even though my upbringing has been principally outside of my community. During the episode at Wounded Knee in 1973, i was a sophomore at Boston University. Wounded Knee transformed me – transformed me from *Joe America* to *Joe Wampanoag*. i've been pursuing my understanding about who *Joe Wampanoag* is for the past 35 years, and still i am learning. Understanding the nature of life, of being responsible, and feeling human in the Wampanoag context is the culmination of my life. Deeply moved by my culture, which respects life on so many profound levels, ensured that my wilful return to my Nation was swift and absorbing. Completing my senior year at university was very difficult for me, after finding my true calling and *real* education in my home community. The significance gained from this experience, and the understanding of the world and spirituality that it brought, would be manifested in my life for many years to come. My new education was formed and shaped by the women of my community. Unbeknownst to me at the time, i was subconsciously following traditional Wampanoag/Wabanaki *Ways of Being*.

The *Ways of Being* are known as the *Longhouse*. Structurally speaking, imagine a great house in the shape of a football; its dimensions could be anywhere from 30 to 60 feet in width, and 60 to 120 feet in length, and approximately 15 to 20 feet in height. This would be the winter house of a family Clan. By definition, a family Clan system would comprise the woman's entire family: grandparents, parents, aunts and uncles, brothers and sisters, and cousins – a total of 50 to 150 people or more, sharing this space. The Clan acts like a cooperative, each member organized and working together for the well-being of the whole family. This is the basic social tenet of Wampanoag people. Each Longhouse has a Clan Mother, a family matriarch, who is the principal 'centre' of the family. Through her, the Clan is organized and functions as a social union. The women of that Clan determine the male representative, who, on behalf of the family, leads by example, the *Sachem*. The family Longhouse is, then, the socio-political and socio-economic power base of the community.

This structural pattern is replicated at the community level, forming political governance. Each Clan has a female and male representative who sits with other Longhouse Clan representatives. Women and Men of each Longhouse form the Women's Council and the Men's Council, who are called together with the Community Sachem and advisors for the Community Council. Like many other Eastern Nations, it is the custom of the women to raise a Sachem (usually a male, but not always) who becomes the community seat of governance – not governance as in Western notions of power and decision-making. The role of the Sachem is to provide wisdom and counsel, to be a deliverer of conflict resolution and economic stability. The Sachem makes no decision alone, as an individual, but with broader community governance. This is made with Elders, Youth, Warrior leaders, and Women's and Men's Councils. Decisions are made through the Community Council, women having the final vote (in Western terms of power-based politics, this would be *veto* power). Decisions are made in a manner where consensus is the norm, everyone has a voice, and all must decide a matter. Family Longhouses have a great influence in community decision-making, and often impasses are returned to each Clan for further review.

This structure is again replicated at regional or national and confederate levels of governance: 'Nations' as regional collectives of communities; and 'Confederacy' as related or non-related groupings of Nations bound together by choice, convenience, and mutual considerations (much like the political body politic of the United Nations). Confederacy and treaty-making experiences are not new concepts to the Nations of this land. As the Longhouse moves further from the community, its power to make binding decisions decreases, so that the power base of sovereignty remains the communities who must approve or reject decisions of the Nation and the Confederacy. The Confederacy is where the treaties with Europeans came to be and each community of the Confederacy either rejected or approved the agreement, local sovereignty being absolutely cherished and never diminished. The whole process took at least a year to complete.

Unfortunately, Wampanoag and Wabanaki people have not lived this way for at least several generations. This gives credence to our present social dilemmas. The Wampanoag, and the Wabanaki Nations in the North, where i moved, are *matrifocal* peoples. Yet there is a big debate in our communities about whether we are matrilineal or patrilineal societies. That debate, in some form or another, has been shaped by the colonial systems around us. For instance, the church has come into our community steeped deeply in patriarchy. Colonial policy, colonization, and aggression are all about patriarchy. Our struggles in the communities are simply because, inherently, the Wampanoag/Wabanaki remain matrifocal peoples and live that way in the context of imposed patriarchy. Stated differently, through all these many years, despite all these many generations of patriarchy and colonialism heaped upon us, we inherently and intuitively understand that we are not whole in patriarchal systems. Western patriarchy's vilest contempt for Wampanoag/Wabanaki *Ways of Being* has not completely convinced us of Western 'rightness,' and has not eradicated our understanding of who we are. Women's voices remain strong in our communities. Patriarchy has proven unable to overpower our sensibilities about the honouring of women. Today, the strength of the women is providing *the* way to community restoration, including restoring men; we are returning to our selves.

i'm doing all that i can to relearn the Wampanoag *Ways of Being*. As a former product of Western education, graduating from university and doing some time in law school, i began to realize, with due respect, that there are some basic dilemmas for First Nations people in becoming professionals outside of our selves, outside of our culture, values, tradition, spirituality, and *world view*. For example, the disciplines of law, medicine, sociology, education, art, philosophy, science, technology, and mathematics are integral to Western education, but when applied to First Nations these disciplines, each in their practice, have furthered the cant of colonialism. While these are normative in Western North American socio-education, these disciplines have also existed in Indigenous country throughout this hemisphere long before the arrival and invasion of Columbus. Western practices consistently rebuke this reality. As a result, even among our own people, we refute the value and depth of our own historic and ongoing knowledge.

Most of my time spent in community is with ceremony. Ceremony provides the framework of my living and my being. Ceremony roots the ways of decolonizing our selves, and works within the context and sociality of Wampanoag/Wabanaki postmodern realities. In the meaning of *Thanksgiving*, i am speaking about the ceremonies, the *Way of Life,* giving *thanksgiving* – which informs us of the nature of Wampanoag/ Wabanaki. Because of this path personally taken, so many times i have been gifted with understanding, with insight. This is truly a beautiful world, if we pay attention and follow the dictates of our heart.

Returning to our original source of knowledge is simply a matter of spending quality time with our common *Mother, the Earth.* Indigenous language embodies the real world view, empowering understanding of place in the world. We are then talking about relationships and relationship-building. i want to encourage us not to be stuck in a homocentric ideology about what relationship means; i want us to *be* inclusive of *all life.* Ultimately, it is the Earth that controls our destiny as a species, it is not humanity. If we are going to have any hope for a future as a species, if we are truly concerned about the well-being of our families, of our children, and the *7th Generation Yet to Come,* the only way that is going to happen is through the women, their leadership and sense of Being, in their own context as women. All of this is contained in our Heart. To be illustrative, we are living on a female planet, acknowledged as such by all Indigenous Nations of this Turtle Island, and the ceremonies suggest to me, as a man, that the *Sacred* is predominantly and pre-eminently female. *The Order of the Universe*, according to the ceremonies, and according to Creation, is feminine-based.

Because we are a people with Clan systems, we are in concordant relationship with Creation. Like our Clanmothers, the alpha female Wolf, not the alpha male, raises the pack to be Wolves; it is the mother Bear that raises her cubs to be Bears. Stated differently, it is the women who teach the men how to be men. It can only happen in that cycle, in that process. The *Great Mothers* in our history, they surround us. We are completely immersed in the spirit of the *Great Mothers.* i am going to suggest to you that the life of the Wampanoag/Wabanaki has always been experience-based in the feminine.

The Work

My community is inhabited by Massachusetts and the United States, so this gives you an idea and reference for understanding where we are from. In our language and context, this land is *Kautanitowit*; the land is the *Creator's House,* not 'North America,' not the 'United States,' not 'Canada.' It is the *Creator's House.* When we begin to think like that, when we begin to use our language, when we really understand the power of *thanksgiving*, that is when i am full of hope, because then the Earth is alive, is moving, and still teaching. Every day we have an opportunity to 'get it right.' In Wampanoag cosmology, to follow our *Heart*, is to immerse our selves in the reality and the state of Creation. This is the state of the Earth, our common Cosmic Mother, *Netimika'ho*, the *First Mother*. For me, this is real life.

Because there is great responsibility as a husband; it is my principal job. i also have daughters, and a son. For me, that is my work. To be a *Father*, to be a *Husband*, to be a *Son of the People* is all i am concerned with; all the other tasks, responsibilities, and opportunities flow from my principal responsibilities, and these extra-familial ones fall into their proper place. This sense of being and purpose, from time to time, creates the opportunity to cross paths with our neighbours.

The cross-cultural experience with the Tatamagouche Centre, the Maritime Conference of the United Church of Canada, the Aboriginal Rights Coalition Atlantic, and with the KAIROS Aboriginal Rights Committee is a wonderful and inspiring opportunity, especially meeting all the people. This work stems from a working principle involving an ongoing reflection and self-education, centring on the series of Eastern *Peace and Friendship Treaties* between the Mi'kmaq, Wulustikwiek, and Passamaquoddy Wabanaki Nations with the Crown – the *Great Covenant Chain*. This work particularly drew all of us together around the outbreak of violence between the Mi'kmaq and the Passamaquoddy First Nations, and their Maritime Canadian neighbours and the government of Canada. Treaties with First Nations present unfamiliar experiences for Canadians. As a social assumption, Canadians hold that all First Nations members are full citizens of Canada and must assent to Canadian laws. However, a paradox exists whereby treaties are held and created between two or more nations and are never held with a country's own citizens. By that principle, First Nations maintain a continuous *nation-to-nation*, government-to-government, legal and political relationship with Canada and the Crown.

In the socio-political context of the Maritimes, the Wabanaki are excluded by government decree and legislation. We have also experienced habitual social relegation to inferior status. Translated differently, the unfounded, unsupportable, provincial-federal possession of recognized legal and political title to Wabanaki land and its coveted resources is a travesty of justice and the *rule of law*. The courts of Canada are paradoxically entrapped in recognizing the binding promises of the *Peace and Friendship Treaties*, but, in doing so, must also recognize the content *and spirit* of those treaties. *Treaty law* demonstrates the unremitting conclusion that these particular treaties gave no title, no resources nor authority to the Crown over Wabanaki First Nations' territories and resources (unlike the *Numbered Treaties* with First Nations' land). In September 1999, in the *Marshall Decision*, the Supreme Court of Canada declared that Mi'kmaq fishermen have a right to fish for a moderate livelihood, basing this decision, unanimously, on the ongoing validity and authority of seventeenth-century Wabanaki-Crown *Peace and Friendship Treaties*. This validity is *mandated* by Canada's Constitution.

In October 1999, fishermen in the Miramichi region assaulted the Burnt Church Community Fishery, destroying 75 per cent of the entire material resources, $50,000 to $75,000 worth of traps, lines, and equipment, and robbing the community of catch. The fishermen justified their actions in order to 'conserve' and 'protect' the lobster resources developed for the past 30 years (a convenience overlooked before the *Marshall Decision* and the opening of the Mi'kmaq fishery). The resultant violence catapulted the profile of the Burnt Church Mi'kmaq Community to national and global status and placed the entire Maritime region on alert. Suspicions between Mi'kmaq, other Wabanaki communities, and Maritime Canada grew into hysteria. Social powder kegs quickly consumed the imagination and escalating fear. Many Miramichi fishermen and neighbours were congregational members of the United Church and Catholic Church, and the tension mounted between neighbouring communities surrounding Burnt Church. Violence perpetrated by the government of Canada, specifically, the Departments of Oceans and Fisheries, Justice, the Prime Minister's Office, and mainstream media (CBC, CTV, ATV) networks and affiliates, encouraged and exacerbated contagious tensions, violence, and misunderstanding.

For example, the CBC would address the issues frequently, but with innuendo and subtle characterizations suggesting the criminality of the Mi'kmaq fishery. Rather than focusing on the criminality, violence, and thuggery by Maritime fishermen, the Department of Fisheries and

Oceans, with the compliance of the RCMP, threatened the peace and social stability, not only of the specific localities but also throughout the region. The RCMP would characterize as 'peaceful protest' white fishermen destroying Mi'kmaq equipment, habitually *firing* weapons into the Burnt Church Mi'kmaq Community, and assaulting Mi'kmaq community members who were not fishermen. The CBC would repeatedly 'report' on violent Mi'kmaq community actions, falsely attributing these actions not to the white neighbours but to the Mi'kmaq people, the CBC habitually describing the Mi'kmaq fishery as 'illegal.' When confronted by community members and challenged by human rights observer groups about these false reports, both the CBC and the RCMP, through public broadcast, would make invalid claims of 'fact' and distort circumstances; they would acknowledge their mistakes personally but never publicly recant or apologize, leaving regional listeners to continually believe the false stories, based on previous broadcasts.

The Maritime Conference of the United Church of Canada responded to the violence and false reporting by calling for calm and peace while insisting on negotiations. Efforts included submitting numerous resolutions calling for the church to recognize the legitimacy of Mi'kmaq claims, legal obligations of the government to Aboriginal neighbours, and the church's duty to promote non-violent means to persuade key players to talk. The Conference also began to acknowledge the necessity to recognize Mi'kmaq people and leadership through a series of invitations to speak to and share concerns, particularly in light of the violence. One other important development of the Conference was the creation of a *Task Group on Aboriginal Concerns and Affairs*, mandated to guide the Conference in developing relationship-building and policy with the Wabanaki First Nations in the Maritime region.

The Aboriginal Rights Coalition Atlantic (ARCA), an advocacy rights-based social justice organization in partnership with Aboriginal people and communities, concentrates its mission on self-education and relationship-building with Aboriginal people and communities throughout the Maritime region. ARCA responded to the violence of the fishery by creating a witness project designed to work with the Burnt Church community as a means to defuse violence and encourage peaceful ways of addressing issues between Aboriginal peoples and Canadians. *The Observer Project* enlisted the support, leadership, and guidance from the Burnt Church community, concerned maritime Canadians, and the experiential and technical services of the Tatamagouche Centre, near Amherst Nova Scotia. This program emanated from the Centre's experience of sending witnesses to Guatemala and developing collaborative ecumenical dialogue. *The Observer Project* reported and recorded the activity at Burnt Church during the fishery crisis, which aided community members in various ways, including providing testimony, news releases, and accurate media accounts surrounding the violence. The actions, initiated by ARCA, contributed to the de-escalation of violence and provided an influence that saved lives.

The work continued. As the violence waned, a new approach to the relationship-building formed. This approach developed as the *Lnapskuk-Neighbours Project*, which involved efforts to bring regional First Nations and Maritime Canadians together. As a result of the previous work of the *Observer Project* and *Task Group*, many requests came from the public for greater understanding of the issues, through education and a desire to develop concrete active relationships. *Lnapskuk* initiated activity to support efforts to build relationships based on 'respect, justice, and mutuality.' Possibly for the first time in Canadian history, this project based its education work on *Peace and Friendship Treaties* and on individual citizens' *treaty obligations*. Reflecting the formality of treaties as the foundation of relationship with First Nations, *Lnapskuk* has evolved into an organization that can take on advocacy and action roles for a variety of significant challenges that continue to stress and alienate First Nation communities and Maritime Canadians. Fisheries, logging, federal and provincial politico-legal relations, treaty and *Indian Act* complexities, and trans-border mobility issues are among the challenges manifesting in the Maritime region.

The importance of gaining recognition of the Passamaquoddy by the federal government of Canada is especially challenging in light of the socio-economic developments brought about by the *Marshall Decision* of 1999. The Passamaquoddy First Nation is a member of the Wabanaki Confederacy and is specifically named in the Marshall Decision under the *Peace and Friendship Treaties*. The Passamaquoddy have the special distinction of being one of the many First Nations whose people and territories are partitioned by the Canada-U.S. international border. The Passamaquoddy on the Canadian side, located near the town of St Andrews, New Brunswick, stake their claims and property titles on Passamaquoddy territories, but have no official 'status' with the federal government and are not, subsequently, 'recognized' by Indian Affairs. Having that distinction, Passamaquoddy territories and resources have no protection from the *will* of development and exploitation from municipal, corporate, and provincial communities in New Brunswick. The

Passamaquoddy have petitioned the federal government for such recognition with piecemeal success. The Passamaquoddy are reminding
the Crown that political and legal relations with the Passamaquoddy
will not stem from the Indian Act, but rather will be based on the treaties that the Passamaquoddy have with the Crown, the *nation-to-nation*
agreement. While other Wabanaki First Nations have the treaty-based
relationship, this relationship is falsely premised by the Canadian
Indian Act, which significantly places a nation under the tutelage and
dominion of federal domestic ministries rather than foreign affairs. The
Passamaquoddy argue that the relationship they seek is based on constitutional prescripts, such as section 35 of Canada's Constitution Act,
and international treaty protocols. This is the legal and political mandate needed to resolve many historic and contemporary questions
plaguing First Nations.

In Conclusion

Teaching at the University of Maine is a current, enjoyable opportunity
to further enrich efforts to respond to and break out of the colonial academic persona and talk the truth in ways that empower us as sisters
and brothers. In an Indigenous, global reality, subscribed and pre-
scribed by the Sacred and Creation, the Earth is *Mother*, the *Great Mother*,
to all beings even though humans come from different places. We must
all understand that at one time, all cultures were entwined with
Creation. We are all *tribal peoples*. Human beings only know tribal life.
Our present social structures all stem from historic, inherent tribal consciousness. The only difference between tribal life in any mainstream
Canadian city and tribal life in 'Indian Country' is that our tribal life in
Indian Country is still connected to the land, to the *Great Mother*. Tribal
life in the cities is connected to abstracts like economics, nationalism,
capitalism, and militarism. These, as ideologies, are not connected to
the *great source of life*. They are connected to an indirect, obtusely sub-
conscious, misogynistic, mini-reality. That is the only difference between us; we all carry the same heart, the same blood, the same breath.
In a real way, the reality of the relationship between us is that there is
nowhere you can hide from us. Our burials, material remnants, and
ancient, sacred sites are everywhere, from pole to pole and coast to
coast. There is no way you can run away. If you intend to stay here, you
have the choice of being our friends or being our enemies, and being
our enemies can simply mean *You do nothing with us*. The world intends

to stay here on this island. If this is true, then there is only one respectful way to live here, and that is to live with the *Great Instructions* of the Creator, in the manner given to the Indigenous Nations of this land. This, then, becomes your world too, and you have responsibilities and obligations to make it so for a*ll life*. For me, this is the true meaning of being neighbours.

Now we can speak your language; now we understand what is important to you; and now we understand your values. We have the moral, social, and political advantage because you do not have a clue who we are. We are as mysterious to you as we were to your predecessors.

This is prompting great change. For those of us who are learning about the real power of love seen radiating in the ceremonies, there is shared *understanding* of the *Principles of Life*. That is where the change is coming from, in my opinion. It is a good time to be on this planet in this time, in this era. We are going to have a lot of help because Creation is alive, has global consciousness, and is watching and participating with us. Family is not just the inclusivity of ancestors and the unborn generations, but all those ones that we call the Earth, the Sky, the Stars; everything is alive and is all *Family*. i am really interested in you and us; there is so much that i want to know from you and about you. i do not think we have to worry so much about what is coming down the road, even though what is coming is real, life-altering challenge. We need to concern our selves with 'getting it right,' acquiring and working with real love, being one with all of life, being with one another as sisters and brothers, as *family*, in the global society of human life.

i'm working for this change. My association with the projects at the Tatamagouche Centre that my colleague Margaret Tusz-King and i have been working on have been a real blessing for me and a real thrill. The relationship we have is itself the very nature of *peace and friendship*. For those of us who are involved with this work, and for those of us who are coming into it, if this work does not transform you then you are not paying attention. If you are immune, complacent, indifferent, and untouched by the horror of human avarice and aggression, then you are not paying attention. It is not possible to be engaged in this work and not behave differently. It is not possible if we are really doing what we are supposed to be doing with this work. We have only really scratched the surface. In *thanksgiving*, gkisedtanamoogk.

PART 2

From the Front Lines

'From the Front Lines' records the experiences and analyses of Indigenous and non-Indigenous leaders and activists who are involved in specific struggles for Indigenous self-determination and social and environmental justice. Their first-hand experience in negotiating Indigenous/non-Indigenous relationships provides the rich ground for their accounts. They write from different contexts: from the defence of Indigenous sovereignty and protection of Indigenous territories; to planning and implementing initiatives to ensure that future generations of Indigenous peoples can live with integrity within their homelands; to developing organizational and institutional linkages between Indigenous and non-Indigenous peoples to carry out joint education, reconciliation, justice, and research projects.

After decades of negotiation, the *United Nations Declaration on the Rights of Indigenous Peoples* (see Craig Benjamin, Jennifer Preston, and Marie Léger) was finally adopted by the United Nations on 13 September 2007. This chapter provides an account of a global campaign by a coalition of Indigenous leaders and non-governmental organizations to ensure support of the *Declaration* at the United Nations, despite Canada's efforts to obstruct its adoption.

Grassy Narrows (Judy Da Silva), Caledonia (Tom Keefer), Nawash (Rick Wallace, Rick Bauman, and Marilyn Struthers), Sharbot Lake (Paula Sherman), and the Great Bear Rainforest (Merran Smith and Art Sterritt) are readily identifiable markers of land and resource disputes in Indigenous homelands. They have been in Canadian news headlines as flashpoints over sovereignty, resources, and territorial protection. Adversaries may be governments, global corporations, neighbours, and outside groups. As these confrontations unfold under extreme political, social, and economic pressures, diverse interests are at play. These examples offer important opportunities for understanding different forms of alliances and coalitions that might form, possibilities of joint action, and also the tensions in trying to work together.

Alliances and coalitions can also take the form of partnerships to work on specific projects while actively decolonizing relationships. Victoria Freeman records the efforts of a group of Indigenous and non-Indigenous activists to promote reconciliation by establishing an educational web site for Indigenous/non-Indigenous exchange. Institutional partnerships are also important sites for forging relationships of respect, including joint arts-based community research projects in Central America, Mexico, and Toronto (Deborah Barndt and Laura Reinsborough), the creation of The Nakwatsvewat Institute to resolve land disputes based on traditional Hopi understandings of land distribution (Justin Richland and Patricia Sekaquaptewa), and the development of a Native American Studies program at Virginia Tech (Sam Cook and Karenne Wood). These chapters identify challenges in confronting the many manifestations of colonization today, and in navigating complex and often contradictory power relationships at institutional, organizational, and individual levels.

Within each of these chapters, there are lessons learned about working in alliances between Indigenous and non-Indigenous peoples, sometimes indicating successes and often revealing tensions that arise in the course of taking action. The contribution of these chapters is to bring forward the deep learning that is inherent in action, knowledge that can illuminate what it takes to re/envision relationships beyond the language of partnership.

4 The UN Declaration on the Rights of Indigenous Peoples: Partnerships to Advance Human Rights

CRAIG BENJAMIN, JENNIFER PRESTON,
AND MARIE LÉGER

The co-authors are part of an ad-hoc coalition that is composed of Indigenous representatives and human rights and faith-based organizations. This group came together in common work to achieve the *United Nations Declaration on the Rights of Indigenous Peoples*. We collaborate in Canada and with the global Indigenous caucus at the UN. This chapter draws from keynote and workshop presentations at the Re/Envisioning Relationships Conference, and gives a summary of our collective work on the *UN Declaration*.

The *United Nations Declaration on the Rights of Indigenous Peoples*[1] was under development within the UN system for more than two decades. In June 2006 the newly formed UN Human Rights Council voted to adopt the *Declaration*.[2] Less than six months later, in an unanticipated move, the UN General Assembly voted to delay final adoption of the *Declaration* to allow more time for consultation. This created a real fear that the *Declaration* might be lost. After just under a year of intense negotiations, on 13 September 2007, the General Assembly voted overwhelmingly in favour of adoption.

Speaking on behalf of the global Indigenous peoples' caucus, an Indigenous rights advocate from Australia welcomed the adoption of the *Declaration*, telling the General Assembly:

> The *Declaration* is a framework for states to link and integrate with the Indigenous Peoples, to initiate new and positive relations, but this time without exclusion, without discrimination, and without exploitation. These rights in the *Declaration* are already recognized in international law, but they are rights which have been denied to Indigenous Peoples everywhere.[3]

Indigenous peoples' representatives from North America stated:

> We affirm that this is an historic day for Indigenous Peoples in the international community, and indeed for humanity as a whole. We hope, and dedicate ourselves to working for our vision, that it will be carried out by Indigenous Peoples and states in good faith, with good will and with integrity, so that Indigenous communities and Peoples of North America and around the world will be able to experience real benefits. The survival, dignity, and well-being of Indigenous Peoples require nothing less. We remain committed to lifting the spirits of our peoples according to the teachings of our ancestors, for the benefit of all members of our communities and for the future generations.[4]

Indigenous peoples were the primary advocates for the *Declaration* throughout this long and often frustrating struggle. For the majority of the process, non-Indigenous organizations played only a limited role in the advancement of the *Declaration*, largely out of respect for the fact that Indigenous peoples were speaking for themselves and were directly engaged in negotiations with states as the rights holders. As the *Declaration* moved closer to adoption, non-Indigenous organizations were able to identify an important role for themselves working alongside and in support of Indigenous partners.

The Urgent Need for the Declaration

In every region of the world, Indigenous peoples are among the most marginalized and frequently victimized sectors of society. Deeply entrenched patterns of racism and systemic discrimination in law and policy leave Indigenous peoples vulnerable to grave abuses. Decisions imposed for the benefit of other wealthier and more influential groups bring little benefit but cause much harm for Indigenous peoples. The forced assimilation programs, the destruction and theft of Indigenous lands and territories, the forced uprooting of Indigenous communities, and the targeting of Indigenous activists have led to widespread impoverishment, ill-health, social stress, and violence.

Kofi Annan, the former UN Secretary General, has described the situation of Indigenous peoples in this way: 'For far too long the hopes and aspirations of indigenous peoples have been ignored; their lands have been taken; their cultures denigrated or directly attacked; their languages and customs suppressed; their wisdom and traditional knowledge overlooked; and their sustainable ways of developing natural resources dismissed. Some have even faced the threat of extinction ... The answer to these grave threats must be to confront them without delay.'[5]

In the *Declaration*, Indigenous peoples and states have re-conceptualized Indigenous and state relations in a fashion that promotes the basic principles that guide the United Nations. The *Declaration* is a way forward for Indigenous peoples and states that is based on collaboration, mutual respect, and a common goal of promoting human rights for all.

Rights Deferred

A draft declaration was first brought forward for adoption by the UN Sub-Commission on Prevention of Discrimination and Protection of Minorities in 1994.[6] By that point, the text had already been the subject of many years of deliberation among state representatives, independent human rights experts, and Indigenous peoples at the UN Working Group on Indigenous Populations. However, a significant number of states were unwilling to support the initial text proposed by that Working Group and endorsed by the Sub-Commission. Instead, the UN Human Rights Commission established a new Working Group to continue deliberations.[7]

Indigenous peoples had played a central role in the development of the initial draft. Many felt that further deliberation could only undermine the rights framework that they had helped shape. These fears were confirmed by states that tried to use the new Working Group on the Draft Declaration to introduce changes to the text that would eliminate critical rights altogether, or require that fulfilment of these rights should always be at the discretion of the state. In response, the caucus of Indigenous peoples' organizations participating in this process took a collective position to oppose all changes to the draft Declaration.

This stalemate continued through almost eight years of deliberations. During these years, protections for the rights of Indigenous peoples continued to evolve, with important precedents set by domestic courts and by international and regional human rights bodies.

The first breakthrough in resolving the deadlock over the *Declaration* came at the eighth session of the Working Group, when a number of state and Indigenous representatives were able to agree on additions to the *Declaration* that would not alter its provisions but would clarify that the legitimate interests of states could be addressed by understanding the *Declaration* in the broader, evolving context of international law. The positive spirit established by these initial collaborative proposals opened the door to the Indigenous caucus entering into renegotiation of the 1994 draft text with the intention of clarifying but not weakening its provisions.

By the final session of the Working Group, held in 2005–06, states and Indigenous peoples had reached agreement on just over half of the articles. Common ground had also been established on all or nearly all the remaining articles, with only a handful of states, led by the U.S., continuing to strongly oppose recognition of Indigenous rights in key areas of self-determination and land rights.

At the end of the eleventh session, the chairman/rapporteur stated that further negotiations would be unlikely to establish broader consensus than already existed, and that he was not prepared to recommend any further extension of the Working Group. Instead, he brought forward a summary that included the articles that already enjoyed consensus, and, for the remainder, the proposed text that appeared to have achieved the broadest agreement in the Working Group.[8] The text presented in the final Working Group report was endorsed by a wide range of Indigenous peoples' organizations, by the European Union, and by almost all Latin American states, as well as the UN Permanent Forum on Indigenous Issues and the UN Special Rapporteur on the situation of human rights and fundamental freedoms of Indigenous people. It was this text that was adopted by the Human Rights Council and brought forward to the General Assembly in the fall of 2006.

Meeting the Distinct Needs and Aspirations of Indigenous Peoples

Human rights instruments such as the *Declaration* are intended to inspire and guide states and civil society on the principles and measures needed to respect, protect, and promote human rights. Declarations are not legally binding in themselves, but may include provisions that have already been accepted as binding in domestic laws or international treaties. Declarations should also help shape the future development of law and policy.

The *UN Declaration on the Rights of Indigenous Peoples* does not create new rights. Rather, it responds to the past and current global denial of the human rights of Indigenous peoples and elaborates a framework of human rights protections based on the specific circumstances of Indigenous peoples. In particular, the *Declaration* responds to the necessity for Indigenous peoples to maintain and pass onto future generations their distinct cultural identities, traditions, and practices.

One of the most important breakthroughs in the *Declaration* is the affirmation that Indigenous peoples are PEOPLES, and as such are entitled to the right of self determination, as are all peoples. The third article of the *Declaration* mirrors the language of the International Covenant on Civil and Political Rights and the International Covenant on Economic, Social and Cultural Rights, which affirm that all peoples have the right of self-determination.

Recognition of Indigenous peoples as *peoples* establishes a basis for protecting both the individual and the collective rights critical to Indigenous societies as a whole. The second article states: 'Indigenous peoples and individuals are free and equal to all other peoples; and individuals have the right to be free from any kind of discrimination, in the exercise of their rights, in particular that based on their indigenous origin or identity.' Other articles provide specific protections against discrimination, forced assimilation, and other forms of cultural destruction.

The *Declaration* also reflects the centrality of the land to Indigenous peoples' distinct cultures and to their health and well-being. At least 10 articles of the *Declaration* deal directly with measures needed to maintain Indigenous peoples' unique relationship with the land. As the preamble states: 'control by indigenous peoples over developments affecting them and their lands, territories, and resources will enable them to maintain and strengthen their institutions, cultures, and traditions, and to promote their development in accordance with their aspirations and needs.'

Finally, the *Declaration* affirms that the distinct rights of Indigenous peoples must be interpreted and applied in the context of the wider body of international human rights laws and standards.

The Role of Non-Indigenous NGOs

A number of non-Indigenous non-governmental organizations (NGOs) closely followed the development of the *Declaration*. Some played a critical support role by providing funding and other resources, such as interpretation, to enable Indigenous representatives to travel to Geneva to participate effectively in the Working Group. Only in the last final years did non-Indigenous organizations play an active role in advocating for the adoption of a strong *Declaration*.

Key to this shift was the recognition by many Indigenous leaders that non-Indigenous NGOs could play an influential role in convincing receptive states to engage more collaboratively with Indigenous peoples. Many of the non-Indigenous organizations that came to be involved, such as Rights and Democracy, the Quakers, and Amnesty International, were seen by states as defenders of the human rights system as a whole, rather than as advocates for Indigenous rights. The support of these organizations was important in refuting states' objections that were often cloaked by the claim of defending universal rights against 'special interests.' The fact that some of these organizations also have a global membership base was also important in demonstrating to states that there was a public interest in seeing a timely and positive resolution of the debates.

Non-Indigenous NGOs sought to use their distinct influence in a number of ways, both publicly and privately. This included issuing press releases, making statements to the Working Group, convening informal meetings of states and Indigenous representatives, and hosting side events at related UN meetings.

In this work, non-Indigenous organizations were respectful of the distinct role of Indigenous peoples as spokespersons and advocates for their own rights. Non-Indigenous organizations who became engaged in the process in Geneva were guided by a number of informal understandings about their own role and contribution to the process:

Non-Indigenous organizations were careful never to appear to speak for Indigenous peoples or to enter into specific negotiations with states over the text.

Non-Indigenous organizations tried to speak with a distinct voice based on their specific knowledge and experience in the broader area of human rights.

Non-Indigenous organizations worked closely with Indigenous partner organizations, to benefit from their expertise in the issues of Indigenous rights and to coordinate efforts.

Non-Indigenous organizations purposely took no position on issues of process or substance where the Indigenous caucus itself was still working to achieve a common position.

In Canada there is an ad-hoc coalition that worked collectively on the *Declaration*. It consists of national Aboriginal organizations, Indigenous Nations, human rights groups, and faith-based organizations. This coalition was built around the common goal of advancing the *Declaration*. We meet regularly – often by conference call – and establish joint strategies. We prepare joint statements, hold press conferences, and share information, which is invaluable.

The partnerships work because we trust and respect each other; we understand that we all have different roles to play, and that these roles not only complement each other, they also strengthen the work of all partners. The partnerships took time and energy to build, and we are mutually supportive in maintaining those partnerships.

The work in Canada has been particularly important because of the critical role – both positive and negative – that has been played by the Canadian government. In our joint work we influenced the Liberal government in a positive direction during the final years of the Working Group process. Unfortunately, these gains were lost when Canada reversed its position with the election of the Conservative government in 2006.[9] Since the adoption of the *Declaration*, coalition members have continued to work together to promote its implementation. This work is seen to be particularly critical given the continued opposition to the *Declaration* by the Conservative government of Prime Minister Stephen Harper.

Canada's Shift

After the election of the Conservative government, Canada's position on the *UN Declaration* abruptly shifted. Without any consultation with Indigenous peoples, Canada aligned itself with the United States, Australia, and New Zealand (a coalition known as CANZUS), and declared that the *Declaration* was now unacceptable. When the *Declaration* came before the UN Human Rights Council, Canada, the only CANZUS state with a seat on the body, led an unsuccessful vote against the *Declaration*. These four states continued to lobby against the *Declaration* when it proceeded to the UN General Assembly for final adoption. Their success in generating concerns among states that had not taken part in the two decades of debate led to an unfortunate decision to delay adoption for a year to allow further 'consultation.' At the time, many feared this delay could lead to further negotiations that would either block adoption of the *Declaration* or drastically weaken its provisions.

Canada's opposition during the crucial period of debate over its adoption is made all the more disappointing by the knowledge that under the previous government, Canadian officials had played a major role in building state support for the *Declaration* during the working group process. Although the Harper government claimed that its position was consistent with that of previous governments, Canadian officials were now repeating extreme and unfounded claims they had once refuted and were denouncing provisions they had helped draft.

In fact, government briefing papers obtained through an access-to-information request confirm that senior Canadian bureaucrats who reviewed the text in advance of the Human Rights Council decision recommended that the government support the *Declaration*. The *Declaration* is also supported by the three opposition parties, resulting in two decisions by the Parliamentary Committee on Aboriginal Affairs calling on the government to support it.

Government ministers and Canadian representatives have tried to justify Canada's sudden change in position by offering extreme interpretations of its potential impact. For example, when the *Declaration* was before the Human Rights Council, the Minister for Indian Affairs and Northern Development told Parliament 'the proposed wording is incompatible with our Constitution, the Canadian Charter of Rights and Freedoms, various Supreme Court decisions, the National Defence Act and federal policies on aboriginal land claims and self-government.'[10]

Although such claims continue to be made by the Harper government, they have never been substantiated. A position paper posted to the Department of Indian Affairs website in September 2006 states instead that '[i]nterpretive uses of the draft *Declaration* could go beyond the current state of Canadian law' and that 'the rights provisions in the *Declaration* could be interpreted to provide for a different balance [between rights protection and public interest] than that already provided for under the Charter.'[11] This is far from identifying an incompatibility between the *Declaration* and domestic human rights commitments. In fact, international human rights instruments are, of course, expected to encourage states to do more to protect the rights of the most vulnerable, and would not be worth lengthy negotiation if they merely restated and endorsed the current status quo.

What is most disturbing about the government's claims is that they rely upon assumptions that any advancement in the rights of Indigenous peoples must necessarily come at the expense of society as a whole – a claim that would not be made about the human rights of any other group.

This message found a sympathetic ear in some of the corporate media in Canada. In an editorial titled 'Hard-headed on the Native File,' the *National Post* praised the Harper government for opposing 'the UN's innocuous-sounding motherhood statements,' warning that 'In the hands of more radical bands or associations ... [the *Declaration*'s recognition of the right of self-determination] could potentially have explosive effects on Canadian sovereignty.' The *Toronto Star*, a paper usually known for its liberal sympathies, also published an editorial supporting the government's position, repeating the government's assertions about the negative impacts of the *Declaration* without question.

The success of the government's media spin illustrates the need for continued solidarity and collaboration between Indigenous and non-Indigenous activists. When politicians or the media can cast the protection of human rights as a threat to Canadian values because the rights holders are Indigenous, non-Indigenous activists and organizations need to be prepared to speak out.

The Harper government has interpreted media support as enabling Canada to exempt itself from any application of the *Declaration*. Canada has claimed that UN mechanisms should not make any use of the *Declaration* when examining human rights in Canada, that it should not be used to aid in the interpretation of other human rights instruments to which Canada is a party, and that future instruments do not need to be consistent with the *Declaration* and can fall below its standard. This assertion that states can opt out of universal human rights standards at their convenience is unprecedented in Canadian foreign policy and sends an alarming message about the triumph of politics over principle.

Despite this opposition there are numerous opportunities to advance the *Declaration* as a living human rights instrument within Canada. Indigenous peoples' organizations, the media, state institutions such as courts and human rights commissions, and civil society can all play a role and should not be deterred by the obstructionist position of a particular government.

The efforts of the ad-hoc coalition have influenced and gained the support of the three opposition parties and two parliamentary committees. As a response to our joint efforts, on 8 April 2008 the House of Commons adopted the following motion: 'That the government endorse the *United Nations Declaration on the Rights of Indigenous Peoples* as adopted by the United Nations General Assembly on 13 September 2007 and that Parliament and the Government of Canada fully implement the standards contained therein.'[12]

Conclusion

On 13 September 2007 the UN General Assembly voted overwhelmingly to adopt the *Declaration*. A total of 144 states voted in support, four voted against, and 11 abstained. The four opposing states were Canada, the United States, New Zealand, and Australia. This marked the end of the long and often tumultuous journey of more than 20 years. It also marks the beginning of a new journey – as we embark on the implementation of the rights affirmed in the *Declaration*.

Victoria Tauli-Corpuz, as chair of the UN Permanent Forum on Indigenous Issues, spoke to the General Assembly after the vote:

> This day will forever be etched in our history and memories as a significant gain in our long struggle for our rights as distinct peoples and cultures. The 13th of September 2007 will be remembered as a day when the United Nations and its Member States, together with Indigenous Peoples, reconciled with past painful histories and decided to march into the future on the path of human rights. I thank very warmly all the States who voted for the adoption of the Declaration today. All of you will be remembered by us ... This is a Declaration which makes the opening phrase of the UN Charter, 'We the Peoples,' meaningful for 370 million Indigenous persons all over the world ... I call on governments, the UN system, Indigenous Peoples, and civil society at large to rise to the historic task before us and make the UN Declaration on the Rights of Indigenous Peoples a living document for the common future of humanity.

The *Declaration* is being implemented at the global level with UN bodies such as the Special Rapporteur on the situation of human rights and fundamental freedoms of Indigenous people, the Permanent Forum on Indigenous Issues, and the new Human Rights Council Expert Mechanism on the Rights of Indigenous Peoples adopting it as the appropriate frame of reference for Indigenous rights. From the grassroots to the national level, there are countless examples of implementation already happening around the globe. Our Ad Hoc Coalition will continue to work towards education and implementation in Canada.

NOTES

1 United Nations Declaration on the Rights of Indigenous Peoples, UNGA Res. A/RES/61/295, 13 September 2007, Annex.
2 The *Declaration* was adopted by the Human Rights Council by resolution: Working Group of the Commission on Human Rights to Elaborate a Draft Declaration in Accordance with Paragraph 5 of General Assembly resolution 49/214 of 23 December 1994, Human Rights Council Res. 2006/2, in Human Rights Council, *Report to the General Assembly on the First Session of the Human Rights Council*, UN Doc. A/HRC/1/L.10 (30 June 2006), 56.
3 Les Malezer, Chair, Global Indigenous Peoples' Caucus. Statement to the UN General Assembly, New York, 13 September 2007.

4 Statement of Indigenous representatives from the North American Region, 13 September 2007.
5 Third session of the United Nations Permanent Forum on Indigenous Issues, 10 May 2004.
6 Draft United Nations Declaration on the Rights of Indigenous Peoples, UN Sub-Commission on Prevention of Discrimination and Protection of Minorities Res. 1994/45, in Commission on Human Rights, *Report of the Sub-Commission on Prevention of Discrimination and Protection of Minorities on its Forty-Sixth Session*, UN Doc. E/CN.4/1995/2, E/CN.4/Sub.2/1994/56 (28 October 1994) 103.
7 *Establishment of a working group of the Commission on Human Rights to elaborate a draft declaration in accordance with paragraph 5 of General Assembly resolution 49/214*, ESC Res. 1995/32, UN SCSOR, 1995, Supp. No. 1, UN Doc. E/1995/95 (1996) 44.
8 *Commission on Human Rights, Human Rights and Indigenous Issues: Report of the working group established in accordance with Commission on Human Rights resolution 1995/32 of 3 March 1995 on its eleventh session*, UN Doc. E/CN.4/2006/79 (22 March 2006).
9 For a detailed analysis of the actions of the government of Canada, please see 'UN Declaration: Achieving Reconciliation and Effective Application in the Canadian Context' in the Continuing Education Society of British Columbia, *Aboriginal Law Conference – 2008: Challenges and opportunities on the road to reconciliation*, Paper 2.2.
10 Hansard, 21 June 2006.
11 Indian and Northern Affairs Canada. 'Canada's Position: United Nations Draft Declaration on the Rights of Indigenous Peoples. 29 June 2006. http://www.ainc-inac.gc.ca/nr/spch/unp/06/ddr_e.html.
12 The text of the Motion is contained in House of Commons, Status of Women Standing Committee, 'Third Report of the Committee (United Nations Draft Declaration on the Rights of Indigenous Peoples)' Sessional Paper No. 8510-392-55 (13 February 2008).

REFERENCES

Battiste, Marie, and Henderson, James (Sa'ke'j). *Protecting Indigenous Knowledge and Heritage: A Global Challenge*. Saskatoon, SK: Purich, 2000.
Grand Council of the Crees (Eeeyou Istchee), et al. 'Assessing the International Decade: Urgent Need to Renew Mandate and Improve the U.N. Standard-Setting Process on Indigenous Peoples' Human Rights.' Joint Submission to

the Office of the High Commissioner for Human Rights, Geneva, Switzerland, March 2004. http://www.gcc.ca/archive/article.php?id=240.

Moses, Ted. 'Invoking International Law.' In *Reclaiming Indigenous Voice and Vision*. Marie Battiste. Ed. Vancouver: UBC Press, 2000.

Saganash, Romeo, and Joffe, Paul. 'Indigenous Peoples and International Human Rights: Eliminating State Discrimination.' Oxford Amnesty Lectures, Oxford, England, February 2005. http://www.gcc.ca/archive/article.php?id=229.

5 Grassy Narrows: Advocate for Mother Earth and Its Inhabitants

JUDY DA SILVA

Judy Da Silva (AnishinabeKwe, Lynx Clan) has been one of the leading spokespeople for the Grassy Narrows community (Asubpeeschoseewagong Netum Anishinabek), where a blockade, first initiated by the youth, has been underway since 2002. It is the longest-standing Indigenous blockade in Canadian history. The Anishinabe of Grassy Narrows have been fighting clear-cut logging in their traditional territory, which comprises over 2,500 square kilometers of forests, lakes, and rivers north of Kenora, Ontario. Judy, together with her sisters Roberta and Barbara, works in alliance with organizations such as Friends of Grassy Narrows, Rainforest Action Network, Christian Peacemakers, and Amnesty International in carrying out their front-line work, lobbying, organizing, and public education. Judy delivered this keynote address at the Re/Envisioning Relationships Conference.

We have been doing a whirlwind tour of cities. We joke around a little bit saying that it sounds like we're in a band or something, but it's the three grandmas travelling together. We're all grandmas, my sisters and I, and we come face-to-face with a lot of young people who are interested in protecting the earth. And we've stayed in their homes. A lot of the times they have really healthy foods, organically grown vegetables or just really healthy foods. And they're kind of like the hippie age.

We started the Grassy Narrows blockade in 2002. It's been a really, really long process. It started out with the mercury pollution being found in the water in 1972. The paper mill that was there from 1952 had been dumping mercury all that time, and in 1972 people started seeing the fish popping up in the water and dying. That was an eye-opener for us. That's when we started seeking compensation. I was too young, then, to think about compensation, but I remember the doctors coming from Japan, taking pieces of our hair, and doing blood samples, and then leaving. As a child, I didn't know why these people were doing this. It was the start of how I began seeing how other people, NGOs, started working with us. It's in a very simple way, and part of that is the caring that comes from them. And since then we have made so many alliances, so many relationships because of our struggle. We have met so many brothers, so many sisters, of the earth.

Kenora, where we are located, is six hours from Thunder Bay; I think it's over 2,000 kilometers, one way, from Toronto. There are 28 reserves around the Kenora area. That's 20,000 Anishinabe that live in that area of our traditional territory. We have 1,200 or more registered members on our band list, but about 700 live on reserve, and about 250 of those are eligible voters. So, in your mind, you can figure out how many youth and children under 18 we have on the reserve. It's a very high population of youth.

At Grassy Narrows, a lot of our people live in Third World conditions. Some of us who have jobs can escape those conditions. I always tell my children that we are the poorest-richest people on this planet because our land is so full of resources, so-called 'resources for development.' There are minerals, there's gold, there's titanium, there are spring waters, there's granite, and there's tourism. It just goes on and on. And yet we still live in poverty, and that was part of our stand. Because we get a lot of complaints that we live off taxpayers, and we feel like, 'Ok, everybody get out of our traditional territory. Leave us alone, and let us live how we want to live.' We could be self-sufficient; we could decolonize our own people and empower them again, and get back on the land. We can do the stuff we were doing, and be who we are, the Anishinabe. It doesn't mean going backwards, because a lot of people think that when you go back to hunting, when you go back to fishing, when you go back to living from the forest that you're going backwards. But it's not. It's just our natural way of living. And my brother, who's been hunting for the last few weeks, was saying, 'I don't think I can be Anishinabe anymore because I have to always go back to my work, so I can pay for my trucks, so I can pay for my gas, so I can go drive away into the forest and go hunting.'

It's like a process of assimilation that we're going through, adapting to this new lifestyle today. We feel that this transition is inevitable, but at the same time, we're going to fight as hard as we can to keep our traditions, to keep our language. Someone said that in 50 years most of the languages are going to disappear. The languages are part of our culture. They tie us to the land and our ceremonies.

We still hunt, we still fish, we still eat wild animals, the moose, the deer. And my sister has a trapline, but that's the name given to it by the Ministry of Natural Resources. Actually it's her traditional hunting grounds, where she gets wild game. And she survives from that, she eats from there, and she tries not to buy cows and chickens and that kind of stuff. She tries to eat in as traditional a manner as she can. But she does buy the occasional thing from the store. So I'm just letting you know that a lot of the traditional peoples still live from the land. We have not disappeared; we have not died off. And we are not going to disappear, because there's still a lot of us out there in the forest who are invisible.

With the blockade that started in 2002, we have met a lot of compassionate people like us. I'll just name a few. The first organization that really kind of stuck up for us was the Wilderness Heritage and Community Keepers Organization (WHACKO) in Kenora. They're one of the first people that stepped up to help us when we were trying to fight to protect the forest. I honour them because, to be realistic, we live in a really racist community in Kenora, and I think these people were brave to step forward and to invite us to one of their meetings. That was a long time ago, and since then we have met so many people. We have the Friends of Grassy Narrows, and they made a website; they're like these hippies that are really poor, but they care about the earth and they care about us. And the Boreal Forest Network, and the University Network and Forest Action Network, and most recently the Rainforest Action Network, and Amnesty International, and the numerous universities that invite us to speak.

So I want to tell the NGOs that the part you can help us with is to see us as human beings, that we have a heart and that you can work with us. But it's up to you to go past those apologies that you have made for yourself or that have been put on you. We can do a lot together to save the earth, to save our common earth. The racism and the discrimination that have been put on us through our own history, they can be put aside, and then we can walk together on this earth.

With the help of the Rainforest Action Network we set up a direct action internship program. All these young people came from Maryland in the United States, and from Hamilton, Ontario, and from British Columbia – mostly from big cities. They lived with us. I don't know if any of you watch television and have seen that *Survivor* series, but that's kind of how it was. I felt sorry for those young people. Sometimes they'd be covered in those mosquito clothes, and they looked pretty scary. Some of them were just adapting to the forest; there's so many blackflies, so many mosquitoes, they'd have all these bites on them. But eventually they'd settle down, and those bug bites started going away, and they started seeing how we operate. We operate in a low time zone. We'd go visit them, maybe 10 o'clock at night, when they were getting ready to go to bed and we're really wide awake. We'd just go and sing songs and wake them up and things like that. They learned to snap out of that scheduled kind of lifestyle and to go with the flow a lot of the times.

When we went on the Highway 1 blockade, it was a huge learning experience for our interns. The experience showed them that direct action is not violent. We worked together, and we stood together, and created awareness of what was happening to the forest. Anishinabe and non-Native people could stand together and stand strong together and work together and operate together. That was the biggest learning experience that I received, that we can actually work with people like that, and not to be so afraid of them. I'm hoping that more internships like that will happen because it was a very good tool. It was a new idea. I have seen the *Survivor* series, and *The Amazing Race*, and we're such adaptable people, the way the Creator made us. And sometimes we give ourselves lines like, 'Oh I can't do that, I can't go there, it's too cold, it's too far,' but if you just give yourself a little shove and go that extra step in doing something, you can make it possible to achieve what you want to achieve.

Our area is one of the biggest reservoirs of fresh water in the world. It's called the Land of the Thousand Lakes. It's very, very precious to the earth. It has its own ecosystem to filter out the poisons that are coming through the air – namely, the trees. I don't know all the scientific terms for it, but I do know that cutting down the trees is affecting the earth, because I see many green lakes with a lot of algae, and we see water levels dropping very rapidly.

Keys Lake is a spring, and the water comes from under the earth. It's one of our most sacred sites. A lot of tourists come there every summer, and they camp there. It's really nice there, but then the thing I'm starting to see is big boats going on there. It's an independent lake; it's just in a circle, and people can easily canoe across, and go along the sloped cedars.

One of the things my sister was saying is that we're hardly seeing any moose. We usually see moose when we are going to Kenora; we see two or three. But now we hardly see any, and we don't know why. But we'll figure it out; the elders will probably tell us why eventually.

In Kenora, one guy was yelling at me and told me that I was cutting a contractor's job because I was protesting. And he said that the contractor had to make $33,000 a day, $300,000 a month to break even, because he has a lot of people working under him, and a lot of logging trucks. They have a machine that costs $500,000, which does a lot of the work. It does the job; it cuts the tree up and breaks the branches. It cuts it into a certain size and then loads it onto a truck. It's really mechanical. This is how they clear-cut. It's very complete. The way my husband describes it, it's like a razor cut, like when you shave your beard off. It just shaves everything off and it doesn't leave anything. It doesn't leave medicines. It destroys everything. And I heard one hunter saying that sometimes bears get in the way, and sometimes there're five or six bears in a row that the loggers have to kill because they were in the way. So there are many different types of devastation going on besides tree and plant life. There's also animal life that gets destroyed, in addition to us.

A lot of times the propaganda messages from the logging companies say that they replant trees, but what they leave out is that they cut them afterward for the mill. They also don't plant anything else except the trees that they want. If trees fall naturally, there's all the other plant life around, and it regenerates the forest. But the logging companies take everything out and just plant the trees they want. These trees grow sick, not healthy and strong. They're very skinny; you see logging trucks now with really skinny sticks on their trucks. But lately I've been seeing poplars that are really fat. So I know they're going further north to old-growth forests to get their quotas for the day, to break even.

Those machines take a lot of jobs from people, and, as the logging industry gets more mechanized, the fewer people you need. In the first information paper that we wrote, in 1999, we predicted that the Abitibi mill would shut down, because it's just the general way these big corporations operate. They come and swoop down, create a few jobs, take what they need, and then leave and drop the workers. So it's not a very sustainable way of living on this earth – just come, destroy, and leave. That's what this machine does. There are a lot of them operating in our forests.

A lot of the trees that are planted have been injected with genetically modified things, so they can grow to be robust and compete with all the plant species. They tell women tree planters that if they are going to have a baby, do not have a baby within four years after you tree-plant, because the chemicals that are on the tree will go inside the woman and hurt the baby. But they won't explain that. They'll just say, 'Don't have a baby for four years.' I'm pretty sure the men that go on planting, it affects them too somehow, if it's that toxic that a woman can't have a baby for four years after she plants trees.

Sometimes we find a lot of waters on the site that are full of oil slicks, different rainbow colours. We assume that they are chemicals that are in the water from the trucks. Sometimes we find oil spills and rotting trees on site, so there's a lot of waste. I was told that back in 2002 each truck was worth $4,000 a load. One time when I was driving by a Trus Joist Weyerheuser mill, I saw six trucks waiting in line to be unloaded. That was just driving by Trus Joist.

In Seattle there is a project called Quadrant Homes, and they've marketed 'green homes,' which means environmentally friendly homes. But what they use is the strandboard from our forest to build these beautiful 'green' homes in Seattle. And it's not the only city that does that. It's all over North America that they say 'green homes.' It's all an illusion to the people who buy these homes.

Abitibi Consolidated in Kenora is closed down now. There's no more smoke coming out of the stacks, but it is still probably finding a place to go and cut in another city, in another community, when it finished with us here. I assume that another company will just come and take over, and continue to try to get a forest licence for our area.

At the Separation Lake Bridge Blockade there were nine adults and four children; eight women and one man. There were 40 police officers that came there and took the protestors away. With those arrests there were very, very clear acts of discrimination, because the white women were put in one paddy wagon and the Native women were put in another, along with the lone man. The Aboriginal women were treated differently. At least one was handcuffed. So they were taken away very violently when they were just there in a very gentle way to protect the earth and the forest and our traditional way of life. And there were little children there.

One young woman activist stopped a logging truck by standing in front of it. And a lot of times when we were doing the blockades, the loggers would pretty much cooperate with us, and they would just listen to the contractor, like if they were told 'go forward' or 'go back.' But, pretty much, if we told them we were not going to leave the area for that load, they'd say, 'Okay,' and they would go back off. But at this particular site it was a 12-hour stalemate where nobody could go either way, and in the end the loggers went back the long way to take the logs to the mill. We didn't allow them to come through.

We built a log cabin, mainly constructed by the young people of Grassy Narrows, at the Grassy Narrows blockade site. Like I said, we are trying to decolonize our youth and get them back on the land so we're more visibly on the land. Our wigwam is very pitiful, but we do our sacred ceremonies in there. It's really big inside, but we tried to make it like a wigwam; and now we have canvas on there, but at the time we had just white plastic. We've had it there for three years now at the blockade site. And part of that is to decolonize our people and get them back on the land and be comfortable.

One of the things people do is called a tree-sit, where they sit in a tree and try to protect the forest. Different people can do that, make different platforms all over the forest to protect that area. Another young woman handcuffed herself under the logging truck, and she was under there a long time, about 10 hours. Ten hours she was under there, and the truck was running the whole time. So there's exhaust and the heat. I honour her for how far she went for us, for the land, and the earth.

A lot of young people came from the cities to stand with us. The police, they stayed there with us the whole time, too. It was really, really hot that day, there was no shade, and we were between rocks. An elder came by trying to tell us to stop, tell us we did enough, we created enough attention, to go home now. We were kind of mixed up there, between listening to an elder and also honouring the spirit of what these young people were doing. The elder was saying that we had done enough, and to continue may bring harm on the people. This was a spiritual warning. However, that one young woman activist had gone so far as to handcuff herself to the undercarriage of a logging truck, and in our mind we needed to honour her determination to support us. In the end we told the elder, 'We're going to stand by this young woman.' We explained that we would take whatever she was saying into consideration, but we had to follow our heart and stand with these young people, to honour what they were doing.

Another young woman had put herself 10 feet in the air on a wooden tripod. It was really, really hot, and she was up there 10 hours without going to the bathroom once. If she came down the police would grab her, so she had to stay there. She was tied to the tripod, like she's sitting on the rope which was holding it together. I could see her sometimes trying to stretch her legs and her back. We kept asking her, 'Are you okay?' and she'd say, 'I'm okay.' So she made a big sacrifice when she was up there for 10 hours. The fire trucks were there, I think more as a barricade for the other people, not as protection, to prevent other people from coming in. Singing always gives us courage, because everything we do is about praying, and singing is part of that.

When creating banners we sometimes use the symbol of the company we are protesting, but use words to get people to think about this company in a different way, words like caution. We try to show how that company's symbol is not a friendly symbol because they are hurting the earth. We use really huge banners at the blockade sites, and when people drive by, they can't help but notice these signs. Another tool is the media, using mainstream media to get the message across. Another tool is to use a projector at night and project the banner onto a huge building. You can put up those words so it shocks people when they drive by and read these signs.

There are the people that stand with us, that are helping us, NGOs such as friendsofgrassynarrows.com and freegrassy.org. If you go anywhere on those sites you'll see all the beautiful, powerful people that stand with us, that help us, that encourage us, that give us strength. We do a lot of things to give us strength, and part of that is we have a sacred fire that we light. This Sunday is a full moon, and hopefully we'll get home before the full moon, before the night ends, and we'll probably light that sacred fire and burn our tobacco. What we do is ask the Creator and Mother Earth to walk with us to protect this land and this earth and that our people be protected and be safe.

It seems like the places that mostly open their doors to us are places of education. It's good to learn about these struggles. Why is this happening? Why are these people struggling? Go back in history and read more books on it, and so on, but the biggest education is hands-on. Come and be with the people, come see the devastation of the land, and feel how the people live. Come into their homes, see the people face-to-face, and talk to them. See if you can come from the heart, and come feel the land, and the earth. Our fight is not finished. We are a long, long ways from finishing this fight. Because as we speak there's still logging going on in the north part of our traditional territory, and it's really massive. You can go to Google Earth and click on Grassy Narrows, and just go to the north part of our traditional territory and you'll see the massive clear-cuts. It's still going on.

Thank you for inviting me to share our story with you, and how the NGOs can form alliances with the Anishinabe, not just at Grassy Narrows. There are a lot of Indigenous struggles across Turtle Island that are happening.

6 Contradictions of Canadian Colonialism: Non-Native Responses to the Six Nations Reclamation at Caledonia

TOM KEEFER

On 28 February 2006, members of the Haudenosaunee Confederacy in the Grand River Territory at Six Nations reclaimed 40 hectares of their lands by taking occupancy and halting the construction of a subdivision on the outskirts of the town of Caledonia, near Hamilton, Ontario. This subdivision, named the Douglas Creek Estates by the developer, was one of the few remaining 'buffer zones' between the town of Caledonia and the Six Nations reserve, which itself occupies less than 5 per cent of the 950,000 acres of land granted to the people of Six Nations 'in perpetuity' for their services to the British Crown by British General Frederick Haldimand in 1784.[1] The standoff between the people of Six Nations and the federal and provincial governments over the Douglas Creek Estates land reclamation, which continues to this day, has drawn thousands of people, both Native and non-Native, into political action, and produced hundreds of media stories about the confrontation. The reclamation has been at the forefront of a resurgence of Indigenous activism taking place across the Canadian state. This chapter will focus on the ways in which non-Native people have intervened in the ongoing standoff in Caledonia. I will argue that the non-Native activism taking place around the reclaimed Douglas Creek Estates subdivision marks a new and significant turning point in both the positive and negative engagement of settlers with the concrete questions posed by the assertion of Indigenous sovereignty.

I am focusing this chapter on the interventions of non-Native activists, not because I think the actions of Indigenous people are not worthy of study, but because I am trying to counteract the tendency of Canadians to view land claims struggles as a 'Native problem,' when in fact it is a 'non-Native' problem, both in its initial construction and in its perpetuation. This means that an important part of any resolution to the historic injustices imposed upon Indigenous people will require active struggle against colonialism on the part of non-Native people. Indigenous led and directed struggles will, of course, provide the concrete instances and socio-political context around which non-Natives are moved into action. But with Indigenous people making up less than 5 per cent of Canada's population, how the non-Native majority of the population responds to Indigenous activism will have a fundamental impact in shaping the success or failure of twenty-first-century anti-colonial resistance movements. In looking at the dynamics playing themselves out in the struggle over the Douglas Creek Estates, this chapter will examine the efforts of two activist groups based in the local settler population that have taken diametrically opposed positions on this issue: Caledonia Wake-Up Call, a group associated with Richmond Hill resident Gary McHale; and Community Friends for Peace and Understanding with Six Nations, a group which has worked to support Six Nations and the reclamation.

Setting the Stage: The Reclamation of the Douglas Creek Estates

The responses of non-Native activists to the reclamation of the Douglas Creek Estates were originally related to the level of confrontation at the site. From 28 February to 20 April 2006, the site consisted of a small encampment by the entrance to the Douglas Creek Estates. Even though the land had been secured by people from Six Nations and construction had been halted, interactions with Caledonia residents were by and large quite cordial. Then, early in the morning of 20 April, hundreds of members of the Ontario Provincial Police (OPP) stormed the reclamation site without warning and attempted to clear the area of its occupants. However, the OPP did not count on the rapid and sizeable community response from the people of Six Nations, and within hours hundreds of Six Nations residents pushed back the police and retook the land. Indigenous activists established checkpoints to control access to the site, and blocked nearby roads and rail lines. Over the following weeks Six Nations community members were joined by hundreds of non-Native supporters and Indigenous activists from across Canada and the United States.

Although Caledonia residents had been very quiet during the first phase of the reclamation, the mood changed once Highway 6 was blocked.

With memories of the death of Dudley George still fresh in the public's mind as a result of the ongoing public inquiry into the Ipperwash affair,[2] and aware of their own inability to disperse the people of Six Nations without recourse to potentially lethal force, the OPP refused to move onto the site or against the road blockades, and instead created a police line to stop anti-Native Caledonia residents wanting the road reopened from clashing with the people of Six Nations. On 24 April, local business leaders and influential members of the Caledonia community, led by lo- cal businessman Ken Hewitt, organized a public rally to demand that the municipal government take action in clearing the reclamation site. Hewitt's group brought out over 3,000 people to the rally, and later that night 500 protestors marched up Argyle Street with the intention of push- ing past the blockades and clearing protesters from the site.

The protest never made it to the reclamation site, although it did try to pass the police line – leading to one arrest and damage to an OPP cruiser.[3] Practically every weekend from 28 April until 22 May, when the barricades on Argyle Street finally came down, hundreds of Caledonia residents would gather in the nearby Canadian Tire parking lot and then make their way to the OPP lines that stood in front of the Six Nations road blockade. At this stage of the conflict, the main spokes- people for those demanding an end to the highway blockade and oc- cupation of the Douglas Creek Estates were the leaders of the Caledonia Citizens Alliance (CAA), an organization established by members of the Caledonia Chamber of Commerce and other business groups.[4]

After the barricades came down in late May of 2006, calm was by and large restored in Caledonia, and with the road opened the level of ten- sion in the community declined. However, a group of residents living in the subdivision adjacent to the reclamation claimed that not only had they been victimized by people from Six Nations during the time of the road blockade, but also that this 'harassment' continued after the bar- ricades came down.

By the end of August, some of these residents had coalesced into a loose-knit group dubbed 'Caledonia Resistance,' which undertook to monitor events at the reclamation site with electronic scanners, tele- scopes, video cameras, and binoculars. Caledonia Resistance lacked a public profile or political leadership, although people associated with the group did attend meetings of the Caledonia Citizens Alliance and critiqued the group for not being more aggressive in confronting the Natives occupying the reclamation site. One chilling example of just how far certain members of the group were willing to go was revealed by *The Globe and Mail,* which quoted Caledonia Resistance spokesperson Steve Tong as stating that 'there's times the trigger locks have been off … There's times when I had my gun out of the cabinet and the gun sitting there ready.'[5] In contrast to the violent and confrontational approach pushed by some members of Caledonia Resistance, the mainstream leaders of the CCA preferred to work closely with government spokespeople, and publicly distanced themselves from the possibility of organizing further clashes with the reclamation site or public protests against the government.

Gary McHale and Caledonia Wake-Up Call

The retreat from open anti-Native activism by the Caledonia Citizens Alliance and the extremism of Caledonia Resistance created a political vacuum that Gary McHale, a resident of the Toronto suburb of Richmond Hill, filled. Beginning in June of 2006, McHale, a card-carrying member of the federal Conservative Party, came into town with a clear political message. Citing the experience of non-Natives living near Stony Point, where the Ipperwash standoff occurred in 1995, McHale claimed that the Natives were unfairly enjoying a 'two-tiered' justice system in which they broke Canadian law with impunity. In essence, McHale was calling for the OPP (and, if required, the Canadian Armed Forces) to decisively move into action against the people of Six Nations in order to crush any Six Nations resistance to the expropriation of their lands that did not operate within the 'legal' boundaries established by the Canadian state.

McHale, an effective public speaker adept at handling the media, first came to prominence with his plans to organize a 'March for Freedom' on 15 October 2006. He argued that since the Ontario government (as part of its response to the crisis) had purchased the disputed land from the developers who had been blocked from the site, the reclamation site now belonged to the people of Ontario and that they could and should exercise their rights by enjoying a 'one day' use of the land. Since the OPP would not let anti-native protestors onto the reclamation site, McHale argued that a mass, 'peaceful' civil disobedience action would pave the way for the ending of 'two-tiered' justice in Caledonia. In attempting to force the OPP either to make mass arrests of Caledonia residents or to allow them onto the Douglas Creek Estates, where a confrontation with Native protesters would undoubtedly occur, McHale claimed to be following in the footsteps of U.S. civil rights leader Martin Luther King, Jr. Speaking at a public meeting in Caledonia,

Mark Vandermaas, a close associate of McHale, explained that the strategic goal of their non-violent protests in Caledonia were best summarized by a passage from King's 'Letter from a Birmingham Jail':

> We who engage in nonviolent direct action are not the creators of tension. We merely bring to the surface the hidden tension that is already alive. We bring it out in the open, where it can be seen and dealt with.
>
> In your statement you assert that our actions, even though peaceful, must be condemned because they precipitate violence. But is this a logical assertion? Isn't this like condemning a robbed man because his possession of money precipitated the evil act of robbery?
>
> We must come to see that, as the federal courts have consistently affirmed, it is wrong to urge an individual to cease his efforts to gain his basic constitutional rights because the quest may precipitate violence. Society must protect the robbed and punish the robber.[6]

As bizarre as it may seem, McHale's strategy for Caledonia is modelled on the discourse of the U.S. civil rights movement and should not be underestimated. In claiming 'equal rights' for all under Canadian law, and in framing the issue as one of 'two-tiered justice' in which Native people are coddled by state authorities while non-Natives are 'terrorized' by violent 'land claim terrorists,' McHale manages to turn the tables on Indigenous people who are, in fact, the true victims of the 'two-tiered' Canadian law enforcement system, and to evade charges of racism by claiming to stand in support of unbiased and universal standards of justice.[7]

One of the most significant aspects of McHale's protest was that it featured its own security team drawn from Caledonia residents, some of them members of Caledonia Resistance, who monitored the crowd and coordinated logistics. Also significant was the fact that a dozen neo-Nazis from the 'Northern Alliance' group based in London, Ontario, attended the protest, handed out literature, and spoke to the media.[8]

When asked in an interview for the *Hamilton Spectator* about his position on the neo-Nazis who attended his events, McHale stated that '[white supremacists] show up (to events) all the time. That's no proof of anything.' Speaking of himself in the third person, McHale added that 'Gary has been condemning white supremacy, the KKK, in the same breath he condemns Muslim terrorists, warriors who do serious crimes …'[9] Disclaimers notwithstanding, at the time of the writing of this article, a Google search of his website turns up no critical statements directed either towards white supremacists in general, or towards those who have regularly attended his demonstrations. Indeed, McHale argues that the neo-Nazis 'have a right to be there. I can't stop them. They are an element which I have no control over. I have no say in their beliefs or actions, and they are the element from my side that I see can create potential problems …' But while refusing to explicitly speak out against the presence of white supremacists at his events, McHale has been very good in not letting the uglier side of his base of support show. He says, 'I tell every person (at the start of each protest) to use no racial slurs. I tell every person not to swear. I tell every person not to use any violence.'[10]

After McHale's 15 October protest, which never actually attempted to march onto the reclamation site, Caledonia remained quiet. In the months that followed, McHale tried to keep the issue of the reclamation in the news by organizing 'flag raising' events, where he attempted to place Canadian flags on hydro poles across from the road where Six Nations flags were flying on the Douglas Creek Estates.

McHale has established through his activities a well-rehearsed and internally consistent political argument against Native land claims that has resonated among certain parts of Canadian settler society. Unlike groups like the CCA, which are essentially elite-based groups focusing their activities on efforts to lobby government officials for financial compensation and a seat at the negotiating table, McHale embodies a kind of radical populism that hopes to 'wake up' the 'silent [white] majority' and push them into vocally demanding that their government repress 'illegal' Native protests. Critical of politicians of every political stripe at all levels of government, McHale calls for Canadian citizens to get active at the grassroots level by organizing protests, monitoring police and Native protests, and circumventing the mainstream media 'blackout' on 'land claim terrorism' by strategic use of the Internet.

Having already built the largest and most comprehensive website on Caledonia – Six Nations related matters, McHale is branching out to discuss the issue of Native land claims more generally, and he is providing a pole of attraction around which a range of groups and individuals opposed to Indigenous sovereignty can gather. A dozen or so right-wing, anti-Native bloggers are linked to McHale's website, and white supremacists, including prominent Holocaust denier Paul Fromm, have been present at a number of McHale's events. Even if McHale is not explicitly working with organized white supremacist groups, it remains possible that relatively discrete white supremacists could penetrate his networks in order to gain recruits and influence the direction of his activities. Although McHale's arguments are largely facile, based as they are on the premise that Indigenous people have no claim to sovereignty and should be treated as if they were no more than assimilated, albeit disobedient, Canadian citizens, his arguments have gone largely unopposed in the constituencies in which he organizes. With the exception of a few pro-Native electronic discussion bulletin boards and a couple of (mostly outdated) websites archiving mainstream coverage of the Six Nations reclamation, non-Native solidarity activists have not produced anywhere near the same level of analysis and opinion that McHale and his compatriots have on these matters.

Many progressive activists have hoped that McHale and his compatriots will go away if they are ignored. They have argued that McHale is simply seeking attention, and that confronting him directly by counter-protesting his activities or by holding public debates with him will only increase his own sense of self-importance. While at a certain level McHale may indeed enjoy being at the centre of attention due to his new-found political importance in Haldimand County, this kind of argument personalizes the matter and fails to take into account the larger forces that are at play in this conflict. Indigenous activism over rights to the Haldimand tract is supported by a relatively large, well-organized and growing Indigenous population, and opposed by a significant number of landowners, entrepreneurs, and developers who have a lot to lose should Six Nations succeed in controlling economic activity on their historic lands.[11] Coupled with the deep undercurrents of anti-Native racism in Canadian society, McHale's populist rhetoric and his appeal to grassroots organizing represents a serious, if not fully actualized, threat. If McHale continues in his activism, it is possible that anti-Native activists across the country will connect to his network as local Indigenous struggles develop in their local area, and will continue his strategy of pressuring the Canadian state to swiftly and decisively intervene against any Native activists taking direct action to advance their interests.

Community Friends: Non-Native Support of Six Nations

Activism in support of Six Nations has not had the same level of mass media coverage as the work being done by McHale's group and the CCA, despite the fact that dozens of different activist groups, trade unions, student groups, and international solidarity movements have passed motions expressing support for the Six Nations reclamation; and many of these groups have sent solidarity delegations, supplies, and financial donations to the reclamation site. While the people of Six Nations held the barricades, dozens of non-Native activists, many of whom had long supported Indigenous causes, were present at the site to help by cooking food and doing camp chores. However, for the most part these non-Native supporters put little or no effort into reaching out to or connecting with non-Native people in Caledonia, the constituency that McHale's Caledonia Wake-Up Call and the CCA were organizing within and claiming to represent.[12]

One exception to this tendency of intermittent support from a distance has been the work of the Caledonia-based group Community Friends for Peace and Understanding with Six Nations, which brought together Caledonia residents, people from Six Nations, and trade union activists from the surrounding area. The group formed in May of 2006 after half a dozen non-Native supporters of the reclamation met up after observing an anti-Native protest in Caledonia on the evening of 28 April.[13] Disturbed by the racism and the size of the crowd at the protest, members of Community Friends decided to focus their activities on trying to defuse the racism and tension within Caledonia by directly engaging with people in Caledonia, and they sought to build and connect pro-Native solidarity groups in surrounding non-Native communities. This approach was based on the argument that the dispute was not simply one of conflict between Natives and non-Natives, but one between those supporting fundamental issues of human rights and self-determination and those upholding colonial practices of oppression. It was on this basis that the Community Friends group began meeting at the home of Caledonia resident Jan Watson, a woman with no prior political involvements or any connection to Six Nations, but who felt compelled to do something in support of what she saw as a fair and just struggle for dignity and justice by the people of Six Nations.[14]

One of the most significant things about the Community Friends group was the joint participation of roughly equal members of Native and non-Native people within it. Although the practical political focus of the group was on intervening in non-Native society, the presence of people from Six Nations provided direct links to activists at the reclamation site, as well as a political grounding in the life and political culture of the Six Nations community itself. Especially in the early days of the group, it was clear that the meetings served as one of the few places where Native and non-Native people from the area could interact in a space of mutual respect and understanding. One of the main results of this ongoing relationship has been the development of strong links of trust, friendship, and political solidarity between Native and non-Native group members.

In contrast to more liberal approaches, Community Friends took an unambiguous perspective of support for Indigenous sovereignty, arguing that, 'We believe that the Six Nations people have been cheated of their land rights, and that the Canadian government needs to honor existing treaties with Six Nations and deal with them on a nation-to-nation basis.' The political goals of the group involved supporting the reclamation of the Douglas Creek Estates and the transfer of the land to the people of Six Nations; defending all Six Nations people criminalized for activity in defense of their lands; pressuring the Canadian government to 'swiftly, fairly, and peacefully' resolve all outstanding land claims relating to the Haldimand tract; and educating the people of Caledonia in particular and the Canadian public in general about the issue of Six Nations land rights and the larger questions of Indigenous sovereignty in the North American context.[15]

The first action of the Community Friends group was to set up a phone hotline and place ads in the local newspapers inviting people who were opposed to the racism and hatred being directed against the people of Six Nations to get in touch with other Caledonians wanting to work for peace and justice. The response to these ads was significant; more than 20 people, the overwhelming majority of whom were women, called the hotline. Many of the callers were afraid to come forward as supporters of Six Nations land rights; they felt that they would be targeted and victimized by their partners, friends, family members, or co-workers if they got politically involved. That repercussions existed for non-Natives who supported Six Nations was made clear by the way Community Friends founder and Caledonia resident Jan Watson was targeted by anti-Native elements in Caledonia. Watson's house was egged on a number of different occasions, someone attempted to kick in her door in the middle of the night, property from her front lawn was stolen, at an anti-Native rally she was confronted by an angry crowd wielding baseball bats and clubs threatening to overturn her vehicle, and on one occasion she was even karate chopped in the neck by a man outweighing her by 100 pounds.[16] Several other non-Native members of Community Friends have faced similar types of harassment and intimidation for supporting Six Nations, and this climate of fear has made it difficult for the Community Friends group to build a base in Caledonia.

In September of 2006, Community Friends organized a public meeting headlined by non-Native speakers in support of Native rights. The meeting featured Caledonia resident Jan Watson, United Steelworkers Local 1005 president Rolf Gerstenberger, and Kate Kempton, a lawyer specializing in Indigenous land rights. Both the speakers and the topics they discussed were selected in order to try and break the myth that the political conflicts taking place over the reclamation site were taking place simply on the basis of ethnicity. Held in a Caledonia high school, the event was attended by over 100 people, showing that support for Indigenous struggles existed among non-Natives.

Members of Community Friends also began a petition drive in support of the reclamation site, and met with representatives from the *Hamilton Spectator* and CHCH TV to complain about specific and general examples of biased coverage against Six Nations. Meetings were also organized with local elected representatives to show that there was a non-Native constituency supporting the demands of Six Nations. Another important role that Community Friends members played was in going to the town hall meetings held by the Caledonia Citizens Alliance and critiquing their anti-Native positions from the floor. This was effective, both in showing that the CCA did not speak for all Caledonia residents and in countering the one-sided flow of anti-Native information spread by the CCA to Caledonia residents.

Another major area of work by Community Friends lay in initiating public support campaigns for two Six Nations political prisoners, Trevor Miller and Christopher Hill, who had been jailed for charges related to their defence of the reclamation site. Miller was incarcerated for six months before getting bail, while Hill spent three months behind bars waiting for bail. Members of Community Friends visited Miller and Hill in jail, and while working closely with the prisoners' families, raised funds, produced two short videos on the issue, and organized a series of protests and vigils outside the jail.[17] In June of 2007, Community Friends helped to organize a hip-hop benefit concert for Hill, which brought dozens of Black community activists and hip-hop artists from Toronto to Six Nations to perform alongside Six Nations youth. The lead-up to the concert saw the holding of a public meeting in Toronto at the offices of the Black Action Defense Committee, where people from Six Nations shared the history of their struggle with activists in Toronto.

As Community Friends developed it became clear that one of the group's strong points lay in the fact that the majority of its non-Native members are rank-and-file union members. The high level of unionization in the area surrounding Six Nations, and the large number of union members involved in Community Friends meetings, led to the group trying to organize support in their respective unions for the reclamation site. From the beginning of the reclamation, several union locals whose members participated in Community Friends activities have been at the forefront of offering support to the reclamation site. In an attempt to consolidate the work being done through trade unions in support of the Six Nations struggle, Community Friends organized a daylong meeting for union activists in March of 2007, which was addressed by reclamation site activists and released political prisoner Chris Hill and his family. Over 50 people attended the meeting, with representation from a dozen different unions.

The greatest weakness of Community Friends has lain in its relatively weak capacity to reach out to residents in Haldimand County and to build a broad-based organization capable of doing the long-term educational work that is necessary to build support for Indigenous sovereignty in non-Native communities. As I have argued elsewhere, opposition to Indigenous land rights in non-Native communities is heavily conditioned by class, race, and social location, and there are very real possibilities for building support for Indigenous sovereignty in specific groups in non-Native communities, the trade union movement, and racialized non-Native communities in particular.[18] But the problem in small communities like Caledonia is that the institutions of local civil society, the media, the Lions and Rotary clubs, the Chamber of Commerce, the churches, and so on, are almost entirely in the hands of a local business elite (e.g., developers, bankers, lawyers, realtors), who are opposed to recognizing Native land rights because such recognition will halt development and thus the growth of their profits in the area. Added to this is the fact that the organized left in most small towns in rural Ontario is minimal or non-existent, meaning that there are no ready-built bases from which to construct support for Indigenous struggles. Given this situation, the growth of support for Six Nations in surrounding white communities is highly contingent on building or rebuilding vibrant left groupings and institutions in towns and cities near Six Nations that can provide a consistent source of non-Native support and solidarity for the people of Six Nations at the same time as they advance a broader agenda of social and economic justice.

In the small towns and cities surrounding Six Nations this will be a difficult task due to the long-standing tensions that exist between Indigenous and settler communities, but it is by no means impossible. This will ultimately mean that outside activist groups must put serious resources into coordinating their efforts and identifying people in places near Six Nations who might be willing to make connections between their struggles and those relating to Indigenous rights. There are lots of poor people, working-class people, and disaffected youth in the regions who have the potential to build activist groups if given logistical and political support. Building a lasting framework to counter anti-Native activism is essential. Although the work that Community Friends has done in this regard has been important, it has been limited by the minimal institutional resources of the group and its failure to receive significant support from other left formations.

Conclusion

Caledonia Wake-up Call and Community Friends are examples of initiatives taken by non-Natives who have been moved to political action by the ongoing contradiction that is Canada's colonial reality. The majority of progressive non-Natives currently rely on the Canadian courts and provincial or federal governments to incrementally achieve a 'fair deal' for Native people, and the majority of conservative non-Natives expect the coercive apparatus of the state to contain Native protests that create economic or political consequences for them. The Caledonia example shows what can happen when a Native struggle in the public eye is not easily resolvable by either the repressive or co-optive agency of the state. In such a context, organizations such as Caledonia Wake-up Call or Community Friends might provide important indications of the future shape that non-Native responses may take in an ongoing conflict over Native land rights. Neither group is necessarily a permanent feature on the political scene, and neither has yet gained a mass following or sustained support by groups with serious financial or institutional capacities, but the possibilities for such development are there, with consequences that could reshape the way that Native and non-Native relations are viewed in this country.

NOTES

1 The Haldimand proclamation was made to compensate Six Nations people for the loss of much of their traditional lands in upstate New York when they sided with the British, who were defeated in the American Revolutionary War. The proclamation allotted six miles of territory on either side of the Grand River, from its source to its mouth, to the people of Six Nations in perpetuity.

2 Dudley George was a 30-year-old Chippewa (Anishnaabe) man who was shot and killed by OPP Sergeant Kenneth Deane on 7 September 1995 during an Indigenous reclamation of lands occupied at Ipperwash Provincial Park in southwestern Ontario. His death sparked a provincial inquiry into what became known as the 'Ipperwash affair.'

3 Nichole Jankowski, 'First Nations ... Last Resorts.' *The Silhouette.* McMaster University's student newspaper. 4 July 2007. http://www.thesil.ca/article.pl?sid=06/07/04/2258225.

4 As the 12 May 2006 News Release from the CCA notes, 'The Alliance is made up of groups such as the Caledonia Regional Chamber of Commerce, the Caledonia Business Improvement Association, Real Estate representatives, local businesses, and a variety of community citizens' groups.'

5 Alex Dobrata, 'Caledonia Standoff Threatens To Heat Up Again. Residents frustrated with slow pace of negotiations over land rights,' *The Globe and Mail,* 2 September 2006.

6 Mark Vandermaas, 'Why we must go to Deseronto.' *Voice of Canada Blog,* 8 June 2007.

7 Indeed, McHale's rhetoric is quite similar to that used by so-called 'father's rights' groups, or by U.S. white supremacists like David Duke, who use the same kind of rights discourse by portraying fathers or white people as victims of 'reverse discrimination.'

8 Photo galleries on the Northern Alliance web site show members of the neo-Nazi group attending anti-Native protests in Caledonia on 15 October 2006 (see http://northernalliance.ca/Protests/Caledonia/index.htmland), and 20 January 2007 (see http://northernalliance.ca/Protests/Caledonia_Jan_2007/index.html).

9 Marissa Nelson, 'It's about accountability: McHale,' *Hamilton Spectator,* 20 January 2007, A12.

10 Ibid.

11 See John Burman ,'Developer says economic chill has hit Haldimand.' *Hamilton Spectator,* 5 July 2007. Archived at http://www.caledoniawake-upcall.com/updates/070705spectator.html.

12 See Tom Keefer, 'Caledonia's Fifth Column: White Anti-Racism and Solidarity with Six Nations.' *Briarpatch Magazine,* August 2006.

13 Video footage of this demonstration is available at http://video.google.com/videoplay?docid=3107072711881835098.

14 See 'Jan Watson talks about supporting Six Nations struggle near Caledonia' [video interview] at web address http://video.google.com/videoplay?docid=5729096695037214179&hl=en.

15 See the Community Friends mission statement at http://www
.honorsixnations.com/mission.pdf.
16 See 'Jan Watson on harassment of Six Nations solidarity activists,' at http://
video.google.com/videoplay?docid=-6172475830419304716&hl=en.
17 These two videos detailing a protest outside of Hamilton's Barton Street
Jail, and a statement in support of the people of Six Nations from former
Black Panther Party member and U.S. Political Prisoner Robert Seth
Hayes, are available at http://video.google.ca/videoplay?docid=
5462657935945847693&hl=en-CA , and http://video.google.ca/videoplay?
docid=-7336742613256533399&hl=en-CA.
18 See Tom Keefer, 'Six Nations and the Politics of Solidarity.' *Upping the Anti*,
vol. 4, May 2007, available at http://uppingtheanti.org/journal/
article/04-the-politics-of-solidarity.

7 Winning Fishing Rights: The Successes and Challenges of Building Grassroots Relations between the Chippewas of Nawash and Their Allies

RICK WALLACE, MARILYN STRUTHERS,
AND RICK COBER BAUMAN

On Labour Day Weekend of 1995, 100 white anglers marched down the main street and into the Farmers Market in the heart of the quiet rural town of Owen Sound, Ontario. They were intent on registering protest about Aboriginal fishing rights won three years earlier by Howard Jones and Francis Nadjiwon on behalf of the Saugeen Ojibway on the Bruce Peninsula. The march touched off a range of activity, from the stabbing of young Nawash men later that weekend, to burning fishing boats and nets slashed from their buoys and set adrift in Georgian Bay. Community members and provincial anti-racism organizations worked uneasily over the next two years to create alliances with Nawash First Nation, and, in the end, the overt violence was contained into a short period of time. This chapter explores the lessons learned from that experience, particularly from the perspectives of non-Indigenous allies.

In the 1990s, the Chippewas of Nawash Unceded First Nation (Anishnaabe peoples, Cape Croker, Ontario) mounted a successful communications and community relations strategy that added strength to a legal campaign to win recognition and implementation of inherent fishing rights in the Saugeen-Bruce Peninsula, Ontario. Faced with local acts of community violence, and opposition from local sports fishers closely allied with both the Ontario Federation of Anglers and Hunters (OFAH) and the Ontario Ministry of Natural Resources (OMNR), they utilized an extensive support base to counter local opposition, racism, and provincial intransigence in fisheries enforcement. This is the context in which the Chippewas of Nawash and their allies (primarily unions, community groups, faith-based organizations, and academics) worked together to advocate and build support for court-confirmed fishing rights.

As three non-Aboriginal social justice activists, we search in this chapter for understanding about the strategies and locations from which to build alliances[1] that give Aboriginal people[2] and their non-Aboriginal allies[3] greater leverage in Aboriginal/non-Aboriginal conflicts around social justice issues. This is part of a larger discussion in the field of conflict resolution concerning large-scale social conflicts and the seldom acknowledged importance of grassroots community-based peace-building.[4] Simply put, effective inter-communal conflict resolution must be addressed not only at the state/global level, but also at the community level through local peace-building efforts and partnerships between communities of interest. Indigenous knowledge, local capacities, and grassroots alliances can combine to offer alternative paradigms and practices about collaboration and inter-group relationships. These collaborations become important intersections of building peace globally and locally.

In asymmetrical power relationships like those in Canada between the state and Aboriginal peoples, what roles can grassroots alliances between Aboriginal and non-Aboriginal peoples play in building respectful and just relations across conflicting communities or nations? First, how can non-Aboriginal allies concretely support Aboriginal peoples in securing, and once secured, implementing their sovereign rights? Second, how can non-Aboriginal people transform our own cultural communities' world views, a paradigm consciously and unconsciously rooted in a history of colonialism, structural violence, and systemic racism? Third, and perhaps most important, how can we (Aboriginal and non-Aboriginal peoples) develop a future for relationships between peoples based on equity, respect, and reciprocity that is truly mutually beneficial?

In this chapter we explore (1) the strengths of different allies, as well as their limitations, motivations, and impact on sustaining alliances; (2) the effectiveness of anti-racist strategies used; and (3) lessons learned on community-based peace building.

Reflecting on the experiences of past community-based efforts, strategies, and successes can strengthen new approaches to sustaining alliances and broadening relationship-building between communities in conflict, locally and nationally. Thierry Drapeau (Chapter 14, this volume) refers to 'glocality' to describe the intertwining and reshaping of global and local situated places of experience.[5] Glocality involves more than hegemony and resistance; it is the porous boundary intersecting power, space, and everyday social practices where the forms of the global and local are being independently and mutually produced, influenced, reproduced, contested, challenged, and made alternate. So, too, the shaping and sharing of allies' knowledges and concrete practices become spaces where the vertical hierarchies of global domination and Canadian colonialism can be horizontalized and at times reversed, a place where the local practice creates different possibilities and configurations of relationships.

Such an analysis of community-based and locally situated efforts can potentially re-orient our thinking so that we can more clearly appreciate the importance of communities as sites of both effort and transformational change in large-scale inter-group conflicts. Examining the experiences of allies in the fishing conflict in the Saugeen-Bruce Peninsula in the 1990s is an opportunity to explore the fundamentals of community-based peace-building, how people learned to create an inter-group collaboration able to devise common and diverse strategies, and to mobilize support for larger social change.

This discussion on allies also needs to frame the analysis from the perspective of the Chippewas of Nawash (Band Council, key actors). What did non-Aboriginal allies bring to the Chippewas of Nawash and their direct concerns over their fishing rights? What is their own assessment of the need for and role of their allies?[6] This chapter utilizes this context and asks how non-Aboriginal allies understood the impact of their community-level actions within their own constituencies. What were the processes of collaboration with the Chippewas of Nawash? How were local strategies intended to overcome opposition and create greater community support for the goals of the Chippewas?

Using the case study and the experiences of two key non-Aboriginal allies, the chapter is structured in four parts, which explore (1) a number of interlinking elements relevant to the success and challenges of building this grassroots partnership; (2) partner priorities; (3) the strengths and limitations of non-Aboriginal allies; and (4) racism as a focal point for action and social change. We conclude by reflecting on lessons learned.

1. Interlinking Elements

The relationship between the Chippewas of Nawash and their allies is a useful case study from which to examine community-based peace-building and its intersection with the issues of identity and Canadian colonialism. It is emblematic of the larger Canadian conflict while simultaneously serving as a window into the interaction of diverse allies as they responded to specific crisis moments.

This conflict extends beyond simple fish quotas and into an examination of relationships in community, revealing an entangled relational web of continued colonialism, settler culture, racism, and structural inequality.

First, the conflict was, and continues to be, embedded in the struggle for access to dwindling Great Lakes fish stock in the context of established treaty and inherent rights[7] of Aboriginal peoples in Ontario and Canada, and an ongoing sports fishery with economic impact in the non-Aboriginal community. As such, it serves as a good macro- and micro-study of the dynamics and challenges of alliance work between Aboriginal and non-Aboriginal peoples in a Canadian setting.

Second, the opportunity to draw upon the experience and reflection of the participants in this conflict offers a window into the nature of grassroots alliances with Aboriginal communities, and between local and non-local organizations. It provides concrete examples and insights into how the allies worked as partners, and some of the successes, limitations, and tensions they faced.

Third, the alliance-building or partnerships involved a diverse spectrum of external allies, each playing a different role. They were most notably the Canadian Auto Workers (CAW), a community group called Neighbours of Nawash created as a result of the crisis, and several faith-based groups, most particularly the Mennonite Central Committee and Project North (now part of KAIROS). At the same time, individual allies included academics from the disciplines of biology, ecology, zoology, and history involved in supportive research on fisheries. Additionally, coalitions of national churches, including the United Church, the Hamilton Roman Catholic Diocese, and the Quakers, participated.[8] In terms of broader movements for social change, or new social movements, this alliance-building experience offers lessons in process and strategy, and in negotiating differences.

Fourth, this conflict, like many, was punctuated by specific and escalating crisis moments which had an impact on the respective communities and on the dynamics of alliance-building. On the positive side, these crises fuelled an urgency for greater collaboration and greater action between partners. They also were a catalyst for a deeper analysis, especially by non-Aboriginal allies, of systemic patterns of violence and racism directed at Aboriginal peoples. Sadly, these same crises were also the cause of greater trauma for an already historically trau-matized community, Cape Croker (the Chippewas of Nawash), and di-vided social dialogue in the nearby non-Aboriginal communities of Wiarton[9] and Owen Sound.

There are many ways to tell the story of this specific conflict.[10] Here, our own socially constructed perspectives as academic, local resident, and representative of a faith-based organization both define and frame the narrative.[11]

By the late 1980s, impoverished First Nations communities in Grey and Bruce Counties had begun to look to commercial fisheries to bring employment and a measure of self-sufficiency, yet were obstructed by the disregard of inherent and treaty fishing rights by the local Ontario Ministry of Natural Resources (OMNR). In the late 1980s and early 1990s, fishers from Cape Croker, operating under a problematic group fishing license and limited quota, were repeatedly charged with both fishing over the OMNR-imposed quota and of illegally selling those catches to the public. The quota allocated to the Chippewas of Nawash constituted roughly 1 per cent of the overall allowable catch, whereas the remaining 99 per cent was assigned to the non-Indigenous commer-cial fishery in the area.

By the early 1990s, the Chippewas of Nawash were engaged in a le-gal challenge that eventually recognized their right to commercially harvest fish.[12] In 1992, the Band Council decided to legally challenge these OMNR-laid charges of over-fishing, and on 23 April 1993 the Ontario Provincial Supreme Court agreed with their argument, that un-der Section 35(1) of the 1982 Constitution Act they retained collective and treaty rights to fish for trade and commerce.[13] Further, Judge David Fairgrieve stated that the OMNR had violated constitutional rights of Nawash through the use of a quota system, and that the Chippewas of Nawash were entitled to priority allocation to fishing resources over other users; that the OMNR regulatory scheme was 'tantamount to "ex-propriation" in transferring economic benefits to the non-Indigenous commercial industry.'

At the same time, the issues of control, management, and access to the fish stock were linked to increasing emphasis on tourism in the nearby town of Owen Sound, to reproduce the economic stability dam-aged by the recession of the 1980s and the erosion of the farm economy. The local sports fishers affiliated with the Ontario Federation of Anglers and Hunters (OFAH)[14] were deeply connected to OMNR strategies of fisheries management, with volunteers engaged in habitat management and fish stocking. The local association was also highly visible and politically influential because its membership included local professionals, politicians, and local elite.

But by 1995 it had become clear that the fish stock in the Great Lakes was in serious trouble. Native fishers and sports anglers were on a seemingly inevitable collision course over entitlement and control of the remnants of a once abundant fishery. That collision of interests, known by some as the 'fishing wars,' was played out on the landscape of racial conflict.

It is within this context that opposition arose in the nearby communities of Wiarton and Owen Sound: local sports fishers, including members of OFAH and the provincial government (MPP), led a protest in the nearby Owen Sound market (August 1995); three youth from Cape Croker were stabbed by non-Aboriginal youth in Owen Sound (September 1995); Nawash fishing tugboats, nets, and gear were vandalized and cast adrift (1995–96). One boat was burned by arson (September 1995).

Finally, in 2000, despite the countering forces of opposition, a fishing agreement was signed involving the Saugeen Ojibway Nation (the Chippewas of Nawash and the Saugeen First Nation), OMNR, and the Federal Department of Indian Affairs. This entailed an agreement between the Province and the Saugeen Ojibway people to fish within an agreed-upon area, and for monies to the Saugeen-Ojibway Nation for research and monitoring of the commercial fisheries within that area.

2. Partner Priorities

In the following section we examine the issues of developing collaborative partnerships and suggest that the strategies devised and approaches taken were the result of differing priorities and motivations between the Chippewas of Nawash and non-Aboriginal allies.

An example of differing priorities was the Chippewas of Nawash strategy to individually become, along with non-Aboriginal allies, OFAH members, in an effort to monitor and influence policy vis-à-vis Aboriginal fisheries. Rick Bauman of the Mennonite Central Committee (MCC) identifies that strategy as indicative of a continuum of potential strategies between allies: 'We in the Mennonite church community needed to find advocacy strategies that had integrity and real backing in our congregations, and were still of sufficient strength and seriousness to be helpful to the Chippewas of Nawash. This was hard work, and at times Nawash representatives felt we let them down. But I do think we found some common ground that both educated and moved our people, and was still "useful" to the Nawash endeavours for a more just sharing of the resource.'[15]

There was a strong common interest between the Chippewas of Nawash and their non-Aboriginal allies to support the inherent rights of Cape Croker in the fishing conflict, yet differences in motivation and priorities surfaced during the crisis and at times threatened the entire relationship – for example, where the MCC was interested in coordinating a citizen's inquiry on the fishing issues in the Bruce Peninsula. The intention was to have a third-party team composed of an historian, a biologist, and faith-based officials to listen to the diverse stakeholders and develop recommendations on potential solutions to the conflict. On the other hand, the Chippewas of Nawash were leery of such an effort. As Rick Bauman, who was coordinating MCC's support for the Chippewas, recounted: 'This [MCC-led citizen's inquiry on the fishing issues] may have been the most delicate of all our involvements. On the one hand, MCC leadership was concerned that we not lead an inquiry process whose results were predetermined to the extent that they would be dismissed [by local opposition and OFAH members]. And, on the other hand, were the concerns of the Nawash leadership that we not produce a report that was unhelpful to their goals.'[16]

David McLaren, former communications director for the Chippewas of Nawash, however, had this to say about the Nawash Band Council's instructions to MCC: 'We basically had to say to them point-blank that if you come up with any recommendations that show a bad light on the First Nations, then your relationship with us is over. So they were in a terrible spot, and I have to admit that their report was pretty good considering all of that, but they weren't very happy about it because they felt they were being manipulated – and to certain extent they were. We had to. The stakes were too high.'[17]

The MCC Citizen's Inquiry project reflected a number of different assumptions about the importance of dialogue and a priority about bridge-building in conflicts. The response of the Chippewas of Nawash showed that they held limits on what kind of dialogue would be valued and a clear priority for Nawash stories to emerge in a good light. Immediate, pressing, and specific strategic goals of securing fishing rights were paramount for the Chippewas of Nawash. A combination of limited resources and a specific strategic focus created priorities that didn't necessarily extend to an emphasis on creating ongoing, deeper transformative relationships with partners. Rather, allies were primarily understood as short-term resources to secure fishing rights.

Meanwhile, the Mennonite Central Committee was motivated by a general vision of social justice embodied in a religious ethos and morality emanating from their faith-based perspective. Their priority was to support the Chippewas of Nawash, to act as a third-party facilitator, and to educate and engage their own constituency on the wider issues of Aboriginal peoples. Similarly, the community group of Neighbours of Nawash was relationship-driven, and their priority was both to increase support for the Chippewas of Nawash and to counter the effects of conflictual behaviour that disrupted their own community relations, space, and identity.

Differences in motivation and priorities raise a number of issues that point up the impact of the differently situated standpoints of partners, and how standpoint affects and mediates issues of power, strategic collaboration, and approaches to racism. The impact of power includes issues of structural inequalities and the historical, political, and economic underdevelopment of First Nations in a Canadian colonial system. These historical and contemporary power dynamics created a focus within the Chippewas of Nawash community, where members were both engaged and constrained by a daily emphasis on addressing immediate socio-economic needs at Cape Croker. Fishing rights had clear and immediate economic benefit for the Nawash community in providing employment in a community geographically at some distance from the nearest small town employment.

As a consequence, Nawash community resources were centred on the struggle to secure fishing rights. The Chippewas of Nawash's immediate focus on reducing poverty and meeting basic needs resulted in external allies being understood and used as short-term resources to help address these pressing needs. Ongoing relationships with external allies as part of some wider social justice movement or undoing racism in the non-Indigenous communities were more nebulous and less pressing goals.

Second, it is important to contextualize Aboriginal peoples' historical experience of disenfranchisement and usurpation of pre-contact self-government,[18] resulting in a contemporary asymmetrical power relationship with the dominant non-Aboriginal society. Located in a context of racist state policies and external social relations,[19] the approach of the Chippewas of Nawash was to understand the conflict as part of an ongoing process of political and cultural empowerment/decolonization in Aboriginal communities generally. Specifically, it meant replacing external colonial authority with community-driven intentions. Allies were of mixed importance to some key people in Cape Croker, whereas a community-driven form of political authority and community development was the strategic choice. As Darlene Johnston of the Chippewas of Nawash stated, 'I don't rely on them [external allies]. If I had money to put into research or alliance-building, I would put it into research. I would make a priority of community education to make sure that our members know what happened and what we are going to do, because that is where there is determination. And I feel way more confident in the determination and stubbornness of our community.'[20]

Limited resources, historical mistrust,[21] and retention of the political authority of the Cape Croker community translated into a cautious approach to strategic collaboration. For the Chippewas of Nawash, leadership and strategic decision-making were foremost an internal decision, not one jointly constructed with external allies. The development of alliances and collaboration was confined to tactics and building support for the specific goal of fishing rights. It did not include having external allies participate in creating the overall strategy and goals, or in exercising co-leadership.

At the same time, non-Aboriginal groups such as Neighbours of Nawash and the Mennonite Central Committee were, themselves, situated differently as Euro-Canadians. The MCC and its constituency were not directly affected by this conflict or its consequences. Their intersection of identity and class positioned them inside the mainstream discursive public arena where they could act as change-agents within their own dominant society, with certain privileges of access to resources, media, political power, and organizing capacity – tools of power not equally available to the Chippewas of Nawash.

As discussed by Marilyn Struthers (Chapter 22, this volume), individual members of Neighbours of Nawash could also figuratively step away from the conflict, but chose to stand in resistance to the sports fishermen and create a public forum based on the principle of neighbourliness. While they had access to few financial resources, they did have both the capacity to organize locally and a more privileged access to the mainstream media, which they used to generate an alternative storyline about the conflict and the response of the non-Aboriginal community to Nawash fishing.

These larger social relations, deeply connected to power, identity, and location, manifested themselves in allies' differing priorities, historical experiences of colonialism, and socio-political privileges, and, lastly, in their respective interests and strategic targets. In fact, they circumscribed the development of collaborative strategies and the sustainability of the relationship between allies. Interestingly, these differences were never explicitly named. Would it have made collaboration more effective if they had been able to clarify and acknowledge an analysis of difference from the outset, and how difference implicates different motivation and choice of strategies? Would the efforts have lead to greater strategic collaboration, more effective outcomes, or sustained relationships? Or, is the capacity of any collaboration inherently limited in some ways at the historical moment and the extent of unfolding crisis?

3. Strengths and Limitations of Non-Aboriginal Allies

Our next theme concerns the connection of local space to the capacities and knowledge available to the respective non-Aboriginal allies. There is a useful comparison to be made between geographically embedded local allies and those who are externally based, or regional, for they occupy different territory in the non-Aboriginal community, both literally and figuratively speaking. These different locations also brought varying strengths, limitations, and approaches to peace-building.

The Neighbours of Nawash organization, rooted in the Owen Sound and area community, offers a powerful illustration of the importance of local space and localized knowledge:

> The Neighbours of Nawash was a small, loosely organized and leaderless group that could articulate a different politics and understanding of our community than that of the fishermen in their both social and political identities. By creating a public structure we too took up a public position representing what we valued most, the articulation of our community as peaceful, tolerant and neighbourly, regardless of race and fish. We used traditional rural organizing methods – a public bank account to support the Nawash fishers' ability to replace their equipment when the boats began to burn, a public forum to explore ideas, a phone tree to draw people together.[22]

The strength of the Neighbours of Nawash organization, as a strategy, grew directly from an intimate awareness of community space – its power dynamics and structures. This awareness was mobilized to assist in building influence and eventually local platforms for the Chippewas of Nawash within the community. The credibility and influence of community members, combined with their local knowledge and organizing capacity, enabled them to identify strategies that offered an alternative message. This contributed to setting the stage later in the conflict process for strategies of restoration of relationship, rather than challenging strategies that might have further divided the community.

The strategies of Neighbours of Nawash were all focused on creating local space to tell an alternate community story about the relationship between the non-Aboriginal community and the Chippewas of Nawash. The first strategy was one of resistance, standing in the market areas, taking up space between the marching anglers and the Nawash fish sellers. The second strategy included opening a public bank account and establishing the organization, which were deliberate creations of public institutional space in support of Nawash fishing rights, and subsequent access to the media to spin an alternative story of relations. Only after the crisis had settled did Neighbours of Nawash begin to take up the more traditional roles of peace-builders, creating public forums for learning and reconciliation.

The capacity to develop a relationship with the Chippewas of Nawash was strengthened by the Neighbours of Nawash's members' existing personal, professional, geographic, and spiritual connection to the community. As community members, they had had longer-term relationships, some interpersonal, with the Chippewas of Nawash that preceded the fishing crisis. Second, they shared a wider sense of meaning through an appreciation of a shared spiritual connection to the land they both inhabited. Third, they understood themselves as tolerant and peaceful people, taking up the rubric of neighbours to the Chippewas of Nawash to address the crisis. On the other hand, they were also limited by a lack of organizational and financial resources; they were inexperienced in anti-racism analysis; and they faced risks of social exclusion, repercussions, and economic hardship, personally and professionally, within their own community because of their solidarity work.

Externally based allies like the Mennonites and the Canadian Auto Workers (CAW) brought greater organizational strengths and resources: paid staff, regional communication networks, expertise in campaigning, research, advocacy, and the capacity to engage memberships numbering in the tens of thousands. They also could, as in the MCC Ontario case, create broad, community-based public advocacy events like their 'Fish and Loaves' supper – where Nawash fishers supplied then 'illegal' fish – as well as an important educational opportunity for

Mennonite participants.[23] At the same time, they were hindered by a lack of intimate associations in the community.

> We don't really have any strong Mennonite churches until you get two hours away from the Cape. On the other hand, Neighbours of Nawash were a neighborhood group: Owen Sound people, rural people in the townships there. That was just a practical reality that anything we did, did not have the flavour of something that folks could drop in on. You could go up and camp for the weekend but it's not the neighbour-to-neighbour reality.[24]

Further, externally based allies (such as MCC, CAW, local and national churches) were troubled by internal factions of opposition or fear within their organizations towards Aboriginal people and their interests. This had the effect of limiting the degree and type of support offered. In hierarchical organizations such as these, support from the organizations' leadership became essential if educators or activists on the front line were to continue their alliance work. Whereas the CAW leadership was supportive of the actions taken by its regional unionists,[25] a local church minister in nearby Tobermory was ejected from his ministry for actively supporting the Chippewas of Nawash. Further, they lacked what locally based activists clearly had: an intimate knowledge, connection, and set of already established relationships within the Nawash community.

The differing capacity of local and externally based regional non-Aboriginal supporters suggests the possibility for greater effectiveness when they are combined.

Insider's knowledge of appropriate strategies and attachment to local space offers greater possibility of sustainability and effectiveness of strategy, but being locally situated simultaneously limits strategic analysis and vision, and risks confrontation and repercussion from within their own communities. The location of externally based allies, like the Mennonites, offers an organizational and constituency-based capacity that allowed them to take different risks, such as their Citizen's Inquiry, without the same consequences. Not being from inside the community, however, hindered regional allies in two ways. The absence of meaningful connection between the local and regional allies of Nawash meant they lacked the capacity to combine local and strategic knowledge to discover what strategies might have been most effective; and, second, the absence of local legitimacy worked against local acceptance of regional activities such as the Citizen's Inquiry Report (called the Report of the Fisheries Listening

Team). The capacities and knowledge of non-Aboriginal partners were inextricably linked to their location. Strategically, the question arises as how best to maximize collaboration between local and regional allies in such a way that joint efforts result in mutual capacity-building, thereby allowing each group to leverage their skills and knowledge.

4. Racism as a Focal Point for Action and Social Change

Collaboration was also affected by the lack of explicit dialogue over how to approach conflict resolution and build community simultan-eously, and specifically how best to engage and counter racism within the non-Aboriginal communities. Reflecting their respective constitu-encies, allies held varied perspectives on the centrality of racism as a cause/consequence of the conflict and the means to transform it. For instance, there were differing analyses and approaches as to whether and how to build bridges to opposition forces such as OFAH, the local sports club, and local elites. The conflicting views between partners centred on whether to frame the core conflict as one of racism, and by extension explicitly naming mitigating actions as 'anti-racist.'

A number of key Chippewas of Nawash organizers rejected working explicitly on issues of racism. Their main concern was not focused on un-doing racism in the non-Aboriginal community or the mainstream community; rather, as mentioned earlier, their priority was to get an outcome that was related to economic concerns. Transforming racism was seen as the job of external non-Indigenous allies within whose communities the problem lay. Lenore Keeshig-Tobias, a Nawash story-teller, writer, and community activist articulated this view: 'I stopped doing antiracism work. I realized "okay, I don't want to do this because I feel like a token. I don't want to do it because it's not my problem even though I'm hurt by it and I feel it. It's not my problem, and David [McLaren] being from the white community should do it because he speaks the language, he knows the metaphors and people. He knows the stories, the Christian stories, and the Greek mythology, and stuff like that."'[26]

By and large, the non-Aboriginal allies agreed that the burden of re-sponsibility rested upon themselves and their communities. Rick Bauman of MCC puts it this way: 'We have to own anti-racism as our work. We are not expecting other people to be the educators of our folks; they may be engaged and may want to be. But I think that was the lesson of the last 10 years. We really have to own it and put the resources in it to do that work ourselves.'[27] David McLaren, former communications director for the Chippewas, offered a non-Aboriginal perspective from within the Nawash community, echoing this position: 'It really was the white people's job to take care of their own racism. And in a certain way, that's the way that I approached it. It was our job, mine and the churches, and whoever else wanted to help. It was our job to deal with the backlash out there and to whatever extent we could do with our governments.'[28]

While there was common agreement amongst non-Aboriginal allies on the pivotal role of racism in the conflict, there was little discussion and so no opportunity for agreement on how best to counter or transform it. In particular, interviews with non-Aboriginal allies indicated a significant difference of opinion on whether and how to build bridges to racist opposition forces. Faith-based and community groups believed there was utility in engaging foes in dialogue. The Mennonite Central Committee followed this approach in its efforts to try to create an independent public report on possible common interests between OFAH (Ontario Federation of Anglers and Hunters), MNR (Ontario Ministry of Natural Resources) and the Chippewas of Nawash.

However, any ongoing dialogue with OFAH was deemed a failure by organizers within the Chippewas of Nawash who had already attempted a somewhat similar strategy of directly engaging OFAH at its own meetings. It was also perceived as a naïve strategy to believe that opposition was ready to listen, especially from those who had personally (and as part of a collective identity) experienced the dialogue with OFAH as a continuum of emotional and intellectual violence targeting Aboriginal peoples.[29]

A union, like the Canadian Auto Workers (CAW), historically engaged in solidarity struggles, was more comfortable in directly confronting racism through explicit anti-racist and human rights education than, for example, faith-based groups. In part this speaks to the nature of the organization, its resources, mandate, capacity to frame racism in a larger context, and the opportunity to bring workers into day-long or even several-weeks-long non-formal education settings.[30] As explained by former union educator Ken Luchardt: 'Our union has for years been identified as having social unionism. So, when it comes to issues like racism in the community, First Nations rights come very quickly into the purview of the Education Department. As a result we engaged our members directly on the issues of racism against First Nations communities in the Bruce Peninsula.'[31]

Neighbours of Nawash in Owen Sound did not see the non-Aboriginal community as unitary purveyors of inherent racism. Rather, they focused on developing diversity in the public voice as a means of providing an alternative standpoint and a community voice concerning their relationships with the Chippewas of Nawash. They used a strategy of building relationships amongst community members rather than direct confrontation with opposition elements. Additionally, another faith-based organization, Project North, held the view that solely focusing on 'racism' did not adequately capture the other structural elements of conflict (economic, political, legislative, governance) nor the unique aspects of Indigenous peoples' struggles where their inherent rights and land title set their conflicts apart from others that are solely race-based. Moreover, they contended, using the term 'racism' as the opening for discussion resulted in even greater resistance and defensiveness from non-Aboriginal community members to cross-cultural awareness-building.[32]

Broadly speaking, the perspectives amongst non-Aboriginal supporters and groups varied, from the CAW's explicit endorsement of anti-racism pedagogy on the one hand, to community-based and faith-based groups' reticence on the other, to utilize an explicit 'anti-racism' discourse as a means of transforming the conflict. The willingness or reluctance to use an anti-racism discourse is explicitly tied to the degree one is locally situated, as is the potential for divisiveness and repercussion in that context. The CAW was not directly tied to Owen Sound or Wiarton, whereas community-based organizations and activists were clearly situated locally. Those activists used a 'softer,' interest-based conflict resolution/community development approach that entailed finding common values, concerns, and interests in the fish in order to create movement towards cohesive community action, both within the non-Aboriginal communities and with the Chippewas of Nawash.

These varied approaches to racism raise a number of critical reflections on collaboration and community-based peace-building. First, given the relationship between alliance-building and the specificity of local situations, the discourse of 'anti-racism' may be a much more problematic language and approach in relationally driven community contexts.

Second, the volatility and rawness of inter-group conflict in a rural setting such as this highlight the potential repercussion for local activists using divisive community strategies. It requires courage and enormous risk for local activists, both Aboriginal and non-Aboriginal, to speak up publicly about issues of racism. This suggests the potential for a division of roles that could have utilized externally based supporters to raise more contentious issues in the community. In the same way, the local context of risk and consequence, and the dense web of relationships available to locally based allies, suggest a legitimacy for approaches based on relationship-building. On the other hand, a critical evaluation suggests that the difficulty in speaking up about racism by local organizers and the faith-based groups led to a 'softer' approach, one that missed opportunities to directly confront the systemic roots of structural inequalities of Canadian colonialism as actively lived-in communities.

5. Lessons Learned

The case study of the Chippewas of Nawash and non-Aboriginal allies points to a number of lessons learned in terms of effective community-based peace-building and alliance-building. The three themes of partners and priorities, local capacities and knowledge, and racism and social change provide an initial conceptualization of how to strengthen future practices.

First, efforts at collaboration between the Chippewas of Nawash and non-Aboriginal allies contain lessons concerning the importance of recognizing differently situated group priorities and abilities, and using them as building blocks to construct sustainable relationships across collective identities. Being explicit about identity, interests, and location, both internal to the organization and between allies, could provide a structure upon which to negotiate differences and visualize a continuum of strategic possibilities and roles.

Second, this case study on collaboration also highlights lessons on accepting strategy as an evolving vehicle driven by unforeseen circumstances wherein activities are sometimes ad hoc and simply arise from a reaction to an intolerable situation, as it did for the Neighbours of Nawash in the Farm Market.[33] At other times, it is important to recognize the diverse world views and values from which strategies arise, such as the deeply held values and approaches reflected in the Mennonite Central Committee's tactic of creating public dialogue through a Citizen's Report, or the centrality of concepts of "neighbourliness' and community relations held by the Neighbours of Nawash.

Third, the ability to have collaborative strategies and coordinated priorities is linked to an understanding of an ally's *capacity* to undertake certain actions. The case study experience indicates a spectrum of diverse strategies, and options for participation extending from working in tandem, where there are convergences, to choosing to work separately or differently in terms of tactics and priorities.

Fourth, combining the strengths of an ally's location, whether it be locally or externally based, impacts on the overall effectiveness and appropriateness of strategies. This was demonstrated when the Neighbours of Nawash's public forums succeeded in engaging factions within a community where MCC's Citizen's Report did not.

Fifth, there are lessons about the diverse approaches to engaging with the behaviours and effects of racism within non-Aboriginal communities towards Aboriginal people. This appears to be a clear place where community-based peace-building could have been strengthened by processes explicitly naming the varied positions on anti-racism, and identifying the cultural and political frameworks held by partners. This in turn could assist organizations and communities to outline a typology of localized approaches to racism.

Taken together, these lessons and learning could potentially deepen and broaden the spectrum of strategic options and relationships, as well as offering other locations of collaboration.[34]

Conclusion

In conclusion, the fishing conflict on the Saugeen-Bruce Peninsula in the 1990s became an opportunity for relationship-building and support of the Chippewas of Nawash by non-Aboriginal allies. A combination of legal decisions, public education, advocacy, and leveraging the actions of allies contributed to a recognition and implementation of Aboriginal fishing rights for the Chippewas of Nawash.

While the larger systemic issues of inherent rights, racism, and self-determination still remain contested, the efforts of the Chippewas of Nawash and their non-Aboriginal allies did result in each developing complementary strategies, and perhaps limited further community violence. The cohesion and sustainability of these efforts at conflict transformation were impacted by the different standpoints that reflected larger power and social relations embedded in differently located historical experiences, constituencies, resources, and approaches. This analysis offers new insight into the sites of conversation that could have made the work more effective.

The relationship between the Chippewas of Nawash and allies like the Neighbours of Nawash, the Mennonite Central Committee-Ontario, and the CAW offers a site of exploration to examine how conflicts can be impacted at the grassroots level by various forms of community-based peace-building. Their experiences represent the possibility, hopes, and contemporary challenges of building peace from the bottom up.

Inter-group conflicts in Canada involving Aboriginal and non-Aboriginal peoples seem to be profoundly lurching from crisis to crisis. Community-based peace-building efforts involving alliance-building and partnerships may well offer the basis for a larger social justice movement based on collaboration and reconciliation. Community-based peace-building models between Aboriginal and non-Aboriginal allies may yet become catalysts for a transformative approach to the conflict by building relationships from the bottom up. There are no universal templates that can be transferred from one locality to another, yet there are experiences that can be shared and that can provide lessons in process, strategies, and negotiating differences for other communities seeking to transform deeply rooted social conflicts.

NOTES

1 By alliances we mean coalition, partnership, coordinated actions, or supportive strategies amongst groups of activists/communities considering themselves (and considered by the Chippewas of Nawash) to be allies or supporters of the Chippewas of Nawash in this conflict.
2 We want to acknowledge that there are numerous terms that could be used here, including Indigenous, First Nations, Anishnaabe, Chippewa, Native peoples, all with advantages and/or drawbacks. We have chosen to use the term 'Aboriginal' in referring to the larger community of people. When writing specifically about the Chippewas of Nawash of *Neyaashiinigamiing* (Cape Croker in English), we refer to them as the Chippewas of Nawash and/or Cape Croker.
3 Another issue of terminology is referring to those peoples/communities who are not Aboriginal. We have chosen to use the term 'non-Aboriginal' to refer to those allies, who are often Euro-Canadian, white though not exclusively. Again, there are advantages and disadvantages to different terminologies, including discussions on whether 'white' people re-inscribes a discourse based on colour (rather than culture or social systems), or whether it firmly names the means by which systemic racism has benefited a certain group (white Euro-Canadians) based on association of skin colour.

4 The framework we use is one tied to the transformative approach of conflict resolution called Peace-building. INTERCHANGE: the International Institute for Community-based peacebuilding (http://tlc.oise.utoronto.ca/peacebuilding/about.html) defines it as 'a broad, comprehensive range of activities and processes at all stages of the conflict cycle. Peace-building addresses the causes of conflict, not just the conflict behaviour, and is also concerned with processing the wounds of the past. The aim of peace-building is to promote human security and transform violent conflict towards sustainable peaceful relationships, capacities ,and structures.' Community-based peace-building begins with the agenda and priorities set at the community level while recognizing that process occurs within, and has impacts on a larger global context. Evident in the academic works of Galtung (1996), Lederach (1995, 1997) and Francis (2002), 'peace-building' shifts the paradigm of building peace in a number of key ways. It redirects the focus away from a single-mindedness on state-centered approaches (so often the case in International Relations) to the necessity of including multiple levels of social actors, especially those at the community or local level ('grassroots'), as pivotal for the creation of more peaceful relations. Second, in this definition, 'peacebuilding' intertwines social justice values, diverse processes and actors, and an ongoing social transformation of the deeply rooted causes of the conflict: structural, relational, and cultural contradictions. The necessity of rectifying these structural inequities between communities in conflict also points to the centrality of the community level as social agents of change. As such, there is an emphasis on community capacity-building and the role of indigenous/local knowledges as a means of transforming relationships from the 'bottom-up' (Lederach, 1995, 1997; Francis , 2002).

5 Thierry Drapeau, 'A Glocality in the Making ' (Chapter 14, this volume).

6 There will be only a partial discussion on these issues as seen from the Chippewas of Nawash. It is beyond the scope of this chapter to take it up fully, though it deserves greater focus. None of the authors are from Cape Croker, and the perspectives that are attributed to the community are ones we triangulated through our own experience, PhD research interviews, and in checking back with various community members. However, the Cape Croker community is not monolithic. There were different positions within the community concerning the overall community strategy, processes, relationships with non-Aboriginal allies, and intra-community relationships. This can be seen in the subsequent Band Council elections where some of the key figures were not re-elected to Council. Nor is there attention paid in this article to

partnerships and support extended between the Chippewas of Nawash and other Aboriginal communities and organizations.

7 Canadian Constitution, Section 35 (i).

8 Environmental non-government organizations (ENGOs) were only nominally involved.

9 Wiarton is a town of 5,000 about 15 km from Cape Croker. Owen Sound is a larger regional city of 30,000 about 45 km away.

10 We want to acknowledge our own subjectivity as writers, and the very real issues of legitimacy (Who legitimates? Who is legitimate?) and representation (Who is representing who? And through whose frame?) raised by cultural anthropologists (Pryke, 2003; Wetherell, 2002), political studies (O'Reilly, 2004), and Aboriginal writers (Smith, 1999; Battiste, 2002). We use a social constructionist theoretical understanding of individual and collective identity (our own) and knowledge as being situated in particular cultural, historical, economic, social, and political circumstances (Burr, 1995; Ponting, 1997).

11 This chapter is a joint effort combining personal and theoretical perspectives. All three writers are non-indigenous. One is a PhD researcher, the other two were directly involved in supporting the Chippewas of Nawash as part of undoing and transforming this long-standing conflict. This chapter combines the thoughts from Rick Wallace, PhD researcher on the case study; Rick Bauman, program director, Mennonite Central Committee-Ontario; and Marilyn Struthers, member of the community-based group, Neighbours of Nawash.

12 In 1992, the Band Council decided to legally challenge these OMNR-laid charges of over-fishing and on 23 April 1993 the Ontario Provincial Supreme Court agreed with their argument that under Section 35(1) of the 1982 Constitution, they retained collective and treaty rights to fish for trade .

13 Regina vs, Jones [1993] O.J. No. 893 (Ontario Provincial Division), April 23, 1993; also known as 'the Fairgrieve decision,' or 'Jones-Nadjiwon.'

14 Its members participated in the Owen Sound market demonstration against the selling of Nawash-caught fish. The local association was also highly visible and politically influential because its membership included local professionals, politicians, and local elite.

15 Rick Bauman, program director, Mennonite Central Committee-Ontario (MCC). Interview with Rick Wallace, 14 July 2006. Rick Bauman directly liaised with the Chippewas of Nawash on behalf of MCC.

16 Bauman, Interview with Rick Wallace, 14 July 2006.

17 David McLaren, a former communications director for the Chippewas of Nawash. Interview with Rick Wallace, 26 April 2006. David added that the MCC Citizen's Committee doing the report was already perceived as

biased and outside the Gray Bruce community, paralleling later comments by Rick Bauman, program director for MCC, that its conclusions were already discredited by many before it reported.

18 The colonial polices embedded in the Indian Act of 1876 clearly usurped and replaced traditional Aboriginal governance.
19 See Chippewas of Nawash Unceded First Nation, *Under Siege*.
20 Darlene Johnston, former research coordinator on Land Claims (1991–2001), Chippewas of Nawash. Interview with Rick Wallace, 25 July 2006.
21 The mistrust towards non-Aboriginal allies, and particularly faith-based groups, reflects a well-founded position given their experience of residential schools, sexual abuse by trusted church officials, and the community's cultural marginalization and denigration by non-Aboriginal institutions, civil and religious.
22 Marilyn Struthers, a member of Neighbours of Nawash. Interview with Rick Wallace, 16 July 2006. See also Marilyn's 'Reflections on the Politics of Neighbourliness' (Chapter 22, this volume).
23 Rick Bauman. See note 15, above.
24 Ibid.
25 Interviews with CAW staff also relayed some interesting stories of opposition from some rank and file members towards the union's support of the Chippewas of Nawash.
26 Lenore Keeshig-Tobias, a Nawash writer, storyteller, and community activist. Interview with Rick Wallace, 24 April 2006.
27 Rick Bauman. See note 15, above.
28 David McLaren. See note 17, above.
29 Ibid.
30 Ken Luchardt, a former staff person, CAW Education Department. Interview with Rick Wallace, 19 July 2006. Ken worked in the nearby CAW Port Elgin Family Education Centre. He was part of the CAW solidarity efforts with the Chippewas of Nawash, countering support for the Ontario Association of Anglers and Hunters (OFAH).
31 Ibid.
32 Lorraine Land, a former board member and chair of the Aboriginal Rights Coalition/Project North , 1991–1996 (now subsumed under KAIROS). Interview with Rick Wallace, 26 July 2006.
33 The group was sparked by the infamous march by some community people into the Owen Sound Market to confront a Chippewa of Nawash woman selling her fish.
34 See also Chippewas of Nawash, *Under Siege,* Appendix H: 'Best Practices … What works,' for thoughts on best practices for First Nations, Crowns, police, and relationships in general.

REFERENCES

Battiste, Marie. Ed. *Reclaiming Indigenous Voice and Vision*. Toronto: UBC Press, 2000.

Burr, Vivien. 'What Is Social Constuctionism?' In Vivien Burr. Ed. *An Introduction to Social Construction*. London: Routledge, 1995.

Chippewas of Nawash Unceded First Nation. 'Under Siege: How the People of the Chippewas of Nawash Unceded First Nation Asserted Their Rights and Claims and Dealt with the Backlash.' Accessed 30 March 2007 from http://www.ipperwashinquiry.ca/policy_part/projects/pdf/under_siege.pdf.

Denzin, Norman K., and Lincoln, Yvonna .S. Eds. *The Landscape of Qualitative Research: Theories and Issues*. London: Sage, 1998.

Francis, Diana. *People, Peace and Power*. Sterling, VA: Pluto Press, 2002.

Galtung, Johan. 'Cultural Violence.' *Journal of Peace Research* 27(3): 291–305.

– *Peace by Peaceful Means: Peace and Conflict, Development and Civilization*. Oslo, Norway: Oslo International Peace Research Institute, 1996.

Galtung, Johan, and Carl. G. Jacobsen. Eds. *Searching for Peace: The Road to Transcend*. Sterling, VA: Pluto Press, 2000.

Goodman, Anne, Klein, Edith, and Wallace, Rick. *Intercultural Community-based Peacebuilding: A Comparative Pilot Study*. Ottawa: Canadian Centre for Foreign Policy Development, 2002.

Goodwin, Jeff, and Jasper, James M. Eds. *The Social Movements Reader: Cases and Concepts*. Oxford: Blackwell, 2003.

Koenig, Edwin C. *Cultures and Ecologies: A Native Fishing Conflict on the Saugeen-Bruce Peninsula*. Toronto: University of Toronto Press, 2005.

Lederach, John Paul. *Preparing for Peace: Conflict Transformation across Cultures*. New York: Syracuse University Press, 1995.

– *Building Peace: Sustainable Reconciliation in Divided Societies*.Washington, DC: U.S. Institute for Peace, 1997.

Mennonite Central Committee - Ontario. *Report of the Fisheries Listening Team: Visits to the Communities of Wiarton, Cape Croker, and Own Sound*. Kitchener, ON: Mennonite Central Committee, 1996.

Meyer, David S., Whittier, Nancy, and Robnett, Belinda. Eds. *Social Movement: Identity, Culture and the State*. New York: Oxford Press, 2002.

O'Reilly, Patricia. 'Shapeshifting Research with Aboriginal Peoples: Toward Self-determination.' *Native Studies Review*, 15 (2), 2004.

Ponting, Rick J. *First Nations in Canada: Perspectives on Opportunity, Empowerment and self-determination*. Toronto: McGraw-Hill Ryerson, 1997.

Pryke, Michael. 'Situated Audiences.' In Michael Pryke, Gillian Rose, and Sarah Whatmore. Eds. *Using Social Theory: Thinking through Research*. London: Sage, 2003.

Schwandt, Thomas A. 'Textual Gymnastics, Ethics, and Angst.' In Michael Pryke, Gillian Rose, and Sarah Whatmore. Eds. *Representation and the Text*. Albany, NY: State University of New York Press, 1997.

Smith, Linda Tuhiwai. *Decolonizing Methodologies: Research and Indigenous Peoples*. London: Zed Books, 1999.

Thompson, M., Ken Bush, and Barbara Shenstone. *Local Initiatives for Peace: Community-level Conflict Resolution*. Ottawa: Canadian Peacebuilding Coordinating Committee, 1998.

Wetherell, Margaret. 'Debates in Discourse Research.' In Margaret Wetherell, Stephanie Taylor, and Simeon J. Yates. Eds. *Discourse Theory and Practice: A Reader*. London: Sage, 2002.

8 Picking Up the Wampum Belt as an Act of Protest

PAULA SHERMAN

In the past, Indigenous peoples exchanged wampum belts with each other as a mechanism to establish, maintain, and restore relations across vast lands and waterscapes. This exchange was a component of a system of relating among Indigenous peoples that included inter-clan relations, marriages, and trade alliances.[1] The system served internal and external needs, including subsistence, political, economic, social, and spiritual needs within and among communities.[2] Wampum strings and belts were a product of that system; the beads used for wampum strings and belts were constructed from quahog and whelk shells harvested by coastal Indigenous peoples.[3] The beads then travelled into the interior where they were used to create cultural items that symbolized relationships. Wampum strings containing white beads were often used to send important messages between nations. Norman Jacobs, who was the keeper of belts for the Haudenosaunee Confederacy, offered that wampum was a reflection of honesty and integrity, and the approach of someone carrying wampum signified they could be trusted.[4]

The principles and protocols for relating among Indigenous peoples also applied to relations with European empires when they arrived in the lands of Indigenous peoples. Examples include the Mi'kmaw Concordat, Two Row Wampum, and the Friendship Agreement. The Mik'maq Concordat was an agreement between the Vatican and the Mik'maq people in 1610,[5] the Two Row Wampum was between the Haudenosaunee Confederacy and the Dutch in 1613,[6] and the Friendship Treaty was between the Omamawíníni, the French, and the English in 1701.[7] While the circumstances differed, all three cases emphasize the importance of wampum as a symbol of truth, honesty, and integrity. In the case of the Friendship Treaty, wampum was a reflection of the sacredness of the agreement. The belt signified the presence of Omamawínini people at the centre of the agreement, holding the hands of newcomers who would live within Omamawínini law.[8]

Over the centuries, as European interest in North American lands passed to the British, and then to Canada, understandings of this agreement and the relationship it represented, faded from memory. This resulted in unbalanced relationships between Omamawínini people, European officials, and settlers. Without the principles and protocols for relating that were embedded in the Friendship Treaty, Omamawínini lands were appropriated and used to facilitate settlement and an economic base for the emerging Canadian nation. As the process proceeded over hundreds of years, many lands and watersheds within the homeland of the Omamawínini people were transformed from living, breathing entities imbued with spirituality into exploitable resources that would be used to support the needs of particular human beings.

While English policy put in place to control the lands of Indigenous peoples was a product of the Colonial Office, settlers and squatters ultimately benefitted from these policies through the acquisition of lands and resources. While this suited the economic and political goals of colonial officials and settlers, these policies led to the impoverishment of Omamawínini communities. It also initiated disruptions in the relationships between the Omamawínini people and the Natural World. These disruptions were multi-generational and impacted the maintenance of collective responsibilities within our homeland.

Very little has changed for the Omamawínini people, since the same oppressive policies implemented through the Colonial Office in the eighteenth and nineteenth centuries are in effect today and enforced through provincial ministries such as Ontario's Ministries of Natural Resources (MNR) and Northern Development and Mines (MNDM). The MNR controls access to Crown lands,[9] while MNDM is responsible for administering mineral exploration and mining interests. In addition, MNDM also serves a similar administrative role with respect to deeded private property under the Mining Act. These two ministries alone are responsible for most of the conflicts that arise between developers, exploration/mining companies, multinational corporations, and Indigenous peoples. Ministry officials continually lease, sell, and issue mineral claims on lands that are contested or still under the title or jurisdiction of Indigenous peoples.

These actions are the result of an ideology which relegates Indigenous peoples to the margins of their homelands so that Canada's legitimacy as a nation state can be maintained. The historical foundation underlying Canada is shaky because it was established through conquest and colonization. Canada is not the ideological result of long-standing relationships going back thousands of years. Canada is the result of settler societies established through conquest and the appropriation of Indigenous lands and resources.

Such claims to Indigenous homelands in the Americas began with Columbus's voyages and the subsequent legal doctrine that emerged from that context. This doctrine, known as the Papal Bulls, divided the 'discovered' world between the Spanish and Portuguese empires and provided religious justification for conquest and colonialism. Columbus' voyages created a crisis in European societies that left some Europeans questioning Christian doctrine. If God created all that was known in the world, how were these people left out? As news of the 'discoveries' spread through Europe, Europeans grappled with the contradiction in Christian doctrine that Indigenous peoples represented.[10]

An ideology called the Doctrine of Discovery was developed as a result of the crisis to reconcile Indigenous lands and peoples with European epistemology and history. The Doctrine of Discovery was used to 'maximize European exploration and colonization in the "New World."'[11] The doctrine had its genesis in medieval, Eurocentric, religious, and even racial theories, according to J.R. Miller, who believes it is still 'an active part of American and Canadian Indian law.'[12] It allows Canada and the United States to infringe upon the real property, sovereignty, and self-determination of Indigenous peoples.[13]

The doctrine has at its centre three components that worked together to negate and sidestep the legitimate autonomy and sovereignty of Indigenous peoples. The first component was that of first discovery, allowing any European power to assert a claim against particular lands if they could prove they had 'discovered' them first. At a later date this would come to mean actual occupancy on those lands, but in the early contact period this simply meant actions by traders, missionaries, and colonial officials that signified which European Crown was asserting jurisdiction.[14]

The second component in the Doctrine of Discovery was the concept of *terra nullius*, or empty wilderness. This did not mean that the land was empty of people, but that it was empty, from a European point of view, of civilization. European empires understood without a doubt that the lands in question were already occupied with people.[15] By *terra nullius*, they were referring to the ways Indigenous peoples used land that differed from the practices known to Europeans. Many European societies at the time believed human beings were on an intellectual level above that of the Natural World. This assumption led Europeans from the relationship their ancestors had once enjoyed with the Natural World.

Indigenous peoples, on the other hand, believed the Natural World was comprised of relatives, and adjusted their social and political systems to promote that reality. For those ancestors, including Omamawínini ancestors, relationships with the Natural World were matters of life and death and of paramount importance for all communities. This was evident in the daily practices of Indigenous peoples. It was also reflected in the cultural objects, ceremonies, and language of Indigenous communities. Europeans came to Indigenous lands and territories in the Americas from epistemological worlds that were markedly different from those of Indigenous peoples, including our spirituality and ecological relationships with our homelands. European practices were foreign to these ecosystems, and Indigenous peoples would have considered European systems destructive and incapable of promoting survival and sustainability. This pragmatic understanding of the land by Indigenous peoples, while different, was not the result of inferiority or limited cognitive abilities. It was a deliberate method of management, where human behavior was regulated. Use of land was organized so as to make the lightest footprint, and thus facilitate lasting relationships with the Natural World.

Europeans did not recognize this as legitimate, and believed such practices to be an inferior 'state of nature.'[16] The European ideology was reinforced through Christianity, which was seen as the only path to enlightenment. Following the logic of the Papal Bulls, Indigenous peoples who did not use their land in the expected way, or who refused to abandon their spiritual beliefs for Christianity, could be invaded and their lands appropriated. As long as a colonizing European power was the first to claim possession, the other components of the Doctrine of Discovery fell into place quite easily.

Purporting a claim to land is not the same as having actual legitimacy there. The autonomy claimed by Europeans was a contrived sovereignty, developed through a colonial ideology which enabled Europeans to conveniently dismiss Indigenous peoples' long-standing relationships with Indigenous homelands. Through this ideology, Europeans were able to reconcile the known world with the newly 'discovered' world. The Doctrine of Discovery not only allowed Europeans to connect themselves to land that was outside their frame of reference, it also enabled the development of a universal history that celebrated the struggle of explorers, traders, colonial officials, and settlers. The result was a process that brought previously unknown lands and peoples into the existing European world. As this process of constructing autonomy and relationships with the land progressed through new generations of settlers, a national ideology developed with an associated historical consciousness that justified and legitimated continual cycles of conquest and colonialism against Indigenous peoples. Indigenous autonomy was not carried forward as part of the official historical narrative.

While the primary focus of this chapter is not the Doctrine of Discovery, a brief analysis of its function is necessary to place the contemporary policies of the Ministries of Natural Resources and Northern Development and Mines into their proper historical context. Most importantly, this brief excursion provides the background needed to understand the continued role played by provincial ministries in the colonization of the Omamawíníni people. Mineral exploration is just one of many 'explorations' that are still permitted through the natural resources regime that is maintained by provincial and federal entities within our homeland.

This process remains a colonial process, as we never ceded nor surrendered any part of our homeland to Canada. Regardless of this lack of jurisdiction, Ontario continues to make decisions that impact our homeland. This is evident in the recent decisions of the province to allow mineral exploration and mining development on our lands. When those mineral claims were registered with the province, it resulted in the staking of over 30,000 acres, 29,000 of which remain under Algonquin jurisdiction. Decisions were made about our land without proper consultation, which is a violation of Ontario's fiduciary responsibilities to us as Indigenous peoples.

Omamawíníni people were unaware of the staking until a neighbour, Gloria Morrison, contacted us in November of 2006. As a good neighbour, she felt an urgent need to alert us so that we could take appropriate action.[17] Sixty acres of the Morrison property had also been staked, and the Morrisons had pursued all available mechanisms to seek relief, but found their efforts thwarted by the Ontario Mining Act. The Morrisons discovered that many property deeds in Ontario carry only surface rights, not subsurface rights.[18] Under the Mining Act, mining companies can divert toxic waste from mining production onto private lands. They can also divert water from any stream, river, or lake for use in mining production.[19] In fact, entire lakes can be drained and filled with tailings, which remain radioactive for billions of years.[20]

While the Morrisons and others were concerned that the Mining Act pre-empted their private property rights, the Omamawínini people believed the province to be negligent in its fiduciary responsibilities with respect to Algonquin land that had been staked. The council discussed this failure, along with possible options to stop the development from going any further. By this time winter had set in, with most of the area covered with heavy snowfall. While serious damage to wetlands had already occurred through the construction of service roads, little else could be attempted by the company with respect to preparation work until spring. This gave us time to continue meeting with our neighbors to facilitate the development of an alliance and a sound strategy of resistance.

The two affected Algonquin communities discussed the issue and quickly reached consensus to present a united front against the project. While Ardoch would be directly impacted by the project, Shabot Obaadjiwan faced the possibility of contamination of its community lands through its ground and surface water. Establishing an alliance with Shabot was a difficult prospect for Ardoch leadership because of Shabot's participation in the land claims process. The Ardoch community opposed the claims process on philosophical and practical grounds and was highly critical of Shabot's involvement,[21] but Ardoch and Shabot managed to put aside existing animosity to focus on the threat that uranium exploration and mining posed. After carefully analysis, a decision was reached through consensus that neither community would permit uranium exploration or mining. While disagreement existed on many levels, the one thing Ardoch and Shabot agreed upon was the fact that uranium exploration was dangerous and a violation of Omamawínini law. Under Omamawínini law, we had a responsibility to restore and maintain the ecological balance within the Natural World as much as possible. Uranium exploration and mining carried huge negative impacts that were known around the world. Given the potential danger, Ardoch and Shabot felt they had to prevent the exploration from taking place.

Extending this alliance to include the Morrisons and others made logical sense given the danger the project represented to the region. We began to collaborate on the issue through March and April 2007, and developed an approach that contained four avenues of resistance: education, direct action, legal options, and political solutions. Educating the public on the dangers from uranium exploration and mining was a major focus early on. Non-Aboriginal supporters began a campaign to bring in experts to speak about uranium. Omamawínini leadership also agreed to give presentations and workshops on Algonquin history, culture, and re-lationships with the land so that our supporters could better compre-hend our position on title and jurisdiction. Direct actions were also planned to bring local, national, and international attention to the issue.

In addition, legal counsel was obtained to deal with the consequenc-es of the direct actions. Letters of opposition were sent to Frontenac Ventures Corporation (FVC) and MNDM informing them that we had not been notified or consulted about the proposed project. The letters demanded that FVC cease their work and remove their equipment from our lands, and that MNDM revoke the mining claims and remove the stakes from our lands. Meetings were held to decide on the best possible direct action that would bring the most attention to the issue. We decided to erect a camp at the site of the old Robertsville Mine, which bordered Omamawínìni land and contained the only entrance onto the mining road. The camp was initiated on 28 June and was slat-ed to last 10 days. Various activities were held on the road allowance outside the gate, including an information toll to alert residents and seasonal cottage owners of the proposed project. The press also made regular visits. Later in the week, a protest march was carried out on the Trans-Canada Highway, which had the result of blocking traffic for an hour and a half between Highway 509 and Highway 38 in the Sharbot Lake area. While all of these activities certainly brought insight and understanding to local and regional residents, they did not have the desired effect on provincial government officials, who remained silent. As a result, we knew that the protest would have to be maintained until the province agreed to fulfil its obligations.

This required a change in strategy, since sustaining the camp indefi-nitely would require more resources. Meetings were held to discuss more permanent occupation of the site as well as the structures that would need to be in place to support that. It was important to all in-volved that the exploration company not be allowed on the site. One of the first decisions made by the alliance was to establish a security force to protect the site and the people who would be there for the duration. The security force was put in place in July 2007 under the direction of war chiefs who were appointed from Ardoch and Shabot. The force patrolled the site and parameter to prevent access by anyone associated with the exploration company. In addition to this mandate, the security force also had the responsibility of maintaining the camp as a peaceful, non-violent protest site. Violence and weapons were banned.

Ardoch and Shabot held a joint press conference alerting the media and general public to the continued protest, which was attended by a strong contingent of neighbours who had begun to organize themselves into a community coalition. The coalition established a contact list of people who could be called upon at any time of the day or night to provide assistance at the site. They also organized benefits to support the camp and formulated a plan to deliver food, water, gas, and other basic necessities on a daily basis.

When the non-Aboriginal organization outside the gate took on formal status as the Community Coalition Against the Mining of Uranium (CCAMU) in July and August 2007, relations between the Coalition and the Omamawínini people changed as well. One person was appointed to meet regularly with a representative of the camp to organize external support and the delivery of its supplies. CCAMU also helped with direct actions, education of the general public, and numerous other activities. Some private landowners did not align themselves with the CCAMU, preferring to maintain less formal relations.

The Omamawínini leadership pursued resolution with provincial and federal officials. Since the exploration company refused to remove its stakes from our lands, Ardoch and Shabot followed the only logical course open within our own epistemology and law. While Ontario continued to shirk its responsibility throughout July, the alliance between the Omamawínini people and our neighbours continued to grow and expand. Over that period of a few weeks, the Omamawínini leadership and representatives of CCAMU travelled around southern Ontario giving talks about the issue and the alliance that had been formed to resist the attempts to destroy our homeland. Local landowner John Kittle, for instance, became very active in pushing for townships and municipalities to pass motions demanding a province-wide moratorium on uranium exploration and mining. He convinced five politicians, 10 municipal councils, seven landowner associations, and eight environmental organizations to support a moratorium.[22] In addition, the alliance of Omamawínini and the settlers has resulted in 81 organizations from around the world signing a statement of support against uranium exploration and mining in Omamawínini territory.[23] This statement included 107 signatures from 12 countries,[24] in addition to the support of over 2,500 people who signed a petition supporting our call for a moratorium. All of the statements, petitions, and associated materials were submitted to provincial and federal officials, yet nothing happened through July and August. Instead of acting in a positive way to resolve the issue, Ontario continued to bury its head in the sand.

Once the camp moved from a temporary protest into an occupation, Frontenac Ventures took the protest more seriously: in mid-July the corporation arranged a meeting to bring the parties together to discuss the issue. While Frontenac wanted the meeting closed, the Omamawínini people wanted an open and transparent process, and the meeting stayed open. It began with a presentation from Frontenac Ventures. As part of its strategy, Frontenac offered $10,000 for the right to drill 200 holes. Many people in the room shouted out, outraged at the offer. Chief Randy Cota was openly distraught, fighting back tears as he spoke, insulted by the offer.[25] His highly emotional state was not due to the amount of money being offered, but was the result of Frontenac president George White's assumption that the Omamawínini people could be bought for a few thousand dollars. Many of our neighbours also declared their anger. George White responded to the outbursts through his legal counsel, and insisted that everyone had overreacted to a project he claimed held no danger for the environment or the people.[26]

An Omamawínini mother and grandmother spoke up at that point, asking Frontenac spokespeople if they believed us to be people who lacked intelligence. She offered that Algonquins 'have an intimate knowledge of the land, and of the way things operate there.'[27] She explained our ability to do research, and that we had access to the same 'scientific knowledge and experience from the history of uranium mining around the world that they did, and knew that there was no safe way to mine uranium.'[28] George White left the meeting fully aware that he had little support for his project in the area.

In a very real sense, what developed between the Omamawínini people and our neighbours as a result of this conflict was a continuation of the original relationship begun hundreds of years ago. That relationship, which had been neglected and tossed aside, now looked promising. As our neighbours began to acknowledge that they were living in the homeland of the Omamawínini people, they began to think about Canada's relationship with Indigenous peoples. People, who barely knew we existed previous to this protest, began to see Canada and its history in a new light. They began to critically analyse what was happening around them.

With this understanding, the protest evolved over the summer of 2007. CCAMU and other organizations took on more responsibilities with respect to education, while the Omamawínini people continued to maintain the occupation and deal with the specific political issues related to our status as the original people within our homeland. Through this alliance, we continued to challenge the right of MNND to issue or register mining claims on lands that had never been ceded or surrendered to Canada. We even took this argument a bit further, to insist that our jurisdiction extended beyond reserves or crown land to include those lands that had been appropriated and transferred to the domain of private property. While we certainly respected the rights of our neighbours to enjoy their land and homes, we believe that this right is one of occupation and not of actual ownership of the Earth.

Actual ownership of the Earth does not reside with human beings. Our jurisdiction is therefore not about ownership in the sense of control and domination, but is instead about relationships and responsibilities. Jurisdiction is a necessary mechanism to maintain our relationships with the Natural World around us. In a very real sense, our identity as people is tied to our relationships with the land. If we maintain good relationships with the Natural World, then our identity develops as it should, and prepares us to live in balance with the world around us. If our relationships with the Natural World are out of control, then identity development becomes more difficult as we try and reconcile those fractured relationships.

Acknowledgement of Omamawínini jurisdiction by our neighbours has furthered our collective efforts. It promotes unity, not only against exploration companies but also against the natural resource regime that is operating in Ontario. This regime promotes the development of mining, forestry, and other activities at the expense of Indigenous peoples and private landowners. When our neighbours discuss the issue, they no longer see it as just an issue of private property. As a result of our efforts, we have both come to a fuller understanding of our relationship. While our neighbours have become aware of the long colonial process that continues to limit and deny our autonomy, we also recognize the fact that the portions of our homeland appropriated through colonial policies remain part of our homeland, and thus we have responsibilities to those lands.

While the province is enriched by this process through the profits gained each year from the resources on our lands, the Omamawínini people remain impoverished. Private landowners in our homeland are now aware of this process and how it impacts us directly. What has also become apparent to our neighbours is the reason behind Canada's refusal to ratify the *United Nations Declaration on the Rights of Indigenous Peoples*. The reasons are transparent: Canada's economy is based upon resource extraction, and ratification of the *Declaration* would jeopardize Canada's access to those resources.

Examined in that context, uranium becomes a symptom of a larger problem of resource extraction from our lands and watersheds. We were aware of this problem from the beginning of the protest, which led us to pursue solutions in both the political arena and the courts, separate from the efforts of our neighbours to reform the Mining Act. We employed short-term strategies to deal with the uranium issue while also working towards long-term solutions to the larger issue of development on our lands. The occupation was a short-term strategy that we hoped would lead to meaningful consultation with the province. The council was hopeful that consultation would then lead to the development of a long-term solution to prevent such conflicts in the future.

As a strategic move to facilitate a process with the province, in February 2008 Ardoch and Shabot withdrew from the court process that had been initiated by Frontenac Ventures after we refused to leave the Robertsville site. In addition to a $77 million lawsuit filed against the communities, Frontenac also filed an injunction with the courts to have us removed from the site by the police. Withdrawing from the court process was a dangerous action, since we would not be allowed to offer a defence against contempt charges. An interim order was granted telling all protestors to vacate the site. Ardoch and Shabot ignored the order and continued to call for the province to come to the table to settle the conflict.

For their part, the Ontario Provincial Police (OPP) were working under a new framework for relating to Aboriginal peoples that emerged out of the Ipperwash tragedy.[29] Their mandate was to facilitate public safety through the deployment of the Aboriginal Relations Team (ART) and the Major Events Liaison Team (MELT).[30] The ART team worked with the Omamawínìni people, while MELT worked with non-Aboriginal peoples, including Frontenac Ventures and our neighbours. In spite of the court order, the OPP took no action to arrest or remove protestors from the site over the summer. This opened the door for Omamawínìni people to push particularly hard for a political solution through negotiation, partly because FVC was irritated by the fact that the injunction did not produce results that would allow them to resume exploration activities.

While FVC continued to push for the injunction to be enforced, Ardoch and Shabot released an offer to settle with the province at the beginning of October 2007, which outlined the following conditions:

- Algonquins will suspend the blockade and go home for the duration of this agreement;
- Ontario will agree to a moratorium on mineral exploration and mining in the disputed area;
- All contempt of court proceedings and other investigations and prosecutions will be withdrawn and/or stayed; and
- Ontario will indemnify all peaceful protesters for liability for actions up to time of this agreement.[31]

Of particular importance to the Omamawínini people in drafting this offer to settle was that a joint panel be set up during the period of the moratorium to investigate the issues related to uranium exploration and mining in the Ottawa Valley. The Omamawínini people felt that one important measure that needed to be secured in writing was land withdrawals[32] of the whole area and joint decision-making on any further resources coming out of our homeland.

This offer was, of course, rejected by Ontario government officials, who claimed that such considerations were best dealt with through the land claims process. Omamawínini people within the Ardoch community firmly rejected this idea, as the community remained outside that process. To include the uranium issue in a process Ardoch already considered corrupt was unacceptable. The claims process had done nothing to secure land withdrawals in the 15 years it had been in existence. Ardoch had no faith in that process, and wanted the uranium issue to be settled as part of a separate consultation between Ardoch, Shabot and the province.

On 6 October 2007, Ontario finally proposed mediation, but Omamawínini leaders had to reject participation because of Ontario's insistence that FVC be a party to the mediation and that the process be closed. Sensitive to the alliance and the work that had been done to bring about mediation, Ardoch refused to participate in a process that was not open and transparent. In spite of this initial setback, we worked through it to reach a decision that the meetings would be open and that FVC would not be a party. We were about to announce this to the press when our legal council was notified that Ontario was reneging on mediation because they did not want to discuss the legitimacy of mining claims and staking. They only wanted to discuss where Frontenac could drill, which was unacceptable and not consultation.

Our press conference called Ontario to task for agreeing to mediation and then pulling out to avoid discussions on the legitimacy of staking.

The press conference produced results, because Ontario came back to the table, claiming they had distributed the wrong draft of a letter. As a result of the agreement to enter into mediated discussions, Ardoch and Shabot agreed to leave the Robertsville site. While the protest was not over, the Omamawínini people made the decision to stand down from the occupation to give the mediation process a chance to resolve the issues. While the process to establish the mediated discussions dragged on and on, an initial meeting was finally held in November of 2007. The lawyers began in earnest then to 'discuss the mediation process, and how the parties and their counsel might work together with the mediator to resolve the outstanding issues related to the protest.'[33]

The other components of the resistance strategy were also still in place and operating alongside mediation. The Omamawínini people and our neighbours continued to make appearances, conducting presentations and workshops on the issue of uranium exploration and mining. Likewise, benefit concerts, dinners, and dances continued to take place to fund the resistance. Ardoch also made connections and alliances with other Aboriginal communities such as Kitchenuhmoykoosib Inninuwug (K.I.) and Serpent River. The Omamawínini people also continued to host socials and film nights to maintain the alliance and relationships with our non-Aboriginal neighbours over the winter months.

In February of 2008, it was apparent that mediation had failed to lead to meaningful consultation. Week after week of meetings consisted of nothing more than a discussion of what would be on the agenda for the mediated discussions. Ardoch and Shabot wanted meaningful consultation that would place the legitimacy of staking at the top of the agenda, while the province would not agree to its placement on the agenda at all. While the Omamawínini people were willing to enter into meaningful consultation that would include a wide possibility of outcomes, Ontario wanted to begin from the position that staking had already occurred and the only topic for discussion should be where the holes would be drilled and how many there would be. Ardoch and Shabot rejected mediated discussions that would include the validity of staking, and walked away from the table.

The contempt charges that had been dormant during the mediation process were resurrected, and Ardoch and Shabot leaders were forced into court to answer the charges. Two days of testimony by Ardoch lead negotiator Robert Lovelace offered evidence of Ardoch's position and refusal to abide by the injunction. On 15 February, Ardoch and Shabot were told to report for sentencing for contempt of court. The day before the hearing, Shabot made a deal with the province and undertook to cease all protests related to the Robertsville site; they agreed to enter into a process with the province and Frontenac Ventures that would allow FVC access to Ardoch Algonquin community lands for uranium exploration, including the drilling of core samples.

Ardoch maintained its position of resistance and Ardoch leaders Robert Lovelace and Paula Sherman were sentenced for contempt of court. Robert received six months in jail and a $25,000 fine, Paula a $15,000 fine. The community of Ardoch received an additional fine of $10,000. Robert remained incarcerated in a maximum security institution until 28 May 2008, when the Ontario Supreme Court ruled that the sentence had been unjustly harsh and released him. Since this time, Ardoch has continued to pursue meaningful consultation with the province to resolve the issue, but Ontario had rejected these offers. Ontario will only agree to a consultation process that allows drilling.

Shabot completed its consultation process and signed an agreement to allow Frontenac access to complete its drilling program. Ardoch Algonquin people reject this agreement and do not recognize the authority of Shabot Obaadjiwan or the land claims negotiations table to allow access to our community lands. This agreement has also been rejected by CCAMU and the numerous landowners whose lands will be impacted by such an agreement. In spite of the poverty that exists within the Ardoch community, no amount of money would entice Ardoch to sign such an agreement. Ardoch is committed to community understandings of Omamawínini law and the responsibilities that emanate from the relationships we have with the Natural World.

What is particularly disheartening about this turn of events is the signal it is sending to our neighbours. While they have finally stepped up and grabbed firmly onto that wampum belt that was extended to them so long ago, Shabot Obaadjiwan has decided to drop its responsibilities to the Natural World. They have chosen to pursue a different path, away from Omamawínini law and relationships within the Algonquin homeland. Ardoch and our non-Aboriginal neighbours are now left to hold up this belt alone. While the belt may wobble as we struggle through this process, Ardoch is committed to maintaining its relationships and responsibilities. To do otherwise would not be in keeping with Omamawínini culture and traditions, and would offend our ancestors.

NOTES

1 Paula Sherman, 'Indawendiwin: Spiritual Ecology as the Foundation of Omamawíníni Relations' (PhD Diss.,Trent University, 2007), 57.
2 Ibid.
3 Lynn Ceci, 'The First Physical Crisis in New York,' *Economic Development and Cultural Change,* 28 (4) (1980), 840.
4 Norman Jacobs, *Legend and Memory: First Nations History in Ontario* (CBC Video, 2000).
5 See Henderson, *Mi'kmaw Concordat.*
6 See James W. Ransom and Kreg T. Ettenger., 'Polishing the Kaswentha: A Haudenosaunee View of Environmental Cooperation,' *Environmental Science and Policy,* 4 (2001), 219–28.
7 William Commanda and Romala Vasantha Thumbadoo, *Learning from a Kindergarten Dropout: A Reflection on Elder William Commanda's Work While at Kiche Anishnabe Kumi* (Kanata, Ont.: Circle of All Nations, 2005).
8 William understands this as an agreement for a true partnership between Omamawíníni people, the French and English. That Omamawíníni people as the centre of the homeland, held the relationship together in peace and balance. His understanding was that Omamawíníni people could not be removed from the centre of that relationship or balance would not be retained.
9 The term 'Crown land' is not accepted as a legitimate term by many Indigenous peoples, as it suggests that the lands in question belong to the Crown. In this case, Crown land is really Omamawíníni lands that were never surrendered or sold to the Crown. They remain under our title and jurisdiction.
10 For more information on the crisis created in European psyche by the 'discovery' of Indigenous lands and peoples, see Deloria Jr's *God Is Red*, and Blaut's *The Colonizer's Model of the World.*
11 Miller, 'Doctrine of Discovery.'
12 Ibid.
13 Ibid.
14 Ibid.
15 By some accounts the population of North America alone was in the millions at the time of contact.
16 See Henderson, 'Context,' 11, 15–17. The *state of nature* ideology held Indigenous peoples to be primitive, and in a pre-human state without the cognitive abilities needed to produce rational thought and reason – both of which were seen as indicators of civilization.

17 Gloria Morrison, 'Personal Communication' (Ardoch, Ont.: 2 February 2007).
18 Ibid.
19 Ministry of Northern Development and Mines. 'Facts about Exploration and Mineral Development in Ontario,' Accessed 23 October 2007 from http://www.mndm.gov.on.ca/MNDM/MINES/LANDS/bulbrd/surface_rights/mrvssr_e.asp.
20 Ibid.
21 This conflict over the land claim goes back to the 1990s when the original claim was filed by Golden Lake. At that time, Ardoch was the only historical community involved in that process with the reserve. Ardoch walked away from the process after it was discovered that Golden Lake wanted off-reserve Algonquin people involved to beef up the claim, but had no intention of including them as eventual beneficiaries. Ardoch also objected to representation, since only one member of each historical community would be allowed to participate, while the chief and the entire council of the reserve would participate. Ardoch was also unhappy with the process, which required the community to adopt elections that the council felt compromised traditional governance. A council decision resulted in Ardoch's withdrawal from the claims process, which angered some people who wanted to partake in that process and saw it as a way of gaining recognition from the government. Those families left Ardoch and formed the Sharbot Lake Algonquins, a community which has recently become the Shabot Obadjiwaan First Nation. They have continued to participate in the claims process believing that they can achieve some sort of agreement with the government to protect their interests. Ardoch has steadfastly maintained that the current structure of the land claims process will not permit us to maintain our responsibilities to the land, and thus we cannot participate until such time as those protections are put in place.
22 John Kittle, 'Personal Communication' (Lanark, Ont., 7 October 2007).
23 Ibid.
24 Ibid.
25 'Meeting at Oso Hall,' (*Oso Township*, 19 July 2007).
26 Ibid.
27 Ibid.
28 Ibid.
29 Although there are some concerns as to how well the framework has been implemented, the aspects implemented thus far seem to be working with respect to the protest at the Robertsville site.
30 The MELT team serves the same function with non-Aboriginal people. Their main focus is also to facilitate public safety.

31 'Algonquin Offer to Settle,' document issued to the Crown (1 October 2008).
32 Land withdrawals are one of the first things that should be negotiated between Aboriginal peoples and the federal and provincial governments at the beginning of a claim and treaty process, to protect those lands from any sort of development or mineral exploitation until the claim is settled.
33 Richard J. Moore, 'Mediation Notes,' Mediation Meeting (Toronto, Ont., 22 November 2007).

REFERENCES

Blaut, James M. *The Colonizer's Model of the World: Geographical Diffusionism and Eurocentric History*. New York: Guilford Press, 1993.
Champlain, Samuel de la. *The Works of Samuel de la Champlain*. Vol. 1. Toronto: Champlain Society Series, 1922–1936. Collected volume, 1971.
Deloria, Vine, Jr. *God Is Red: A Native View of Religion*. Golden, CO: Fulcrum Publishing, 2003.
Henderson, James Sa'ke'j Youngblood. 'The Context of the State of Nature.' In Marie Battiste (Ed.), *Reclaiming Indigenous Voice and Vision*. Vancouver: UBC Press, 2000.
– *Mi'kmaw Concordat*, Halifax: Fernwood, 1997.
Miller, Robert J., 'The Doctrine of Discovery in American Indian Law.' *Idaho Law Review*, (42), 2005.
Seed, Patricia. *Ceremonies of Possession in Europe's Conquest of the New World, 1492–1640*. Cambridge: Cambridge University Press, 1995.

9   Towards a Shared Vision: Lessons Learned from Collaboration between First Nations and Environmental Organizations to Protect the Great Bear Rainforest and Coastal First Nations Communities

MERRAN SMITH AND ART STERRITT

On 6 February 2006, a new era of sustainability dawned in coastal British Columbia, in the area known as the Great Bear Rainforest.[1] Conservation groups, First Nations, and forest industry leaders joined British Columbia Premier Gordon Campbell in Vancouver to announce an historic set of agreements to guide the future of this globally unique region. The agreements called for the protection of a vast tract of rare temperate rainforest, laid the groundwork for improved logging practices, and initiated an investment of $120 million into the well-being of the region's communities. The agreements have since been hailed as one of the most comprehensive conservation achievements in North American history.

Behind the transformative change embodied in the Great Bear Rainforest agreements exists a set of relationships between environmental organizations, First Nations, government, and industry. This chapter focuses on the relationship between Coastal First Nations and ForestEthics, one of the three environmental groups involved in the negotiation. In the pages that follow, we will introduce the context in which the initiative was conceived, and provide a chronology of key events leading to the 2006 agreements. We will also discuss six key aspects of the environmental/First Nations collaboration with other sectors we feel were critical to success. These are:

1 BE BOLD: Articulate a compelling vision of change.
2 BUILD POWER: Real change requires real power.
3 NURTURE RESPECT: People make change, not institutions; create relationships with people.

4 USE DIVERSITY: Build alliances of 'Strange Bedfellows.'
5 PLAY SMART: The more complex and entrenched the system, the
   more creativity and innovation is required to change it.
6 BE POSITIVE: Persistent optimism is infectious.

It should be noted that the project described herein involved literally
hundreds of individuals and spanned a decade. Any attempt to characterize broad themes is interpretive, and influenced by the authors' frames
of reference. There are many ways of telling this story. This is one.

The People and the Place

Temperate rainforests are rare ecosystems found in only 11 regions of the
world, mostly coastal zones with heavy rainfall. The Great Bear Rainforest
on Canada's Pacific Coast represents one-quarter of the world's remaining
coastal temperate rainforest and is part of the planet's largest remaining
intact rainforest system. Extending from Butte Inlet north to the British
Columbia-Alaska border, including Haida Gwaii, this 74,000 square-
kilometer (28,500 square-mile) area is larger than Ireland.
   Here, 1,000-year-old trees tower as high as skyscrapers. Rivers sustain
wild salmon; forests, estuaries, and islands support tremendous biological diversity, including grizzly bears, black bears, white Kermode bears
(Spirit Bears), wolf populations, migratory birds, and a multitude of bo-
tanical species. The Great Bear Rainforest is truly an ecological treasure.
   For millennia, the ecological riches of the Great Bear Rainforest have
supported equally rich human cultures. The region is the unceded traditional territory of more than two dozen First Nations. Outside of Prince
Rupert, the region's only urban centre, First Nations in small, isolated
communities such as Klemtu, Bella Bella, Metlakatla, and Oweekeno –
communities accessible only by air or water – comprise the majority of
the population.
   Historically, First Nations carefully managed natural resources from
both land and sea, relying on knowledge of seasonal cycles to harvest
resources without depletion. Colonization, however, brought newcomers to log the forest and catch the abundant salmon. Throughout much
of the nineteenth century, pulp mills, sawmills, logging camps, canneries,
and mines extracted resources from First Nations' Traditional Territories
despite protests. While early resource extraction turned profits for companies and provided employment, few benefits accrued to First Nations,
who suffered economically, socially, and culturally.

By the 1990s, the need for change was dramatically clear. The region's economy had dwindled to isolated logging camps, a remnant fishing fleet, and a few tourist lodges. Most First Nations' communities suffered high unemployment and low graduation rates, limited infrastructures, poor health, substandard housing, and low incomes. Piecemeal attempts at economic reconstruction had all failed, and, with unemployment rates as high as 80 per cent, no group faced a more urgent economic crisis than these communities.

Escalating Conflict

The 1980s and early 1990s were an era of conflict in British Columbia's rainforests. As public concern erupted over logging, forest companies were forced to defend their practices and challenge their critics. On Haida Gwaii, First Nations elders and youth stood with environmental groups to blockade logging trucks. Following the Haida blockades, activists fought valley-by-valley over the remaining 13 intact Vancouver Island watersheds, culminating in 1993 when over 900 people were arrested in Clayoquot Sound – the largest mass arrest in Canadian history. It was time for change.

Hoping that a broadly supported plan might resolve disputes, the BC government initiated a province-wide land-use planning process in 1992. The premise was that those with a stake in the land – residents, resource companies, First Nations, environmentalists, workers, and others – would inform decision-making through consensus recommendations, balancing development with conservation demands.

While their goals were laudable, many land-use planning tables did not reach consensus – and in these cases, the BC government made unilateral land-use decisions. By 2000, BC had doubled its protected lands, but the philosophy persisted that the economy and the environment were contradictory values. First Nations were still regarded as 'stakeholders,' and the BC government remained the ultimate arbiter.

In 1997, the BC government created land-use planning tables (Land and Resource Management Planning processes) for BC's central coast, and later the north coast – the area that became known as the Great Bear Rainforest. These tables constituted the government-sanctioned forum for land-use decisions.

Having experienced five years of BC land-use planning processes, environmental groups recognized that the process was too constrained and avoided the most critical issues: the Great Bear Rainforest's global significance, the need for a scientifically valid resource management, and new economic options for communities. Environmental groups would not sit at the coastal planning tables until the process was improved. Some First Nations reluctantly engaged in the process, providing their communities' and governments' perspectives, but did not endorse recommendations. They opposed being characterized as stakeholders and made this clear at each meeting. Thus, the planning tables were thwarted by the frustrations of First Nations and environmental groups.

Fuelled by a growing concern about the state of the world's forests and dismayed at a flawed planning process, environmental groups launched an international campaign to raise awareness of logging in the Great Bear Rainforest. They developed a new vision for the region which included:

- Protection of a connected network of intact watersheds and key ecological areas;
- A new type of forest management;
- Recognition and accommodation of First Nations' title and rights; and
- Realignment of the region's economy away from industrial resource extraction toward support for the long-term health of the region's environment and communities.

Realizing this vision meant influencing the companies that held the rights to log most of the region's valleys, as well as the BC government, which held decision-making power. Because BC's economic interests were closely aligned with the coastal forest companies, government was not a passive player. First Nations, with unresolved rights and title, were potential allies, but relationships between First Nations and environmental groups were undeveloped.

The environmental groups took their message to the market place – to the international buyers of BC's wood and paper products. ForestEthics, Greenpeace, Rainforest Action Network, and other groups contacted Home Depot, Staples, Ikea, various Fortune 500 companies, and the German pulp and paper industry, among others, and showed them the destruction their purchases caused. Some purchasers cancelled contracts. Others paid no heed, sparking an international environmental campaign that included storefront rallies, blockades, shareholder resolutions, and prominent advertisements.

For the forest companies, a public relations problem became a customer-relations debacle. Both risk and values informed customers' responses:

some wanted to avoid controversy; others did not want to participate in the decline of old-growth forests.

As the markets campaign raised the region's profile in international boardrooms, other BC groups such as the Sierra Club of Canada and the Raincoast Conservation Society took the story to the public. Reporters dubbed it 'The War in the Woods,' a moniker now firmly part of BC's historical lexicon.

Getting to the Table

Customers don't want to buy their two-by-fours with a protester attached to it. If we don't end it, they will buy their products elsewhere.
   – Bill Dumont, Chief Forester, Western Forest Products, March 2000

In 1999, a number of senior forest company representatives met to re-define their approach to the conflict. Denial was replaced by recognition that the Great Bear Rainforest was the focus of growing public concern, and that environmental groups were credible in the eyes of their custom-ers. They realized that to eliminate conflict over coastal logging, they would need to change their relationship with environmental groups, a more strategic land-use planning approach, and renewed efforts to work with First Nations, communities, and stakeholders.

The companies realized they would have to sit down with the environ-mental groups they had long battled and seek a negotiated resolution to the conflict. This would not be easy, as the conflict had entrenched antag-onisms between sectors and created animosities between individuals.

In 2000, the logging companies agreed to halt development in more than 100 intact Great Bear Rainforest watersheds. In return, Forest-Ethics, Greenpeace, and the Rainforest Action Network modified their market campaigns, updating customers on progress in negotiations rather than requesting contract cancellations. This standstill allowed a new beginning.

Following the agreement, the logging companies and the participat-ing environmental groups created the Joint Solutions Project. It was a structure for communications and negotiations, and facilitated a broad-er dialogue with First Nations, government, labour, environmentalists, and communities. It was also a venue for sharing information, solving problems, and discussing policy – discussions that would carry for-ward to the land-use planning and decision-making processes. Two historically disparate sectors were hammering out their differences, pooling their energy and resources to define new approaches. It was a step forward.

First Nations Create a Turning Point

For many years First Nation communities worked in isolation from one another. But in 2000, leaders from communities throughout the Great Bear Rainforest gathered for the first time to discuss the shared problems of unemployment, poor economic opportunities, and inadequate resources.

From the outset, the First Nations' goal was to restore responsible resource management approaches on BC's central and north coast and Haida Gwaii through ecologically, socially, and economically sustainable practices. First Nations agreed they wanted to both promote economic development and protect the environment and quality of life in coastal communities. They recognized that resolving these issues required mutually acceptable solutions.

As First Nations leaders discussed their communities' plight, it became clear they were stronger together. A coast-wide alliance was formed, called Turning Point (now Coastal First Nations). It included the Homalco, Wuikinuxv Nation, Heiltsuk, Kitasoo/Xaixais, Gitga'at, Haisla, Metlakatla, Old Massett, Skidegate, and Council of the Haida Nation.

The Coastal First Nations developed a declaration[2] that laid the foundation for its future work:

> We declare our life source is vital to the sustenance and livelihood of our culture and our very existence as a people. The First Nations of the North Pacific Coast inherit the responsibility to protect and restore our lands, water, and air for future generations. We commit ourselves:
> - to making decisions that ensure the well-being of our lands and waters;
> - to preserving and renewing our territories and cultures through our tradition, knowledge, and authority;
> - to be honest with each other and respectful of all life.
> We will support each other and work together as the original people of the North Pacific Coast, standing together to fulfill these commitments.

First Nations believe that the people who best know, use, and protect biodiversity are the First Nations who call the region home. In order to reach a solution that included a broader range of groups, Turning Point engaged others, including the Truckloggers Association, unions and municipal governments, environmental groups, and logging companies.

By late 2000, the scenario in the Great Bear Rainforest had evolved considerably from the unrest of only a few years previous. Logging in key areas had been halted and three venues for dialogue had been initiated: the Joint Solutions Project, the Coastal First Nations/Turning Point, and the Land and Resource Management Planning tables. Tensions remained, but people were talking. The potential for creating something revolutionary was palpable.

Shifting Philosophy: Agreeing on a New Framework

The first breakthrough came in 2001. The Coastal First Nations and the Joint Solutions Project, along with other First Nations and stakeholders, agreed to a five-part framework for resolving the conflict. Faced with a united message from such diverse groups, the land-use planning tables too adopted this framework, which had five components:

Logging Moratoriums

It was important to maintain future management options while dialogue was underway, so logging was deferred in 100 intact valleys and key ecological areas.

Independent Science to Inform Decision-Making

Because land-use decisions of such magnitude required the best available science, an independent science team – The Coast Information Team – was formed, with funding from the BC and Canadian governments, environmental groups, and the forest companies.

New Forestry and Land Management Approach

Ecosystem Based Management (EBM) recognizes that functioning ecosystems form the basis for sustaining communities, economies, and cultures. Rather than focusing on what resources to extract, EBM focuses first on values that must be maintained to sustain ecosystems.

Commitment to a New Economy

To facilitate an equitable transition to a diversified economy, $35 million was allocated to assist existing workers and contractors affected by logging deferrals and other changes. First Nations, environmental groups, and the BC government also agreed to discuss new financial capital to support biodiversity protection and healthy communities through stimulating new types of economic development.

Government-to-Government Agreement

The General Protocol Agreement on Land Use and Interim Measures, signed by the BC government and eight First Nations, provided for First Nations land-use planning processes to take place parallel to the BC government-initiated planning processes. Signatories agreed that once First Nations land-use plans were complete, government-to-government negotiations would reconcile them with the BC government's land-use plans.

For First Nations, the Agreement helped create a level playing field with government, environmental organizations, the forest industry, and other stakeholders. It changed the way business was conducted in their Traditional Territories, providing them with the power to make land-use decisions.

The Coastal First Nations believed the General Protocol Agreement should address other issues related to land-use planning, including:

– Recognition of history of First Nations in their Traditional Territories and their Aboriginal Rights and Title as articulated by the Constitution of Canada: Respect and acknowledge Aboriginal Rights and Title as defined by the Constitution and case law.
– Ecological principles: Sustain the biological richness and the biological services provided by natural terrestrial and marine processes at all scales[3] through time.
– Principles of information and adaptive management: Identify benchmarks against which future management performance can be measured, and adopt a coordinated approach to information management.

From Framework to Solution

Agreeing in principle to the framework for the 2001 agreement – protected areas, new forestry (EBM), a new regional economy and government-to-government relationships – was a significant step. But much work was still required to turn this agreement into a plan that would result in a new on-the-ground reality. This took five years, over a dozen committees and thousands of hours of meetings.

The Coast Information Team (CIT) conducted biophysical and socio-economic research. It developed reports and recommendations for the land-use planning tables, and produced products to inform Ecosystem Based Management, including a framework, handbook, planning guides, spatial analyses, and discussion papers.

Each First Nation worked to gather elders' and hereditary chiefs' traditional knowledge, combining it with Western science to develop land-use plans. Tired of hearing about the promise of a 'new economy' without corresponding promises of supporting resources, they took steps to secure necessary funds for their ongoing work.

First Nations and others had long challenged environmental groups to demonstrate how conservation could promote economic diversification and deliver community benefits rather than hindering development. Environmental groups responded with the idea of attracting conservation financing capital. To advance this concept, First Nations, the BC government, and environmental groups created the Conservation Investments and Incentives Initiative (CIII), the first task of which was to explore the legality and feasibility of conservation financing.

Conservation financing linked clear, lasting conservation commitments to create investments in new businesses and build First Nations' conservation management capacity. Because some of these economic opportunities were unprecedented, Coastal First Nations carried out pilot projects to try new business concepts such as shellfish aquaculture and non-timber forest products. They also explored Ecosystem-Based Management pilot projects.

The government's land-use planning tables continued, and, in 2004, with new information provided by the CIT and CIII processes, consensus land-use recommendations were produced for protected areas and commitments to EBM. Simultaneously, First Nations were completing their own land-use plans and preparing for government-to-government negotiations.

Finally, in February 2006, the BC government, First Nations, environmental groups, and forest companies together announced the Great Bear Rainforest Agreements, the culmination of over a decade of work. More directly, it was the outcome of a year and a half of negotiations between First Nations and the BC government, which used the consensus recommendations of the land-use planning processes along with First Nations' own land-use plans to arrive at final agreements.

The 2006 Great Bear Rainforest Agreements encompass several key elements.

Protected Areas

At the regional level, the Agreements established a network of new and existing protected areas, representing the Great Bear Rainforest's full diversity. These protect ecologically and culturally significant areas from logging and other industrial uses, secure habitat for sensitive plants and animals, and safeguard many of the region's most productive salmon streams, unique natural features, and cultural sites. The protected area network encompasses 21,120 square kilometers (8,150 square miles), or one-third of the land area of the central and north coast. The agreements quadrupled the area of land protected.

Of the 104 protected areas, 65 have been legally designated as conservancies; the remaining areas are in the process of receiving legal designation. To ensure the protected areas respect First Nations' values, each area's management plan will be co-developed by the First Nation in whose traditional territory the area falls.

Managing Land and Resources (Ecosystem-Based Management)

The 2006 agreements followed up on the commitment to Ecosystem-Based Management embedded in the 2001 framework. With help from the Coast Information Team, a broad understanding of Ecosystem-Based Management evolved into a rigorous, scientific-implementation handbook.

At the regional and landscape scales, the protected area network and old-growth reserves safeguard a core of ecologically and culturally significant areas. At the landscape and watershed scales (e.g., a watershed greater than 10,000 hectares, or 20,000 acres), management plans assign high, medium, or low risk to ecosystem integrity, creating reserves in which little or no resource extraction occurs. These reserves maintain wildlife habitat and migration corridors, protect waterways, and preserve threatened species, and other values. At the site scale, (e.g., within a 100-hectare, or 250-acre, forest stand), harvesters must retain 15 to 70 per cent of the trees to maintain key habitat features (e.g., streamside cover, trees for nesting, rare plants, or den sites). Logging plans also seek to sustain ecological processes. For example, leaving large fallen trees in rivers contributes to salmon habitat.

Ecosystem-Based Management plans are matched with socio-economic plans that generate income, enhance cultural and community health, and provide sustainable livelihoods. Under the 2006 agreements, all parties

committed to fully implement EBM by 31 March 2009, a target now successfully achieved through landmark legislation introduced by the
Province of British Columbia in March 2009.

*Economic Transition and the Conservation Investments
and Incentives Initiative*

The 2006 agreements brought the vision of the CIII closer to reality. The
private philanthropy community brought funding commitments that
leveraged government contributions. The Nature Conservancy, along
with First Nations, ForestEthics, and other groups, played a central role
in raising $60 million in private funds.

Conservation financing comprised two complementary investment
streams. First, $60 million in private funds would be dedicated solely to
conservation management, science, and stewardship jobs in First
Nations communities. Second, $60 million in public funds – the Coast
Opportunity Funds – would be invested in sustainable First Nations
business ventures.

In January 2007, the Canadian and British Columbia governments
each committed $30 million, bringing the conservation-financing pack-
age to $120 million.

Ongoing Government-to-Government Relationship

The Great Bear Rainforest saw an evolution in relations between coastal
First Nations and the BC government. This evolution was mirrored in
the 'New Relationship,' a policy endorsed by Premier Gordon Campbell
and BC First Nations leaders (see Chapter 17, this volume).

In its essence, the government-to-government relationship in the Great
Bear Rainforest seeks to establish structured, shared decision-making
and collaboration between First Nations and stakeholders, primarily
through the government-to-government Land and Resource Forums.

Lessons Learned

BE BOLD: Articulate a Compelling Vision of Change

The Great Bear Rainforest initiative was successful because of its
uniquely compelling vision: a global conservation model for an internationally significant area, sufficiently comprehensive to simultaneously address ecosystem health, resource use, and community well-being.

This vision inspired environmental groups, forest companies, and First Nations, and built public support for changes to the status quo.

At the heart of the vision was the place itself, which, until the mid-1990s, was known within the forest industry by the notably unsexy moniker 'Mid-Coast Timber Supply Area.' The name 'Great Bear Rainforest' became integral to the vision, communicating the vastness, uniqueness, and majesty of the region's towering trees and white bears. It conjured up an image of a place worthy of special consideration.

Creating a global model was equally compelling. It was broadly recognized that land-use conflicts between communities and corporations were globally ubiquitous, and the notion that British Columbia could lead the way by developing a workable, replicable solution provided an added incentive.

During the course of negotiating the solution, there were many points at which success seemed distant, even impossible. The vision served as a mantra, motivating participants to push forward. Had the vision been less compelling, it is unlikely people would have dedicated so much of their lives to the project.

BUILD POWER: Real Change Requires Real Power

At the outset, the BC government asserted ownership and legal control of the land base, and forest companies, which held logging rights throughout the region, had primary influence in resource planning. This power began to shift when several court decisions recognized and affirmed First Nations' Aboriginal Rights and Title, and gave First Nations power to advance their agenda. The most notable case was the 1997 Delgamuukw decision, which recognized and accommodated First Nations' rights and clarified the Crown's legal obligations.

At the same time, the international market campaigns became increasingly successful, and environmental groups gained influence approaching that held by forest companies. When environmental groups asserted that the status quo needed to change, government and forest companies listened – knowing that approximately $1 billion in sales hung in the balance. When forest companies, and ultimately the BC government, acknowledged this new sphere of power, negotiations and planning processes experienced a fundamental shift.

New court cases, such as the Haida First Nation's 2004 case against the BC Ministry of Forests and Weyerhauser, further defined First Nations' rights, articulating that neither the BC government nor forest companies could make land decisions without consultation and accommodation. While the courts continue to refine the precise meaning of these cases, they had the primary impact of obligating the BC government and the companies to include First Nations in decision-making.

The General Protocol Agreement marked the first time the BC government had agreed to negotiate on a government-to-government basis with BC's coastal First Nations.

This new power dynamic made First Nations and the BC government equal participants in negotiations, while environmental groups gained political power by threatening forest companies. If environmental groups or First Nations walked away from talks, their respective legal and market initiatives could significantly harm the other parties. Parties were kept at the table due to their unique power and shared interest in arriving at a solution. However, each remained cognizant of alternative courses of action that could be pursued if negotiations went astray.

The shift in power was one of the most critical elements in achieving success in the Great Bear Rainforest. Would companies have sat down with environmental groups if their markets had not been threatened? Would government have signed protocols with First Nations if the latter had not undertaken legal action? All involved agree that without the power shift, the breakthroughs necessary to achieve such a holistic conservation approach would not have occurred.

NURTURE RESPECT: People Make Change, Not Institutions;
Create Relationships with Those People

Few, if any, would have predicted people from opposite 'sides' would form personal relationships based on understanding – much less that they would be seen in hindsight as such an important facet of success. Past land-use conflicts had produced caustic relationships between individuals, which had spread into more broadly held disrespect. A lack of contact between individuals fuelled misperceptions and stereotypes, further eroding relations.

When environmental and forest industry leaders first sat down to discuss the Great Bear Rainforest, they carried this past: there was little respect, no trust, and poor understanding of each other's perspectives. Over hundreds of meetings, something changed. People began to listen and understand the other side's interests and perspectives, rather than simply exchanging demands.

Relationships between environmentalists and First Nations were similarly strained by past tensions, though on a less personal level and to a lesser extent. First Nations saw parks as an extension of the colonization that had so harmed their culture. For their part, environmentalists had spent little time in First Nations communities, and had not adequately addressed their economic and cultural issues.

Later in the project, the issue of financial resources created tension and conflict between environmental groups and First Nations. Both groups struggled to obtain funding to carry out their projects; however, environmental groups had more direct ties with philanthropic foundations. First Nations, who then obtained philanthropic funding through the environmental groups, felt this created a power imbalance. Relationships improved as First Nations, with the support of conservation leaders, developed their own direct arrangements with foundations.

If near-constant meetings broke down interpersonal barriers and helped people gain mutual understanding, tackling on-the-ground issues taught individuals to trust each other's commitment to the solution. The Kitasoo-Gitga'at Protocol Integration Team provides one example.

In 2001, following the first framework agreement, the Gitga'at and the Kitasoo First Nations invited environmental organizations, logging companies, and the tourism sector to sign a protocol with them regarding the development of some aspects of the framework. This agreement led to the Kitasoo-Gitga'at Protocol Implementation Team – a group of protocol signatory representatives who committed to working on ground-level experimentation with the kinds of economic activities envisioned in their proposal. The team served as a laboratory, taking people out of the abstract policy level to wrestle with the myriad challenges of putting ideas into practice.

By working on concrete projects, and supporting one another to acquire necessary resources, participants built the relationships required to make real change.

USE DIVERSITY: Build Alliances of Strange Bedfellows

At the outset, the environmental organizations, coastal First Nations, and forest companies each held distinct world views. The former two – those seeking change to the status quo – held differing views as to what such change should entail. While these differences had fuelled past conflicts, the unique circumstances turned diversity from a weakness into a formidable strength. Overall, diversity can be credited both with the breadth of the solution and with its eventual adoption by the BC government.

Environmental organizations began the Great Bear Rainforest campaign with the perspective that the earth's systems were in peril, that modern society's industrial systems were largely at fault, and that the solution was to codify protection of remaining intact natural systems through mechanisms such as parks. They had applied this approach with great success since the birth of the modern environmental movement. These groups' early work was motivated by an aesthetic appreciation of nature; later, conservation science provided a strong tool for informing and justifying protection.

By contrast, the First Nations who have occupied the BC coast for at least 10,000 years, and have co-evolved with the ecosystems around them, held a more integrated view of nature. They carefully managed the abundant resources of both land and sea, relying on knowledge of seasonal cycles to harvest a wide variety of resources without depleting them. But while they had deep connections to – and concern for – the land, they also faced serious social and economic issues, many of them the legacies of colonization. First Nations' vision of change thus involved both regaining control over their territories by asserting their title and rights, and addressing poverty by providing jobs for their communities. Some First Nations supported conventional resource extraction if it provided economic benefits.

Finally, forest companies held a world view based on business economics and a more utilitarian view of nature. Betrothed to their shareholders, and working within the context of international export markets, they sought to maximize cutting rates, production efficiency, and profits. Some companies also felt responsible for providing employment for communities. They benefited most from the status quo, and until their markets were threatened, had little incentive to change.

A critical phase in the development of the solutions package involved all three parties seeking to understand the each other's unique perspective. This led to a willingness to expand and merge their respective visions of change so that each could see their values and interests reflected in the proposed solution.

In the end, the solution included protected areas, but not conventional parks – they were a new form of protection under new legislation that respected First Nations. It included funds for community economic development, but these funds would be applied to conservation management and sustainable business development; they could not be used for unsustainable resource extraction. Finally, logging would occur, but it would involve the lighter-touch Ecosystem-Based Management approach, not business as usual.

The 'strange bedfellows' approach was powerful: when historically polarized groups presented a solution they had agreed upon, government had virtually no choice but to endorse it and work to make it a reality.

PLAY SMART: The More Complex and Entrenched the System, the More Creativity and Innovation Is Required to Change It

Coastal First Nations consistently referenced their millennia-old cultures and successful stewardship of the land and sea. However, over the past century they had lost their rightful control over the area and were now experiencing high unemployment levels and nearly no control over the land-use decisions in their territories.

Environmental groups had long espoused the belief that economics and conservation were not necessarily mutually exclusive, that there was a way to protect ecosystems *and* have forest economies. However, they had created few working models and none of significant scale.

By contrast, the BC forest industry is a juggernaut. The BC Ministry of Forests makes decisions affecting a land base of millions of square kilometers. BC's forest industry is dominated by large, multinational corporations heavily invested in conventional practices and at the whim of international markets. Despite falling forestry employment, communities also depended heavily on the status quo.

Protecting vast tracts of rainforest within the context of such a complex, deeply entrenched system required an acknowledgement that a solution would need more than existing knowledge and instruments, and a commitment to unprecedented innovation.

The first significant innovation was the creation of the Coast Information Team, a group of independent scientists tasked with producing new information to inform planning. The CIT had buy-in from all parties, breaking a deadlock whereby each presented its case based on its own science.

Another significant innovation was conservation financing, whereby financial investments in communities were linked to conservation outcomes. This approach had not been applied elsewhere, and was aimed at helping communities' transition from an industrial forestry economy to one based on a wider range of activities, including conservation.

Finally, Ecosystem-Based Management had to be built from the ground up using new science produced by the Coast Information Team. This regime offers a more sophisticated approach to planning and harvesting, and considers ecosystem and cultural protection at a number of nested scales: from the forest stand level, to the watershed level, and to the landscape or regional level.

Status quo approaches invariably lead to the status quo; creating new, innovative paths forward is key to developing new models.

STAY POSITIVE: Persistent Optimism Is Infectious

Vision, power, relationships, and innovation are all tools that can be used to successfully change systems; however, without believing one can succeed, their full potential cannot be realized. For the authors, failure was not an option: we believed we could – and had to – succeed. We understand our optimism was infectious and inspirational. Persistent optimism, even when the going gets rough, is fundamental to success.

Conclusion

In the past, First Nations and environmental groups didn't talk directly to each other. They pursued their own paths in addressing their respective issues. Today they are working to bridge that gap.

As responsible groups they recognize they must sit down together and work towards mutually acceptable solutions to common concerns, knowing that these issues can and will be resolved. Certainty will be achieved for First Nations and environmental groups when we succeed in creating a sustainable economy – that is the most important issue we face. No one is going to have certainty if they must continually adjust to an ever-changing political landscape.

Equally important was the fact that relationships between groups of people – not a land use planning agreement – was being negotiated. Often groups focus on pieces of paper and forget the human side of the equation. Yet it is keeping this human aspect healthy that ensures the advancement of everyone's agenda.

This journey has not been easy. There were – and still are – times when our alliances came dangerously close to disintegrating because we forget what made us successful. The greatest lesson we learned is that it was working together that offered the unique opportunity to access the diverse expertise found within both respective communities.

Our alliance demonstrates that complex issues can be resolved, not only for specific groups but for the greater good of all British Columbians.

NOTES

1 The environmental groups named coastal British Columbia as the 'Great Bear Rainforest' in the Mid-1990s. Prior to that it was known as the 'mid-coast timber supply area.' First Nations refer to their own territories specifically with their own names.
2 *Declaration of First Nations of the North Pacific Coast*, 13 June 2000.
3 Examples of scale include the forest stand level, the watershed level, and the landscape or regional level.

10 Reconciliation in Cyberspace?
Lessons from Turning Point: Native Peoples and Newcomers On-Line

VICTORIA FREEMAN

Established in 2001, Turning Point: Native Peoples and Newcomers On-Line – www.turning-point.ca – is a web site that has offered cyberspace for Indigenous and non-Indigenous people in Canada to engage in dialogue, information-sharing, and cooperative action. I would like to talk about how Turning Point came into being, what it achieved, and what we learned from doing it. I would also like to reflect more broadly on its role within what some people call the reconciliation movement in Canada.

'Reconciliation' is a problematic word for many people. To some, it suggests having to put up with or 'be reconciled' to something with which you're not that happy. Others have suggested that it's really premature and even a sell-out to talk of reconciliation when colonialism is still alive, well, and systemic in Canada. Nevertheless, it is a word that a number of activists have used to describe the process of developing and deepening more equitable, sustainable, and respectful relationships between Indigenous and non-Indigenous people in Canada. I say 'more equitable' because I recognize that systemic inequality can't be overcome merely through relationships between individuals or community groups. But those of us in the 'reconciliation movement,' whether or not we actually use that term to define it, see relationship-building as a critical part of the decolonization process, involving learning, transformation, and healing by both parties. Good interpersonal and working relationships are necessary to establish effective and powerful alliances that can fight for Indigenous rights in a world where Indigenous peoples are a small minority of the population in Canada and need non-Indigenous allies. They are essential to the development of longer-term co-management and power-sharing structures that work. Furthermore, Canadians need models of 'right relationship' that can help the whole country envision and move towards just and mutually beneficial relations with Indigenous peoples. And it is through personal and working relationships that we can begin to chip away at the colonial socialization that affects every individual in this country and creates such a huge divide between our peoples. Thus relationship-building is an ongoing and experimental process, and one that benefits from critical reflection. As Turning Point's vision statement says, we believe that:

> 'transforming this historical colonial relationship from one based on domination to one characterized by balance and fairness will take cooperation and mutual effort ...While many aspects of the struggle for justice require Native people to work apart from non-Native Canadians, and non-Native Canadians also have individual and collective responsibilities to challenge and change their own patterns and behaviours, we must also collaborate if we want a fundamental change in our relationship ... We all gain by supporting each other, bound as we are to live together for many generations in a common land, with constitutional, legal, financial, and social obligations to fulfill.'[1]

Activists such as Dorothy Christian, John Ord, Jessie Sutherland, Mary Alice Smith, Ann Pohl, and Cuyler Cotton – to name just a few of the many people doing this work across the country – have in various ways worked to create spaces for dialogue and relationship-building through public forums and meetings, youth programs, Internet exchange programs, web sites, teleconference calls, and other innovative techniques for community engagement. Turning Point is just one of these experiments.

Turning Point started from my own need to continue conversations and explorations that I began through the process of researching my book, *Distant Relations: How My Ancestors Colonized North America*.[2] I needed to understand my own relationship to First Nations people and my potential role in the process of decolonization. It also developed out of two 'community dialogues,' one at a community centre in Kenora, Ontario, and one at the University of Winnipeg, Manitoba, which were held to discuss the past, present, and future of the relationship between Indigenous and non-Indigenous people in those communities. In both cases, the participants commented on how rare it was to have the opportunity to speak to each other respectfully and from the heart, particularly in a group setting and a non-crisis environment. They called for more such opportunities for dialogue.

Face-to-face meetings can only be attended by a small minority of Canada's population, so I became curious about the possibilities of the Internet for facilitating Indigenous/non-Indigenous dialogue. Mary Alice Smith, then president of Kenora Anishinaabekwe (an Indigenous women's organization), agreed to be my partner in developing a web site, which became Turning Point. We were aided by an advisory group of seven Indigenous and non-Indigenous activists, and sponsored by the Seven Generations Education Institute in Fort Frances, Toronto's Centre for Social Justice, the Coalition for the Advancement of Aboriginal Studies, the University of Manitoba Native Studies Department, Under a Northern Sky: Aboriginal Circle for Justice and Healing, and the University of Winnipeg Conflict Resolution Studies Program. K-Net Services, the Internet service provider of Keewaytinook Okimakanak, a Council of Chiefs in northern Ontario, agreed to design and host the site and train Mary Alice and I to manage it. Turning Point was formally launched in May 2001.

What distinguished Turning Point from other sites on the Internet devoted to Native issues was that it was a joint effort to share information and promote thinking about how to improve and facilitate relationships between Indigenous and non-Indigenous people, whether personal, working, or political. In addition to several discussion forums, it featured a large resources section, which was a clearinghouse of information on reconciliation efforts, a question board, and notice board. Visitors to the site could post to any section.

One of the key ideas behind TP was that both Indigenous and non-Indigenous people need encouragement and a certain amount of safety to talk openly about the complexity of our relations, since the personal is indeed political and the political often gets personal. Turning Point was thus not only a place to discuss our political ideas and opinions but also to speak of and examine our personal experiences and emotions, since these are often what prevent us from being able to collaborate. As we wrote in our vision statement:

> We recognize that many Aboriginal people feel alienated and damaged by what non-Native people have done, and feel little hope of ever having a constructive relationship with their non-Native neighbours. We also recognize that a lot of non-Aboriginal people would like this relationship to be better than it is, but don't know what to do and feel immobilized (by helplessness, guilt, fear of doing the wrong thing or of being blamed for everything), particularly if all they hear about is the 'bad' news about our

connections. In our experience as Aboriginal and non-Aboriginal people working together toward a common goal of justice and healing, we have found that hearing each other's truth can be transforming and empowering, if we can speak openly, honestly and respectfully – and listen in the same way. True dialogue is possible and, as the foundation for trust between our peoples, it is a necessary first step along the road to change and any eventual reconciliation.[3]

To facilitate self-disclosure and ensure respect for others, we decided that all submissions to the discussion forums would go to a moderator for approval before posting and we would not publish material that we considered racist or a personal attack. On our home page, we encourage all participants to be 'hard on problems, but soft on people.'

Turning Point was also envisaged as linking individual activists and groups across the country who might never meet face-to-face but who were involved in reconciliation and Indigenous rights work, so that we could learn from each other in an ongoing way, develop joint strategies, and become a stronger force in Canadian society. We had the sense that many more people than we knew were working on reconciliation in various ways, but we were ignorant of each other's work and reinventing the wheel in our isolation.

Turning Point recognized from the beginning the need for each of us to speak from our own particular perspectives. This approach made it a welcoming place for people of mixed heritage, since both sides of their heritage could be honoured and addressed. In my case, as a white woman I felt the need for dialogue and connection with other non-Indigenous people who were trying to work as allies of Indigenous people. It's easy to support Indigenous rights in theory, but much harder for non-Indigenous people to work through these issues in our personal and working relations with First Nations people. As a non-Indigenous person, it's hard to clearly locate oneself in this struggle, so that one is not denying one's own identity or pretending to be Indigenous. I felt that non-Indigenous allies needed to support each other and share their experiences of trying to do this kind of work. Similarly, some of the Indigenous founders of Turning Point spoke of their need to hear from other Indigenous people who were committed to working with non-Indigenous people, because they often felt isolated or even disparaged for their interest in working cross-culturally rather than solely for their communities.

From the beginning, the issues of structure, funding, and independence were intertwined for us. Almost immediately, we were approached by the federal Ministry of Heritage with an offer of funding to be involved in the Canadian Digital Cultural Content Initiative and the development of a national web portal. This was a very tempting offer, but two members of our advisory group argued forcefully that we should not be funded by government, given its historic role and ongoing complicity in the oppression of Indigenous peoples; at the time the government was attempting to impose the First Nations Governance Act. We decided that it was important that Turning Point be, and be perceived to be, independent and beholden to no one, so we refused this offer.

This issue came up again when we applied to two foundations and received short-term funding to upgrade technically, promote the site, expand the number of forums and the resources section, and develop a strategic plan. At that time, we considered the possibility of incorporating or applying for charity status and raising funds for a paid staff position. But based on the experience of how time-consuming it was to apply for even these two small grants, and the fact that there appeared to be no possibility of stable funding, we decided to remain a loosely organized volunteer organization funded by donations. Also, as one of our funders, the Trillium Foundation, had become more politicized under the Mike Harris government (1995–2002), we did not want to be constrained in our ability to comment on the need for an inquiry into the death of Dudley George at Ipperwash in September 1995.

We therefore designed the site to be run by volunteers on almost nothing (about $50 a year), and to be highly participatory. This was made possible by new developments in on-line management software that allowed us to have multiple moderators, who did not need to know hypertext markup language (HTML). The software allowed us to spread out the responsibility for the maintenance of the site to several people rather than having a single paid staff person. Furthermore, visitors to the site were encouraged to contribute to its development. The downside of its being a volunteer site was that all of us were busy people doing many other things, and that limited what Turning Point could be.

Despite this modest infrastructure, Turning Point gained considerable attention. In its first three years, roughly 400 different contributors submitted messages to the Talking Circle and 150 different individuals and several organizations posted information in our resources section. Those were just the active participants. In the year 2003, Turning Point received over 11,000 visits, where people actually went into the site, or between 400 and 550 visits a day depending on the time of year. There were 1,800,000 hits where the site came up on a search list.

Unfortunately, participation rates decreased after this high point when frequent spam attacks on our increasingly out-of-date software necessitated a cumbersome registration process and sometimes paralyzed the site. In addition, the two main people managing the site, Dorothy Christian and myself, enrolled in graduate school and became too busy to attend to the site or even to find new volunteers. But even when we neglected it utterly, people still found Turning Point and started new discussions, reminding us of the site's ongoing utility. We recognize now that the site needed some form of institutional support, perhaps a university, to sustain it.

The Talking Circle, moderated by Dorothy Christian, was the most popular discussion forum, with exchanges on spirituality, identity, cultural appropriation, residential schools, Caledonia, colonialism, white guilt, the proposed First Nations Governance Act, the recent federal election, what constitutes respect, and many other topics. There were some really powerful exchanges. The resource section was also useful to people. There were articles on becoming an ally; resources on conflict resolution; information and links to reconciliation efforts in Australia; success stories in improving Aboriginal/non-Aboriginal relations; resources for healing for residential school survivors; links to on-line Native oral history; information on forestry issues; and a list by region and nationally of organizations working on reconciliation. It was a true sharing of knowledge.

Another strength was the diversity of participants. The site attracted a wide range of participants, not just from Canada, but from the United States, Europe, Australia, and New Zealand. From the beginning, Turning Point attracted an excellent mix of Native and non-Native participants, as well as many people of mixed heritage. Given the tremendous diversity of voices and perspectives represented, it would be hard for a visitor to read postings in the Talking Circle and think, 'Native people think this' or 'White people think that.'

On the downside, we didn't reach many Inuit, and most of Quebec was excluded because we operated only in English. It also proved far easier to involve people voluntarily and individually than through institutional participation, although we had hoped to involve church groups, schools, and university classes. Yet Turning Point avoided the 'preaching to the converted' problem that afflicts many activist groups. We know from feedback we have received that it has been a powerful tool for educating especially non-Indigenous people who have had little contact with Indigenous people and do not know very much about the issues or where to begin to take action.

We learned that Internet communication does not replace face-to-face interaction, but does offer some opportunities that are unavailable in person. Interactions between Indigenous and non-Indigenous people in any medium are often a minefield, with pain and fear easily triggered on both sides. Indigenous people feel the pain of Canada's history of colonialism and racism directly, and must often deal with the ignorance, racism, and denial of individual non-Indigenous Canadians. I've heard many Indigenous people speak of their weariness with having to educate us and deal with our reactions when they try to do so. Meanwhile, what keeps a lot of non-Indigenous people from admitting, let alone addressing, the injustices that have occurred, is their fear of the pain they will feel if they face what has happened, particularly if they experience it as guilt. Non-Indigenous people who engage in a serious way with Indigenous issues are challenged many times to re-examine their actions or beliefs – and it's very threatening because their sense of themselves, their history, their ancestors, and their culture are challenged as well. Yet that inner work is a necessary first step in order to be able to work as true allies, with honesty and integrity.

In face-to-face encounters, people often don't have the courage to say what they feel, or they blow up at each other and never speak to each other again. In on-line discussion, people feel freer to say things they would not be brave enough to say face-to-face or with people they don't know very well, and they also have time to compose their thoughts. Even if the original participants leave the discussion, their interaction is on record and others may take up where they left off or suggest ideas that can bring resolution. Many more people, therefore, have the opportunity to learn from these interactions, and the reader can access a wide variety of perspectives, which helps to break down stereotyping on both sides. As one participant wrote,'I think the only way forward is to see ourselves as all in this together, and try to learn from our reactions to each other, to help us communicate and understand each other better in the future.'

This is not to say that Internet communication about Indigenous/ non-Indigenous relations is easy. It hurts to be challenged or triggered, particularly in an environment where you don't really know who you are talking with or in what tone of voice their words were used. People may not have support off-line for dealing with the painful feelings that may result. But it is possible to reach out on-line and ask others for help. One woman wrote: 'To the readers out there – I don't like the way this conversation is going. I feel helpless, like my words are washing up against a concrete wall.'[4] There were several thoughtful responses to this posting that helped her find her way through.

It took a lot of courage to participate in some Turning Point discussions, such as one where a number of people challenged a non-Indigenous man for his economic use of Native spiritual practices. One Indigenous contributor wrote: 'just to say to all who have been participating in this dialogue how much I've been moved at times as I've read … mostly for some reason by your willingness to put yourselves out there, a courage I feel lacking at times – to say anything, say the wrong thing or say too much … not knowing how it might be taken. It seems the turning points are in those moments!'[5]

The process of reading other people's comments sometimes helped people find the courage to speak and act. A 15-year-old non-Indigenous girl wrote: 'I have actually been visiting this site for a while, but have never mustered up the courage to post anything. I have been afraid of my reactions and other people's reaction[s]. I can truthfully say that reading through the various posts on this site has not been an easy thing to do. I come across things that make me react in ways that I don't want to react, and bring up unexpected emotions. Some things make me sad, others angry; some make me feel guilty, confused, or defensive. I have tried to take note of what makes me react in different ways.'[6]

She proceeded to express her feelings and ask a number of questions, and she received a number of thoughtful responses. This direct communication with Indigenous people could be of help to her in later face-to-face interactions.

What excited me most about Turning Point was when moments of real transformation and learning were visible on-line. Such moments were truly inspiring, and visible proof that change is possible. On the other hand, there were still bullying, dominating people who tried to silence and intimidate others, and even with a moderator, it was sometimes difficult to stop them from doing so.

The flip side of Turning Point's strength in educating the general public was that more seasoned activists stayed away, especially at the beginning, first of all because they didn't know who was behind it (sometimes

Internet networks work better *after* people have met each other face-to-face), and secondly because the level of political consciousness among the majority of the participants was not that high, so the site wasn't particularly useful to activists with a deeper knowledge of the issues. Although academics and activists became aware of the site and recommended it to others who wanted to learn about Indigenous issues, to a large extent we failed in our efforts to link activists in a Canada-wide network and make Turning Point a useful working space for them, which was part of our original vision. Perhaps what there needs to be is two tiers of discussion: one for committed activists and another for the general public.

We also learned that moderators have to actively nurture discussions and it takes a lot of energy to keep such a site current. A major disappointment was the Action Forum. We had hoped to provide a place for calls for action and perhaps even a mobilization network similar to Move-On.org, but as we never successfully engaged the more seasoned activists, this never really worked. It's a shame, because some people asked us how to 'join' Turning Point, but we never had an easy way for them to do so.

Turning Point has been largely dormant since 2006, but it still has a useful on-line presence as an archive, providing a valuable snapshot for historians and others studying Aboriginal/non-Aboriginal relations in the first decade of the twenty-first century. I also continue to believe that there is a role for a web site focused on reconciliation in the broad spectrum of activities that make up the movement for decolonization, and hope that someone will create a new web-based forum – or help us reconfigure Turning Point – to do that work.

NOTES

1 'Our Vision,' Turning Point: Native Peoples and Newcomers On-line, www.turning-point.ca.
2 Victoria Freeman, *Distant Relations: How My Ancestors Colonized North America*. Toronto: McClelland and Stewart, 2000.
3 See note 1.
4 'Spirituality' thread, Talking Circle, Turning Point.
5 Ibid.
6 '"White"shame' thread, Talking Circle, Turning Point.

11 Decolonizing Art, Education, and Research in the VIVA Project

LAURA REINSBOROUGH AND DEBORAH BARNDT

The VIVA Project

'Viva!' is a call to memory and to action. Rooted in Latin American struggles, the cry often recalls past leaders and movements while inspiring future collective action. 'Viva!' is understood in both Spanish and English, reflecting the cross-fertilization of activists in the south and the north. It connotes the fullness of life that cultural action and creative artistic practices nurture in communities. It signals critical hope.

In this spirit, we adopted VIVA as the name for our transnational collaborative research project that began in 2003, and is currently completing its first phase with the forthcoming publication of a book and accompanying videos. VIVA consists of eight partners: four universities and four non-governmental organizations (NGOs) from Central and North America, who each brought a popular education and/or community arts project to the table. The projects were shared, critically reflected upon, and used to stimulate discussion on the intersections of community arts and popular education. An initial framework, called 'Creative Tensions,' was developed at an initial meeting to spark discussion about salient issues within such work. As VIVA now comes to a close, we have identified an emergent framework from the group discussions and individual reflections, that of decolonizing.[1]

This chapter first introduces the VIVA Project and the framing notion of decolonizing. We rethink our understandings of art, education, and research through a decolonizing filter. Finally, we offer a decolonizing analysis of the project, each from our own perspective: Deborah considers VIVA at the macro level as project coordinator, while Laura considers

VIVA at the micro level from her experience as a summer intern with one of the local projects.

VIVA comprises a rich array of community arts and popular education practices. Here is a list of the local projects, to give you a taste (with the sponsoring organization in parentheses):

- Pintar Obedeciendo, participatory mural-making processes with a practice originating in Chiapas, Mexico, and spreading north and south (Universidad Autónoma Metropolitana);
- ArtsBridge, post-secondary arts education training, based in Los Angeles inner-city schools (University of California Los Angeles);
- Telling Our Stories, 'train-the-trainer'-style popular education workshops for artists interested in working with marginalized youth in Toronto (The Catalyst Centre);
- The Kuna Children's Art Project, children's art workshops aimed at recovering Indigenous culture and ecology in Kuna Yala, Panama (Panamanian Social Education and Action Centre);
- Tianguis Cultural, an independent, youth-run, cultural marketplace allied with a popular education centre in Guadalajara, Mexico (Mexican Institute for Community Development);
- The Legacy Work, the development of a performance methodology by theatre artist Diane Roberts, drawing on ancestral and embodied memory (independent artistic practice);
- Jumblies Theatre, elaborate and aesthetically driven community plays in multi-ethnic neighbourhoods of Toronto (York University); and
- BilwiVision, a community television station in Bilwi, Nicaragua, with the motto 'Less Hollywood, More Local Content!' (URACCAN University).

Several of us began to dream up this transnational project in 2003, when Panamanian, Nicaraguan, and Mexican popular educators came to York for two weeks to mount a bilingual workshop, 'Making Art, Making Change.' This hands-on experience with the diasporic community of Toronto revealed our common ground: a commitment to social justice through a practice of Freirean-based popular education and a belief in the power of community arts. We created a proposal for cross-border exploration of the 'creative tensions of community arts and popular education in the Americas,' and were funded by the Canadian Social Science and Humanities Research Council.

When we gathered again in 2004 for our first official meeting, we crafted two key objectives for this three-year project, based on our common ground:

1 Using participatory action research, to recover, promote, and create diverse cultural and artistic practices integrated into processes of popular education and community organization, and aimed at both personal and social transformation that respects diversity.
2 Through gatherings, workshops, videos, and books, to organize exchanges of practices and theories, promoting a critical and self-critical perspective, and strengthening multicultural and transnational solidarity.

While the partners took responsibility for the first local objective, with each researching and documenting one community arts project in its own particular context, we shared the process of organizing our annual gatherings, meeting in Toronto in 2004, in Panama in 2005, and in Mexico in 2006. These week-long encounters allowed us to experience local practices through a conference on popular education at the Native Canadian Centre in Toronto, a popular theatre workshop in Achiote, Panama, and engagement with Unitierra, an Indigenous university in Chiapas, Mexico. As important, these annual meetings gave us solid time to reflect on our eight projects and to analyse the key things we learned from their diverse practices and contexts.

Theoretical Frameworks: From Creative Tensions to Decolonization

While the VIVA project was initially framed around the creative tensions of community arts, other grounded theory soon emerged out of our exchange. Thus, in the Panama meeting in 2005, we crafted a spiral model that focused on three interrelated processes: historical and cultural recovery, transformative processes of ethical representation, and artistic creation, all contributing to popular art and education for social change. The notion of decolonizing, and its potential as a theoretical framework, was only collectively named in our third and final meeting.[2]

Beyond the initial common ground that VIVA partners identified in 2004 – community arts and popular education – a third shared feature began to appear: the context of living in the colonized Americas. Although each partner has experienced and continues to experience colonialism in different ways, it remains a shared context for us all. Our cross-border exchange speaks to an increasingly integrated hemispheric economy, as well as the globalizing of civil society and a growing movement of Indigenous peoples and communities of colour challenging the Eurocentric values driving corporate globalization. All VIVA projects are located in complex multicultural contexts, with Indigenous and diasporic populations being clear protagonists in diverse processes of community-based art-making. However each project or partner chooses to acknowledge it, all of this is taking place in a hemisphere with over 500 years of colonial history.

While such a revelation might seem quite obvious, naming this element of our common ground has led us to collectively consider how we are and could be decolonizing our work. How do the distinct artistic and educational practices address our contexts of colonialism and post-colonialism? How can the VIVA team, engaged in an international research project, decolonize our collective and transnational practices? How does each of us contribute to decolonization processes on personal, institutional, community, and governmental levels?

Like most any term, the word 'decolonizing' signifies a complex notion whose meanings are shifting and evolving. It can, at once, be understood as: a process of *acknowledging* the history of colonialism; working to *undo* the effects of colonialism; striving to *unlearn* habits, attitudes, and behaviours that continue to perpetuate colonialism; and *challenging* and *transforming* institutional manifestations of colonialism.

While acknowledging and addressing the context and enduring effects of colonialism are positive steps towards healing and renewal, using terms like 'decolonizing' or 'postcolonial' runs the risk of re-centring colonialism. If we are seeking to transcend the colonial mentality and re-envision relationships, then what does a term like 'decolonizing' do to the struggle? Does it place colonialism as our only frame of reference? What other phenomena and forces might the term overshadow? On the other hand, failing to recognize the impacts of 500 years of colonial oppression can leave our analyses shallow and misleading.

As the term 'decolonizing' gains more and more currency, particularly in academic contexts, there is also the risk that we will lose sight of whose struggles this term addresses. Its ambiguity, especially in its verb form, offers rich possibilities for imagining what this process could look like. At the same time, however, its vagueness might result in its dilution. Therefore, it is important to remember how some are more negatively affected than others in the struggles that the term addresses.

Margaret Kovach (2005) emphasizes the importance of maintaining the perspective of those people most implicated in her work: 'Indigenous researchers ... can only get so far before we see a face – our Elder cleaning fish, our sister living on the edge in East Vancouver, our brother hunting elk for the feast, our little ones in foster care – and hear a voice whispering, "Are you helping us?"... As Indigenous research enters the academy, this principle needs to stay up close and personal' (31).

While the concepts that 'decolonizing' contains are not exclusive to academia, it should be noted that the term resonates quite vividly within academic discussions: located within postcolonial theory, written about in academic journals, and debated in classrooms. This presents its own set of contradictions. In a graduate-level course on the topic, cross-listed in the Faculties of Education and Women's Studies at York University in Toronto, Celia Haig-Brown (2006) uses the term as such: '(de)Colonizing Methodologies.' The parentheses exist purposefully and politically in order to 'call into question the (im)possibility of non-Indigenous people and people in a university doing this work in light of the histories of research and universities' on-going contributions to colonization.' Questioning the possibility of this notion is a challenge to our faith in emancipatory work: *who* can achieve decolonizing and *where* can it be achieved? Such questions might not seem fruitful if they convince us to lose hope in our efforts; rather, their strength lies in the critical reflexivity that they demand. They ask us to consider our institutional locations and cultural identities as related to the work that we do. In the VIVA project, for example, partners are working in varying institutional locations and from complex cultural identities; the distinctions between Indigenous/non-Indigenous and academic/non-academic are not always so clear. The questions that Haig-Brown poses remain relevant and constructive because they keep researchers on their toes, alert to the contradictions and complexities of such work.

Many of the themes that have arisen in the VIVA project pertain to the complexities of postcolonial identity. Our discussions of decolonizing may have started from the dualism of Indigenous/non-Indigenous identities, but they quickly erupted to make sense in our local contexts. Within BilwiVision, the community television station of URACCAN in Nicaragua, for example, Indigenous and non-Indigenous identities are explicitly complex and overlapping. A person's identity is defined not necessarily by blood or lineage but by self-identification, a right which is enshrined in the autonomy law of the region. Most coastal peoples are actually of mixed heritage, but may choose to identify more strongly as

Miskitu, for example, rather than Creole, Sumu-Mayagna, or Mestizo. One of the goals of BilwiVision is to affirm all ethnic identities and languages, and to challenge the hierarchy reflected in which languages dominate the media. In our bilingual cross-cultural dialogues, we have discussed the different uses of terms like 'pluri-ethnicity,' 'interculturalism,' 'diaspora,' and 'multiculturalism.' Each one frames cultural identity in ways that have distinct meanings in the diverse contexts of the VIVA projects. It is a challenge to find a common language, and perhaps the richest part of our exchange has been to acknowledge the 'untranslatability' of certain concepts, which in effect reflect different cosmovisions (ways of viewing the world).

VIVA partner Diane Roberts reminds us that colonialism is inscribed on our bodies, and that 'colonial products can be instruments, like our projects and how we interact with the cultures we are working with. At the centre are colonial products that are *people* who are continually not considered part of the story. It's an ugly part of the story so we don't talk about it. And when we're talking about interculturality, and it continually gets buried deeper and deeper into the earth, we never get past the idea of interculturality as this happy utopian place if we don't recognize the idea of colonial products as people.'

The VIVA project, with its many diverse local contexts, offers an opportunity to rethink 'decolonizing' in relation to the nuances of cultural identity and survival through colonialism (in its past and present forms).

Decolonizing Art, Education, and Research

The fact that we have chosen to focus on alternative practices – that is, *community* art and *popular* education using *participatory action* research – reflects the potential for decolonizing throughout the entire process of the VIVA project. In this section, we highlight how the interrelated processes of art-making and research can be challenged through the lens of decolonization.

Art

To decolonize art is to first unpack the forms and content of colonial art processes and products. 'Our concepts of art come from Europe; the term "art" itself is colonized,' says Checo Valdez, VIVA partner and Mexican graphic artist who, at a VIVA annual gathering in December 2006, critiqued his own training in European art as egoistic. Through the Painting by Listening Project, he has been training Indigenous groups in Chiapas, Mexico, in community mural production processes in which people bring their own histories and aesthetics to a mural which they themselves paint.

As an Afro-Caribbean woman, Diane Roberts, speaking at the 2006 gathering, asks us to consider who is not represented in an official history of the Americas, which privileges European settlers and less often acknowledges Indigenous nations. It is impossible, she says, to ignore slavery or the slave trade, 'and this river of blood that feeds the land, makes the land grow, and mixes with the blood of all of the ancestors in this room. But there is a devaluing of the contribution of the African culture, a deracination, a removing of race, a removing of culture of race. And we can see it in the music, the dance, the literature.' The Personal Legacy work is a response to her own theatre training in Canada, where all students were expected to perform Shakespeare; her project grounds theatre practitioners in their own bodies and ancestral heritage.

The community arts projects reflected through the VIVA exchange challenge conventional notions of art as elitist, individual, market-driven, or focused only on form, and promote the integration of art in its infinite cultural forms into daily rituals and movements for social change. They offer other stories and other ways of telling stories, to counter the official stories fed to us by mass media and dominant culture.

Education

The VIVA Project grew out of long-term relationships of solidarity and exchange between popular educators in Canada and North America. 'Popular education' is not a term that is commonly understood in the north, but among activists it has come to represent an approach to education that starts with the experiences of groups and communities who have been marginalized by a dominant culture, moves them through a collective process of reflecting on their own history and social situation, and develops critical consciousness and the collective capacity to act more strategically to change the oppressive conditions of their lives. While it is best known internationally through the work of Brazilian educator Paulo Freire (1970) and his seminal work, *Pedagogy of the Oppressed*, popular education has actually been shaped in the cauldron of social struggles of the global south, as integral to social movements.

Because it advocates a critical naming and transforming of historical power relations, popular education could be seen as a decolonizing process. But it is also limited by its Eurocentric origins, as it was very in-fluenced by European Marxist thought and structural analysis, and by a conflict view of history. In the last 10 to 15 years there have been challen-ges to this analysis: it has been critiqued for elements of positivist thought, which keep the dichotomies of object-subject in place, and it is often seen as a very linear, rational, and logical process.

Research

'The word itself, "research," is probably one of the dirtiest words in the Indigenous world's vocabulary,' writes Linda Tuhiwai Smith (1999:1). Whether the research is academic, corporate, arts-based, scientific, community-based, and so on, there remains a dire need to reassess common practices and to enact decolonizing methodologies.

Efforts to decolonize research involve both practices (epistemology, methodology, and methods) and people (researchers and participants). These might include: challenging conventional institutions to include more participatory means of knowledge production; voicing multiple languages (including Indigenous languages) in research; questioning the objectives, ethics, and methods of the research; creating funding oppor-tunities for marginalized people to take ownership of research about their communities; and encouraging a diversity of frameworks (ways of viewing the work) and cosmovisions (ways of viewing the world).

Decolonizing VIVA: From the Macro to the Micro

To further explore the possibilities of decolonizing through the VIVA Project, each of us will reflect on particular aspects of the project and our own roles within it. As coordinator of the VIVA project, Deborah provides an overview of the process by examining particular aspects of the project's organization. As research assistant and international in-tern, Laura explores her position through the intricacies of researching one VIVA project.

Decolonizing the VIVA Project: An Ongoing Process (Deborah)

Since we have begun to reframe our work as a decolonizing process, I have found myself revisiting the four years of our transnational collab-oration through this lens. In what ways have we perpetuated colonizing practices, and how have we tried to address them with decolonizing alternatives? I focus on five aspects of the project: participants and representation, project funding, evolving frameworks, products, and leadership.

1. PARTICIPANTS AND REPRESENTATION

As the project initiator, I invited partner organizations to take part based on our common history of work in popular education in the Americas. Only as the project evolved did other criteria become as important. As it turned out, for example, all southern projects had Indigenous participation, and in a couple of instances they were the key leaders, while none of the projects in North America had strong Indigenous participation. Was it because popular education in the north remains primarily a white, middle-class, Eurocentric practice? Or was it because we often reproduce ourselves by choosing to work with people like us?

How are we redressing this issue of representation? Since Aboriginal/ non-Aboriginal alliances have become important to VIVA, we are making links with Aboriginal community artists and educators in Canada, and connecting them with our Indigenous partners in the south. Questions of representation are complex, and we realize there is no simple answer, but naming the ways we have excluded certain groups helps us clarify our deeper goals and consider how the project itself can be more inclusive.

2. PROJECT FUNDING

When VIVA partners first met in 2003, we decided that each of us (whether in NGOs or universities) should seek whatever resources were available to us in our respective contexts. When I was able to secure funding from the Social Science and Humanities Research Council (SSHRC) of Canada in 2004, however, the responsibility of administering the project became centred in a northern academic context, laden with implications of historical colonial practices (in terms of whose knowledge counts and who has access to funds, for example). SSHRC funding criteria limited the possibility of supporting southern partners directly: we could provide travel to meetings, for example, but could not pay southern NGO staff for their work on local projects, which was often a greater need. We also had access to student research assistant and internship monies, which reproduced the privilege of northern students funded for rich intercultural opportunities, while southern youth had no such resources.

Margarita Antonio, a Miskitu partner from Nicaragua speaking at the VIVA meeting in Chiapas, Mexico, in December 2006, questioned this pattern: 'When I hear the Canadian students speak about the time they have to participate deeply in this project, they're talking about a VIVA that is in the north. I want a VIVA which all of us feel part of. And it is difficult because the initiative and the resources come from the north. I think it also has to do with the material conditions and political situation we live in.'

How do we break the pattern of north-south donor relationships in a context where we do have greater privilege and access to funds? How do we use our privilege strategically? Could we have pushed for more shared responsibility for finding other funding sources? Or perhaps have de-emphasized the monetary element, and proposed ways to continue our exchange that wasn't totally dependent on outside funding?

Decolonizing in the context of funding exchanges, then, engages a historical dynamic of north-south, donor-recipient relationships that are laden with contradictions and not easy to redefine.

3. EVOLVING FRAMEWORKS

The initial partners developed a framework of creative tensions that are common in popular education and community arts: tensions between process and product, aesthetics/ethics, cultural reclamation/cultural reinvention, the spiritual/political, and body/earth. While we brought a Gramscian framework to these tensions, seeing them more as dialectical and dependent on historical moments and places rather than dichotomous, they perhaps belied a deeper epistemology of Cartesian dualisms dominant in Eurocentric thought (body/mind, nature/culture, human/non-human, male/female, emotion/reason).

While able to identify with the notion of 'creative' tensions, partners in the 2005 meeting in Panama expressed concern about reproducing dualist thought, so we crafted another framework based on a spiral model more congruent with Indigenous and non-linear world views. Growing out of a systematization of our diverse projects, we identified three key points in the spiral process: historical and cultural recovery, transformative processes of art-making, and ethic representation, all feeding social change and movement-building (see Figure 11.1).

The emphasis on cultural reclamation resonates with Indigenous groups: Tuhiwai Smith (1999:34) suggests that 'coming to know the past is central to a critical pedagogy of decolonization' (34), especially for communities whose ways of knowing have been driven underground or destroyed by institutions such as the residential schools in Canada.

We also used the spiral to describe three key elements of our methodology: its integrated approach (mind, body, and spirit), its intergenerational

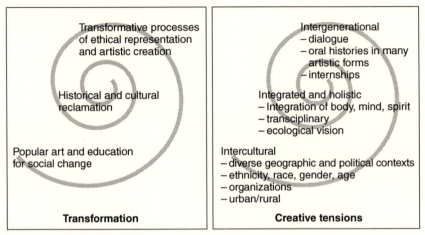

Figure 11.1 Spiral Model: The left spiral refers to the content, the right spiral to the methodology of the project.

dynamic, and its intercultural thrust. These are central characteristics of many Indigenous educational practices, and are also increasingly adopted by progressive popular educators and participatory researchers. For example, Central American popular educators have developed the concept of *integralidad*, or holism, to emphasize a pedagogical practice which embraces embodied and analytical knowing, theory, and practice, and affirms the interconnectedness of all living entities.

4. PRODUCTS

The SSHRC funding of the VIVA project perhaps influenced our decision early on to produce a bilingual collective book. As popular educators we were interested in finding ways to promote the integration of the arts into popular education and social movement-building, and we envisioned a popular book filled with stories and images that would engage grassroots educators, activists, and artists. But the pressures to produce also impacted the dynamics of our exchange, especially in the third year of the project. In a positive sense, it pushed partners to reflect more critically on the work and to articulate the possibilities and tensions of community arts more clearly for themselves and others. Negatively, it demanded time that busy activists didn't have, and focused our exchange on the details of getting a manuscript ready for publishers rather than the evolution of intercultural dialogue following other rhythms. At a deeper level, we run the danger of seeing the culmination of our exchange as a book, which is not only limited in terms of audience, but also reinforces dominant ways of knowing and communicating while the projects themselves draw on embodied practices and knowledges.

Performance theorist Diana Taylor (2003) distinguishes between two distinct though often overlapping ways of knowing: the *repertoire*, our store of embodied knowing and expression that was negated, demonized, repressed, and even outlawed by America's colonizers; and the *archive*, referring to text-based learning, which 'separates the source of knowledge from the knower.'(19). The centuries-old privileging of written texts over embodied ways of knowing still dominates contemporary academic practice, and we may be reproducing this colonizing tendency in our book. The embodied practices themselves may offer a greater integration of thought and feeling, challenging the Cartesian split and reflecting what Central American popular educators have tagged *sentipensando,* or thinking/feeling (Nunez, 1998: 165).

We collaborators in the VIVA project have to recognize as well that we are still working in two colonial languages; while there are intriguing differences between them, there are even more pronounced differences between them and the Indigenous languages represented by two of our partners, in particular, the Kuna in Panama and the Miskitu in Nicaragua. In both cases, we have to be careful not to fall prey to what Marie Battiste and James (Sa'ke'j) Youngblood Henderson (2000:79) call 'the Eurocentric illusion of benign translatability,' a dominant cultural assumption that world views can be translated. Such an assumption has often gone hand in hand with benign neglect in the face of the extinction of up to half of the world's 6,000 Indigenous languages. Our experience has confirmed what the Supreme Court of Canada declared in 1990, that 'Language is more than a mere means of communication, it is part and parcel of the identity and culture of the people speaking it.'[4] Our discussions through translation have revealed not only different terms related to arts and education but also different frames and cosmovisions embedded in the languages we use.

5. LEADERSHIP

While there are obvious contradictions and inequities reflected in the leadership of the VIVA project, based on north-south funding relationships, gendered and racialized practices, and my own way of working (which combines a commitment to collectivizing leadership with a need to have a clear oversight), the annual exchanges, built on very participatory processes, have generated new bilateral relationships and have shifted the power dynamics over time.

A Nicaraguan partner has offered to take on the coordination role of the project into its next publication and post-publication phase, when we hope to broaden the network; our next gathering will be on the Caribbean coast of Nicaragua and will be open to groups from around the hemisphere, no longer limited by an academic project. Decolonizing practices must also take into account the multiple dimensions of power, not simply north-south, but class, race, gender, and age. We understand this to be a collective responsibility and an ongoing process.

We now move from an analysis of the project as a whole to a probing of one particular project within the exchange, through the eyes of an international intern who contributed to research on and documentation of the project.

Tales from an Intern: The Kuna Children's Art Project (Laura)

Situated in Kuna Yala, an autonomous Indigenous region along Panama's southeastern Caribbean coast, The Kuna Children's Art Project consisted of regular art workshops held in five communities between 1994 and 1999. The objectives of the workshops were to reclaim Kuna culture and to transmit knowledge about local ecology. The art workshops used a diversity of forms, such as puppetry, popular theatre, drawing, screen-printing, photography, music, and traditional dancing, to realize their objectives. The workshops were led by local facilitators and were well-integrated into regular community life. Once a year, one of the participating communities would host an arts festival for all workshop participants across Kuna Yala. The festivals served as a networking space for the project facilitators, artists, and participants, and as a culminating opportunity for the project's objectives to be realized through collective mural-making, parades, and celebration.

In the summer of 2005, it was my honour and privilege to interview some of the project participants – including workshop facilitators, organizers, community members, and participants – about the Kuna Children's Art Project. I say that it was an *honour* because the interviews were fascinating and the project compelling. The experiences offered in these interviews have been a rich source of inspiration for my own work, which also dwells in the space where community arts and environmental education intersect.

I also say that this experience was a *privilege*. I use this second adjective to reinforce the honour and responsibility I held. But I also intend to emphasize the one-way privilege that comes with most international development work. For example, the funding agencies that made my trip possible do not allow people from the Global South to come to Canada and learn about community arts projects here. How was my work going to affect the communities that I visited? Would my research about the Kuna Children's Art Project act like a vacuum, sucking the knowledge from an Indigenous region in the South and releasing it for academic consumption in the North? And if not, then what would an alternative look like? Much thought has gone into this from various pockets of the international development field, and yet the vacuum model is repeated time and time again through internships like mine.

I was cognizant of this privilege when I began the internship. I was sensitive to power dynamics in the workplace and careful of how my whiteness was received while living and working in Panama City. But I reached a new depth of understanding when I was whisked off to Kuna Yala for a week, asked by my Kuna supervisor to record some interviews for a participatory reflection process. It was a moment of deep discomfort and dizziness when I found myself walking through a Kuna community armed with a video camera and broken Spanish. My white skin shone more brightly than I had ever seen it before, and the video camera I held took on new meaning, as shown in Figure 11.2. It was obvious that I was from the North, and as much as I wanted to believe that I was researching in solidarity – as an ally from the fields of community arts and environmental education – I had no control over how my presence was perceived. I was treading in the treacherous wake of many researchers before me, many of whom had done more harm than good in their work. Whole histories of past researchers (tourists, explorers, scientists, and anthropologists) had already set a precedent of colonial relationships.

The Kuna Children's Art Project set an incredible example for anti-colonial education in Kuna Yala. While harvesting stories and reflections through interviews with past participants, artists, and facilitators, I was apprehensive that my research would not match the integrity of decolonizing practices that the workshops had established. Many of the stories I heard while conducting interviews spoke to the contrast between the colonial public school system and the community arts workshops of the Kuna Children's Art Project. Not only were the workshops decolonizing in contrast to the formal education system, but their

Figure 11.2 Laura, with video camera, surrouded by Kuna children.

structure fundamentally addressed many colonizing aspects of conventional education. Leanne Simpson (2002), an Anishnaabe educator in Ontario, explains the unfortunate reality of many Indigenous environmental education programs: '... few programs are designed to enable students to address the issues of colonization and colonialism in their communities, effect healing and decolonization at the individual, community and national levels, facilitate resistance strategies in response to current injustice, and promote the building of healthy, sustainable Aboriginal communities and Nations based on traditional cultural values and processes' (14).

The Kuna Children's Art Project was a superb example of how a project can be realized on deeply meaningful principles for an Indigenous community: the facilitators were Kuna; the ideas and values that were being taught were Kuna; the organizational structure was both local and lateral; the bilingual nature of the workshops and festivals reflected Kuna identity as both local and national; and the histories that were taught reflected the community's strength in resisting colonizing forces. Throughout the five years that the Kuna Children's Art Project existed, its success shines through. To this day, it lives on in the hearts of many people, as I was told repeatedly during the interviews I conducted. It as an example of local, place-based, Indigenous education, and speaks directly to the challenge of decolonizing education.

As an intern, I worked out of a popular education centre in Panama City called CEASPA (Panamanian Centre for Social Research and Action), a centre which had contributed popular education training to the facilitators of the Kuna Children's Art Project. During my first week on the job, my Kuna supervisor handed me a manual on *sistematización*, a critical reflection methodology that has come out of popular education practice in Latin America. I had only been learning Spanish for a few weeks when I was advised to read this Spanish-language manual. Within weeks I flew to Kuna Yala to try to enact whatever I had absorbed of its methodology. Many meaningful reflections were gathered through my research, but I wonder how many unanswered questions about my role as researcher remained in my wake.

Since that experience, I have had time to learn more Spanish, to be exposed to writing on decolonizing methodologies, and to reflect upon my time in Panama. I have also had the opportunity to delve more deeply into writings about *sistematización,* and so I now understand why this methodology was chosen. The most important rule of *sistematización* is that only those who have participated in the experience are able to evaluate and reflect upon it. Therefore, the stories of the participants comprise the central elements for analysis and reflection. The process is also collaborative, as it engages the participants in all levels of the research: from gathering people's experiences to sharing their reflections; and from designing the research plan to evaluating and analysing the findings. The role of documentation is emphasized, not just for an archive but also for a deepening of critical reflection. In addition, *sistematización* is considered 'self-research,' meaning that it asserts that the responsibility of theorizing from the lived experiences rests with the participants, not with an outside institution. (Orozco, 2005; Antillon, 2002).

All of the features mentioned above combine to form a research methodology that has much potential for decolonizing. And yet, as I question the intricacies of my involvement with the Kuna Children's Art Project, I wonder if it can be considered *sistematización*. The research that I performed broke many rules: I had not participated in the initial experience, I was not from the community, and I stayed only one week to conduct the video interviews. As Oakley (1981:244) has articulated, there was a 'lack of fit between the theory and practice.' And yet, I can defend my involvement through a number of reasons: I had been asked by members of the community to lend my skills and access to resources for this particular job; the research was approved by the local Kuna government; and the results of the research were returned to the community, not only through the videos that I sent to them but also by the VIVA project's commitment to publish a text intended for activists as well as academics. Here I have exposed the back-and-forth deliberations between 'right' and 'wrong' justifications for my presence in the research process, whereas I have been advised that such 'yes' and 'no' questions can never be satisfied with either answer.

As is the case with any methodology, *sistematización* outlines the *ideal* research scenario. It cannot anticipate all of the dynamics, complexities, and nuances that every *actual* research situation is sure to present. The rifts between methodological theory and its application can be alarming. Such was the case for me as I journeyed through the process of translating my research across language, culture, cosmology, and continent. In the end, much more of the work fell on my shoulders than anticipated: I led the majority of the research interviews (which comprise much of the raw material for the reflections and analysis), and created the video of the project. The video was originally intended to be used internally for deeper reflection within VIVA, but the lack of a video camera and available staff with editing skills at CEASPA resulted in my being asked to produce the final version. Along with more work came more responsibility and editorial control, all the while mediated by my modest knowledge of the Spanish language, the Kuna world view, and the Kuna Children's Art Project itself. Despite being asked by members of the community to carry out this research, I believe it is important to question these sticky situations in order to come to a better understanding of what decolonizing might be.

Inspired by Russell Bishop's framing of five concerns for Kaupapa Maori research in New Zealand (initiation, benefits, representation, legitimation, and accountability), the following questions arise: Who initiated this research? How was *sistematización* selected as the preferred methodology? How does this methodology relate to the Kuna world view and Kuna methodology? Since *sistematización* divides only along the lines of 'participant' and 'non-participant,' and does not account for identity or status, is this appropriate within an Indigenous context? Is something more specific needed to address the context of deeply embedded colonial structures and histories?

Whether or not an explicitly Kuna methodology exists as such today, there is much potential for Kuna ways of being and knowing to influence research that occurs in Kuna Yala. In the case of researching the Kuna Children's Art Project, there were moments of confluence where Kuna research protocols met with *sistematización*. For example, the research began in *Omnaket Nega*, the congress house of the community, explaining the research to the community leaders (facilitated by Blas López, who grew up in the community and accompanied me to translate from Kuna to Spanish). Also, popular education techniques were selected to train the workshop facilitators because they were so closely aligned with the objectives of the work. Such moments reveal the potential for non-Indigenous and Indigenous methodologies to work in tandem, as allies.

Final Words, Multiple Voices

The conversation among VIVA partners about decolonization really began seriously during our third annual meeting in Chiapas, Mexico, in December 2006. Our collective book includes some of the diverse perspectives that partners brought to this discussion, ranging from frames that are more academic, others that are more shaped by direct historical and embodied experiences, and still others that struggle to redefine the colonial and anti-colonial in our present-day relationships and practices. We offer three voices as syntheses of some of the questions, responses, and visions that feed an evolving process.

Heather Hermant of Toronto reminds us to keep a self-reflexive and critical perspective on our own internal processes: 'Even within our own group, we see the colonial story repeating itself – in little bursts – all the time, and that in itself speaks to why we need to be doing this kind of work.'

In offering an Indigenous perspective on decolonization, José Angel Colman of Kuna Yala in Panama refuses to get caught in a narrow dualistic frame: 'I believe that the Kuna Children's Art Project workshops were important because they were flexible and ran with a spirit of accepting others. We don't see ourselves shaping ourselves only as Indigenous people, in order to close ourselves within our Indigeneity. We are forming ourselves in our own traditional school as Indigenous people in order to project ourselves in the broader world.'

And Amy Shimshon-Santo of Los Angeles articulates a vision that moves beyond decolonization to a truly inclusive society: 'Decolonization is to come into that awareness of how your ancestors brought you here, and to engage in an affirming way with who you are, where you came from, and what your potential for creativity and change might be. Cultural and educational institutions should be reflective of who we are as a people. What we consider beautiful, what we consider meaningful, what we consider intelligent and knowledgeable, should be reflective of all of us.'

While we recognize that our various institutions and organizational bases each present their own limitations, we enter into this deeper dialogue with this hopeful vision and a commitment to challenge and transform the practices we engage in – both within our own distinct cultural contexts as well as in our construction of transnational solidarity.

NOTES

1 This chapter was originally to be co-written by two non-Indigenous researchers from the North and two Indigenous researchers from the South. As it turns out, many factors have resulted in only the two non-Indigenous researchers being able to write the piece. While this limits the richness of the discussion, this chapter remains an opportunity to contribute to an emerging discussion about how a transnational, collaborative research project can be decolonizing at both local and international levels.
2 See the introduction in our collective book, *VIVA Community Arts and Popular Education in the Americas*, for an elaboration of diverse understandings of colonization and decolonization by VIVA partners, publication forthcoming, by SUNY Press with the support of the Ford Foundation; anticipated release 2011.

REFERENCES

Antillón, Roberto. 2002. *¿Como lo Hacemos? Para Construer Conocimiento a Traves de la Sistematización de la Practica Social.* Guadalajara, México: Instituto Mexicano para el Desarrollo Comunitario.
Battiste, Marie, and James (Sa'ke'j) Henderson. 2000. *Protecting Indigenous Knowledge and Heritage: A Global Challenge.* Saskatoon, SK: Purich Publishing.

Bishop, Russell. 1996. 'Collaborative Stories as Kaupapa Maori Research.' In *Collaborative Research Stories: Whakawhanaungatanga*. Russell Bishop. Ed. Palmerston North, NZ: Dunmore Press.

Freire, Paulo. 1970. *Pedagogy of the Oppressed*. New York: Continuum.

Haig-Brown, Celia. 2006. 'WMST 6111: (de)Colonizing Methodologies.' Course syllabus, York University, January.

Jara, Oscar H. 1994. Para Sistematizar Experiencias: una Propuesta Teórica y Práctica. Lima, Peru: Alforja.

Kovach, Margaret. 2005. 'Emerging from the Margins: Indigenous Methodologies.' In *Research as Resistance: Critical, Indigenous, and Anti-Oppressive Approaches*. Leslie Brown and Susan Strega. Eds. Toronto: Canadian Scholars' Press.

Loomba, Ania. 1998. *Colonialism/Postcolonialism*. New York: Routledge.

Marino, Dian. 1997. *Wild Garden: Art, Education and the Culture of Resistance*. Toronto: Between the Lines.

Mutua, Kagendo, and Beth Blue Swadener. Eds. 2004. *Decolonizing Research in Cross-Cultural Contexts: Critical Personal Narratives*. Albany, NY: State University of New York Press.

Nuñez, Carlos. 1998. Educar *para transformar, transformar para educar*. Guadalajara, México: IMDEC.

– 2002. *La Revolución Ética*. Guadalajara, México: IMDEC.

Oakley, Ann. 1981. 'Interviewing Women: A Contradiction in Terms.' In *Doing Feminist Research*. Hele Roberts. Ed. London: Routledge.

Orozco, Efrén. 2005. 'Sistematización.' Presentation at the Second Meeting of The VIVA Project (2005). Achiote, Panama: The VIVA Project.

Simpson, Leanne. 2002. 'Indigenous Environmental Education for Cultural Survival.' *Canadian Journal of Environmental Education*, 7, no.1 (spring): 13–25.

Stanley, Liz, and Sue Wise. 1990. 'Method, Methodology and Epistemology in Feminist Research Processes.' In *Feminist Praxis: Research, Theory and Epistemology in Feminist Sociology*, 20–60. Liz Stanley. Ed. New York: Routledge.

Taylor, Diana. 2003. *The Archive and the Repertoire: Performing Cultural Memory in the Americas*. Durham, NC: Duke University Press.

Tuhiwai Smith, Linda. 1999. *Decolonizing Methodologies: Research and Indigenous Peoples*. London: Zed Books.

12 The Nakwatsvewat Institute, Inc.: Helping Hopi Justice Work for Hopi People

JUSTIN B. RICHLAND AND PATRICIA SEKAQUAPTEWA[1]

One of the most difficult social issues that Hopi people find themselves mired in today concern disputes over property and its ownership on the Hopi Reservation (Sekaquaptewa 2001; Richland 2005, 2008). Increasingly, Hopi families are fighting over property but not finding effective resolution either in the Hopi Tribal Courts, or in the traditional authority of their village and clan leaders. As one of us is a citizen of the Hopi nation, and both of us are justices of the Hopi Appellate Court, we have come to know first-hand the suffering experienced by Hopi people struggling with property disputes, and the role that tensions between traditional and non-traditional tribal governance play in their struggles. In our roles as Native nation legal scholars, we have also come to know how fights over land and homes and other kinds of property, and the complications added by divides between traditional and non-traditional Native governance, are crippling Native communities across the United States (see Richland and Deer 2004; Biolsi 2004, 2005). And now we have met many First Nations people, and their non-Aboriginal colleagues and friends, who have told us of similar issues facing Aboriginal peoples across Canada as well.

In this chapter we describe our experiences working to assist Hopi people in addressing their property disputes, particularly those of land and family homes, through the creation of The Nakwatsvewat Institute (TNI). TNI is a national non-profit organization designed to assist Native nations and their members in the development of culturally sensitive dispute-resolution services and legal systems. The Institute emerged from an earlier effort, the Hopi Customary Law Project, an outreach program of the Hopi Appellate Court initiated eight years ago, and based on our 12 years of experience working on various aspects of Hopi law.

After some background discussion about the Hopi Nation and its trad-itional and contemporary governmental organization, and a discussion of the kinds of property dispute issues that Hopis are contending with, we will turn to a discussion of the history and services of The Nakwatsvewat Institute itself. We will focus on how TNI emerged from efforts by the au-thors and their colleagues, who, after some initial false starts, generated a sustainable working relationship based on four principles of Native/non-Native collaboration: (1) 'Listen, don't lecture,' (2) 'Consult, don't con-clude,' (3) 'Provide resources, not regulations,' and (4) 'Follow the tempo, don't try to set it.' These principles have guided not just how TNI ap-proaches its work with the Hopi, but also the very kinds of services it offers them, which include: (1) Legal information exchanges, (2) Village Custom Law Archives, (3) Dispute Resolution Training, and (4) Dispute Resolution Technical Assistance. The TNI, with their Hopi colleagues, have been able to 're-envision' their working relationships in ways that opened bridges between the gaps that all too often divide Natives and non-Natives.

The Hopi Nation: Origins and Organization

There is a Hopi story about their origins that has all of humanity emer-ging from the Third World into this, the Fourth World, through the earth's navel somewhere at the bottom of the Grand Canyon. When they come through they are greeted by *Maasaw*, the caretaker of this world, who asks them to pick from four different ears of corn – the se-lection process will dictate the ways of life each people will lead. The choices are from among several long, beautiful ears and one rather short, plain ear. Some, including the ancestors of Euro-Americans and other tribes, choose the beautiful corn, and head off to discover the fer-tile homelands and easy lifestyles that they represent. The Hopi ances-tors choose the plain ear, and with that pick are told by *Maasaw* that though they must go away, they will eventually migrate back to the arid high desert of the Southern Colorado Plateau, where they now res-ide, to carve out a plain and difficult agrarian way of life.

In more optimistic moments, the Hopi state that among the many messages here is an explanation of how they have managed to stave off the imposition of non-Indigenous society in ways not observable in the circumstances of other U.S. native nations. It is suggested that it is the isolation of their 12 villages on and along three fingers of the Black Mesa in northern Arizona that has been the best defence against the ravages of colonization and other forms of oppression from outsiders.

Thus today, according to the U.S. Census of 2000, of the approximately 11,200 enrolled members of the Hopi Tribe, just over half (approximately 6,500) reside full time on the Hopi reservation, a territorial expanse that occupies 1.5 million acres of those aboriginal lands (*Hopìtutskwa*) promised them by *Maasaw*. Established by executive order in 1882, virtually all Hopi reservation lands are still held in trust today by the federal government for the benefit of the Hopi Tribe. As such, and likely in large part because there has been little non-Indian demand for access to their lands, the Hopi have avoided the territorial displacement that has caused so much suffering among tribal nations in many other areas of Indian Country.

Of course, life today is not what it once was for the Hopi. Their economy has largely shifted from strategies of subsistence dry-farming of crops like corn, squash, watermelon, and beans to a market-based economy. The need for cash sends a portion of Hopi adults off-reservation for work in nearby metropolitan areas. Others who stay on the reservation make ends meet either by making craft items for tourists or by taking positions with the Hopi Tribal Government, the largest employer on the Hopi Reservation. But even these changes have a remarkably recent origin, well within the twentieth century, and many Hopi elders can recall a time when their families largely relied on their planting of corn, beans, and squash, and/or raising sheep and cattle to meet their daily needs (Clemmer 1995; Whiteley 1988; Nagata 1970).

It was U.S. efforts pursuant to the Indian Reorganization Act of 1934 (IRA) that would work the most profound changes to Hopi socio-political organization in the last century. In fact, prior to the 1930s no entity called the Hopi Tribe even existed. Before that time, most of the villages that tribal members occupy today each operated under a largely autonomous village leadership.

In 1932, U.S. Bureau of Indian Affairs officials, with assistance primarily from a few sympathetic tribal leaders, drafted a constitution and by-laws which called for the federation of the several Hopi villages into a single Hopi tribe, to be governed by a representative tribal council made up of officials to be elected by each village. And despite opposition to the constitution, and even abstention by a majority of Hopis from the 1936 referendum to approve it, BIA officials took the yes votes by the majority of Hopis who *did* vote as an affirmation of the constitution. Thus the Hopi Constitution was deemed to have passed, and then subsequently approved by the U.S. Secretary of the Interior.

Of course, the questionable legitimacy of these moves was not lost on Hopi tribal members, and though it is largely the same constitution that still governs Hopi politics today, the validity of federally imposed tribal governance and tribal organization, including the creation of an Anglo-style Hopi Tribal Court, generally has become 'a dominant issue in Hopi politics' (Whiteley 1988: 223; Sekaquaptewa 1998; Richland 2008).

Still, our experiences concur with those of Whiteley (1988:230), that the Hopi Tribe, its council, and court have nonetheless become 'the de facto political form for the majority of Hopi people,' if only out of a need to deal with the exigencies of trans-reservation life and the increasing influence of non-Hopi forces on that life. Today the tribal council, tribal court, and other departments of tribal government possess much of the power and authority to address issues involving *inter*-village affairs, such as overseeing the management and disbursement of funds generated through tribally owned corporations. They also manage affairs between the Hopi tribal nation and other federal, state, tribal, and private entities. But at the same time, establishment of the Hopi Tribal Government has not meant the erasure of authority and at least semi-autonomy for the several Hopi villages. Indeed, written into Article III, Section 2 of the Hopi Constitution are explicit recognitions and reservations of authority to the leadership of each village over certain *intra*-village matters, including family disputes, adoption, and the assignment and inheritance of farming land and property.[2]

Consequently, the socio-political organization that defines internal village politics also continues to play a major role in contemporary Hopi governance. And while each village community is distinct, with its own unique social practices and institutions, there are some aspects of Hopi village social organization that are generalizable across them. Thus, there exits within each Hopi village several kin-based groupings that the Hopi call clans, in which membership is reckoned matrilineally. Village membership and residence is ideally (though often not actually) matrilocal, and upon marriage men are expected to move to their wives' locale. Moreover, these clans are traditionally the holders of property, including homes and land, which are also controlled and passed, like clan identity itself, along matrilineal lines (Titiev 1944; Whiteley 1988, 1998).

Additionally, the Hopi rely upon an elaborate ceremonial cycle that is a central feature of Hopi social life throughout the Hopi year. Like property and identity, ceremonies are understood as 'belonging' to specific clans, constituted in light of efficacious traditional knowledge (*navoti*) concerning the world and its operations that each clan accrued in their migrations before coming to the village (Titiev 1944).

Upon a closer look, the picture of Hopi village life becomes more complex. Again, given their historic autonomy, much of the social and ceremonial organization that can be identified today for one village does not hold for others. The reasons for this vary, but may include the extinction of particular clans and their ceremonies, and the different reactions villages have had to recent historical events that dictate the relations villages and village members have to the traditional religio-political structure (Whiteley 1988).

The complications wrought by non-Native encroachment are also evident in the competing views among members of the same village, and even same clans. For example, clans are ideally understood as the holders of certain lands and homes which pass matrilineally along with clan identity, by mothers to their children, or by matrilineal uncles to their sisters' children. This means that fathers do not, traditionally, pass property to their own children, because they do not share their clan identity. These traditional modes of property distribution conflict with the 'Anglo' style, individual-property concepts (e.g., that fathers can distribute property to their children) that some Hopis today have come to expect with respect to how land and homes should be passed.

It is against this background that we can begin to see the kinds of problems posed by Hopi property disputes. It is to those problems, and the rise of the Nakwatsvewat Institute, that we now turn.

The Problems of Property Dispute Litigation in the Hopi Court

As a law student in the early 1990s, Sekaquaptewa spent her summers at home on the Hopi Reservation as an intern with the Hopi Tribal Courts. During those trips home she was made aware that there were around 40 live cases that had been appealed from decisions of the Hopi Tribal Court, up to a higher level Hopi Appellate Court, but which hadn't been heard because of a lack of court staffing.

Her first summer there, Sekaquaptewa was charged by the Hopi Tribal Council with reading and reporting on the entire backlog of Appellate filings. With the help of fellow law students, of which Justin Richland was one, we started summarizing these files to understand what people were litigating about. Four years later, we were able to prepare a report that catalogued all the issues and subject matter of the whole of the pending appeals. After completing our report, we recommended supplying law students as clerks to the Hopi justices so that they could move these cases forward, and they could be heard. The Council accepted our recommendation, and Sekaquaptewa led a group of law students to undertake legal research and writing in support of the justices. By 1998 the entire log of cases had been either dismissed or adjudicated, and the court was beginning to hear new appeals.

As we discovered, a considerable number of both the backlogged cases and the new appeals concerned very complex property dispute cases. It soon became clear that disputes over homes, over lands, and even over village boundaries was a lasting and pernicious problem for many Hopi people. Indeed, many cases that on their face seemed to involve other matters – including criminal assault and domestic violence – were actually land dispute cases in which people, often family members, had decided to use self-help to resolve disputes that seemed to have no possibility for resolution under the operation of Hopi law.

Consider, for example, *Smith v. James* (1999). In this case, the parties were fighting over a piece of farming land in one of the villages. Specifically, the dispute involved an aunt, who we'll call Rose, and her sister Mary's daughters, Jill, Dolly, and Marie. All were members of the same clan. In any circumstance such intra-family disputes can be painful, but they are viewed as particularly disruptive from a Hopi perspective, insofar as such disputes among kin are thought to bring disharmony and to diminish prosperity for the entire village.

Aunt Ruth claimed to be the inheritor of a plot of land that she says was promised to her by her father before his death in the 1950s. Her three nieces claimed that they inherited the property from their mother, Mary, who was recently deceased, and who had inherited the land from her and Ruth's mother. They argued that Ruth was not able to inherit the property from her father, insofar as the land was clan land that he had no authority to promise to her. They also say that even if Ruth's father could legitimately bequeath land to her, she lost that right because she had moved off the reservation, married a non-Hopi, and never returned to care for the land, all actions that violate the customs of property inheritance in their village.

The Hopi trial judge brought in traditional experts to testify, and ended up crafting a new rule based on their testimony. His conclusion was that it is possible for a Hopi woman to acquire an interest in property if she had participated in the ceremonies, or if she cared for an elder who has an interest in the land, and if she had also participated in the ceremonies. However, once a woman had an interest in land, she had to use and properly care for it in order to maintain a right to it. So he did recognize some of the custom-law concepts that were in the clan-lands system, but he did not recognize necessarily that, today, the only way to have an interest in land is if it passes from mother to daughter.

This decision raised some complicated policy questions. Is it fair, for example, for the court to apply customs and traditions to Hopis who have changed to live a more 'non-traditional' life? Is it fair to tell Aunt Ruth that she has to be participating in the Hopi ceremonies to maintain her land rights? And is it fair to treat people differently under the law? In this case, one of the custom-law rules that the tribal court came down with is that if you are a married woman and you have an interest in land, your husband has to farm it. But if you are a man and you have an interest in land, it's enough that you farm it. So there's a different treatment between men and married women under the rule.

In contemplating Aunt Ruth's appeal in this case, the Hopi Appellate Court struggled to determine how and when Hopi custom law should prevail over other kinds of legal principles in Hopi court. One of the key policy reasons why the Hopi court may want to apply Hopi customs and traditions in contemporary land dispute cases is that through such decisions, the court reinforces the unique principles of Hopi culture that they embody in the context of contemporary disputes. Particularly in property disputes, because the Hopi clan-land system in each village supports that village's ceremonial cycle (by requiring the growing of ceremonial crops and the tending to those crops by clans-women), when the courts reinforce the matrilineal distribution of clan lands, they are also supporting the Hopi ceremonial cycle.

But at the same time, when the court upholds Hopi custom and tradition in these cases, it potentially curtails the Hopi law's recognition of individual property rights. Hopi individuals who want to build on tribal lands will find it difficult to convince banks and other lenders that they have sufficient equity to qualify for the kinds of loans necessary for such projects. The effect may be to create a legal system that dampens Hopi efforts at real economic development and Native self-determination.

Moreover, the whole body of land dispute litigation that came before the Hopi courts, of which *Smith v. James* is just one example, raises fundamental questions about the distribution of dispute resolution authority among the different levels of Hopi governance. Because the Hopi tribe has multiple villages, and multiple clans within each village, each of these social units is seen under Hopi law as having some form of exclusive legal authority. As a result, one clan might have a certain kind of property custom that is different from other clans in the same village, and different again from the customs and traditions of the village more generally, as well as from other villages and from the tribe as a whole. The many different layers of legal authority make it very difficult for the Hopi Court to discern what should be the proper analysis of custom and tradition in any given case, particularly when each party to the dispute offers a different interpretation of tradition from a different legal authority. We saw many cases come before the Hopi Appellate Court in which the parties to the dispute were essentially appealing the determinations of custom and tradition made by the tribal court and/or challenging the authority of that court to resolve the case in the first place.

In short, we began to realize that perhaps the 'Anglo-style' adversarial legal system employed by the Hopi Tribal and Appellate Courts was not the best dispute-resolution alternative for Hopi people themselves. It is out of that recognition – eventually, and with more than one false-start – that The Nakwatsvewat Institute was created.

The Nakwatsvewat Institute: Making Hopi Justice Work for Hopi People

At bottom, cases like the *Smith v. James* litigation revealed to the Hopi Appellate Court that there seemed no clear way to best resolve Hopi land disputes. But this was not for lack of options. As we saw, Hopi litigants had multiple avenues already available to them for resolving their disputes, including: (1) the Anglo-style adversarial procedures of the Hopi Tribal Court, (2) the dispute-resolution authority recognized by the Hopi Constitution as resting in the several Hopi villages, and (3) the traditional dispute-resolution authority recognized in Hopi clan mothers and uncles. Yet not one of these alternatives ever seems to offer a completely satisfactory response to the Hopi peoples' fighting over property.

As a result, in 1999 we were charged by the Hopi Appellate Court to investigate the problems that Hopis were facing in achieving fair and just resolutions to their disputes, and to see if we could come up with some kind of reasoned alternative. So we set out with grants from the U.S. Department of Justice on the course that would eventually lead to The Nakwatsvewat Institute. But, as we shall see, this result was about eight years in the making, and marked by several false-starts, before we settled on the multi-pronged service approach that TNI now offers to Hopi people. The best way to describe the Nakwatsvewat Institute is to examine, in order, the four principles that guide TNI's programming. More specifically, we want to show how the failure of the original idea provoked and promoted the very kinds of principled relationships that are the central theme encompassing the chapters in this volume. We hope that our discussion of each will offer guidance for others as to how setbacks can be converted into successes for achieving working, sustainable interactions and relationships between and among Indigenous and non-Indigenous peoples today.

Four Principles of Collaboration, and the False Start from Which They Emerged

The original idea behind The Nakwatsvewat Institute was the achievement of a great goal: 'addressing the dispute resolution needs of Hopi people,' particularly those caught in property disputes. When the Appellate Court reflected on how the *Smith v. James* and other property cases came to the tribal court, they realized that it was because the traditional village and clan leaders who would normally have the authority to resolve these cases had refused to handle them. These leaders essentially told the parties involved that they were worried about all the legal and political implications, those we described earlier.

The first plan that The Nakwatsvewat Institute put in place, then, was to give the Hopi courts the necessary information about village and clan traditions so that the courts could better resolve the property disputes that the village and clan leaders didn't want to handle. The idea we came up with was to draft a Hopi Custom Law Treatise, a written document compiling all the relevant property and inheritance customs from all 12 villages and every clan that was willing to speak to us, and to then put it into a legal document that could be easily referenced and relied upon by the tribal judges. That was the plan. But when we went to the villagers to tell them of our great plan, and the idea of a legal document that would list the customary laws of the different Hopi villages, it failed. And it failed, we would later realize, because it violated four principles that have come to rest at the heart of the services The Nakwatsvewat Institute now offers.

1. 'Consult, don't conclude.'

This principle stands for our recognition that no collaboration with Hopi people (and we think, with any people) works without the sustained and sustainable involvement of their community. The idea of the

Custom Law Treatise, we now realize, didn't spring from consultations with Hopi people about their needs in resolving property disputes. It actually addressed the Hopi Tribal Court's need for legal research. Our original plan started from the faulty premise that a Custom Law Treatise would address the problems facing Hopi people, not just the Hopi court's problem of access to traditional information.

But this error revealed itself soon enough, when we met with village and clan leaders. Among the tough questions they posed to us was the basic one, 'Why does the court need to know village and clan traditions, many of which are secret and sacred?' Some asked, 'Those judges aren't from our village. Why do they need this information?' Others challenged, 'If we have waived our jurisdiction to hear a case, it means that we don't want our customs and traditions even talked about in court. So why should we tell them to you so you can write them down?'

What we began to realize, after several of these kinds of meetings, was that Hopi community members didn't have a clear sense of what exactly the tribal court was doing with these property disputes – how they were addressing them and what kinds of law (traditional or non-traditional) they were trying to apply in them. Moreover, they explained that a central reason why villages and clans were waiving their traditional authority to resolve property disputes was because they thought that their decisions, particularly if they were based on custom and tradition, would not be respected or enforced by the 'Anglo-style' adversarial legal system of the tribal court.

So, after that experience, we realized that we had failed to properly *consult* with the clans, villages, and Hopi people directly affected by property disputes, before *concluding* that a custom law treatise was the best way to address their needs. Subsequently, we rethought our efforts, and initiated one of the four services that The Nakwatsvewat Institute currently offers to Hopi communities, namely use of quarterly legal workshops in which information is exchanged with Hopi people about the rules, procedures, and relevant case law of the Hopi tribal legal system. In these meetings we update Hopi village and clan leaders on particular cases pending before the court which concern members of their communities, in a pro-active effort to keep them apprised of the legal matters affecting their friends and families.

2. 'Listen, don't lecture.'

To say that we should be 'listening' more and 'lecturing' less to Native peoples about their social and political circumstances seems almost obvious. Likewise, it goes without saying that Indigenous peoples can speak for themselves about their dispute-resolution needs, and that their voices deserve to be heard on those issues. And yet, affording Indigenous peoples the opportunity to do this still seems not to happen nearly often enough. This is true even, or perhaps especially, in contexts where non-Indigenous people claim to be working for and on behalf of Native peoples. Unfortunately, the Hopi Custom Law Treatise was a perfect example of the latter.

Recall all the complexities involved with determining what Hopi customs and traditions concerning issues of property dispute are, and how they differ among the 12 Hopi villages, among the numerous clans within each of those villages, and even, as we saw in the Smith v. James case, among members of the same clan. When it came time to actually start writing the Hopi Custom Law Treatise, those of us working on that project had to ask ourselves, 'Whose customs and traditions exactly were we going to be writing down?' Were we really going to be able to get every different version of Hopi custom and tradition on these matters, from every village and every clan in every village? If not, whose voices were we going to include and whose were we going to exclude? Moreover, isn't it really the case that when you transfer what are essentially oral traditions it into a written format and put it in a form of legal rules, the voice that would be speaking the loudest would be the person doing the writing? If we were going to be going out there and writing this information down, wouldn't this treatise start to sound an awful lot more like the Anglo-style statutes and legislation that we had been trained to write and read as law students? And if that were true, who then would be able to access that information, if you'd then need a law degree to be able to read and apply the information collected in that treatise.

So the alternative approach that we came up with, and which is a service we continue to provide at The Nakwatsvewat Institute, is what we call the Hopi Custom Law Video Archives. The Archives consist of digital video recordings of Hopi people engaging each other, in discussions spoken in both Hopi and English, concerning what they understand to be their customs and traditions of property holding, use , and distribution. These discussions are then transcribed in Hopi and English, using a software program that allows viewing of the transcript alongside the running video. The result is a searchable database of recordings in which Hopi people can see and hear Hopi people talking about their customs and traditions.

For example, if a Hopi person wanted to learn about one particular topic of property traditions – say, women who leave the reservation but still want to inherit property – they can enter that topic into a search engine that will link to every instance in which that topic is discussed in the video. Of course, access to each archive is determined by the Hopi social unit that agrees to be recorded, whether that be village, clan, or family. We see these Video Archives as the most direct way to keep a searchable record of Hopi customs and traditions about property in and through which Hopi people can maintain both maximum control over the information, while also making it accessible in ways that allow Hopi people to *listen*, without being *lectured*, to Hopi voices speaking about the complex customs and traditions surrounding their property disputes.

3. 'Provide resources not regulations.'

In our work as Hopi justices and scholars of contemporary Native law and politics, we are keenly aware that the Hopi, like all Indigenous peoples, need to be supported, not supplanted, in exercising their sovereign powers for themselves. Indeed, the Hopi Tribal Court got started when it replaced the U.S.-run Court of Indian Offences that had operated on the Hopi Reservation from 1950 to 1972. But while this act today stands as a strong expression of Hopi self-governance, interestingly enough, the original impulse to create a Hopi court came from non-Hopi lawyers of the Hopi Tribe who recommended the change in the face of potential legal violations being committed by the U.S.-run court. The Hopi Tribal Council passed a resolution creating its own court, but when it came time to running the court, they relied upon non-Aboriginal lawyers to draft rules and civil and criminal procedure that adhered largely to the 'Anglo-style' adversarial procedures found in U.S. federal and state courts.

While most Hopi people have worked with this system effectively, and some have come to understand the court as the main forum for resolving disputes, many still challenge the legitimacy of the court, its decisions, and its enforcement powers, on the grounds that it is fundamentally a non-Hopi institution.

We came to realize that we were in fact running the risk of the same kinds of legitimacy problems with the Hopi Custom Law Treatise. Who is empowered by such a treatise? As mentioned before, treatises are legal documents that assume knowledge of legal procedures, and which are first and foremost meant to provide information to be used in 'Anglo-style' courts, and not necessarily by Hopi village and clan leaders themselves. And what about the sovereign powers of the villages that are recognized by the Hopi Tribal Constitution but which were not being exercised in the resolution of property disputes? Many Hopi village and clan leaders expressed a desire to use those powers, even as they were waiving their jurisdiction over property disputes, but were concerned with how their actions and decisions in such cases would be recognized by the court. Additionally, a treatise can't address the concerns of Hopis who may not want to use custom law to resolve their disputes, but who also may not want to spend the money and time to hire a lawyer to go to court.

We thus realized that village and clan leaders were asking that we not *replace* their authority with a written treatise that would serve as sort of a Hopi custom 'crib sheet' that the tribal court justices could turn to in deciding their cases. Instead, what they were saying they wanted was to be provided the kinds of informational and technical assistance *resources* to help them further develop the kinds of village and clan dispute-resolution systems that would best meet their needs. And they were clear that such systems would have to be ones that came from them – whether they be systems based in traditional or non-traditional Hopi practices – insofar as that was the only way they would be viewed as legitimate by the Hopi people themselves.

So The Nakwatsvewat Institute has been working with Hopi villages to provide technical assistance to explore different modes of traditional, mediational, arbitrational, and adversarial dispute resolution. In so doing, we in TNI have come to recognize our role as putting resources before Hopi village and clan leaders, listening to their views and concerns about each, and allowing them to generate their own dispute-resolution processes. This, of course, is a long process, insofar as the legacies of colonization have created a situation where even Hopi people, despite their successes in maintaining their culture, have nonetheless been disempowered. It will thus take time to reverse this process, to remind Hopi village and clan leaders that the powers they are now wanting to exercise in the resolution of property disputes are powers that they have always had and that really can never be taken away. The Nakwatsvewat Institute is thus prepared to work in the long term on this component of its services, insofar as we know that this is the only way real, lasting, and sustainable change will be accomplished for Hopi people. This in fact is our fourth principle:

4. 'Follow the tempo, don't try setting it.'

Those of us who have experience trying to get funding from private and public agencies to do work in Indigenous communities think that this is perhaps one of the most important of the four principles, and one about which we must try constantly to remind ourselves. It refers to the tension between the kinds of 'progress' that funding agencies want to see, versus the kinds of progress that are ever really tenable in Indigenous communities like the Hopi. It took us a long time to realize – and there are still moments that we need to be reminded – that for justice reforms to work out for the Hopi, as we suspect for any Indigenous nation, no other time frame matters but that of the Aboriginal nation you're working with and serve. While it may matter to you as the recipient of funding to attend to the timelines imposed by those agencies, and while it may matter to you as a conscientious professional to attend to your own personal project schedule for accomplishing your goals, you must do whatever you can not to expect or attempt to impose those time frames on the Indigenous nations you are serving. Not only will they not let you impose them, your project will almost certainly fail if you try.

The idea of a Custom Law Treatise was designed with funding agency reporting in mind. It was designed to be what we call in the non-profit world a 'deliverable'– some material realization of our efforts that we could send off at the end of the funding period to show what a community's money had been used for. 'Deliverables' are undoubtedly critical in the competitive world of non-profit fundraising. To get funding, you need to be able to promise concrete goals when you write funding proposals, and you need to 'deliver' on those promises in order to maintain and renew funding. But real, sustainable progress among Native communities will take decades and generations, because such progress only comes through the rectification of decades and generations of injustice wrought by colonization. This is something that cannot and will not be rushed.

So TNI's information workshops, custom law archives, and dispute-resolution system-development programs are designed to be ongoing. They are designed to be progressive and to continue to be improved upon while running independently of TNI once we give the tools to these communities. Built into these services are options in which any Hopi or other Indigenous community that has worked with us can ask that we come back out to help them address specific dispute resolution issues or assist in answering specific dispute-resolution questions as they emerge. This is the case because, just as we discovered that the Custom Law Treatise would offer no 'quick fix' to the problems of property disputes among Hopi villages, neither could we now expect villages to design and implement their own dispute-resolution systems in the one or two years dictated by the timelines of our funders.

At the same time there are Hopi people who are currently suffering with the uncertainty of their unresolved property disputes, and there are more disputes seeming to emerge every day. These people should not have to wait for decades and generations to pass before Hopi village and clan leaders are ready to run their own dispute-resolution systems. So, in addition to the other three ongoing services that TNI provides to insure the long-term sustainable legal reforms that Hopi people have called for, The Nakwatsvewat Institute also had to become prepared to offer dispute resolution services for those Hopi people who need them right now. As officers of TNI, and based on our experiences as justices of the Hopi Tribal Court, we felt it would have been irresponsible for us to acknowledge the dispute-resolution needs of Hopi people but not offer them any immediate resource for addressing those needs. We felt that if Hopi people wanted our help, it was important to offer our help as an option, perhaps the last option.

And TNI is prepared to offer that help in multiple ways. We are prepared to sit alongside clan and village leaders to assist them in live disputes to exercise their constitutionally recognized dispute-resolution jurisdiction, and under the auspices of their authority. We are also prepared to offer dispute-resolution services independent of village or clan authority, as a service available to private Hopi parties. TNI has its own set of dispute-resolution rules designed specifically to address the unique cultural circumstances that surround our work with Hopi communities and their property disputes. And those rules are flexible to accommodate the different ways in which Hopi people currently in disputes can seek our help in resolving those issues.

Moreover, as a side issue, this aspect of the services provided by TNI can provide clear proof of progress, a 'deliverable,' to our funders. We can give them figures concerning the number, type, and community distribution of disputes addressed by TNI. In this way we can meet the many and varied expectations of the people and communities we serve in Hopi country, and we can also insure that we are making productive use of the resources given to us by funding agencies, so that we can continue to call upon them to support and maintain our efforts in the future.

Conclusion

As you have seen, four principles emerged from our failed attempt to compile a Hopi Custom Law Treatise, and those principles gave birth to the four programs that today constitute the services offered by the Nakwatsvewat Institute. This entire process then constituted one in which we 're-envisioned our relationships' with the Hopi community so that our efforts would address their justice needs, as they saw them, and in flexible and responsive ways. This is, of course, a continuing effort, and 're-envisioning' TNI's relationship with Hopi and other Indigenous communities is an ongoing process. From our initial plan to draft a Hopi Custom Law Treatise, to our current multi-pronged and multi-principled approach to serving Hopi people, we have come to recognize four central principles that, we hope, will lead to real and lasting changes towards the achievement of justice for Hopi people. We now understand that we must be guided by these four principles if we hope to achieve a working relationship that is rooted in mutual trust and commitment. Self-determination is a process, one that can often easily be talked about as a goal, but which takes time and effort to undertake and enact. Indigenous nations who are raising their voices for self-determination and sovereignty should be 'listened to, not lectured,' they should be 'supported, not supplanted' in making efforts to achieve that self-determination. And when non-Indigenous organizations like The Nakwatsvewat Institute are given the opportunity to assist Native Nations in those efforts, they must do their best to 'consult with, not conclude about' Indigenous peoples and their needs, and be ever careful that they 'follow the tempo, not set it' when attempting to set timelines for the accomplishment of real and lasting change for Indigenous peoples.

The name of our institute comes from the Hopi word *Nakwatsvewat*, which also has a corresponding Hopi symbol, the *nakwatsveni*: two hands clasped together. *Nakwatsvewat* means 'going along together in a friendly way.' This 'going along together in a friendly way' is not just what TNI sets out to help Indigenous peoples achieve for themselves – amicable, non-violent resolution of their disputes. It is also the overriding principle by which we aim to accomplish that goal – entering into respectful, responsive, and empowering working relationships with Indigenous peoples as they address these matters themselves.

NOTES

1 Authorship is listed according to alphabetical order and does not reflect a difference in amount of contribution to, or responsibility for, the content of this chapter. Both authors contributed equally.
2 The Constitution and By-Laws of the Hopi Tribe (1936), Article III, Section 2, reads, in relevant part:

The following powers which the tribe now has under existing law are reserved to the individual villages:

(a) To appoint guardians for orphan children and incompetent members
(b) To adjust family disputes and regulate family relations of members of the village
(c) To regulate the inheritance of property of members of the village
(d) To assign farming land, subject to the provisions of Article VII.

REFERENCES

Barsh, Russell L. 1999. 'Putting the Tribe in Tribal Courts: Possible? Desirable?' *Kansas Journal of Law and Public Policy*, 8: 74–97.

Biolsi, Thomas. 2005. 'Imagined Geographies: Sovereignty, Indigenous Space, and American Indian Struggle.' *American Ethnologist*, 32(2): 239–59.

– 2004. *A Companion to the Anthropology of American Indians*. Oxford: Blackwell.

Clemmer, Richard O. 1995. *Roads in the Sky: The Hopi Indians in a Century of Change*. Boulder, CO: Westview Press.

Geertz, Armin. 1994. *The Invention of Prophecy: Continuity and Meaning in Hopi Indian Religion*. Berkeley: University of California Press.

Levy, Jerrold. 1992. *Orayvi Revisited: Social Stratification in an 'Egalitarian' Society*. Santa Fe, NM: School of American Research Press.

Nagata, Shuichi. 1970. *Modern Transformations of Moenkopi Pueblo*. Urbana: University of Illinois Press.

Pommershiem, Frank. 1995. *Braid of Feathers: American Indian Law and Contemporary Tribal Life*. Berkeley: University of California Press.

Porter, Robert B. 1997. 'Strengthening Tribal Sovereignty through Peacemaking: How the Anglo-American Legal Tradition Destroys Indigenous Societies.' *Columbia Human Rights Law Review*, 20: 235–304.

Richland, Justin B. 2005. 'What are you going to do with the village's knowledge? Talking Tradition, Talking Law in Hopi Tribal Jurisprudence.' *Law and Society Review*, 39(2): 235–72.

– 'Pragmatic Paradoxes and the Ironies of Indigeneity at the "Edge" of Hopi Sovereignty.' *American Ethnologist*, 34 (4): 540–57.

Richland, Justin B., and Deer, Sarah. 2004. *An Introduction to Tribal Legal Studies*. Walnut Creek, CA: AltaMira Press.

Rushforth, Scott, and Upham, Steadman. 1992. *A Hopi Social History: Anthropological Perspectives on Sociocultural Persistence and Change*. Austin: University of Texas Press.

Sekaquaptewa, Pat. 1999. 'Evolving the Hopi Common Law.' *Kansas Journal of Law and Policy*, 9: 761.

Thompson, Laura. 1973. *Culture in Crisis: A Study of the Hopi Indians*. New York: Russell and Russell Press.

Titiev, Mischa. 1944. 'Old Oraibi: A Study of the Hopi Indians of Third Mesa.' Harvard University. *Peabody Museum of American Archaeology and Ethnology*, 22(1).

Tsosie, Rebecca. 2002. 'Symposium: Cultural Sovereignty: Native Rights in the 21st Century. Introduction.' *Arizona State Law Journal*, 34: 1-14.

Valencia-Webber, Gloria. 1994. 'Tribal Courts: Custom and Innovative Law.' *New Mexico Law Review*, 24: 225.

Vincenti, Carey. N. 1995.'The Reemergence of Tribal Society and Traditional Justice Systems.' *Judicature*, 79(3): 134–41.

Whiteley, Peter. 1988. *Deliberate Acts: Changing Hopi Culture through the Oraibi Split*. Tucson: University of Arizona Press.

– 1998. *Rethinking Hopi Ethnography*. Washington DC: Smithsonian Institution Press.

CASES AND LEGISLATION CITED

Constitution and By-Laws of the Hopi Tribe (1936)

Hopi Indian Credit Association v. Thomas, AP 001-84 (1996)

Hopi Tribal Ordinance 21 (1972)

Resolution, Hopi Tribe H-12-76 (1976)

Smith v. James, 98AP00011 (1999)

13 'To Lead and to Serve': American Indian Studies in Virginia

SAMUEL R. COOK AND KARENNE WOOD

The publication of the edited volume *Native American Studies in Higher Education* by Duane Champagne and Jay Stauss (2002) marked a milestone in American Indian Studies (AIS). Not only does it commemorate the formal existence of programs focusing on this broadly defined field at various academic institutions for more than 30 years, but also the sheer fact that so many long-standing Native/American Indian Studies programs exist in North America is an indication that the academic canon has changed, if only slightly and stubbornly. While accounts of each program vary, all authors agree on specific guiding principles that make American Indian Studies programs legitimate endeavours – namely, that such programs must constitute holistic, praxis-oriented pursuits designed to serve and to work collaboratively with Indigenous peoples in ways that complement and enhance tribal sovereignty, and that recognize the legitimacy and value of Indigenous knowledge. This book understandably focused on those AIS programs that have endured the test of time and 'that have developed and deepened their philosophy about American Indian studies and their commitment to students, community, scholarship, and in many cases, traditional knowledge and language' (3).

In this chapter we offer a glance at a fledgling American Indian Studies program that has embodied the guiding principles of most salient AIS programs from the outset of its short existence. This program was born at Virginia Polytechnic Institute (Virginia Tech) in 1999, specifically at the request of some of the state's Indigenous peoples, and it has been guided by a collaborative mandate ever since. It is important to chronicle and report on such programs in the early stages, because these are the points at which some of the greatest obstacles to development present themselves, as do some of the most creative innovations for overcoming such obstacles and for nurturing and sustaining programs. While hindsight may provide a better perspective from which to glean generalized models and observations, it does not provide the best vantage point from which to observe the critical nuances and realities of what it takes to develop an American Indian Studies program in the face of localized institutional idiosyncrasies and peculiar, if not hostile, political climates.

History

American Indian Studies programs that exist at land grant institutions (which, in the United States, have a legal mandate to serve communities within their home states) are theoretically well-situated to gain institutional support as service-oriented programs. The irony is that those involved in such programs find themselves continually evoking the land grant mission and philosophy in attempts to stir up university support (Albers et. al., 2002: 149; Stauss, Tippeconnic Fox, and Lowe, 2002: 84–6). In the case of Virginia Tech, which was established as a land grant college in 1872 (Kinnear, 1972: 1), it proved to be a critical factor in setting the gears in motion for developing our AIS program.

In June of 1999, the tribal council of Virginia's Monacan Indian Nation sent a letter to then-Virginia Tech president Paul Torgersen and several other key administrators and state legislators suggesting that Virginia's land grant institution consider establishing an American Indian Studies program. In that letter, the Monacans provided a basic blueprint for a program that would not only educate the general public on American Indian history, cultures, and issues in a culturally sensitive way, but one that would – first and foremost – exist in service to Indigenous peoples. They envisioned a program that would not treat Indians as subjects, but as partners and colleagues in collaborative efforts to develop curricula that would engage the state's Indigenous communities in joint ventures designed to bolster their cultural, political, and economic autonomy, and would create a wider awareness and space in the academic canon for the legitimacy and value of Indigenous knowledge (Virginia Tech American Indian Studies Steering Committee, 2000).

In order to realize the full significance of the Monacan letter, it is necessary to place their request and the subsequent development of the program in historical context of Indian and non-Indian relations in Virginia. Following the 1677 Treaty of Middle Plantation between the

Colony of Virginia and most of the tribes within its boundaries, Virginia Indians faded from the limelight of political significance in the eyes of European – and, later, Euro-American – sovereigns. The 1677 treaty technically reduced Virginia Indians to the nebulous status of 'tributary Indians' (Robinson, 1959), which subsequently meant that they were neither militarily nor territorially powerful enough to draw the political interest of the American government following the Revolution. Concomitantly, Indians were not distinguished legally from other persons of colour in Virginia until 1866, when the General Assembly passed a law stating that 'Every person having one-fourth or more Negro blood shall be deemed a colored person, and every person having one-fourth or more Indian blood will be deemed an Indian' (Commonwealth of Virginia, 1866: 84–5). Unfortunately, prior and subsequent renderings of Virginia miscegenation law seemingly negated the 'Indian' portions of this statute, beginning with a 1705 colonial Virginia law which declared that the offspring of an Indian and any person of African ancestry 'should be deemed, accounted, held, and taken to be mulatto' (Henning, 1823: 252).

The rising tide of the eugenics movement in the late nineteenth century made it imminent that many prominent Virginians would launch a legal vendetta against the state's Indigenous peoples for their alleged (and often unsubstantiated) violation of miscegenation laws. Among those prominent citizens was Walter A. Plecker, the state's registrar and director of vital statistics from 1912 to 1946. An internationally known eugenicist, Plecker devised a policy of 'documentary genocide' (Smith, 1993) in which he identified all surnames listed as anything other than 'White' on vital records dating back to the Civil War, and issued a mandate among county clerks, medical doctors, and midwives stating that anyone bearing these surnames should thereafter be classified as 'colored.' Because many Indians had been forced to register as free people of colour prior to the Civil War, this left them with little recourse in asserting unique tribal identities in the eyes of the law. As this policy became codified under the 1924 Virginia Racial Integrity Act, Plecker became more determined to eradicate Indians from the record in Virginia. This policy, in turn, was subject to some rather creative and discriminatory interpretations where Indians were concerned, especially in the context of county political economies. Thus, Virginia Indians were systematically denied access to public schools into the 1960s. For most tribes, church-operated mission schools offering up to a sixth-grade education (on an irregular basis) provided the only option for formal schooling (Rountree, 1990: 219–424; Cook, 2000: 84–114). Even after public school integration in the early 1960s, Indians found it difficult to access meaningful education for years to come. For instance, in Amherst County, Indians were integrated into public schools in 1963 (although African Americans had been accepted earlier, and the county then proposed a bond issue to build a separate school for Indians), but the first Monacan did not graduate from public high school until 1971 (Cook, 2000: 114–16).

Although social, political, and economic conditions have improved significantly for Virginia Indians since the 1960s, the aforementioned policies of 'racial integrity' and their peculiar manifestations created a formidable obstacle to Indian education in the state, one that continues to pose problems. It is worth mentioning that until recently no Virginia institution of higher education had formally reached out to the state's Indigenous population since the College of William and Mary closed its Brafferton Indian School with the inception of the American Revolution (of course, the Brafferton fund originated in England, not Virginia). Some Virginia tribes, including the Pamunkey, Mattaponi, and Chickahominy, were able to send students to federally funded Indian schools in North Carolina (Cherokee), Kansas (Haskell), and Oklahoma (Bacone College) during the mid-twentieth century, largely through the advocacy of anthropologist Frank Speck (Rountree, 1990: 168–70). Hence, these tribes have seen a significant number of members attain degrees in higher education since the 1950s. Tribes such as the Monacan, however, have had a longer road to travel in adjusting to changing political economic conditions, and have just begun to see a few members matriculate through institutions of higher education on a regular basis. In either case, the state of Virginia did not make a solid commitment to Indians in the realm of education.

Birth of Virginia Tech's Program

There are currently eight state-recognized tribes in Virginia: the Chickahominy, Eastern Chickahominy, Mattaponi, Upper Mattaponi, Monacan, Nansemond, Pamunkey, and Rappahannock. None of these tribes is currently federally recognized, and only two – the Mattaponi and Pamunkey – have official reservations, established through colonial treaty. The total population of these tribes is approximately 4,500 (compared with a statewide population of about 45,000 American Indians and Alaskan Natives of all tribes), according to the latest census estimates.[1] Thus, compared to most states with institutions hosting salient AIS programs, our Indigenous constituency is small. Interestingly, the development of Virginia Tech's program has paralleled, and in some ways worked in concert with, important political movements from within Virginia's Indian community.

In the 1999 letter that spurred the development of Virginia Tech's program, the Monacan tribal council expressed two broad sets of interests that set the tone for future dialogue: (1) we would like to foster an affiliation [with Virginia Tech] in order to educate our young people, and other Indian students, in Native American Studies so that they would be well prepared for positions of tribal leadership, and would be educated in the issues facing Native people today; and (2) we believe that through such affiliation, we would be better able to develop tribal programs that would serve our members in the areas of tribal economic development, agriculture, land management, and social programs' (Monacan Indian Nation, 1999). The Monacans did not simply rehash the land grant mission, but insisted that such a program must be based on true collaboration and partnering with Indigenous communities.

Virginia Tech officials responded surprisingly fast to the letter, perhaps reacting in part to increased media coverage concerning public scrutiny of diversity at state universities in Virginia. Whatever the case, then-provost Peggy Maeszaros contacted key administrators and heads of departments with potential interests, or faculty with expertise in American Indian issues, to determine what resources were available for the development of such a program and which department or academic unit should house the program, if it were developed. The group had very little difficulty in determining that the program should be located in the Center for Interdisciplinary Studies (CIS, reorganized as the Department of Interdisciplinary Studies in 2003), a unit within the College of Arts and Sciences that serves as a home for several ethnic studies and humanistic interdisciplinary programs.

The next step was to determine the parameters of the prospective program. Accordingly, Dr Maeszaros convened a meeting of all administrators, deans, and faculty who might be potential affiliates with this program, and representatives from the Monacan Indian Nation, in the fall of 1999. Monacan Council Chief John L. Johns and then-tribal director of social and economic development (and co-author) Karenne Wood attended the meeting and elaborated on the earlier letter, explaining that any AIS program must deal holistically with Native issues, and must not only be concerned with educating the general public but also with bolstering the presence of Indians in the academy and with serving Indigenous communities in ways that would enhance tribal sovereignty. They summed up university tribal relations in one word: diplomacy. Significantly, Johns and Wood insisted that a legitimate AIS program must provide a conduit through which Indigenous knowledge would be seen as relevant. The administration was quite receptive to this proposal and encouraged the further development of the program, with one major caveat: the program must be developed *without* requiring additional resources.

On paper, we were to develop an academic minor under the auspices of the Humanities program at the Center for Interdisciplinary Studies. In practice, we knew we must develop a more holistic entity from the outset, one that operated in service to, and relied on input from, Indigenous people statewide (and ultimately nationwide). Then-associate dean of arts and sciences Myra Gordon oversaw the development of the program, relying on a core group of faculty from various departments who comprised an internal steering committee, and on sustained input from Monacan tribal representatives. During the first year, each faculty member developed proposals for curricula and the minor according to respective fields of expertise. These we then subjected to scrutiny from Monacan tribal council members, although we realized at the time (as discussed below) that future scrutiny would have to include rigorous input from representatives of all Virginia tribes. In the fall of 2000, proposals were refined and submitted through departmental and college review processes. At that point, Sam Cook (co-author) became the official coordinator for the program, thus assuming the first and only full-time position reserved exclusively for American Indian Studies.

Program Accomplishments

In the fall of 2002, the minor program became official. Course offerings have included: Introduction to American Indian Studies, Oral Tradition, American Indian Literatures, American Indian Languages, American Indian Spirituality, Indigenous Peoples and World Politics, and a variety of courses under the Special Topics designator, including American Indian Cultures and Societies, American Indian Law and Policy, American Indians in Film, American Indian Arts, and Native Peoples of the Southeast. While the courses and requirements may seem peculiar compared to those of other AIS programs, it is important to realize that we had to develop this minor with no additional resources. Thus, we had to streamline the proposal by limiting the number of new courses, restructuring existing courses (as in the case of the oral tradition course), and including more specialized courses under the heading 'Special Topics.' These courses have been and will continue to be developed through increasing collaboration with Virginia's Indigenous peoples, and eventually with other tribes in the region. This collaborative spirit, in fact, has been at the heart of all other initiatives. However, these developments have not come without major obstacles and challenges from various directions, nor without great sacrifices on the part of Virginia Tech faculty and tribal representatives.

Challenges

Not surprisingly, our greatest challenge in developing Virginia Tech's AIS program has been financial. The administrative mandate to develop the program without drawing on additional resources remains in place. The only permanent funding for the program is the director's salary, which means that Sam Cook has spent many hours soliciting funds from internal and external sources in order to support our public and outreach programs. Likewise, there is only one tenure-track faculty line and a more recent – albeit tenuous – full-time instructorship. For the first four years of the program's development, affiliated faculty – particularly Jeff Corntassel (Political Science) and Harry Dyer (English) – devoted a disproportionate amount of time towards seeing the program become a reality. Fortunately, Harry Dyer was transferred full time to American Indian Studies, although his instructorship remains non-tenured. This situation has been complicated by a prolonged financial crisis in the state of Virginia that impacted Virginia Tech in profound ways. The possible advantage that the American Indian Studies program has had – one that differentiates our program from any other on campus – is that our Indigenous constituency is quite willing and able to mount formidable political pressure on the university. This was made clear during our most recent budget-related crisis, when Harry Dyer's position was targeted for possible elimination in response to an impending 5 per cent budget cut statewide. The potential termination of the only American Indian faculty member employed in Virginia Tech's American Indian Studies program was met with a swift bombardment of letters from our Indigenous constituency and supporters across North America. For the moment, Dyer's position has been secured, but we have taken this event as yet another reminder that complacency is never an option when trying to sustain the rights of Indigenous peoples within and without the academy.

A similar problem is the fact that those faculty most directly involved in the development of our program find themselves serving as the de facto agents for outreach and recruitment in Indigenous communities and as the providers of services for Indigenous students. As M. Annette Jaimes (1987: 3–4) has argued, this can potentially cause faculty to compromise scholarly activity. Indeed, most participating faculty were aspiring towards tenure during the first years of the program and were expected to fulfil a base research requirement. It is safe to say that they put in more time on the university clock than many other colleagues who were junior faculty, simply because of the integrated, holistic nature of the program. Faculty members dealt with this in creative ways – namely, understanding that work on this program might be incorporated into a research agenda. Faculty members have also been concerned with the mission of nation-building, and for scholars such as Jeff Corntassel, work with Virginia's Indian nations on this and other programs opened a new dimension of scholarly activity and collaborative research (see e.g., Corntassel and Cook, 2002).

Finally, in spite of the initial enthusiasm that seemed to brim from Virginia Tech's administration when the Monacans sent their query, we have experienced certain political obstacles to the development of the program, some of which reflect state and local controversies that are not devoid of racial overtones. First, certain officials in the administration have expressed concerns that our program is developing in conjunction (rather than simultaneously) with a current campaign among six of Virginia's Indian nations for federal recognition through joint legislation. The initial concern reflected opposition from several state lawmakers and religious and social organizations that such recognition would open the doors to casino-style gaming in the state (see e.g., Hardin, 2000). While many AIS faculty members endorsed the federal recognition project, these concerns from within the university seem to have subsided with the current bill, which has a specific provision prohibiting tribes from engaging in gaming activities without state approval (an unnecessary reiteration of the 1988 Indian Gaming Regulatory Act that the six tribes were willing to live with in order to bolster political support).

Nonetheless, we continue to contend with bureaucratic implications that our program and curricula are over-politicized. For instance, the

minor proposal and most of the courses would probably have matricu-
lated much faster through the various layers of curriculum committees
had certain individuals on the Arts and Sciences Committee not suggested that our program was too closely aligned with local politics –
specifically, with a movement to change the Blacksburg High School
Indian mascot to something non-offensive to Natives. Indeed, many
faculty members did speak in favour of a mascot change (including
Virginia Tech's vice-president for multicultural affairs), but our immediate response to this scrutiny of our professional integrity was to
point out the contradiction in the anonymous critic's implication –
namely, that such a claim implied a disturbing possibility that the college curriculum committee had itself become a caucus for local
(partisan) political interests. Fortunately, the chair of the committee and
Dean Myra Gordon tactfully reminded the committee of the proper
parameters of its duties.

Our greatest loss came in December of 2002, when Jeff Corntassel accepted a position as co-director of the graduate program in tribal governance at the University of Victoria. We fully supported his decision
because his research and activism became globally oriented, and that
was the place where Dr Corntassel is going to make the greatest impact
in the field of American Indian Studies. His loss, however, was one we
still feel in terms of his commitment to the program.

Developing a Collaborative Model

The title of Duane Champagne's article, 'American Indian Studies is for
Everyone' (1998), bears volumes of wisdom for those who understand
the nature of our field. American Indian Studies programs do not exist in
a vacuum, nor should they. Such programs are necessarily about cross-
cultural interactions as much as they are about inter-and intra-cultural
affairs. However, whether students, faculty, or other university representatives are American Indians or not, there is always a responsibility to
the institution's prospective Indigenous constituency, which, if un-
fulfilled, nullifies any legitimate claim to holism that an institution might
make. At Virginia Tech, we have tried to meet such obligations by keeping the state's Indigenous peoples involved in our program at every step
of development. Our approach builds on certain existing collaborative
models emphasizing research methods (see, generally, Mihesuah, 1998;
Lassiter, 2000, 2005) as we seek to transform not only scholarly approaches within the field, but the very academy of which we are a part.

The philosophy behind such a model is at the very essence of the initial mandate for our program as outlined in the letter from the Monacan Tribal Council. However, we realized early on that we had to get all of the tribes in Virginia involved as partners and colleagues in the program, and, eventually, to move out in concentric circles and involve other tribes in the same manner.

Thus, in the spring of 2001 Virginia Tech hosted the first Virginia Indian Nations Summit on Higher Education (VINSHE). The purpose of this gathering was to break the ice – to dissolve barriers between our institution and the state's Indian nations, many of whom were openly suspicious of any state institution in light of Virginia's previously mentioned track record of dealing with Indigenous peoples. The AIS program invited representatives from each of the eight tribes to come to our campus at our expense and to engage in two days of informal and open dialogue. Although many tribal representatives were initially reserved, they were not afraid to express their concerns and to adopt a 'wait and see' approach.

The end result was overwhelmingly positive. We opened the summit with a powerful keynote from then-chair of American Indian Studies programs at the University of Arizona, Jay Stauss, who appealed to both tribal representatives and university administrators in his assessment of the obligation of land grant universities to Indigenous peoples. Dr Stauss's explicit emphasis on the obligation of Indian Studies programs (and the institutions that house them) to prioritize tribal nation-building offered an important diplomatic catalyst that prompted many tribal representatives to feel confident in venting their concerns thereafter. In fact, an important component of the summit, one that became an ongoing part of this annual gathering for several years, was a public forum called 'What It Means to be a Virginia Indian in the 21st Century.' During this session, tribal representatives were invited to speak from the heart about their lives, cultures, and histories, and to convey to the general public what they thought was truly important to know about Virginia Indians and Indigenous people in general. This forum gradually evolved into a frank conversation between tribal representatives and audience members, and constituted a remarkable interactive platform in which the Indigenous speakers were able to convey their realities on their own terms while engaging the audience in a fluid and non-threatening manner.

The first VINSHE yielded two other important and very positive results. First, we established a standing tribal advisory board consisting of representatives from all of the tribes in the state, as well as a few 'at-large' members from other tribes. Members of the advisory board serve as liaisons between their respective nations and Virginia Tech while exercising a certain degree of oversight in monitoring activities directed by the American Indian Studies program. Champagne (2002) and others have commented on the difficulty in sustaining such community advisory groups, especially where institutional, financial, or infrastructural support is lacking, while the demand for research and publication does not lessen for the sake of community interests. To be sure, it has not been easy to 'sponsor' this group and the joint initiatives that we have pursued with our advisors, especially since most of our funding has come from external grants or from hard-sought, internal 'soft monies.' Yet all of the tribal advisors have devoted a tremendous amount of their time, energy, and money to our program. They see the development of this program as complementary to, and part of, their larger political agenda. The pressure these advisors have exerted – as a group and as individuals – on university officials has constituted a crucial element in sustaining the program thus far. Indeed, without their support the program would be nothing more than a struggling academic minor at best.

A second important initiative stemming from the first VINSHE is the Virginia Indian Pre-College Initiative (VIPCI). At that first summit, tribal representatives expressed a qualified enthusiasm for seeing more of their youth enter higher education. The main concern was that while higher education may empower individuals, as with Western education in general, it had historically been a primary means of destroying Indigenous communities. The representatives at the summit insisted that if Virginia Tech and other state institutions work with tribal communities in promoting higher education, they should do so in a manner that recognized the importance and legitimacy of Indigenous knowledge. By the same token, representatives were concerned that while some of their students needed long-term guidance in preparing for college, all should be encouraged to make the most of whatever education they receive, regardless of whether they attend college or not. Thus, the VIPCI emerged as a two-tiered mentoring program in which Virginia Indian youth in grades eight through twelve are invited to our campus two weekends each year, along with parents and elders, to take part in specific programs that exhibit the possibilities afforded through education. Such programs have included tours of our university's state-of-the-art virtual reality facility, natural resource management hikes at a remote wildlife preserve maintained by Virginia Tech, and an

Indigenous art exhibition. The presence of elders is crucial to this program, because their presence conveys a message to the youth – namely, that the university values their knowledge and input. Indeed, these elders have been both enthusiastic participants and substantive critics of our program.

At least eight Virginia Indian students who have taken part in the VIPCI since its inception have entered (or will be entering) Virginia Tech, a rather impressive ratio given the small number of Virginia Indians and the historical odds they have faced in pursuing higher education. While some might argue that the VIPCI is an outreach program that belongs in a non-academic unit, we regard it as an integral part of the American Indian Studies mission, regardless of whether participants are involved in the minor program or not.

The academic minor received full and final approval at a time when the top university curriculum committees at Virginia Tech were tabling or refusing to approve many new courses and minors in light of budget and personnel reductions. Nevertheless, and other obligations notwithstanding, the tribal advisors along with several of the chiefs from Virginia's Indian nations have attended subsequent VINSHE meetings with full force and vigour, and they have openly expressed their praise and concerns during special sessions with university administrators.

Our latest initiative, one that was conceptualized during the second VINSHE, is referred to as 'Virginia Indian Nations 101' (VIN 101). This is a multifaceted project intended to provide various media through which Virginia Indians can educate both the general public and educators on Virginia Indian cultures, histories, and realities. As a result, the tribal advisory board has for the past three years held a series of summer symposia for schoolteachers in which Virginia Indians and other Indigenous representatives serve as the primary instructors, in collaboration with scholars who have worked closely with these tribes for years. We are now developing an on-line course based on these symposia that will be taught by Virginia Indians.

Currently, a smaller committee, including some VINSHE members, is working with the tribal leaders and the Virginia Department of Education to revise the state Standards of Learning for Social Studies, which public school educators are mandated to follow in teaching about Virginia and other American Indians. Another immediate goal is to develop a set of resource materials for schoolteachers at various levels, with sections for each tribe in the state containing information prepared in collaboration with (or by) members of each tribe.

Our annual VINSHE meetings have matured in several important ways. Four years ago, faculty and staff from the University of Virginia joined our meetings, and UVA began hosting annual Tribal Leaders' Summits as well as hosting VINSHE meetings in alternate years. Accordingly, we aligned the VINSHE meeting with the Virginia Festival of the Book in Charlottesville so that our advisors could attend panel discussions about the mythology surrounding Pocahontas, Jamestown, and other historical distortions concerning Virginia's Indigenous peoples and American national development.

As of this writing, the alliance between Virginia's Indian nations and the state's two most prominent academic institutions was reaffirmed as the summit once again convened at the University of Virginia. In 2008 the College of William and Mary provisionally joined the VINSHE alliance. The inclusion of this institution represents a cyclical transformation, since William and Mary was the first state institution to reach out to Indigenous peoples – albeit for the purposes of assimilation. Now the tide has turned to embrace Indigenous knowledge.

Conclusion

The year 2007 saw the first-ever Monacan student graduate from Virginia Tech, completing the circle we began in 2000. If we have done one thing right in developing our program, it has been to maintain an open line of communication with our Indigenous constituency and the students they send us, thereby fostering a true collaborative enterprise.

We honour the tribal advisors and their respective communities by acknowledging them as colleagues and not mere subjects of academic fascination. In return, they gift us with knowledge and values they have retained throughout their history, despite obstacles we cannot now imagine. This kind of knowledge is priceless. Through it we have learned to work together, to develop our relationships with one another and our larger communities, and to respect and trust one another as colleagues and friends.

REFERENCES

Albers, Patricia C., Brenda J. Child, Vicki Howard, Dennis Jones, Carol Miller, Frank C. Miller, and Jean M. O'Brien. 2002. 'A Story of Struggle and Survival: American Indian Studies at the University of Minnesota – Twin Cities.'

In *Native American Studies and Higher Education: Models for Collaboration between Universities and Indigenous Nations,* 145–64. Duane Champagne and Jay Stauss. Eds. Walnut Creek, CA: AltaMira Press.

Champagne, Duane. 1998. 'American Indian Studies is for Everyone.' In *Natives and Academics: Researching and Writing about American Indians,*181–9. Ed. Devon Mihesuah. Lincoln: University of Nebraska Press.

– 2002. 'American Indian Studies at the University of California Los Angeles.' In *Native American Studies in Higher Education: Models for Collaboration between Universities and Indigenous Nations,* 43–60. Duane Champagne and Jay Stauss. Eds. Walnut Creek, CA: AltaMira Press.

Champagne, Duane, and Jay Stauss. Eds. 2002. 'Native American Studies and Higher Education: Models for Collaboration between Universities and Indigenous Nations.' Walnut Creek, CA: AltaMira Press.

– 2002. 'Introduction: Defining Indian Studies through Stories and Nation Building.' In *Native American Studies and Higher Education: Models for Collaboration between Universities and Indigenous Nations,* 1–16. Duane Champagne and Jay Stauss. Eds. Walnut Creek, CA: AltaMira Press.

Commonwealth of Virginia. 1866. *Acts of Assembly, 1865–1866.* Richmond, VA: Commonwealth of Virginia Division of Resources and Supply.

Cook, Samuel R. 2000. *Monacans and Miners: Native American and Coal Mining Communities in Appalachia.* Lincoln: University of Nebraska Press.

Corntassel, Jeff J., and Samuel R. Cook. 2002. 'Federal Recognition Strengthens Native Communities – It Is Not a License to Gamble.' *Native American Policy Network Newsletter,* 17 (3): 2–4.

Hardin, Peter. 2000. 'Group Opposes Sovereignty for Tribes: Elks, Petroleum Markets Cite Potential Economic Effect.' *Richmond Times-Dispatch* (5 November), B1–B2.

Henning, William Walter. Ed. 1823. *Statutes at Large: Being a Collection of All the Laws of Virginia.* Philadelphia: DeSilver.

Jaimes, M. Annette. 1987. 'American Indian Studies: Toward an Indigenous Model.' *American Indian Culture and Research Journal,* 11 (3): 1–19.

Kinnear, Duncan. 1972. *The First 100 Years: A History of Virginia Polytechnic Institute and State University.* Blacksburg, VA: Virginia Polytechnic Institute Educational Foundation.

Lassiter, Luke E. 2000. 'Authoritative Texts, Collaborative Ethnography, and Native American Studies.' *American Indian Quarterly.* 24 (4): 601–11.

– 2005. *The Chicago Guide to Collaborative Ethnography.* Chicago: University of Chicago Press.

Mihesuah, Devon. Ed. 1998. *Natives and Academics: Research and Writing about American Indians.* Lincoln: University of Nebraska Press.

Monacan Indian Nation. 1999. Letter to Dr Paul Torgersen, president, Virginia Polytechnic Institute. 26 June.

Robinson, W. Stitt. 1959. 'Tributary Indians in Colonial Virginia.' *Virginia Magazine of History and Biography*, 67: 49–64.

Rountree, Helen C. 1990. *Pocahontas's People: the Powhatan Indians of Virginia through Four Centuries*. Norman: University of Oklahoma Press.

Smith, J. David. 1993. *The Eugenic Assault on America: Scenes in Red, White, and Black*. Fairfax, VA: George Mason University Press.

Stauss, Jay, Mary Jo Tippeconic Fox, and Shelley Lowe. 2002. 'American Indian Studies at the University of Arizona.' In *Native American Studies and Higher Education: Models for Collaboration between Universities and Indigenous Nations*, 3–96. Duane Champagne and Jay Stauss. Eds. Walnut Creek, CA: Altamira Press.

U.S. Bureau of the Census. 2007. 'Profile of General Demographic Characteristics.' Accessed 3 August 2007 from http://www.census.gov/prod/2006pubs/censr-28.pdf.

Virginia Tech American Indian Studies Steering Committee. 2000. 'A Proposal to Establish a Minor in American Indian Studies at Virginia Tech.' 6 June.

PART 3

Linking Theory and Practice

Theory can be a potent source of analysis for practice, and practice can be a wellspring for theoretical formulation. The authors in this section, all academic-based researchers from different disciplinary bases, ground their work in existing and emerging scholarship. Their gaze is firmly fixed on ways in which theory can be useful for practice, and, at the same time, how practice can make theory relevant for re/envisioning relationships. Examples both in Canada and internationally are the focal point for discussing the possibilities and limitations for partnership in specific political contexts.

Thierry Drapeau examines the Secwepemc Watershed Committee's struggle with the Sun Peaks Resort in their homelands near Kamloops, British Columbia. He introduces the concept of 'glocality,' which describes a political space created at the intersection of global and local forces, a space which is both circumscribed by its naming, protected through government and industry alliances, and incorporated into the global market economy. Such a space can be described not only by the repressive forces it embodies, but also by the new opportunities created for local/global alliances of resistance.

Lily Pol-Neveu critically examines normative theories of recognition, and suggests that their pitfalls might be overcome by turning to insights gleaned from practice; here, she shares her experiences as an interpreter at Fort-Témiscamingue/Obadjiwan, a national park co-managed by Parks Canada and Timiskaming First Nation. Beneesh Jafri documents both possibilities and tensions in developing alliances between Indigenous peoples and 'people of colour' through anti-racist work, and offers the case study of the National Secretariat Against Hate and Racism in Canada. Caitlyn Vernon analyses the conditions needed to achieve both social justice and ecological sustainability on the British Columbia West Coast, and takes a critical look at the BC government's 'New Relationships' approach to relations with First Nations. Writing from the context of Guyana, Tanya Chung Tiam Fook examines the complex epistemological, cultural, and political dimensions in conservation partnerships with Indigenous peoples, and offers the example of the Iwokrama program to illustrate how the Makushi of North Rupununi have been engaging in a collaborative community-led partnership based on traditional and modern knowledge frameworks.

Adam Barker challenges individuals of Settler society to 'unsettle' themselves, to undertake a journey of deep self-examination, to decolonize one's own mind and behaviours, and to find ways of taking action to support the self-determination of Indigenous peoples. Lynne Davis and Heather Shpuniarsky share the 'lessons learned' from case studies in the Alliances research project, including the Coalition for a Public Inquiry into Ipperwash and relationships between First Nations and environmentalists on the West Coast.

By the end of this section, the reader will have had a rich encounter with some of the diverse, interdisciplinary frameworks that are informing the theorization of Indigenous/non-Indigenous relationships at this moment in history. However, these chapters are not about theory alone. All of these authors test theoretical insights in the cauldron of concrete experiences. Linking theory and practice provides the ground for penetrating critiques and new pathways towards re/envisioning relationships.

14 A Glocality in the Making: Learning from the Experience of Resistance of the Secwepemc Watershed Committee against Sun Peaks Resort, British Columbia

THIERRY DRAPEAU

Introduction

For the past 20 years or so, there has been a massive increase in the activities of Indigenous minorities in the world.[1] Born in the margins of established society and struggling for control over their conditions of existence, the rise of this 'global Indigenous movement' has been capable of presenting important challenges to the capitalist world-system (Edelman, 1998; Yashar, 1998; Friedman, 1999; Harris, 2002; Hall and Fenelon, 2004). One of the most challenging tensions seems to be the reassertion of control over the territories they have historically occupied (Zibechi, 2005). Indeed, from places which up to now have been the locations most favourable to the neoliberal model, Indigenous struggles have been creating new sites of resistance and political organization which set themselves up as de facto autonomous regions or places, whether explicitly or not. By doing so, the old concept of 'habitat' takes a new radical meaning: it becomes a critical site where Indigenous people create new political subjects who shape the geographic space, appropriate it, and endow it with their meanings and practices, their senses and sensibilities. To borrow from Henri Lefebvre (2000), what Indigenous people bring with their exigencies of struggle is a conception of space based on *use* value rather than *exchange* value. This global panorama of Indigenous resistance is not only located at the periphery of the world economy. It also occurs in countries at the centre.

In effect, since the summer of 2000 in the Secwepemc territories, located in the Interior plateau of British Columbia, many Elders, traditional land users, and youth of the Neskonlith and Adams Lake Bands of the Secwepemc Nation have been maintaining protests against the expansion of Sun Peaks Resort (SPR), an international resort owned by Nippon Cable, a Tokyo-based multinational corporation. Rather than carrying their struggles through their respective band councils, the official political bodies installed by the federal government from the late 1800s to contain Aboriginal politics, these Secwepemc peoples founded a grassroots organization called the Secwepemc Watershed Committee (SWC), which immediately called for action against this ongoing urbanization of their land. Helped by other Aboriginal and non-Aboriginal organizations,[2] this grassroots committee has sought to build a local occupation movement to protect their land by erecting many Skwelkwek'welt Protection Centres (SPCs) next to Sun Peaks Resort. From these centres, the SWC started out as a powerful movement of occupation in order to stop the urban expansion and to secure their traditional activities, such as hunting, fishing, collection of medicines, and traditional spiritual practices in which many Secwepemc people still engage and upon which they depend. In addition, the Committee launched an international boycott of the resort, which has brought them to experience transnationalism, that is to say, a social experience of struggle and solidarity in the world economy.

Thus, drawing on my three months of fieldwork research at the Neskonlith reserve in the summer of 2006, what follows is the story of this Secwepemc resistance filtered through my own understanding.[3] First, I will describe the history of the resistance and its outcomes. Next, I will try to illustrate that through the dialectics of power and counter-power between the Secwepemc Watershed Committee and Sun Peaks Resort, there is a new significant place in the making in our contemporary world, a place that needs to be theoretically acknowledged. Borrowing from other analyses that have already given a name to this process of place-making, I will call this place a *glocality,* and try to think about its particularities as a contingent site of struggle in the world economy. Finally, I will elicit some elements regarding what could be learned theoretically and tactically from this experience of resistance.

The Secwepemc Resistance against Sun Peaks Resort

The Secwepemc Nation is located in the Interior plateau of British Columbia, their homeland traversed by the Fraser and Thompson Rivers. In this Aboriginal territory, each consisting of a number of bands, there are seven Secwepemc divisions: Shuswap Lake, Kamloops, Bonaparte, Canyon, Fraser River, Lake, and North Thompson. Like anywhere else where colonial settlements have been established, the Secwepemc people have been forced into a history of political resistance that began with the British colonization and continued throughout the twentieth century. In 1992, about 200 years after European explorers – Alexander MacKenzie, Simon Fraser, and David Thompson, to name the most prestigious – first came to spread the fur trade westward across the North American continent; and, to incorporate the region into the world system of capitalist accumulation (Wolf, 1982; Hudson and Ignace, 1995; Thomson and Ignace, 2005), the Secwepemc territories have once more been drawn into global capitalism's orbit.

Facilitated by an internationally oriented provincial tourist incentive law (the Mountain Resort Association Act), this encounter with transnational capital, a Tokyo-based multinational corporation named Nippon Cable, specializing in ski lift development and ski resort management in Japan, came to one of the last unspoiled and sacred places in the territories of the Secwepemc people, a traditional land historically called 'Skwelkwek'welt' (high alpine mountain). Skwelkwek'welt encompasses three big mountains known as Tod Mountain, Mount Cahility, and Mount Morrisey. It also includes McGillivray Lake, Eilenn Lake, Morrisey Lake, Cahility Lake, and watershed systems. The area is a valuable provider for the Secwepemc people in terms of medicinal plants, foods, and spirituality.

On this traditional land, located 40 kilometres northeast of Kamloops, Nippon Cable purchased Tod Mountain, a modest ski station, from the previous owners and contracted a 50-year lease from the British Columbia Assets and Lands Corporation (BCALC) on 4,139 hectares of Crown Land.[4] Along with its global (Delta Hotels, ReMax, Ecosign), national (Canadian Commission on Tourism, SkiCan), and local partners (Kamloops Chamber of Commerce, BCALC), Nippon Cable renamed the place Sun Peaks Resort. To help achieve social consensus between Nippon Cable and the Secwepemc Band Councils, the provincial government initiated a series of formal and informal meetings in which they served as a mediator between the two parties. As a result, in 1997, a Protocol Agreement was signed by the six Secwepemc Band Councils[5] and two economic partnerships were reached (with the Little Shuswap and the Whispering Pines Bands).[6] According to Janice Billy, former spokesperson of the Secwepemc Watershed Committee:

[The Protocol Agreement] was made by a few chiefs and the people didn't know what they were signing. After we saw it we didn't agree with it, because we didn't even give consent to the development let alone sign any kind of protocol agreements with them (Sun Peaks Resort). When we (the few Secwepemcs of the Neskonlith Band) were first really actively involved up there, one of the bands, the Adams Lake Band, pulled out of the Protocol Agreement and said that they didn't want to be part of it ... So, I guess it was null and void, and there has never been a meeting ever since about that protocol.[7]

Hence, because this agreement was made in a quasi-private manner between Nippon Cable and the band councils, the Secwepemc people were never meaningfully consulted. Accordingly, as soon as the project's destructive effects on the environment became apparent, tension began to grow between the Secwepemc Band Councils and their communities – mostly from the Neskonlith and Adams Lake Reserves, the closest to Sun Peaks.

In 1997, disagreeing both with their chiefs and the project, the Secwepemcs of the Neskonlith and Adams Lake Bands began their diplomatic actions against Sun Peaks by setting up the Secwepemc Watershed Committee (SWC) in order to do legal research on their historical titles. This coincided with the *Delgamuukw* decision made by the Supreme Court of Canada that same year (*Delgamuukw v. British Columbia*, 1997). This decision stated that 'Aboriginal title is a property right to exclusive use and occupation of land, and that it is protected under s. 35 (1) of the Constitution Act, 1982' (Dacks, 2002:240). In the beginning, then, the Secwepemc resistance was played out mainly in the legal and diplomatic arenas, taking their case to court and presenting their claims to the land directly to the Nippon Cable owner, Masayoshi Ohkubo, informing him that they wanted all development stopped until there was a resolution to the outstanding land issue. The land issue was – and still is – their core grievance.[8]

In September 2000, despite three years of diplomatic negotiations, the Japanese corporation launched concretely its Master Plan for a $70 million expansion at Skwelkwek'welt. This plan was one of clear-cutting three more mountains-worth of ski runs, developing the drainage basin for commercial and residential real estate, expanding a nine-hole golf course into an 18-hole golf course, and constructing a Delta Hotel with an international reach. The full implementation also calls for a massive construction project on Tod Mountain, one of upgrading the lift and trail systems to a level consistent with current international mountain planning and development standards, and one of upgrading and expanding the existing base areas to provide a resort centre complete with accommodation, restaurants, retail space, and other visitor amenities. This set in motion a series of more militant actions by the SWC. One month later, direct actions began at Sun Peaks Resort.[9]

In October 2000, the SWC launched a movement of occupation and re-appropriation of the land by erecting the Skwelkwek'welt Protection Center (SPC) at the entrance of the resort, in which members of the Secwepemc community lived permanently. By establishing this SPC, the Secwepemc peoples were not only claiming Aboriginal title and rights to the land. They were also reanimating a 'politics of place' that has characterized other anti–ski resort struggles in British Columbia, specifically in Penticton in the early 1990s and in Lillooet in early 2000. The purpose of the SPC was to monitor development at Sun Peaks Resort, to inform the public and tourists of their opposition to the expansion project, and, more importantly, to re-establish themselves on their lands in order to protect them.

Direct actions continued throughout 2001 and 2002, with many demonstrations being held at the resort and at other locations on and beyond Skwelkwek'welt. In May 2001, a protest was held in front of the BCALC in Kamloops. In June, they began their occupation at McGillivray Lake, but as Sun Peaks did before when they were not able to prove 100 per cent jurisdiction over the land, they again applied for a lease, which they got. A couple of days later, a cordwood house built for a Secwepemc family at McGillivray Lake was torn down by the Sun Peaks employees and the Royal Canadian Mounted Police (RCMP). In early August, directed by their Elders, the family built a traditional winter home on Mount Morrissey. This winter home has been used as a cultural, spiritual, and healing centre where the Secwepemc people gather to learn cultural and spiritual teachings from the Elders, as well as other cultural skills such as hunting. However, when they returned to this winter home at the beginning of winter, they found the road to Mount Morrissey totally demolished by Sun Peaks officials, with the approval of the BC Ministry of Forests. In response, members of the newly formed Secwepemc Chapter of the Native Youth Movement (SCNYM) and other supporters blocked the main road into Sun Peaks and were criminally charged.

It was from these local actions of resistance that the SWC launched an international boycott of Sun Peaks Resort and Delta Hotels in 2000. Among Aboriginal people, this boycott received support from the Assembly of First Nations, the Interior Alliance, the Shuswap Nation

Tribal Council, the Union of British Columbia Indian Chiefs, the League of Indigenous Sovereign Nations of the Western Hemisphere, the Indigenous Sovereignty Network, and many regional Aboriginal activist groups, such as Grassy Narrows. At the national level, they had support from Toronto Native Youth, which has held many information pickets at the Delta Hotel in downtown Toronto, and from the Ontario Coalition Against Poverty, which occupied the Toronto office of the SkiCan Corporation, a company that has a near monopoly on ski vacation bookings in Canada.

A crucial step was reached when the boycott was carried out from Skwelkwek'welt with the help of the Interior Alliance's political structures. Through this channel, the Secwepemc resistance was placed at the forefront of the Alliance's International Forest/Tourism Campaign against mass tourist development and logging in the BC Interior. They conjointly targeted the two major companies that had commercial interests in the region: Interfor, which held most of the provincial logging permits, and Nippon Cable.

In December 2001, echoing the blockade of the Mount Morrissey road by Sun Peaks officials, militants of the Munich-Based *Aktionsgruppe Indianer und Menschenrechte* (Action group for Native Americans and Human Rights) organized a picket line at the Canadian Consulate in Munich as they symbolically heaped up snow in front of the main entrance and put a Christmas Tree on top, decorated with complaints about violations of Secwepemc rights. Two months later, in February 2002, they disturbed the arrival of Team Canada's trade mission, led by then-prime minister Jean Chrétien, at the Munich city hall. This protest was to inform the Canadian government about human rights violations at Skwelkwek'welt and to make German tourists aware of the international boycott against Sun Peaks and Delta Hotels.

In early October 2003, the campaign reached and had support from the Oakland, CA-based transnational institution DataCenter. For SWC, this social justice institution provided technological infrastructure and consultation services to help them settle their camp and identify what type of research on Nippon Cable and the Canadian government would advance their campaign's goals. From the perspective of global social movements, DataCenter clearly shows how a transnational organization established itself locally as a link – a global hub – with a place-based struggle in the world economy.

Through the actions of the Interior Alliance, the DataCenter, and the Aktionsgruppe in Munich, the issues of the SWC's international campaign were modified and radicalized. What had started as a local

struggle against commodification of the land and for Aboriginal land titles became an international struggle for human rights, and the protection of the Aboriginal way of life against mass tourist development and
forest exploitation in the Secwepemc's homelands. This is not to say that
the SWC's local issues of struggle ceased to be relevant politically. Rather,
they were re-articulated within the broader narrative of human rights. It
was because of this very cosmopolitan issue that nearly 200 people came
to Skwelkwek'welt to participate in the protest of Sun Peaks' expansion
at the 'Sun Peaks Convergence' on 28–29 August 2004.

Hosted by the SPC, the event was significant because it was the biggest demonstration staged by this resistance, gathering people from
BC's Lower Mainland, from the West Coast of the United States, and
from as far east in Canada as Montreal. There were activists from the
Anti-Poverty Committee, the Council of Canadians, No One Is Illegal,
the Veteran Troublemaker, and the Canadian Auto Workers, Local 111.
Less spectacular but still very significant, it was because of the human
rights issue that the journalist and activist Naomi Klein and the chair-
person of the Austrian Chapter of the Society for Threatened Peoples
(ACSTP), Peter Schwarzbauer, visited the SPC in 2004 as well.

However, despite the international campaigning, the many supporters,
and the direct actions taken at Skwelkwek'welt, the Secwepemc resistance
is today still extremely weakened by many court injunctions, police repres-
sions, and racist intimidations from the Sun Peaks inhabitants.

To date, there have been seven SPCs, two traditional cedar bark homes,
a hunting cabin, two sacred sweat lodges, and one cordwood home of a
Secwepemc family that have been bulldozed or torn down by Sun Peaks
and the RCMP. There have been 54 arrests, with charges ranging from
criminal contempt and intimidation by blocking roads to resisting arrest.
Over a dozen Secwepemc Elders, traditional land users, and activists are
still prohibited by courts from going within a two-to-10-kilometre radius
of the Sun Peaks Resort. At the moment of writing, their last political
stand-off was in 2005, when the SCNYM held a short demonstration in
Sun Peaks Village. This was a response to the announcement of a
$285 million real estate investment in Phase II of the Master Plan. Phase
II seeks eventually to develop 10,352 bed units over the next 10 years.

Yet, by 2006, besides 5,858 bed units distributed among 11 hotels and
hostels, Sun Peaks Village had 1,300 private properties (estimated between $249,000 and $255,000) in 22 neighbourhoods, for a seasonal
population of 500 residents (Sun Peaks Municipal Incorporation Study,
2007). With those numbers, Sun Peaks Resort is now the second largest
ski resort in British Columbia, following Whistler Blackcomb (near

Vancouver), and is one of the most internationally visited, all-season resorts in North America.

Theoretically, what the Secwepemcs' encounters with Sun Peaks Resort and the Canadian government show us is how a glocality emerges not only as the site for control and domination of global capital, but also as the site where new political possibilities for everyday transnational resistance might occur.

I will now illustrate that, through the dynamic crossroads of local, national, and transnational everyday relations of power and counter-power born out of Skwelkwek'welt, the world economy is becoming a concrete place of social practice.

The Making of a Glocality

Rather than focusing either on the local or the global, I will try to look at the Secwepemc resistance through a perspective that seeks to articulate the dialectical relation between the two scales. In order to get a wider perspective on this dynamic of power and counter-power, I start my analysis from the world economy itself, which is considered here to be 'a new, relatively indeterminate and permeable field of political practice' (Drainville, 2004:9). Arguably, the world economy is now becoming a concrete space for social forces to meet; it is, to borrow Doreen Massey's phrase on space of politics, 'a *place as meeting place*' (1993: 235, emphasis added). This spatial assumption is linked to an historical argument that I will now present.

Like many anthropologists (Kearney, 2004; Gupta and Ferguson, 1997), sociologists (Beck, 2000; Castells, 1996), and political scientists (Held, 1995; Guehenno, 1995; Ohmae, 1996) have argued since the collapse of the Bretton Woods system,[10] the nation state has lost the structuring power needed to keep social relations grounded on the national level. In fact, during the post-war period, but significantly after the crisis of Fordist regulation in the 1970s and the subsequent rise of neoliberalism, global forms of policies (monetarism, structural adjustments, global governance), along with the making of a transnational capitalist class, saw the light of day and became increasingly more central than the state in regulating socio-economic and political practices in national social formation. This global effort throughout the world economy to discipline localities and people in the realm of neoliberal globalization has parachuted social forces onto this new global terrain and redefined historical relationships between people and territories.

Consequently, the rescaling of social and political practice towards the world economy has had a considerable impact on social movements in that the interstate relations have ceased to be their only conditioning framework, thereby opening up room to manoeuvre for new transnational movements.[11] The Secwepemc resistance must be situated, then, in the light of this new global conjuncture.

In order to understand this new dynamic through the Secwepemc resistance, my analysis begins with a situated and contingent concept of place-making, a concept that gives analytical coherence to the process of spatial restructuring of order and counter-order in the world economy. Presenting both material and metaphorical aspects of this dialectical structuring process of place-making, I suggest that *glocality* is such a concept. Although it has been used elsewhere to grasp places perhaps more perfectly circumscribed than Sun Peaks Resort – places such as global neighbourhoods (Deckha, 2003), export zone factories (Armbruster-Sandoval, 2005), or cybernetic spaces (Meyrowitz, 2004; Gunkel and Gunkel, 1997) – the concept of glocality is nevertheless accurate to materially seize the process of place-making engaged through the dialectics of power and counter-power on the 4,139 hectares of Sun Peaks Resort.

According to Arturo Escobar (2001), one of the leading figures in the growing field of transnational anthropology (Appadurai, 1991; Gupta and Ferguson, 1997; Kearney, 2004; Hannerz, 1996, 1997; Marcus, 1995), a glocality consists of 'cultural and spatial configurations that connect places with each other to create regional spaces and regional worlds' (166). To put it simply, a glocality is a global place locally situated, where the local-global relations are being mutually constituted through socio-spatial practices of power. To borrow from Erik Swyngedouw (1997), we need to understand glocality as a life *milieu* 'that is produced; a socio-spatial process that is always deeply heterogeneous, conflictual, and contested' (140). Thus, we emphasize the influence of local actors and power relations on living conditions, as well as on the form taken by globalization. What is needed now is an understanding of how a glocality is produced, contested, and negotiated through the concrete of everyday actions. This is, I think, where the Secwepemc resistance contributes to the analysis.

Glocally Incorporated Structures

In British Columbia, the frontiers of the First Nations' reserves were organized and articulated around the colonial concepts of the gold rush and state settlements. The frontiers of the glocality-like Sun Peaks Resort are now formulated around the neoliberal – or neocolonial – concept of capitalist expansion, yet are based on expropriation. In this section, I suggest that the first set of contours of this glocality derive from the making of what I call an 'incorporation processing zone' that enables global tourism.[12]

As mentioned earlier, with the neoliberal restructuring of the world economy after the collapse of the Bretton Woods system, spatial practices are no longer exclusively confined within the boundaries of the nation state, and tourism is no exception (Britton, 2004; Meethan, 2004; Hawkins and Mann, 2007). Sun Peaks Resort is a clear example of how a pristine and unspoiled territory is economically incorporated into the world economy. The process of incorporation zoning in Sun Peaks imputes its own spatial structures that seek to attract global capital and cater to the international class of mass tourists. From a wider perspective, this process has made Sun Peaks Resort – and, arguably, the new Whistler Blackcomb and Sun Peaks economic axis – another transnational site of correspondence for global capital to commodify space. In effect, the same global routes that lead, for instance, to global cities, export processing zones, and global destinations of leisure are being used. But how does this incorporation work day-to-day?

First, as many writers have argued elsewhere (Bienefeld, 2004; Panitch, 2004; Peck and Tickell, 2002; Robinson, 2004), this process of incorporation zoning illustrates how the role of the state is still very crucial for mediating encounters between transnational capital and internal social forces, which, as a result, embeds localities within wider networks and structures of transnational capitalist accumulation. Two neoliberal principles seem to be carried out together by the federal and provincial governments in this conflict: (1) economic enabling of privatization and deregulation, and (2) political and legal protection of a 'correct business climate' (Hoogevelt, 1997). Second, this process of incorporation, which, as such, is a trademark of the global spread of capitalism, seems to bear a colonial idiom on its shoulder which is reanimated everywhere in the world economy where the discipline of accumulation is sought. I call this principle the 'interdiction of proper.' According to Michel de Certeau (1990), a 'proper' is a triumph of place over time. It is an exercise of power over specific wants by controlling a specific place. It allows one to capitalize acquired advantages, to prepare future expansion, and thus to give oneself a certain independence with respect to the variability of circumstances. In Sun Peaks, by making their own enclave for tourists and consumer-citizens, the federal and provincial governments along with Sun Peaks officials have established a spatial matrix of power that, de facto, annihilated every kind of political possibility for emancipation of the Secwepemc people. Then, through the effort of Nippon Cable to domesticate their transnational operations in the Secwepemc territories, Sun Peaks Resort consequently appears as an apolitical space.

However, when we look closer into the most critical threshold in the continuum of everyday relations of power and counter-power between the federal and provincial governments, Sun Peaks Resort, and the SWC, we then gain a measure of this interdiction of 'proper': it is clearly marked by a cycle of dispossession, resistance, repossession, and repression through which the interdiction is constantly actualized. As such, we can postulate that the interdiction of proper is more than a simple hegemonic instrument of domination but also mediates social relations of power in relation to space – that which mediates social relations of power in the world economy as a new social space. This is what happened when SWC activists launched direct actions in the reserve despite many court injunctions to leave the land purchased by Sun Peaks. By refusing to obey the court the SWC activists became trespassers on their own land, and the interdiction became the basis for lengthy periods of police repression and incarceration of SWC activists whose presence in Sun Peaks has been criminalized.

To restate what I have said so far, we know that the process of incorporation structures a first set of spatial contours – the 4,139 hectares-wide Sun Peaks' territory – by locally inscribing the global interdiction of proper into it as the structural basis of social relations. As a result, every time the members of the SWC gathered in Sun Peaks to protest, they were constantly in a situation known as 'crime of presence' – that is, they were breaking the law simply by being present not as commodified and entertaining exotic products nor as consumers, but rather as whole human beings claiming their right to the land.

We also know that this process is a part of the dominant form of the global spatial practices of capitalism and a nodal point in worldly circuits of capital, and that it is characterized by representations of space defined at the global level but ensured at the national level by state apparatus. Overall, through this complex of power, the development of global tourism in Sun Peaks appears not only as a local means to attract well-off tourists, but also as a global mechanism to discipline capitalist accumulation by the privatization and commodification of territories

(Harvey, 1990). As such, what is happening now in Sun Peaks Resort gives us a good example of how a region has been economically re-scaling itself to the capitalist world economy. Nevertheless, though this incorporation zoning seems to be one such site in its own right, it is also a contested terrain that offers the *maquette* of radical political possibilities of emancipation.

Glocally Exported Structures

The second set of contours of this glocality is made of the links between the SWC occupation movement in Skwelkwek'welt and its transnational campaigning in the world economy. As Michael Kearney (2004) put it, 'The form that resistance takes, whether passive or active, rebellious or revolutionary, is shaped in part by the forms of repression'(240). In Sun Peaks Resort, the privatization of Secwepemc lands has shaped the SWC resistance. By privatizing and transforming Skwelkwek'welt into a space of capital accumulation, Sun Peaks Resort has deprived the Secwepemc people of an Aboriginal space where both their culture and identity are performed. Indeed, this process has severed their onto-logical relationship with nature. As Janice Billy mentioned, 'The resist-ance is how the land is important to us. [...] The other resistance is maintaining our cultural integrity and identity. Being able to hunt and eat those foods from the land, being able to practice our traditions in those mountains and our languages. That is to say, just to have a free access to our lands and spirituality.'

In a remarkable way, it is from this very contradiction entailed by the construction of Sun Peaks on Skwelkwek'welt that the SWC resistance came into being. It was within Nippon Cable's newly 're-territorialized' territory – a space conceived to be empty of politics – that the SWC has been creating new sites of resistance. Moreover, it was precisely by re-mobilizing Aboriginal cultural traditions, such as building traditional winter homes and sweat lodges that the Secwepemc of the SWC tried to re-establish the historical unity between Skwelkwek'welt and their cul-tural identity. In that sense, what was radical about the SWC occupation movement in Sun Peaks was not that it took place in a site perfectly in-tegrated into the global tourism system, but rather because it was explic-itly informed by the Secwepemc place-based, cultural practices. By and through those cultural-space practices, mobilized in the specific context of power relations in Sun Peaks Resort, the Secwepemc of the SWC instituted a counter-territoriality and developed as a political subject; that is, an Aboriginal political subject rooted in restoring its ontological relationship to traditional lands. In doing so, the Secwepemc's Aboriginal habitat meaningfully became a critical site whereby they could challenge Sun Peaks Resort as a glocal space by re-appropriating it and endowing it with their Aboriginal meanings and practices.

It is from this local production of an Aboriginal counter-territoriality at the core of Sun Peaks Resort that the SWC resistance transnationalized itself. From there, the SWC has been able to build what Michael P. Smith (2001) has called 'translocal connections;' that is, those relations that are constituted within historically and geographically specific points of origin and destination, and established by transnational political activists. Indeed, just after the launching of the international boycott against Sun Peaks Resort and Delta Hotels, four significant political moments fuelled the transnationalization of the SWC resistance.

The first transnationalizing moment was that of the *Aktionsgruppe Indianer und Menschenrechte* in Munich. As I have said above, what was significant about this relation of solidarity is that the *Aktionsgruppe* re-territorialized the SWC's issues of struggle in the same politics of place which occurred at Sun Peaks Resort. This translocal connection is a good illustration of how local contexts of resistance reproduce themselves elsewhere in the world economy through modes of political practices informed by the local point of origin.

The second and third moments can be taken together, as they represent the involvement of two transnational institutions in the SWC resistance, that is, the ACSTP and the DataCenter. Although these two institutions were transmission belts, transmitting and diffusing the issues of the SWC resistance transnationally, they nevertheless had different modes of doing so. Indeed, while the ACSTP aimed at deterritorializing and re-articulating the SWC's issues around the broader spectrum of human rights in order to broaden the social basis of transnational solidarity, the DataCenter sought to re-territorialize political tactics and strategies that were effectively occurring elsewhere in the world so as to strengthen the SWC's local occupation movement. To put it simply, the ACSTP worked at transnationalizing local issues of struggle, whereas the DataCenter worked at localizing a field of transnational political tactics and strategies.

Finally, the fourth transnationalizing moment of the SWC resistance was that of the 'Sun Peaks Convergence' in August 2004. As a matter of fact, the Convergence had been the first re-territorialization in Sun Peaks Resort of the transnational movement of solidarity since the international boycott launched in 2001. The Convergence was, indeed, the concrete fusion between the local occupation movement that had been arduously maintained in Sun Peaks Resort and the long and slow movement-building of transnational solidarity in the world economy. While three years had passed since the international boycott was launched, the transnational movement of solidarity with the Secwepemc's resistance helped give them back the political momentum, especially by helping them with the construction of another Skwelkwek'welt Protection Centre near Sun Peaks. It somewhat reanimated the local occupation movement by re-embedding it into counter-hegemonic, Aboriginal cultural practices. Thus, the Convergence illustrates how the reterritorialization of a transnational political momentum radicalizes political positions maintained at the local level. It is also another good example of how the contemporary movement of social forces into the world economy is structured; that is, as a collection of campaign-centred movements that are both increasingly linked to one another by national and transnational institutions, and grounded by, and constitutive of, a global sense of place (Drainville, 2004).

So, through the links between the local occupation movement in Skwelkwek'welt and the transnational campaigning in the world economy, the Secwepemc's relationship with Sun Peaks Resort was radically modified. Skwelkwek'welt, too, became a glocality of its own where the social relations of solidarity forged by transnational networks linked this Secwepemc habitat with other places in complex ways, generating translocal discursive and spatial practices that had reconfigured relations of power with Sun Peaks and the Canadian and provincial governments. Those social relationships between the local occupation movement rooted into the affirmation of the Secwepemc Aboriginality in Sun Peaks Resort and the transnational campaign of solidarity in the world economy forged a new mode of being-in-the-world which challenged that imported by the re-territorialization of Nippon Cable in Skwelkwek'welt. To the alienating, consumerist mode of social relations attributed to Sun Peaks Resort, the Secwepemc of the SWC along with their allies recreated a mode in which Secwepemc Aboriginality could be fully, yet temporarily, relived.

However, as I have said, a glocality is a socio-spatial process that is always deeply heterogeneous, conflictual, and contested. The making of a Secwepemc Aboriginal presence both in Sun Peaks Resort and in the world economy occurred only periodically and for a short period of time.

The members of the SWC had been constantly squeezed between state repression – at once politically and legally – and the privatization of their land. To this effect, the court injunction of 2004, which prohibited over a dozen Secwepemc Elders, traditional land users, and activists from going within a two-to-10-kilometre radius of Sun Peaks Resort, was precisely the reply by the provincial government to the success of the 'Sun Peaks Convergence.' Indeed, the SWC has not been able to ensure a strong occupation movement in the national social formation. The lack of resources and a kind of politics of immediacy and spontaneity, combined with the Canadian government and Sun Peaks' ability to enforce repression and make strategic integration – recall the Protocol Agreement – resulted in an inability to sustain mobilization locally.

Moreover, the Canadian and provincial governments have sought to take advantage of their discretionary-like power in the Secwepemc territories by opening them up for further economic development. This has become the case especially in British Columbia, where the globally growing interest for sports tourism is at its peak with the hosting of the 2010 Olympic Winter Games at Whistler Blackcomb ski resort near Vancouver.[13] The sum of all this considerably weakened both the SWC positional struggle in Sun Peaks and its transnational campaign movement in the world economy. The former (local struggle) was literally extinguished, while the latter (transnational movement) worked considerably for itself; that is to say, without being translated and materialized into political forces at the local level.

Conclusion

Weakened mostly by state repression, the SWC occupation movement did not endure long enough for the transnational campaign to be really effective locally. In turn, the transnational campaign, even though it has merely worked alone, has considerably strengthened committee resolve and broadened the local social basis of its resistance. Nonetheless, in the end, mainly because the connection between the local resistance and the transnational campaign has been severed, neither has strengthened the other in a way that really radicalizes their position both in Canada and in the world economy. Although the transnational campaign began from a concrete and situated struggle, it has remained throughout its journey in the world economy a goal unto itself, without constituting a broader, more radicalized political sense of place in Skwelkwek'welt. Thus, the SWC needs to find ways to really strengthen positions locally to gain in political power from the social forces of movements in the world economy. Although many of the international activists who visited the SPC have spoken about being inspired to support their struggle, in the absence of a clear grasp of what solidarity could be and how it could be politically translated into an active will of force, this inspiration leads to little more than political tourism. In other words, transnational social relations of solidarity have to go beyond political moral support by being capable of challenging concretely – if not destroying – specific structures of power and domination. To actualize the potential of local resistance, transnational institutions like the DataCenter and the ACSTP are fundamental as transmission belts between real concrete struggles.

Of course, the way of doing politics changes as the historical power relations change. These relations are now changing in Canada, as the state is now flanked by transnational capital in dominating Aboriginal people. It is more than urgent, then, that Aboriginal people adapt their politics to the new conjuncture they are now facing, and also that non-Aboriginal people join them in a more durable way. But the question is, to what extent is this realizable. More importantly, to what extent is this politically sustainable over time.

NOTES

1 In this chapter, I use the terms 'Indigenous' and 'Aboriginal' interchangeably to refer to people who 'were in that place' when some others came and usurped some or all of their political control and power and their economic resources.

2 By 'non-Aboriginal organizations' I mean organizations that are mainly composed of people – often white people, though not exclusively – who are not Aboriginal in the sense that I gave this term in the previous note.

3 Because many Secwepemc Bands were in favor of the establishment of Sun Peaks Resort on their territories (mainly those bands close to the city of Kamloops), by 'Secwepemc resistance' I do not mean the resistance of the entire Secwepemc Nation. Instead, it refers to the Secwepemc people who were actively engaged in the resistance against Sun Peaks Resort, that is to say, mainly those from the Neskonlith and Adams Lake Reserves.

4 Historically, the first economic development for skiing on the Neskonlith reserve began in the early 1960s when a local entrepreneur ran a ski shop at Tod Mountain in cooperation with the Secwepemc people. Although there have been a few developments around the mountains, up until the 1990s

this recreational area has remained very small, with only one skiable mountain and a day lodge along with a few small cabins, which have caused little damage to the natural environment.

5 They are: Adams Lake Indian Band, Bonaparte Indian Band, Kamloops Indian Band, Little Shuswap Indian Band, Neskonlith Indian Band, and North Thompson Indian Band.

6 This protocol agreement stipulates: 'Now therefore, Nippon Cable and Sun Peaks Resort Corporation, along with the Chiefs of the Secwepemc (Shuswap) Nation, hereby declare their mutual intention to develop and pursue a formal relationship based upon mutual respect and trust, to ensure to the benefit of their respective communities, investors and the economy of the region; and, in furtherance of this mutual intention, Nippon Cable and Sun Peaks Resort Corporation, and the Secwepemc Chiefs, undertake the following commitments: (1) To hold formal joint meetings, at least twice a year, to discuss matters of mutual concern and to develop specific cooperative initiatives in respect of the long term benefits which flow from the aforesaid developments within the traditional territory; (2) To develop and maintain effective, open communications between each other at all times, particularly through the establishment of working committees to deal with specific matters as identified in ongoing joint meetings' (Protocol Agreement, 1997).

7 Janice Billy, spokesperson of the Secwepemc Watershed Committee (SWC) and the Skwelkwek'welt Protection Center (SPC). Interview with Thierry Drapeau, 21 July 2006, in Kamloops, BC. Janice Billy directly liaised with the two Secwepemc Bands (Neskonlith and Adams Lake) and engaged against Sun Peaks expansion on behalf of SWC and SPC.

8 As a matter of fact, there have been few treaties signed in British Columbia, and a tri-partite treaty-making process has been in progress since 1992, a process boycotted by many First Nations. Without treaties, jurisdictional issues in British Columbia have been highly complex, and this has a considerable impact on Aboriginal praxis in terms of political targets and strategic choices.

9 The reference to the concept of struggle, 'direct actions,' is not gratuitous here. It refers to the anarchist philosophy of politics. The distinguishing feature of direct action is that it aims to achieve people's political goals through their own activity rather than through the action of others. Direct action seeks to exert power directly over affairs and situations which concern us. Examples of direct action include blockades, pickets, sabotage, squatting, tree spiking, lockouts, occupations, rolling strikes, slow downs, and, at the extreme of this spectre, the revolutionary general strike. Thus, direct action is about people taking power for themselves. According to

the Secwepemc political *praxis* that took place in Sun Peaks Resort, the concept of 'direct actions' then gives coherence to their struggle because it was carried and organized 'from below' by the Secwepemc people, who explicitly repudiated and avoided the political rectitude of the their band councils.

10 The Bretton Woods system was an international monetary system that lasted from 1944 to the economic crisis of 1973. It was the first example of a fully negotiated monetary order intended to govern monetary, commercial, and financial relations among the world's major industrial states. Setting up a system of rules, institutions, and procedures to regulate the international monetary system, the planners at Bretton Woods established the International Bank for Reconstruction and Development (IBRD), (now one of five institutions in the World Bank Group) and the International Monetary Fund (IMF).

11 For a good historical account on the transformation of the world economy as a concrete space for social movements, see Drainville, 2004 (especially Chaps. 2 & 3).

12 Here I use the term 'incorporation' in a broader sense than the narrow and strictly economistic signification the world-system theorists have given to it. Hence, by 'incorporation' I mean a scalar process of power through which the historical centre of gravity of a particular place has shifted to the world economy. The incorporation occurs when historically and locally situated modes of being-in-the-world are disarticulated from their places and re-articulated within the logics of accumulation of transnational capital.

13 The fact that there have never been treaties signed between Aboriginal peoples, the provincial and the federal governments in the BC Interior makes it easier, both legally and politically, for the Canadian government to ignore and to repress them when they become *irritants* to non-Aboriginal development projects.

REFERENCES

Appadurai, Arjun. 1991.'Global Ethnoscapes: Notes and Queries for a Transnational Anthropology.' In *Recapturing Anthropology: Working in the Present*, 191–210. Richard Fox. Ed. Santa Fe, NM: School of American Research Press.

Armbruster-Sandoval, Ralph. 2005. *Globalization and Cross-Border Labor Solidarity in the Americas: The Anti-Sweatshop Movement and the Struggle for Social Justice*. New York: Routledge.

Beck, Ulrich. 2000. *What Is Globalization?* Cambridge, MA: Polity Press.

Bienefeld, Manfred. 2004. 'Capitalism and the Nation State in the Dog Days of the Twentieth Century.' In *The Globalization Decade: A Critical Reader*, 94–129. Leo Panitch, Colin Leys, Alan Zuege, and Martijn Konings. Eds. London: Merlin Press and Fernwood Publishing.

Britton, S. G. 2004. 'Tourism, Capital and Place: Towards a Critical Geography of Tourism.' In *Tourism: Critical Concepts in the Social Sciences*. Vol. 1, *The Nature and Structure of Tourism*. Stephen Williams. Ed. London and New York: Routledge.

Castells, Manuel. 1996. *The Rise of the Network Society. The Information Age: Economy, Society and Culture*. Oxford: Blackwell.

Cunningham, Hilary. 2001. 'Transnational Politics at the Edges of Sovereignty: Social Movements, Crossings and the State at the US-Mexico Border.' *Global Networks*, 1(4): 369–87.

de Certeau, Michel. 1990. *L'Invention du Quotidien: Tome 1: Arts de Faire*. Vol.146. Folio/Essais. Paris: Gallimard.

Dacks, Gurston. 2002. 'British Columbia after the Delgamuukw Decision: Land Claims and Other Processes.' *Canadian Public Policy/Analyse de Politiques*, 28 (2): 239–55.

Deckha, Nitin. 2003. 'Insurgent Urbanism in a Railway Quarter: Scalar Citizenship at King's Cross, London.' *ACME: An International E-Journal for Critical Geographies*, 2 (1): 33–56.

Delgamuukw v. British Columbia, 3S.C.R. 1010, 1997.

Drainville, André. C. 2004. *Contesting Globalization: Space and Place in the World Economy*. New York and London: Routledge.

– 2005. 'Beyond Altermondialisme: Anti-Capitalist Dialectic of Presence.' *Review of International Political Economy*, 12 (5): 884–908.

Edelman, Marc. 1998. 'Transnational Peasant Politics in Central America.' *Latin American Research Review*, 33 (3): 49–86.

Escobar, Arturo. 2001. 'Culture Sits in Place: Reflections on Globalism and Subaltern Strategies of Localization.' *Political Geography*, 20: 139–74.

Friedman, Jonathan. 1999. 'Indigenous Struggles and the Discrete Charm of the Bourgeoisie.' *Journal of World-Systems Research*, 5 (2): 391–411.

Guehenno, Jean-Marie. 1995. *The End of the Nation State*. St Paul: University of Minnesota Press.

Gunkel, David J., and Ann H.Gunkel. 1997. 'Virtual Geographies: The New World of Cyberspace.' *Critical Studies in Mass Communication*, 14: 123–37.

Gupta, Akhil, and James Ferguson. 1997. 'Beyond "Culture": Space, Identity, and the Politics of Difference.' In *Culture, Power, Place: Explorations in Critical Anthropology*. Akhil Gupta and James Ferguson. Eds. Durham, NC, and London: Duke University Press.

Hall, Thomas D., and James V. Fenelon. 2004. 'The Futures of Indigenous Peoples: 9/11 and the Trajectory of Indigenous Survival and Resistance.' *Journal of World-Systems* Research, 10 (1):153–97.

Hannerz, Ulf. 1996. *Transnational Connections: Culture, People, Places*. London and New York: Routledge.

– 1997. *Flows, Boundaries and Hybrids: Key Words in Transnational Anthropology*. Transnational Communities Programme. Working Papers. Oxford. Accessed 14 March 2007 from www.transcomm.ox.ac.uk.

Harris, Richard. L. 2002. 'Resistance and Alternatives to Globalization in Latin America and the Caribbean.' *Latin American Perspectives*, 29 (6): 136–51.

Hawkins, Donald E., and Shaun Mann. 2007. 'The World Bank's Role in Tourism Development.' *Annals of Tourism Research*, 34 (2): 348–63.

Harvey, David. 1990. *The Condition of Postmodernity*. Oxford: Blackwell.

Held, David. 1995. *Democracy and the Global Order: From the Modern State to Cosmopolitan Governance*. Cambridge, MA: Polity Press.

Hoogevelt, Ankie. 1997. *Globalization and the Postcolonial World: The New Political Economy of Development*. Basingstoke, UK: Macmillan.

Hudson, Douglas, and Marianne Ignace. 1995. 'The Plateau: A Regional Overview.' In *Native Peoples: The Canadian Experience*, 342–52. R. Bruce Morrison and C. Roderick Wilson. Eds. Toronto: Canadian Publishers.

Kearney, Michael. 2004. *Changing Fields of Anthropology: From Local to Global*. Lanham, MD: Rowman and Littlefield.

Lefebvre, Henri. 2000. *La Production de L'Espace*. Paris: Anthropos.

Marcus, George E. 1995. 'Ethnography in/of the World System: The Emergence of Multi-Sited Ethnography.' *Annual Review of Anthropology*, 24: 95–117.

Massey, Doreen. 1993. 'Power-Geometry and a Progressive Sense of Place.' In *Mapping the Futures: Local Cultures, Global Change*. J. Bird et al. Eds. London: Routledge.

Meethan, Kevin. 2004. 'Tourism Development and the Political Economy.' In *Tourism: Critical Concepts in the Social Sciences*. Vol. 1, *The Nature and Structure of Tourism*. Ed. Stephen Williams. London and New York: Routledge.

Meyrowitz, Joshua. 2004. 'The Rise of Glocality: New Senses of Place and Identity in the Global Village.' Conference proceeding. In *The Global and the Local in Mobile Communication: Places, Images, People, Connections*. Budapest: Hungarian Academy of Science. June 10–12. Accessed 21 November 2006 from http://www.fil.hu/mobil/2004/meyrowitz_webversion.doc.

Ohmae, Kenichi. 1996. *The End of the Nation State*. New York: Free Press.

Panitch, Leo. 2004. 'Globalization and the State.' In *The Globalization Decade: A Critical Reader*. Leo Panitch, Colin Leys, Alan Zuege, and Martijn Konings. Eds. London: Merlin Press and Fernwood Publishing.

Peck, Jamie, and Adam Tickell. 2002. 'Neoliberalizing Space.' *Antipode*, (34)3: 380–404.

Protocol Agreement. 1997. Kamloops, BC: In hands.

Robinson, William I. 2004. *A Theory of Global Capitalism: Production, Class, and State in a Transnational World*. Baltimore and London: Johns Hopkins University Press.

Ruggie, John. G. 1981. 'The Politics of Money.' *Foreign Policy*, 43: 139–54.

– 1982. 'International Regimes, Transactions, and Change: Embedded Liberalism in the Postwar Economic Order.' *International Organization*, 36 (2): 379–415.

Skwelkwek'welt. 2002. *Newsletter*, 8 January. Chase, BC: Skwelkwek'welt Protection Centre, c/o Neskonlith Indian Band.

Smith, Michael. P. 2001. *Transnational Urbanism: Locating Globalization*. Malden, MA: /Oxford: Blackwell.

Sun Peaks Municipal Incorporation Study. 2007. *Technical Report*. Sun Peaks Resort, BC: Sussex Consultants Ltd.

Swyngedouw, Erik. 1997. 'Neither Global nor Local: 'Glocalization' and the Politics of Scale.' In *Spaces of Globalization: Reasserting the Power of Local*, 137–66. Kevin. R. Cox. Ed. New York and London: Guilford Press.

Thomson, Duane, and Marianne Ignace, 2005. '"They Made Themselves Our Guests": Power Relationships in the Interior Plateau Region of the Cordillera in the Fur Trade Era.' *BC Studies*, 146: 5–36.

Wolf, Eric. R. 1982. *Europe and the People without History*. Berkeley: University of California Press.

Yashar, Deborah. J. 1998. 'Contesting Citizenship: Indigenous Movements and Democracy in Latin America.' *Comparative Politics*, 31 (1): 23–42.

Zibechi, Raul. 2005. 'Subterranean Echos: Resistance and Politics "Desde el Sótano."' *Socialism and Democracy*, 19 (3): 13–39.

15 Beyond Recognition and Coexistence: Living Together

LILY POL NEVEU

The issues of recognition for Aboriginal peoples and coexistence between Aboriginal and non-Aboriginal populations have gained greater importance since the 1960s. This reality brings up important political and ethical questions. Canadian political philosophers such as Charles Taylor, Will Kymlicka, and James Tully have entered the debate by developing what is known as normative theories of recognition. These theories suggest norms on which collective decision-making can be based. They question the universality and well-founded principles of the traditional liberalist ideology in North America and throughout the world. The basic principle of normative theories of recognition states that a different identity deserves a different treatment.

This chapter includes the case of Fort-Témiscamingue/Obadjiwan, National Historic Site of Canada, Parks Canada, where an agreement of co-management between Parks Canada and Timiskaming First Nation is in progress. In 1998, the discovery of Algonquin remains completely transformed the relationship between the different communities of the Témiscamingue region. After a difficult period, the historic site is now working towards an agreement of co-management, and the activities are operating in that spirit. Throughout my work as an interpreter at Fort-Témiscamingue/Obadjiwan, I have observed that dialogue, openness, and exchange are crucial in order to build a good relationship.

In the first part of this chapter, I will adopt a theoretical approach to the relationship of Aboriginal and non-Aboriginal peoples. I would like to argue that contemporary normative theories of recognition are useful to understand how reconciliation between Aboriginal and non-Aboriginal peoples can be done in practice. Practical cases like Fort-Témiscamingue/Obadjiwan can help make sense of theories by pointing out their pitfalls.

Indeed, some important aspects have been neglected in these theories. First, the question of what will bring the majority and the minority societies together to enter into a dialogue of real openness and mutual recognition remains unsettled. Second, individual-to-individual as well as community-to-community relations are important factors often overlooked by these theories and by higher political orders in the process of agreements. Thus, it is important to consider practice as well as theory when thinking about the relationships between Aboriginal and non-Aboriginal peoples. Beyond recognition and coexistence, I suggest that 'action, time, and path' are three elements that are part of the answer to these problems. These elements contribute to our understanding and building of a better 'living together.'

I will start by explaining briefly the normative theories of recognition through the works of the aforementioned Charles Taylor, Will Kymlicka, and James Tully; their ideas are distinct from one another, but they themselves are commonly looking for norms legitimating special rights on the basis of different identities. I will then outline the main critiques of these theories. I will finally give an explanation of the context of Fort-Témiscamingue/Obadjiwan from my point of view as a non-Aboriginal and interpreter on the site. This case study demonstrates the relevance of considering both theory and practice in finding solutions to practical problems.

Origins of Contemporary Normative Theories of Recognition

I would like to introduce normative theories of recognition by explaining how they responded to liberal claims.

American political philosopher John Rawls, in his book *Political Liberalism*,[1] describes liberalism as the quest for a just society.[2] Rawls attempts to answer the question of how collective decision-making, necessary in ordered societies, nations, or entities, can be possible when pluralism seems irreducible: 'How is it possible that there may exist over time a stable and just society of free and equal citizens profoundly divided by reasonable though incompatible religious, philosophical, and moral doctrines'?[3] We have to build a 'political' or a 'public' conception of justice, says Rawls. All individuals, having the same rights to participate in collective decision-making, must be 'reasonable' in the justification of their position on basic and fundamental rights. According to Rawls, what is just is what can be accepted by all citizens rather than what is stated by transcending and absolute notions such as spiritual beliefs, religions, and distinctive cultures. These comprehensive doc-trines shall be kept in the private sphere when justifying collective deci-sions.[4] Public reason is a political ideal of democratic citizenship, and is the cornerstone of Rawls' political theory of living together.[5]

German critical theorist Jürgen Habermas, like Rawls, attempts to solve the problem of collective decision-making in a pluralist world. He develops a theory of communicative action based on communicational reason as an acting force. According to Habermas, it would be possible to arrive at a just decision through rational discussion.[6] A just norm ex-ists when everyone agrees to conform to it in comparable situations.[7] Discussion and universalization are the two principles underlining Habermas' theory of communicative action.[8]

Rawls and Habermas have been criticized on the grounds that liber-alism is not neutral, nor is it universal.[9] Their theories suggest a certain neutrality of the liberal state, which has caused harm to minorities in the past and still does today.[10] In Rawls' political conception of justice, being 'reasonable' is approximately the equivalent of eliminating the particularities which shape one's identity and decisions. Although Rawls recognizes moral pluralism – the idea that individuals hold dif-ferent conceptions of what is good based on different fundamental principles (religious, cultural, spiritual) guiding our actions and choic-es in life – he trivializes this pluralism by stating the possibility of an existing universal 'reasonable' quality in each individual.[11] Universal beliefs are deemed to be universal simply because they are supported by a majority of people. Paradoxically, the imposition of the majority's beliefs is often against the very principles they defend: for example, equality and freedom. In the case of Aboriginal peoples, Rawls and Habermas' conceptions of justice raise problems, since it is exactly their specificity as first peoples of Canada that they want to be recognized as legitimate and deserving of differentiated treatment. Notably, in re-sponse to this fundamental problem of theories of justice developed in the 1970s by Rawls and Habermas, normative theories of recognition have emerged. Although these theories value equality and liberty, they emphasize group identity as important sources in the interpretation of these principles. In the theories of recognition, equality does not mean identical treatment for all individuals.

Contemporary Normative Theories of Recognition

Charles Taylor, Will Kymlicka, and James Tully are three important Canadian political philosophers who are part of a critical movement sparked by contemporary theories of justice. These authors can be placed under the umbrella of normative theories of recognition, as they are defending the idea that differentiated group rights are legitimate. The principles central to their theories can easily be applied to Aboriginal peoples in Canada, and are often used as examples by these authors.

Charles Taylor is one of the first thinkers who presented a strong justification for recognition. In his important article, 'The Politics of Recognition,' published in 1994, Taylor says that 'misrecognition of a person's identity by others can have negative effects on his/her identity and self-esteem: misrecognition shows not just a lack of due respect. It can inflict a grievous wound, saddling its victims with a crippling self-hatred. Due recognition is not just a courtesy we owe people. It is a vital human need.'[12] According to Taylor, the definition we have of our 'self' is acquired in dialogue with others. A human is a dialogical being and cannot be thought of outside a dialogical context. If other people project an inferior image of you, your beliefs, and practices, misrecognition and low self-esteem can be internalized and become part of your identity.[13] Taylor defends more than a simple right to difference, but a right not to be 'misesteemed.'[14] A different identity than the majority deserves to be valued and considered. Based on these claims, public decisions have to be culturally sensitive.[15] Substantial recognition is required; that is, political powers have an obligation to recognize difference.

Will Kymlicka is an influential political philosopher who developed a theory of minorities using liberal theory. In his book, *Multicultural Citizenship: A Liberal Theory of Minority Rights*, Kymlicka states the importance of cultural belonging in the achievement of individual liberty and equality, two core values of liberalism. A liberal society must recognize minority rights because of the special link each individual holds with his/her culture. Therefore, according to Kymlicka, minority rights are consistent with liberal democratic principles of individual equality and freedom.[16] Kymlicka differentiates two types of minority groups: national minorities and polyethnic minorities. Aboriginal peoples are part of the former, and most immigrants of the latter. Whereas polyethnic minorities ask for better integration as full members of the system and institutions, without necessarily wanting to assimilate to the majority's culture, national minorities seek to be recognized as distinct societies with a right to self-government.[17] According to Kymlicka, effective equality for national minorities such as Aboriginal peoples is acquired by self-determination.

Patrick Macklem uses Kymlicka's ideas and applies them specifically to Aboriginal peoples in Canada. He states that Indigenous difference is composed of four social facts: (1) distinctive culture, (2) prior occupation, (3) sovereignty over the territory, and (4) the treaty process. These constitute the unique relationship Aboriginal peoples hold with the Crown, which deserves constitutional protection.[18] Based on Kymlicka's argument, Macklem also states that special protection to Aboriginal peoples is justified by the imperative to reduce the burden imposed on them to reproduce their culture compared to the reproduction of the non-Aboriginal majority culture.[19] Identical rights do not result in equality for all individuals. It favours the majority and imposes a burden on minorities that have to abandon vital parts of their culture to integrate with the majority. Thus, special measures or special rights have to be put in place in order for everybody to feel free and equal.

James Tully is the last thinker I would like to briefly examine in relation to theories of recognition. In his book, *Strange Multiplicity: Constitutionalism in an Age of Diversity,* Tully looks for a way to manage cultural diversity in a just manner through constitutionalism. A broader contemporary vision of constitutionalism open to dialogue should be adopted. For Tully, 'A constitution should be seen as a form of activity, an intercultural dialogue in which the culturally diverse sovereign citizens of contemporary societies negotiate agreements on their forms of association over time in accordance with the three conventions of mutual recognition, consent and cultural continuity.'[20]

In Tully's book, acclaimed Haida artist Bill Reid's sculpture, *The Spirit of Haida Gwaii*, embodies his ideas. Reid's sculpture is a large bronze canoe with 11 strange and diverse characters from Haida mythology on board.[21] In the middle of this canoe stands an imposing character that Tully calls, at the end of his book, 'the mediator.' This sculpture shows how the characters in the black canoe are different from each other, but also within themselves. Identities are multiple and interconnected. The sculpture also demonstrates how it is possible to move forward, and at the same time stay grounded in who you are. Through this demonstration, Tully shows that languages are diverse. It is impossible to claim that there exists only one perception of the good. Allowing dialogue between these different ways of seeing the world enables a better 'living together,' a better understanding of each other and ourselves. By bringing together equality and difference in dialogue, Tully solves the challenge of how majorities and minorities should live together in a just manner.

In another article, entitled 'Aboriginal Peoples: Negotiating Reconciliation,'[22] Tully uses five principles to define a just and practical relationship that can be shared both by Aboriginal and Western sets of values.

These principles are (1) mutual recognition, (2) intercultural dialogue, (3) mutual respect, (4) sharing, and (5) mutual responsibility.[23] The first principle of mutual recognition offers a definition of recognition which must be in place in order to establish a true partnership between Aboriginal and non-Aboriginal peoples. Before taking a collective decision, Aboriginal and non-Aboriginal peoples have to recognize themselves mutually as being equal, living in coexistence, and self-governing.[24] These are Tully's three criteria for mutual recognition, which have to be accepted publicly by the two parties and entrenched in a constitution.[25] It has to become a habit which would be part of every collective decision. It implies understanding and openness to the other.[26]

Looking at the present situation in Canada, it seems clear that mutual recognition, in the sense presented by Tully, is far from being central to the relations between Aboriginal and non-Aboriginal peoples. Power struggles currently seem more representative of the context in negotiations, for example. Mutual recognition and dialogue appear nonetheless central to better relations between Aboriginal and non-Aboriginal populations. Indeed, the key to reconciliation cannot be found in the creation of watertight compartments of cultures closed to external influences. Dialogue allows people to understand each other, and it transforms their identities. Is dialogue powerful enough to push governments into the recognition of Aboriginal peoples in the sense of Tully, that is, as being equal, self-governing, and coexisting? The question as to what would bring Aboriginal and non-Aboriginal peoples into an equal dialogue remains unanswered. Tully does not tell us how we can arrive at a mutual recognition. This is an important shortcoming of recognition theories.

Critiques of Normative Theories of Recognition

Despite their differences, Taylor, Kymlicka, and Tully's theories all stand for the recognition of Aboriginal peoples. These theories have been criticized on different levels. In order to strengthen our understanding, I would like to look at their main weaknesses and pitfalls.

One critique has been that giving self-determination rights to different groups erodes the national identity, unity, and stability of a country.[27] As Alan Cairns puts it, 'What will hold us together?'[28] According to this interpretation, when recognition of groups takes place, the allegiance of people would be directed towards the identity group that represents them better, rather than towards the larger national identity.

The country would then be fractionalized into different identity groups. The state would lose its stability and decisional capacity. This critique is not without resonance for the believers in a strict conception of equality where all individuals are entitled to identical rights. Indeed, a few authors believe that giving special treatment to people with a different identity threatens the equality principle. Tom Flanagan is one of them. This controversial author, who served as the Conservative government advisor on Aboriginal policy, suggests that integration of Aboriginal peoples into democratic liberal society is the solution to their difficulties.[29] According to Flanagan, different treatment would mean giving privileges to people simply in the name of their differences. This differentiation would disadvantage 'normal' citizens, since they would not have access to the same benefits.

Such a strict interpretation of equality and freedom favours a partial majority. A strict conception of equality is insensitive to the history and context of most Aboriginal communities. Historical injustice has been discredited by politicians, some academics,[30] and the general public as a justification for the recognition of Aboriginal peoples. The idea of being held accountable for unjust actions committed by their ancestors seems unacceptable to them. This interpretation is unfair to Aboriginal peoples and not worthy of the principles of justice and equality defended by Canada. In Duncan Ivison's words, 'Insofar as it remains unaddressed, the moral rupture that occurred in the past persists in the present.'[31] History might not be the principle on which reconciliation can be based, but it has to be acknowledged. It can act as a starting point in the discussion. Not to recognize historical injustice is not to recognize the difficult socio-economic situation Aboriginal peoples now find themselves in as a consequence of the history of cultural repression, land erosion, and appropriation by non-Aboriginal peoples. Aboriginal peoples still see their lives affected daily by this history. They see the actual system as illegitimate because of the misrecognition of their population. Non-Aboriginal peoples benefit today from this history.

Recognition can be seen as a factor of stability rather than as a factor of instability. Misrecognition leads to the repression of identity groups by the majority government, which is not neutral in its own identity. Governments' (federal, provincial, territorial, and Aboriginal) continuing dialogue can lead to a greater feeling of belonging to the vast and diverse political association existing within the boundaries of this country.[32] Such a discussion could bring a change in the political system – a better representation of the different political systems within the country's institutions, for instance.[33]

A second critique directed against the general claim of theories of recognition is that they essentialize and freeze the identity of individual members of a group. This critique has been directed particularly towards Taylor's work, 'The Politics of Recognition.' As already stated, the basic proposition of normative theories of recognition is that a different identity deserves a different treatment. The essentialization critique states that by recognizing the existence of a cultural group, the members of this group see their identity tagged and imposed upon them. Some members of an Aboriginal community could see their identity fixed in the traditional past even if they consider themselves to be living a modern lifestyle, for example. This critique misunderstands the theoretical claims of normative theories of recognition which defend the multiple and changing nature of identities. However, in practice, the essentialization critique remains a challenge to the ways identities can be recognized.

The essentialization critique is linked with what Kymlicka has named the 'illiberal minorities' problem. It consists in the danger of 'individual rights breach' when minorities are given special rights.[34] Minorities trying to have their claims recognized could inflict a harmful treatment to identity groups within their own group.[35] One example of this critique can be represented by the movement for Aboriginal women's rights within the broader Aboriginal community. There is a danger that a minority asking for recognition attributes a uniform identity to its members. The group would then be wrongly presented as homogeneous. In reality, the identities of Aboriginal peoples have been reduced and frozen by the Canadian government and its institutions rather than by the authority of the communities themselves.[36] The Indian Act, introduced in 1876, for example, reduces Aboriginal identity to a 'blood' identity and to a registered status. The Supreme Court of Canada, on the other hand, reduces Aboriginal identity to practices, customs, and traditions. They use a cultural interpretation anchored in the past, which requires a demonstration of the continuity of an activity from the pre-contact period in order to be recognized as an ancestral right.[37] In the end, the Court encouraged communities to negotiate with the government rather than enter into lengthy and disappointing judicial battles.[38] The 'essentialization' critique may in fact reflect the fears of the majority losing their monopoly on the conception of the good. Moreover, the communities defending their right to self-determination on the basis of mistreatment from the majority are likely, in order to legitimate their claims, not to inflict such a treatment on their own population.[39] Although the essentialization critique remains powerful, making sure dialogue is central to the relationship between communities is probably the best avenue to answer fears of human rights breaches within communities.

The essentialization problem in identity recognition could also be answered by the way a minority group is recognized. Should a group be recognized through constitutional specificity, Parliament seats, public recognition, or academic program adaptation? To a certain extent, these methods are all homogenizing identity. They do not leave enough room for the flexibility of identity. The primacy of a particular part of one's identity – as a Quebecer, as a woman, or as an Aboriginal person, for instance – depends on diverse elements. Most practical methods of recognition cannot account for the fluidity and subtlety of identities. They separate identity in boxes of recognition more or less hermetically, not allowing for the pursuit of dialogue that opens individuals to the understanding of others and the self. Does that mean that recognition should be rejected altogether? I don't think so. The creation of a constitutional enclave might not be the best solution for the recognition of Aboriginal peoples, but principles, accepted by both Aboriginal and non-Aboriginal peoples and open to change in the future, can be elaborated in order to guide the relation between Aboriginal and non-Aboriginal peoples.

If Aboriginal communities are to achieve the recognition of their right to self-determination, discussions between Aboriginal communities and the non-Aboriginal majority have to continue. Aboriginal communities often share territory with non-Aboriginal peoples, they undertake economic activities together, and they have agreements with municipalities, health services, and other cooperative arrangements. Self-determination does not necessarily mean the creation of watertight compartments. Based on the history of consequences of the imposition of a foreign system onto Aboriginal communities, recognizing their right to make decisions for themselves while keeping the lines of dialogue open, seem more coherent than preventing them from doing so on the basis of essentialization fears.

Many questions remain unanswered by normative theories of recognition. They do offer principles of justice on which a new relationship can be based, including identity, self-esteem, cultural belonging, diversity, mutual recognition, and dialogue.[40] But how can we ensure that those principles are implemented? The report of the Royal Commission on Aboriginal Peoples (RCAP), for example, is an extensive document representing an important source in understanding the principles that should be used when thinking of reconciliation and a new relationship between Aboriginal and non-Aboriginal peoples. However, not much action has been taken following the RCAP report to implement these principles. Normative theories of recognition are now at an impasse because of their incapacity to resolve identity conflicts in a specific and permanent manner.[41] The question of how theories of recognition can work in practice is thus an important test of these theories.

Another practical aspect that has been neglected in normative theories of recognition is individual-to-individual and community-to-community relationships. Great principles do not mean much if they are not endorsed by the communities of Aboriginal and non-Aboriginal peoples. The success of an agreement depends on grassroots relationships between communities and the individuals involved in negotiations.[42] Their will to make their environment a better world for both parties is a crucial factor in the success of the implementation of principles of justice. This grassroots level is often forgotten in higher political analysis. Experiences of Aboriginal and non-Aboriginal peoples' working together become opportunities to know more about each other's realities. This level of study could become a vehicle for genuine mutual recognition. If the communities involved in a conflict have the will to reconcile, dialogue, and find solutions to living together better, it will make a significant difference in the negotiations at the political level because of popular support.[43] A bottom-up approach where people are brought together in improving their lives has more chance of success than an imposed agreement.

These last two critiques of normative recognition theories are related to their practical implementation. Firstly, the community-to-community and individual-to-individual relations have been neglected by higher political orders, and in academic studies. Secondly, the question of how the principles of the normative theories of recognition can be implemented in practice remains unaddressed. The failure to provide a complete theory having permanent and practical effects has led academics to turn to process-oriented approaches. The theories of deliberative democracy have been regarded as an alternative to solve diversity and pluralism issues. Theories of recognition and deliberative democracy could learn from one another.

Melissa S. Williams, in her article 'Représentation de groupe et démocratie délibérative: une alliance malaisée,' reflects on the practical reasons that would push groups to dialogue.[44] She examines what would bring a privileged group (the government or the Canadian majority, for example) to establish a dialogue with the unprivileged group (a minority, or Aboriginal peoples in our case), and what would incite the unprivileged group to engage in dialogue with the privileged group. If the marginalized group does not feel there is a will on the part of the privileged group to find a solution and arrive at a just agreement, then why would the unprivileged group even want to engage in dialogue? There has to be a desire from both groups to find a just solution. Is the will for justice strong enough? According to Williams, privileged groups will let go of some of their privileges when the costs of the conflict become too high – the risk of the conflict getting worse in the future, or the public display of the disrespect of principles they defend (liberty, equality), for instance. Threatened interests would push a privileged group to engage in dialogue with marginalized groups.[45] Seeing that the privileged group is willing to offer something, the marginalized group would be ready to negotiate. Williams brings a practical sense to the idealized discourse of recognition. She integrates political interests to deliberative theory as well as acknowledging the legitimacy of group identity in power politics.[46]

Normative theories of recognition, just like theories of justice and deliberative democracy, have the same will to restore justice in today's society. The challenge lies in the recognition of each and every one's individuality and unique character, while acknowledging that this unique character can depend on the sense of belonging to a group different from the majority. Normative theories of recognition are instinctively appealing, but attention must be brought to the way these theories can be implemented in practice and to the actors involved day-to-day in this process. Deliberative democracy theories can bring insights to the shortcomings of normative recognition theories.

I would like to finish this section by looking at Dale Turner's critical approach to the ideas of recognition. In his book, *This Is Not a Peace Pipe: Towards a Critical Indigenous Philosophy*, this Aboriginal scholar evaluates different ways in which liberal theory attempted to deal with the 'Aboriginal question.' In the first three parts of his book, he critically assesses White Paper liberalism, a strict conception of equality where everybody is granted the same rights, and special rights to Aboriginal peoples should be repealed; Alan Cairns' 'Citizen Plus' concept, where the idea of a shared common citizenship is developed; and Kymlicka's liberal theory of minority rights, where Aboriginal rights are seen as rights of minority cultures. According to Turner, these concepts to accommodate Aboriginal rights have failed in four ways: '… these three liberal theories are not peace pipes, for four reasons: 1. They do not adequately address the legacy of colonialism. 2. They do not respect the *sui generis* nature of Indigenous rights as a class of political rights that flow out of Indigenous nationhood and that are not bestowed by the Canadian state. 3. They do not question the legitimacy of the Canadian state's unilateral claim of sovereignty over Aboriginal lands and peoples. 4. Most importantly, they do not recognize that a meaningful theory of Aboriginal rights in Canada is impossible without Aboriginal participation.'[47] The lack of participation of Aboriginal peoples in the evolution of the discourse on Aboriginal rights is one of the main problems of liberal recognition theories, says Turner.

Turner suggests that Indigenous intellectuals need to engage the legal and political discourses while respecting both Indigenous philosophies and Western European intellectual traditions.[48] Any theory about Aboriginal rights has to evolve out of a dialogue between Aboriginal and non-Aboriginal peoples. Turner therefore entrusts Indigenous intellectuals with the role of mediator to undertake the bridging task between the two groups to better articulate the concept of Aboriginal rights. As he puts it: '*If* Aboriginal peoples want to assert that they possess different world-views, and that these differences ought to matter in the political relationship between Aboriginal peoples and the Canadian state, they will have to engage the Canadian state's legal and political discourse in more effective ways.'[49]

Turner's account is interesting in the way he critiques important liberal trends in the theories of recognition by addressing the role of Aboriginal peoples, particularly Aboriginal intellectuals, as a solution in building a new theory of Aboriginal rights without interrupting the dialogue between Aboriginal and non-Aboriginal groups. He tries to bridge the Western academic culture with Aboriginal traditional knowledge. In that sense, his book is very interesting and brings up an important question for non-Aboriginal people like myself who try to think about these questions. At this point of my reflection, I believe that the issues raised by Turner are key to Aboriginal peoples. As Turner suggests, if non-Aboriginal thinkers should not engage in discourse *about* Aboriginal peoples but enter into a relationship *with* them, then one of the most effective ways we can deal with these questions is to be open to this dialogue and find ways to be involved in grassroots relationships and initiatives. Better knowledge of each other at the local level will create a climate to engage in dialogue.

This brief overview of normative theories of recognition and their critiques enables us to understand better the relationship between theory and practice. Theoretical research can help us see what principles should legitimately lead our discussions. However, practice teaches us the problems of theories.

I would now like to turn to a practical case which helped me make sense of the normative theories of recognition.

Theories in Practice: Problems and Solutions

Despite the fact that Tully, Taylor, and Kymlicka root their arguments in practice, we have just seen that there are still some unanswered questions when applying their theories in real-life contexts. I would like to talk about my experience as an interpreter at Fort-Temiscamingue/ Obadjiwan. Practical examples are useful to point out what works, and how we can improve theories.

I will start by giving a brief explanation of the history of Fort-Témiscamingue/Obadjiwan. A Parks Canada National Historic Site, Obadjiwan is an Anishnaabe word meaning 'where the lake is narrow,' or 'meeting point,' and Témiscamingue means 'deep water.' Fort-Témiscamingue/Obadjiwan is located at the narrow of Lake Témiscamingue, where opposite shores are less than 200 metres from each other. This unique location makes the site a strategic point from which to control the territory on this 110-kilometre-long lake. This lake has been used extensively by Aboriginal peoples,[50] fur traders, and settlers, as it is an extension of the Ottawa River and was part of the Northern Trade Route. It also holds an important place and value today in the identity of Aboriginal as well as non-Aboriginal peoples of the Témiscamingue region.[51] Several archaeological digs on the site have shown evidence of the presence of Aboriginal peoples for more than 5,000 years.[52] Obadjiwan was a meeting point for the Anishinabegs. It was used for seasonal meetings and ceremonial purposes.[53]

The French Compagnie du Nord, the Scottish North-West Company, and the English Hudson's Bay Company subsequently owned the site from 1720 to 1902 for its rich pelt territory. The relationship between Anishinabegs and the fur-traders was characterized by interdependency. The fur traders needed the Anishinabegs, who had a good knowledge of the territory and brought the pelts back to them. On the other hand, the companies provided goods, work, and help to the Anishinabegs through the harsh winters. An important number of weddings were representative of the good relationships between the traders and the Anishinabegs. The site has also seen the establishment of the first religious mission in the area, at the beginning of the nineteenth century. In 1851, a reserve was created at the head of Lake Témiscamingue (today's location of Timiskaming First Nation and the town of Notre-Dame-du-Nord). Aboriginal peoples were encouraged to live on the reserve. In 1886, the first settlers established themselves at Baie-des-Pères (today Ville-Marie), only six kilometres from Obadjiwan. At the end of the twentieth century, the fur trade was declining, and the site was abandoned by the fur traders in 1902.

Slowly, European settlers created their own traditions and myths associated with Obadjiwan. In 1924, they celebrated Saint-Jean-Baptiste, the holy patron of French Canadians, for the first time at Obadjiwan, which they called, and still call today, 'le Vieux Fort' (the Old Fort). They used the site to enjoy its natural beach and the 'enchanted forest,' a thuya forest of crooked trees. Timiskaming First Nation still used the site for occasional ceremonial purposes. Written sources tell us that the nomination of chiefs was still taking place at the site as late as 1880.[54] Most of the buildings were destroyed during the twentieth century. In 1931, the site was given historical designation, a process sparked by the municipality and the Oblates, and, in 1970, Parks Canada acquired the site from the Oblates. Parks Canada conducted three archaeological digs between 1975 and 1995, which were meant to be the source of information for the renovation of the site in order to make it a central attraction for tourists visiting the region. The focus of the research was on the fur-trade period, rather than on the life of the Anishinabegs pre-contact. During these archaeological digs, Parks Canada discovered that the Anishinabegs, without necessarily living on the site permanently, had been coming to it regularly for more than 5,000 years. In 1997, Parks Canada adopted an official commemorating statement whose focus was the importance the site held for the fur trade, the fierce competition between companies, and the French and English presence. The site's long significance for Aboriginal peoples was secondary in this statement; little was said about the ancient presence of Aboriginal peoples in Obadjiwan.[55]

In 1997, Parks Canada started the renovation of the site to build a new interpretation centre with an exhibition and platforms of interpretation located on the original space of the company buildings. During these important changes, in 1998, they accidentally discovered Aboriginal remains. There were already two identified graveyards on the site: one

Protestant and one Catholic. The latter contained many Catholic Anishinabeg. They had no records, however, of a more newly discovered burial ground. The remains were from the fur trade period, since they also found objects that were exchanged with the fur traders. The bodies were buried according to Anishinabeg tradition. It was a major discovery that transformed the relation between Timiskaming First Nation and the non-Aboriginal population in Témiscamingue.

A period of crisis followed this discovery. The site was closed for two years. Anishinabegs held a blockade at the entry of the historic site. A lot of frustration was expressed by both sides of the population. The people of Timiskaming First Nation were frustrated at having been excluded from the process of historical recognition of a site they had been coming to regularly for thousands of years, a site that has been part of their heritage and tradition as much if not more than that of non-Aboriginal peoples.[56] The non-Aboriginal population were frustrated because they felt that their 'old fort,' which over time had become a place of leisure, was being 'taken' by Aboriginal peoples. Both Aboriginal and non-Aboriginal communities have feelings for this special site. After negotiations, Timiskaming First Nation and Parks Canada negotiators agreed to reopen Fort-Témiscamingue/Obadjiwan to the public while continuing the negotiations for a co-management agreement concerning the site. The remains were put back in the ground during a private ceremony with Elders from Timiskaming First Nation. The site is now working in a spirit of co-management. The agreement has not been signed yet, but it is on its way.

This co-management agreement is meant to be a real, effective method in which both parties will share equally in the management of the site – it represents co-ownership of the site. It has been named a 'Trust Patrimony Agreement,' meaning that a trust has been created, external to the Parks Canada entity, which is to be managed equally by Timiskaming First Nation and Parks Canada. Each party will hold equal decision-making power as part of the trust. It is the first agreement of its kind in Canada.

The agreement of Fort-Témiscamingue/Obadjiwan means a shared commitment of bringing Aboriginal and non-Aboriginal communities' histories together and working together to transmit them to the general public. Since the reopening, Fort-Témiscamingue/Obadjiwan has a team from Timiskaming First Nation who explain and demonstrate to the public Anishinabeg cultural activities, like building birchbark canoes, wigwams, and birchbark baskets. In 2006, for the first time, National Aboriginal Day was celebrated by Timiskaming First Nation at Obadjiwan instead of at the reserve. In 2007, the team from Timiskaming First Nation was not on the site. At the time of writing, Parks Canada and Timiskaming First Nation are working to secure their permanent presence at the site and to provide the public with more information about the history and culture of the Anishinabegs based on information coming from the community.

For me, the interesting element that has happened on the site has been the interaction between workers from Parks Canada and the Timiskaming First Nation. The very mandate of this site, to transmit history to the general public, has made this relationship very meaningful, and this relationship is transmitted to the public. Visitors leave the site with a personal experience that can transform their original perceptions. As an interpreter at Fort-Témiscamingue/Obadjiwan for three years, I learned a lot about myself and about the history of the land I grew up on. How can we live only a few kilometers away and know so little about each other? My job suddenly took on much more significance. People had to know about that. The good relationships built between colleagues show visitors how it is possible to talk to each other, live together, become friends, and laugh together. The fact that this site provides a place for everybody to meet and talk in a casual setting changes perceptions. In my opinion, and based on my experience, what happens daily at Fort-Témiscamingue/Obadjiwan can have implications for negotiations in higher political contexts. What happens on the ground is what makes an agreement work. Despite the fact that the co-management agreement has not been signed yet, the people on the ground are ready to accept it.

With the signing of the agreement, things will change even more at Fort-Témiscamingue/Obadjiwan. There will be more support for research on Anishinabeg history before the contact with the Europeans, and on the relationship between the two communities in the region. This information will be transmitted to the public. The institutional support of a written agreement should help, but the way the agreement will be lived on the ground is what matters the most. At the moment, following the *Haida Nation v. British Columbia (Minister of Forests)* judgment of the Supreme Court in 2004, the text of the agreement has been submitted to the neighbouring Anishinabeg communities of the region for consultation.

The story of Fort-Témiscamingue/Obadjiwan is a small example of a collaborative relationship, but we can learn from it. Of course, I do not want to portray a perfect image of the relations between Aboriginal and non-Aboriginal peoples in Témiscamingue. At the historic site, every year is a different year. Different people work on the site, and the relationship is still fragile. A solid relationship takes time to build. This chapter is based only on the relationship at Fort-Témiscamingue/ Obadjiwan, and not on the wider scale of Timiskaming First Nation and the non-Aboriginal population of Témiscamingue. However, to focus on the positive outcomes of this case study can help us build on what works.

Theories are helpful in conceptualizing what a good relationship is, and what principles we should look for in building that relationship: the importance of cultural belonging, mutual recognition, group-sensitivity, equality, and justice. Practice and theory are interrelated. The experience of Fort-Témiscamingue/Obadjiwan made me reflect on these theories. They do not show us the path to bring these principles to life, and they do not consider the grassroots support necessary in the making of agreements. However, a formal agreement is also necessary to support continuing relationships on the ground. The desire for justice and mutual recognition is not a strong enough incentive to change the actual situation. Sometimes, to change the status quo, things have to be forced by an event, a conflict, or an action. In the end, these actions will bring people together to discuss the questions at stake, and it will help people understand and know each other better. More effort has to be given to bring populations together. In this case, the discovery of Aboriginal remains has been a catalyst for change in the relationship between Aboriginal and non-Aboriginal peoples in this region. However, there is still a lot of work ahead. It will take time – time to recover, time to understand, time to listen to our story.

Beyond recognition and coexistence presented by the normative theories of recognition, I suggest that 'action, time, and path' will help us live together. Action will bring us together. It provides an opportunity for change. Path is the way we should take in that change. This path can be guided by the principles of the normative theories of recognition and deliberative democracy, the grassroots level, and the actual people involved in that change. Time is necessary to understand ourselves and our history. It is time that we started living together, not just co-existing. This is, of course, my humble opinion and vision. This is how I understand the relationship from a non-Aboriginal point of view. However, I hope these arguments can serve as powerful reasons for people who wish to bring populations together, and convince the one who doubts. This would open the discussion, a discussion that could transform the way we see ourselves and others.

NOTES

This chapter is based on a previous paper presented in Saumur (France) for the International Conference of the French Association of Canadian Studies in June 2006, entitled 'Co-existence et reconnaissance au Fort-Témiscamingue/Obadjiwan.'

1 Rawls, Political Liberalism.
2 Ibid., 10–11.
3 Ibid., xviii.
4 Ibid., 13, 152.
5 Ibid., 212–13.
6 Habermas, *Between Facts and Norms*, 39–40, 108–9.
7 Ibid., 163–4.
8 Ibid., 109.
9 Taylor, 'Politics of Recognition.' 44.
10 Weinstock, 'Le concept du 'raisonnable,' 4.
11 Ibid., 3–32.
12 Taylor, 'Politics of Recognition,' 44.
13 Taylor has been influenced by Hegel, an important German philosopher, who wrote about the well-known 'master-slave' dialectic stating that it is difficult for slaves to liberate themselves since their condition becomes part of how they see themselves.
14 Pourtois, 'Luttes pour la reconnaissance,' 291.
15 Ibid., 287.
16 Kymlicka, Multicultural Citizenship, 75.
17 Ibid., 10–11.
18 Macklem, *Indigenous Difference,* 4–5, 49. Adam Barker in this volume is highly critical of the way Macklem suggests we recognize Aboriginal difference (constitutional protection). However, the four social facts stated by Macklem remain widely defended among Aboriginal and non-Aboriginal academics.
19 Ibid., 74.
20 Tully, Strange Multiplicity, 30.
21 Ibid., 17–18. See Tully's insightful description of Reid's sculpture.

22 Tully, 'Aboriginal Peoples,' 413–41.

23 Ibid., 417.

24 Ibid., 419–20.

25 For a complete explanation of Tully's conception of constitutionalism, see *Strange Multiplicity*, 4, 34–43, 183–7.

26 Based on these principles, Tully later develops a system of multinational democracy where nations can coexist and govern within the same territory. See Tully, 'Introduction,' 1.

27 Tully, *Strange Multiplicity*, 196.

28 Cairns, *Citizens Plus*, 177.

29 Flanagan, *First Nations?* 192–8.

30 Ibid., 194–5; see also Waldron, 'Superseding Historical Injustice,' 4–28.

31 Ivison, *Postcolonial Liberalism*, 100.

32 Tully, *Strange Multiplicity*, 197. See also Marilyn Struthers' 'Reflections on White/Native Alliance Building from the Fishing Wars of 1995' (Chapter 22, this volume), concerning the concept of identity and neighbourhood.

33 On the integration of a precolonial system of justice, see Borrows, *Recovering Canada*, 27.

34 Kymlicka, *Multicultural Citizenship*, 94.

35 Shachar, 'On Citizenship,' 65.

36 See, for example, Rotman, 'Creating a Still-Life,' 6.

37 See R .v. Van der Peet, [1996] 2 S.C.R. 507; and Delgamuukw v. British Columbia, [1997] 3 S.C.R. 1010.

38 Delgamuukw v. British Columbia, [1997] 3 S.C.R. 1010; and, later, Haida Nation v. British Columbia (Minister of Forests), [2004] 3 S.C.R. 511.

39 Maclure, 'La reconnaissance,' 86.

40 See, among others, Tully, *Strange Multiplicity*; Kymlicka, *Multicultural Citizenship*; or Ivison, *Postcolonial Liberalism*.

41 Maclure, 'Politics of Recognition,' 3.

42 Rick Wallace, Marilyn Struthers, and Rick Bauman (Chapter 7, this volume) suggest something similar in 'Winning Fishing Rights: The Successes and Challenges of Building Grassroots Relations between the Chippewas of Nawash and their Allies.'

43 Wallace, Struthers, and Bauman (Chapter 7, this volume) suggest that initiatives have to be undertaken by the non-Aboriginal population (anti-racism campaigns). See also Adam Barker's Chapter 19 (this volume), which asks the question, 'What can "we" (the non-Aboriginals) do?'

44 Williams, 'Représentation,' 215.

45 Ibid., 236–7.

46 Ibid., 237.

47 Turner, *This Is Not a Peace Pipe*, 7.
48 Ibid., 7.
49 Ibid., 5.
50 The territory around Lake Témiscamingue is Timiskaming First Nation's traditional territory. It is currently subject to specific and comprehensive land claims undertaken by TFN. The co-management agreement of Fort-Témiscamingue/Obadjiwan offers room for further developments on the land-claims front, as well as allowing co-management to take place now, before these issues are settled.
51 The lake is also a natural border between the provinces of Ontario and Quebec. Fort-Témiscamingue/Obadjiwan is located in Quebec.
52 Côté, 'L'occupation amérindienne,' 7–22.
53 Ibid.
54 Morrison, *Report on Aboriginal Presence*.
55 For more information on the history of Fort-Témiscamingue, see Allan Mitchell, *Fort Timiskaming;* Riopel, Le Témiscamingue; and Neveu, 'Le Fort-Témiscamingue.' Accessed 11 February 2009 from http://www.ameriquefrancaise.org/fr/article-21/Fort-Temiscamingue_Obadijiwan_:_lieu_de_rencontres_et_d'echanges.html.
56 For more information on the point of view of Timiskaming First Nation, see their web site «Timiskaming First Nation – Obadjiwan, National Historic Site» *Algonquin Nation Secretariat*, accessed 25 April 2007 from http://www.algonquinnation.ca/timiskaming/obadjiwan.html.

REFERENCES

Allan Mitchell, Elaine. *Fort Timiskaming and the Fur Trade.* Toronto: University of Toronto Press, 1977.
Borrows, John. *Recovering Canada: The Resurgence of Indigenous Law.* Toronto: University of Toronto Press, 2002.
Cairns, Alan. *Citizens Plus: Aboriginal Peoples and the Canadian State.* Vancouver: University of British Columbia Press, 2000.
Côté, Marc. 'L'occupation amérindienne au Témiscamingue. L'exemple du Lieu historique national du Canada du Fort-Témiscamingue (Obadjiwan), une présence multi-millénaire.' *Recherches amérindiennes au Québec*, 36, no. 1 (2006): 7-22.
Delgamuukw v. British Columbia, [1997] 3 S.C.R. 1010.
Flanagan, Tom. *First Nations? Second Thoughts.* Montreal: McGill-Queen's University Press, 2000.

Habermas, Jürgen. *Between Facts and Norm: Contributions to a Discourse Theory of Law and Democracy*. Trans. William Rehg. Cambridge, MA: MIT Press, 1996.

Haida Nation v. British Columbia (Minister of Forests), [2004] 3 S.C.R. 511.

Ivison, Duncan. *Postcolonial Liberalism*. Cambridge: Cambridge University Press, 2002.

Kymlicka, Will. *Multicultural Citizenship: A Liberal Theory of Minority Rights*. New York: Oxford University Press, 1995.

Macklem, Patrick. *Indigenous Difference and the Constitution of Canada*. Toronto: University of Toronto Press, 2001.

Maclure, Jocelyn. 'The Politics of Recognition at an Impasse? Identity Politics and Democratic Citizenship.' *Canadian Journal of Political Science/Revue canadienne de science politique*, 36, no. 1 (March 2003): 3-21.

– 'La reconnaissance engage-t-elle à l'essentialisme?' *Philosophiques*, 34, no. 1 (2007): 76–96.

Morrison, James. 2002. *Report on Aboriginal Presence and Burial Grounds at Obawjewong/Fort Temiscamingue - Final Report*. Prepared for the Algonquin Nation Secretariat and Parks Canada, Quebec region, Winnipeg.

Neveu, Lily Pol. 'Le Fort-Témiscamingue/Obadjiwan: lieu de rencontre et d'échanges.' *Encyclopédie du patrimoine culturel de l'Amérique française*. Accessed 12 May 2009 from http://www.ameriquefrancaise.org/fr/article-21/Fort-Temiscamingue_Obadijiwan_:_lieu_de_rencontres_et_d'echanges.html.

Pourtois, Hervé. 'Luttes pour la reconnaissance et politique déliberative.' *Philosophique*, 29, no.2 (fall 2002): 287–309.

R. v. Van der Peet, [1996] 2 S.C.R. 507.

Rawls, John. *Political Liberalism*. New York: Columbia University Press, 1993.

Riopel, Marc. *Le Témiscamingue. Son histoire et ses habitants*. Québec: Fides, 2002.

Rotman, Leonard I. 1997. 'Creating a Still-Life Out of Dynamic Objects: Rights Reductionism at the Supreme Court of Canada.' *Alberta Law Review*, 36, no. 1 (1997): 1–8.

Shachar, Ayelet. 'On Citizenhip and Multicultural Vulnerability.' *Political Theory*, 28 (February 2000): 64–89.

Taylor, Charles. 'The Politics of Recognition.' In A. Gutmann. Ed. *Multiculturalism: Examining the Politics of Recognition, 25–73*. Princeton: Princeton University Press, 1994.

'Timiskaming First Nation – Obadjiwan, National Historic Site.' *Algonquin Nation Secretariat*. Accessed 25 April 2007 from http://www.algonquinnation.ca/timiskaming/obadjiwan.html.

Tully, James. *Strange Multiplicity. Constitutionalism in an Age of Diversity*. Cambridge: Cambridge University Press, 1995.

– 'Aboriginal Peoples. Negotiating Reconciliation.' In J. Bickerton and A-G. Gagnon, Eds. *Canadian Politics,* 413–41. 3d ed. Peterborough, ON: Broadview Press, 1999.

– 'Introduction.' In A-G. Gagnon and J. Tully, Dir. *Multinational Democracies,* 1–33. Cambridge: Cambridge University Press, 2001.

Turner, Dale. *This Is Not a Peace Pipe: Towards a Critical Indigenous Philosophy.* Toronto: University of Toronto Press, 2006.

Waldron, Jeremy. 'Superseding Historical Injustice.' *Ethics,* 103 (1992): 4–28.

Weinstock, Daniel. 'Le concept du "raisonnable" dans la "démocratie deliberative."' In A. Duhamel, D. Weinstock, and L. Tremblay, Eds. *La démocratie délibérative en philosophie et en droit: enjeux et perspectives*, 3–32. Montréal: Thémis, 2001.

Williams, Melissa S. 'Représentation de groupe et démocratie délibérative: une alliance malaisée.' *Philosophique,* 29, no. 2 (fall 2002): 215–49.

16 Indigenous Solidarity in an Anti-Racism Framework? A Case Study of the National Secretariat against Hate and Racism in Canada (NSAHRC)

BEENASH JAFRI

> While we do have some empathy from other organizations of colour, they're also like the rest of the Canadian public. They understand the situation of racism, but they're not too well versed on Canadian history or the history of the Americas to filter through the propaganda that sometimes the Canadian government uses to make it sound like Aboriginal people are such wealthy welfare recipients.
>
> – Former NSAHRC member

What does it mean for people of colour to work in solidarity with Indigenous peoples in Canada, and is it possible to do so within the rubric of anti-racism politics? As an anti-racism organizer, this is a question that I have struggled with for several years, and one that I have heard echoed by other anti-racist organizers. I have struggled with knowing that despite my desire for my anti-racist work to include Indigenous peoples, it has not. Yet, when our organizing work happens without certain groups at the table, it is mostly an indication of power relationships we ourselves are reproducing. In this chapter, therefore, I engage Bonita Lawrence and Enakshi Dua's (2005) suggestion that '[t] here is a strong need to begin discussions between anti-racist and Aboriginal activists on how to frame claims for anti-racism in ways that do not disempower Aboriginal peoples' (137). To do so is not to deny the importance of anti-racism organizing. However, anti-racism strategies are problematized when considered in relation to Indigenous struggles for decolonization in Canada.

Specifically, I present here a case study of the National Secretariat Against Hate and Racism in Canada (NSAHRC). Active from 2004 to 2006, the NSAHRC was unique as an anti-racism organization involving both 'Aboriginal peoples and diverse ethno-racial and faith-based communities' that also operated under Indigenous leadership. The organization was formed out of a recommendation made at the Hate and Racism Conference organized in 2004 by the Indigenous Bar Association (IBA) and the Quebec Native Women's Association (QNWA), in collaboration with non-Aboriginal partners. The conference, in turn, was a strategic response to the incendiary anti-Semitic comments made in 2002 by the former national chief of the Assembly of First Nations (AFN), Federation of Saskatchewan Indian Nations (FSIN), Senator David Ahenakew (NSAHRC, 2005: 2). The conference was also, however, a response to some mainstream reactions to Ahenakew. For example, Member of Parliament Jim Pankiw asserted that Ahenakew and the FSIN were racists and criminals, and that assimilation was the solution (NSAHRC, 2004c). There were also more general assumptions that Ahenakew's comments reflected the beliefs of Indigenous peoples collectively.

By taking the opportunity presented by the Ahenakew incident to work in coalition and advance an anti-racism agenda, the NSAHRC's formation challenged the idea that racism is limited to prejudice and discrimination. Also critical was the prioritization of Indigenous leadership within the NSAHRC. What have been the strengths and challenges of the NSAHRC's unique model? To explore this question, I spoke to four NSAHRC members.[1] Their insights revealed that the development of shared political agendas has been an important means of addressing the differential marginalization of communities of colour and Indigenous communities. However, the politics of community organization and anti-racism also threaten to undermine this work when they silence Indigenous struggles. This chapter will discuss the ways that the NSAHRC members negotiated these issues, as well as the challenges they faced.

The Context of Anti-Racism Advocacy in Canada

Some Indigenous organizations have drawn upon anti-racism frameworks when mobilizing around particular issues.[2] However, as NSAHRC members attested, Indigenous communities as a whole have been excluded from anti-racism organizing. To a great extent, this reflects the marginalization of Indigenous histories and perspectives within anti-racism theory (Lawrence and Dua, 2005). However, the internal challenges facing anti-racism organizing pose a challenge to coalitional possibilities as well. I highlight three of these challenges here: lack of cohesion, institutionalization, and a post- 9/11 context.

A central issue facing anti-racism organizers in Canada has been a lack of a cohesive organizing body. As activist Beverly Bain has noted, it is difficult to identify an anti-racism 'movement' in Canada; 'anti-racist perspective' is more accurate, because an anti-racism framework has not been adequately formulated at a practical level (cited in Robertson, 1999: 310). Furthermore, much of this work has been fragmented, sporadic, and not always identified as 'anti-racist.' Those who do organize around anti-racism have done so with a range of political agendas. For example, liberal approaches to anti-racism have simply been about representation and equal opportunity of non-whites within societal institutions. Meanwhile, integrative anti-racism approaches (Dei, 1996) and anti-racist feminist approaches (Dua, 1999) have offered more critical frameworks emphasizing interlocking systems of oppression, power, and privilege.

The institutionalization of anti-racism advocacy has not supported the development of a cohesive movement. Many anti-racism advocates are paid workers carrying out their activism through non-governmental organizations. It is useful to briefly trace the genealogy of this particular form of anti-racism activism here. Tania Das Gupta (1999) writes about a constellation of events in the mid-seventies, including the opening of the Immigration Act in 1976 to people from Third World countries; people of colour's resistance to police brutality, institutional racism, and racialized violence; and the publication of academic studies confirming the increase of racism, which motivated shifts in Canadian multicultural policy towards a race relations framework in the 1980s. Racism and equity concerns were thus added as they reinforced the primary goal of national identity consolidation (i.e., in terms of attitudinal/behavioural changes and barriers to participation in Canadian society and institutions). White supremacy and colonialism were not included in the discussion.

Indeed, an anti-racism framework encapsulating these critical ideas and concepts has never been taken seriously by the federal government; thus far, the federal government has not endorsed anti-racism within official policy. Multiculturalism itself has been downsized into a governmental program, rather than a department. In the face of official multiculturalism, anti-racism activists are faced with the constant challenge of articulating a more critical political agenda. The events leading to the NSAHRC's creation are indicative of this. For example, while acknowledging the incendiary nature of Ahenakew's comments, the IBA and the QNWA drew greater attention to the broader question of racism as 'a root cause of the discrimination suffered by Indigenous Peoples in Canada' and '[other] communities and individuals in Canada' (NSAHRC, 2004a: 2).[3]

At the same time, the relationship between anti-racism advocates and the state has not been solely antagonistic. Ironically, community organizations also use state funds to carry out anti-racism programs that may be critical of the state. With the identification within multicultural policy of racial discrimination as a priority area in the 1980s, some limited funds for community groups were made available through the multiculturalism program, which supports researchers and non-governmental organizations (NGOs) in undertaking projects advancing the government agenda for multiculturalism.[4] Community groups are able to leverage funding for anti-racism programming,[5] and to advance their respective agendas. As will be discussed later, however, the utility of this funding in supporting movement goals is contested.

Provincial contexts of anti-racism organizing add an additional layer of complexity to the discussion. The federal vision of multiculturalism has not been uniformly realized across the provinces. Anti-racist activism has been perhaps the strongest in Ontario (e.g., see Carrington and Bonnett, 1997), and it is not surprising that the majority of NSAHRC members come from this province. 'Race relations' became a catchword in Ontario in the late seventies and eighties; a race relations directorate associated with the Ontario Human Rights Commission was established in 1981 (Wallis et al., 1988). In 1991, following through on an election campaign promise, an Ontario Anti-Racism Secretariat was established by Bob Rae's NDP government (Harney, 1996). The establishment of the secretariat was a pivotal moment in the history of anti-racism organizing in Canada. Funding was made available for programs and policies furthering systemic anti-racist change through the education system and through employment equity (Harney, 1996: 37–8). But it was also the beginning of a shift in anti-racism organizing towards bureaucratization and co-optation by state interests. Activist Angela Robertson (1999:325–6) reflects:

> Looking specifically at Ontario, in 1988 and prior, what I was seeing was on-the- street activism, on-the-street mobilizing, public mobilizing to build mass support. And what happened, ironically, is with a left-leaning government we moved into consultations. Our protests became bureaucratized,

they were no longer public and that only benefited a privileged few who became part of the consulted. Many of us benefited from the privatization of anti-racism as an industry. It's not even that people aren't making challenges to regressive changes. But it is happening in these very bureaucratic ways, in these things called state consultation.

In 1995, Mike Harris's Conservative government came into power and axed the Secretariat, the employment equity policy, and various other equity-related initiatives that had been established under the NDP. At the same time, the organizing structures that had been developed during this time, as noted by Robertson above, have remained in place.[6]

Anti-racism organizing in Canada picked up momentum as a result of the United Nations World Conference against Racism, Xenophobia and Related Intolerances (WCAR), held in Durban, South Africa, in August 2001. Networks and coalitions, such as the National Anti-Racism Council of Canada (NARCC), the Pan-Asian Anti-Racism Network and the African Canadian Coalition Against Racism developed as a means to build common agendas and strengthen positions, while resisting multiculturalist notions of community organization and formation (e.g., see Siemiatycki et al., 2001). Shortly after, on 11 September 2001 (9/11), terrorist attacks led to the collapse of the World Trade Center in New York City. The response of the U.S., Canada, and the UK has led to a heightening of security concerns that have reinforced existing notions of nationhood, citizenship, and race by emphasizing distinctions between who belongs and who does not (e.g., Thobani, 2007). In a post-9/11 climate of increased paranoia, fear, and racialization, anti-racism mobilization is more important than ever. It also presents potentially challenging circumstances, as dissent is criminalized and state funds are diverted towards the strengthening of security and military needs.

NSHARC's Strategies

In many regards, the NSAHRC had much in common with other anti-racism organizations. Like other such organizations, it struggled with articulating a critical anti-racism analysis in the face of liberal approaches to anti-racism. The NSAHRC also followed in the footsteps of other anti-racism groups in the institutional character of its activism. For example, non-Aboriginal member organizations in the NSAHRC were recommended by the Department of Canadian Heritage, and were groups that the department consulted with on a regular basis. In this sense, the NSAHRC's composition was a product of the shift from grassroots mobilization towards the centralization of state consultations noted by Robertson, above. The NSAHRC arguably re-articulated a bureaucratic strategy of the state.

However, the NSAHRC also differed significantly from other anti-racism organizations in its prioritization of Indigenous leadership. Indeed, the centralization of Indigenous leadership was a key component of the NSAHRC's work. Meeting minutes from 30 July 2004 stated that 'this secretariat is particularly helpful to participating organizations as it provides an opportunity to do anti-racism work with the Aboriginal community... this is where this secretariat will be most valuable as most anti-hate/anti-racism networks, while sometimes crossing several communities, tend not to include Aboriginal communities' (NSAHRC, 2004b). By placing Indigenous peoples at the forefront of the organization, the NSAHRC recognized the ways in which Indigenous struggles have traditionally been sidelined within anti-racism organizing. An Indigenous member of the secretariat reflected on the evolution of this particular dynamic:

> I think that there was a willingness for both Aboriginal people and non-Aboriginal people to work together, and there were some commonalities, but the agendas started to compete and Aboriginal peoples were feeling that they were not exactly the [right] fit in some of this anti-racism movement; that their issues were quite distinct. And they then found that they became subsumed in somebody else's agenda. And there was a feeling that they were being used, but not understood. And I don't think it's because the people who are anti-racist activists intended that, but it's easy for the Aboriginal people to fall by the wayside and not say anything.

Within the NSAHRC, placing the Indigenous Bar Association (IBA) in a leadership position was a key means through which the silencing described by this participant could be addressed. However, critically centring an Indigenous agenda was a difficult process. As one participant expressed it, the process was uncomfortable for many, raising feelings of helplessness and frustration as members struggled to come to terms with issues of citizenship and settler privilege.

Several strategies were used by the NSAHRC to fortify the IBA's leadership position within the organization. Some of these strategies were organizational. For example, according to the Terms of Reference, the IBA was responsible for setting meeting agendas (NSAHRC, 2004d). In addition, in a March 2005 meeting it was agreed that the first item on every meeting agenda should be an update by the IBA 'concerning issues it wishes the NSAHRC to consider'; that all meetings be chaired by IBA representatives; and that 'in the event no IBA representative is present at NSAHRC meetings, no new business ... be discussed and members ... focus on actions agreed upon to implement NSAHRC positions' (NSAHRC, 2005).

Other strategies focused more on programming. For example, meeting minutes of the NSAHRC from 6 March 2005 stated that:

> iii. Non-aboriginal members will consider how best to make connections between their organizations and Aboriginal leadership. For example, it would be useful for members to invite IBA representatives to their organizations to discuss issues of concern to Aboriginal peoples and actions being taken by the NSAHRC;
> iv ... issues concerning Aboriginal peoples will be given priority and linkages to other communities will then be considered. Further, public education regarding these matters is critical to engaging the public on Aboriginal issues, perspectives and history. The networking provided through the NSAHRC membership can be very useful to reaching out to non-Aboriginal communities on these matters.

In light of the stated commitment to prioritize 'issues concerning Aboriginal peoples,' NSAHRC members strongly supported a campaign by the Indigenous Bar Association to have Aboriginal appointments to the Supreme Court of Canada. The decision to support this campaign came out of a mutual agreement that employment equity and representation were points of commonality for all, and that Indigenous communities needed to be prioritized in this endeavour.

NSAHRC members also successfully identified a few points of commonality around which to organize advocacy strategies, determined initially through an 'environmental scan.' This involved a discussion of each organization's respective goals, priorities, and programs, as well as an identification of key issues in which member groups were engaged. There was consensus that 'it was important to concentrate on priority issues that affect all of our organizations so as not to exclude organizations that are not involved in those other issues' (NSAHRC, 2004d). The priority issues/projects which were decided upon included: effective relationships; youth partnerships; education; racial profiling; hate crimes; speaker's bureau; national anti-racism campaign; core funding; race based litigation; redress/reparations; and race/gender (intersectionality). The secretariat did not work on all these issues, but members did produce position papers on the collection of race-based data and racial profiling. In addition, they identified a common project around policing, criminalization, and hate crimes.[7]

Defining the Terrain of Struggle

The issue of framing struggles was an ongoing one for the NSAHRC. This was not surprising; at the time of this research, the NSAHRC was only in the beginning stages of coalition building. In addition, the challenges of defining struggles reflect broader debates happening within anti-racism and Indigenous activism. My critical examination must be read in this context. Furthermore, as I did not speak to all NSAHRC members, this assessment is neither exhaustive nor definitive. I attempt to provide constructive critique, rather than point out 'flaws.'

A central ambiguity within the NSAHRC concerned defining racism. For instance, within the overall goals of the secretariat – including in the name itself – 'anti-hate' activism curiously appears alongside 'anti-racism.' This is interesting because discourses of anti-hate tend not to include an analysis of race; while hate crimes may be a manifestation of racism, anti-hate advocacy is not necessarily anti-racist.[8]

In addition to the general inconsistency in understandings of racism, there were notable differences between the ways that Indigenous members and members of colour were conceptualizing racism. This is not surprising given the different ways that Indigenous peoples and peoples of colour are positioned within the Canadian state through official policy. For example, one member of colour understood racism as a human rights concern but also suggested that 'if we move along further to racial incidents … racism is … the ideology of white supremacy.' Meanwhile, an Indigenous participant, explaining the consciousness-raising aspects of her work, understood racism as just one aspect of the struggles of Aboriginal peoples in Canada, and defined it primarily in terms of discriminatory acts and racial slurs.

Evidently, the frameworks were wide-ranging across the board. Of course, a consensus on definitions is not a prerequisite for coalition work. However, it raises important questions around how 'shared political agendas' might be built in the context of ambiguity. For instance, the ambiguity around definitions of racism is important not only in principle, but because of the way it impacts which issues are chosen, prioritized, and framed. This was evident in the common project around policing, criminalization, and hate crimes identified by NSAHRC members. They chose to examine these issues by drawing attention to the inadequacies of the administration of the criminal code,[9] and, according to one participant, 'how people who are experiencing hate crimes, or at minimum, racism, are not apt to want to engage that process, because they have very low faith in the people that are running.' Although inclusion in these administrative processes is important, the unanswered question was, how might this be situated within the broader context of social movement goals?

Contradictions also arose with respect to defining Indigenous struggles. For example, in reference to the NSAHRC's campaign to lobby for an Aboriginal appointment to the Supreme Court, one Aboriginal member noted: 'It's not just that [Aboriginal people] are people of colour, they're actually one of the founding nations of this country... [NSAHRC members] understood the distinction; they all supported the initiative. So we were very successful in convincing many legal groups and many high-profile legal thinkers about the necessity to have more Aboriginal people represented in the judiciary, for example.'

The justification given for the campaign was that Aboriginal peoples were founding nations of Canada, and therefore needed to be represented in the judiciary – an argument which does not necessarily challenge the existence of the Canadian nation, but suggests that the underlying issue is of Aboriginal peoples' exclusion from the official narrative of the nation. However, earlier, this same participant had noted that a primary focus of Indigenous struggles was around challenging the institution of Canada: 'People who are fighting anti-racism who have joined Canada as part of the whole embracing [of] Canada [are] not indigenous to Canada, [whereas] Indigenous people are actually fighting the establishment of Canada.'

Accordingly, the relationship between anti-racism and Indigenous struggles as understood by NSAHRC members was not entirely clear either. For example, one member suggested that the primary linkages between Indigenous communities and communities of colour were around representation and employment equity, but failed to draw attention to experiences with colonization. Meanwhile, there was also recognition within the organization that differences existed between anti-racist activism and Indigenous activism. In meeting minutes from

6 March 2005, it was suggested that First Nations may have different views with respect to human rights approaches and the Charter of Rights and Freedoms, and that the 'NSAHRC may wish to work with Aboriginal leaders in educating the public about these differences and why they are important' (NSAHRC, 2005).

Clearly, the NSAHRC's membership recognized the differences between anti-racism activists and Indigenous activists in Canada. They also recognized the power relations existing between Indigenous and non-Indigenous communities, through which Indigenous peoples have been silenced. Furthermore, through their collective efforts, they affirmed the common concerns around hate and racism through which Indigenous and anti-racism activists can build shared agendas. However, several questions remained unanswered. For example, are anti-racism and Indigenous self-determination primarily discrete spheres of struggle, which overlap at particular moments? How are the Indigenous organizations affiliated with the NSAHRC situated with respect to Indigenous communities in Canada? Where do the anti-racism groups in the NSAHRC situate themselves with respect to communities of colour? These are important questions to consider, as a lack of clarity around framing struggles can lead to the development of advocacy strategies that inadvertently reinforce existing power relations.

Conflicting Strategies of Resistance

Another challenge to coalition work identified by NSAHRC members was conflicting strategies of resistance. As highlighted by Cherokee scholar Andrea Smith in the context of women of colour organizing in the United States, colonization and white supremacy do not subordinate people of colour and Indigenous peoples in the same ways, despite similarities in experiences of subordination (Smith, 2006: 66–7). Accordingly, respective resistance strategies are not necessarily congruous with one another. As Smith's work suggests, one community's definition of their struggles can make invisible, and thereby further reinforce, the oppression of other communities.

This argument could be extended more broadly to people of colour and Indigenous peoples in Canada. In this section, I draw attention to the consequences of such assumptions of shared oppression by examining three examples of NSAHRC members' advocacy work. I demonstrate through these examples how resistance strategies undertaken by communities of colour may reinforce the subordination of Indigenous communities in Canada. The first example is the Canadian Charter of Rights and Freedoms. The second example is campaigns for head tax redress, which I examine alongside campaigns for residential school redress. The final example is campaigns for reparations for the African slave trade.

Charter of Rights and Freedoms: Possibilities and Limitations

NSAHRC members discovered a tension in discussions around the way in which many non-Aboriginal member groups of the NSAHRC rely on the Canadian Charter of Rights and Freedoms as an advocacy tool. The National Anti-Racism Council of Canada (NARCC, 2002) notes that the Charter 'among other things, grants every individual in Canada equal protection and equal benefit before and under the law' (6). For many communities, the Charter has been crucial means of holding the Canadian state accountable to its stated commitment to equality.[10]

This has not necessarily been the case within Indigenous communities, where there has been considerable debate regarding the Charter. Some, like the Assembly of First Nations, have argued that the isolation of individual rights from collective rights within the Charter leads to increased discrimination and conflicts with Indigenous philosophy (cited in NWAC, 1991: 17). Meanwhile, Indigenous women have strategically deployed Charter principles to draw attention to gender discrimination within the Indian Act (e.g., see Monture-Angus, 1999). However, they have also problematized their use of a law developed by a settler-colonial state, contextualizing it in terms of colonialism's role in creating gender inequity. The contextualization is key. For example, the conflict for communities of colour may not be that deployment of the Charter itself, so much as the failure to situate that deployment in the context of struggles for Indigenous self-determination. Viewed in that context, the liberal paradigm of equality can be challenged. By historicizing the Charter within this framework, the struggles of Indigenous communities and communities of colour can be more clearly linked.

'Conflict and Competition': Head Tax Redress and Residential School Redress

Conflicting strategies of resistance must also be linked to state practices. One of the impacts of state bureaucracy has been the production of conditions of apparent competition. A focus on competing agendas for change can obscure the structural forces creating these animosities, undermining the potential for coalition work. NSAHRC members grappled with this issue in 2006, when Prime Minister Stephen Harper's Conservative government issued a formal apology to Chinese Head Tax survivors while continuing to refuse to apologize to residential school survivors (until 2008).

For a better understanding of the context of this conversation in the NSAHRC, some background on these campaigns is useful. Briefly, residential schools were first established by missionary societies in the seventeenth century, and were subsequently supported by the Canadian government from 1879 to 1986 (Milloy, 1999). In line with the assimilationist agenda of the Indian Act, the policy of residential schooling was a strategy to 'civilize' Native children so that they could 'integrate' into Canadian society. Under the leadership of Canadian churches, children were separated from their families and lived in deplorable conditions, often enduring multiple forms of abuse and violence.

The trauma of residential schools has had a collective impact (e.g., see Simpson, 2004). Dian Million (2001) notes that a campaign by 'Aboriginal parents, students, and their allies' led, in the 1940s and 1950s, to heightened awareness of the injustices being perpetuated as a result of residential school policies (98). She further observes that Celia Haig-Brown's book, *Resistance and Renewal* (1988), which centralized residential school survivors' voices, sparked widespread debate on the issue (100). In 1996, the *Report of the Royal Commission on Aboriginal Peoples* made several recommendations towards reparations for survivors, including financial compensation and a formal apology (RCAP, 1996). In 1998, the federal government announced a grant of $350 million towards establishing a healing foundation for residential school survivors, and offered an unofficial apology (Demont, 1998). In late 2005, an agreement in principle was reached by the Canadian government and the Assembly of First Nations that would ensure $1.9 billion towards compensation for living survivors. Funds were finally allocated to survivors in 2007. However, the compensation was individually based.[11] A formal apology was finally made in June 2008.

The Chinese Immigration Act was brought into effect in Canada in 1885, in roughly the same period that the residential school policy was implemented. Central to the Canadian nation-state's development as a 'white man's country' was the management of Indigenous peoples, the restriction of non-white immigration, and labour for capitalist expansion. Many Chinese men had migrated to Canada in the mid-1800s during the gold rush and were later hired contractually to build the

Canadian Pacific Railway in British Columbia (Bolaria and Li, 1988: 102). Once the railway was completed and Chinese labour no longer required, a head tax of $50 (increased to $500 in 1923) was enforced for all Chinese immigrants, as stipulated in the Chinese Immigration Act (Backhouse, 2005: 24). From 1923 to 1947, the Chinese Exclusion Act virtually banned all Chinese immigration (Dyzenhaus and Moran, 2005: 7; see also Li, 1994).

The campaign for Chinese Head Tax redress was initiated by a head tax payer in 1983 and subsequently taken up by the Chinese Canadian National Council (CCNC) a year later (Go, 2005: 20). A grassroots mobilization was underway for over two decades, lobbying for a formal apology from the Canadian government and financial compensation for head tax payers. The campaign situated its analysis in the context of anti-Chinese sentiments, and race, capitalism, and dominant discourses of Canadian nationhood (Mawani, 2004). In 2006, the campaign achieved a milestone when the Conservative government issued a formal apology to the Chinese Canadian community, as well as symbolic payments for head tax survivors, and community projects (CCNC, 2006b).

The contrast between the federal government's respective responses to Chinese Head Tax redress and reparations for residential school survivors is consistent with the Canadian state's positioning as a multicultural nation where colonization has been completed and racism exists only in the past. For example, until 2008 the state refused to apologize to residential school survivors, and the agreement in principle that has been reached focuses primarily on individual survivors' experiences. In general, the state's approach fails to contextualize survivors' experiences within colonial structures. Meanwhile, in the campaign for head tax redress, both the campaign and the state's reaction to the campaign reaffirmed official narratives about Canadian nationhood. For instance, as suggested by Mawani (2004: 24), those in the campaign for head tax redress were articulating a critique highlighting Canada's racist nation formation that continued through present-day immigration policies. However, this approach obscured questions around the policies of Indigenous genocide and displacement, which facilitated any Chinese settlement at all. As Lawrence and Dua (2005) note, 'military subjugation of [Cree and Blackfoot] peoples on the plains made possible the settlement of newcomers and was the precondition for restrictions that ensured that the settler population replacing Native peoples would be white' (134). Meanwhile, in the reactions of the courts, the state situated the head tax issue as a blot in the past of an accommodating nation, as evidenced in Prime Minister Stephen Harper's assertion that '[w]e have the collective responsibility to build a country based firmly on the notion of equality of opportunity, regardless of one's race or ethnic origin' (Office of the Prime Minister, 2006). This government's reaction made invisible both ongoing colonial relations and colonial policies that prefaced the development of racist policies.

'Conflicting' Strategy of Resistance: Africville and Reparations for the African Slave Trade

Another issue demonstrating 'conflicting' strategies of resistance is the case of Africville. Africville was a tight-knit African Canadian community on the outskirts of Halifax, Nova Scotia, dating from approximately the mid-1800s (Clairmont and Magill, 1999: 30). It was poorly serviced by the city, and a dumping ground for the city's wastes (McCurdy, 1995). In the 1960s, the community was demolished, without consultation with the residents. Residents were relocated and dispersed with minimal compensation (Clairmont and Magill, 1999). In 2004, a United Nations report by Special Rapporteur Doudou Diène called on the province of Nova Scotia to provide compensation for families who had been displaced. With respect to some of the campaigning that had been happening around this, one NSAHRC member commented: '… you could look at the example of the historic Black movement in the Maritimes, which may sometimes conflict with the Aboriginal people … There was a report from the UN on human rights and they recommended that Africville be recognized and that reparations be made, and they wanted the Indigenous people to support them. And I don't know if that happened to the degree that the community of the Indigenous Black people on the East Coast wanted.'

The 'historic Black movement' in the Maritimes which this member mentions references the movement for reparations for Black Loyalists,[12] who were promised land by the Crown upon relocation to Canada but were later denied this or given poor land, as well as reparations for descendants of the African slave trade. This movement may 'conflict with Aboriginal people' for two reasons. First, as Lawrence and Dua (2005) note, the Mi'kmaq people, who are Indigenous to the Maritimes, fought English settlers for over a century (139). They note furthermore that '[w]ith the 18th-century peace treaties, the British Crown unleashed a concentrated campaign of extermination efforts, including the posting of a bounty for the scalps … "scorched earth" policies to starve out survivors, the absolute denial of land for reserves ... and the accompanying spread of epidemics that brought the Mi'kmaq people to near extinction' (ibid.).

In other words, there is a history of genocidal policies that is easily erased in calls for reparations for descendants of the slave trade. A second reason for conflict is that reparations movements have often included demands for the acquisition of land from the settler state. Reparations for slavery were identified as a priority issue at WCAR, and the tensions between Indigenous communities and Black communities on the land issue were evident. The argument made by Indigenous peoples was that settler states cannot give out land that is not theirs in the first place (Smith, 2005: 47).

Hope in Reparations?

Although these examples may appear to render coalition-building possibilities bleak, some scholars/activists suggest otherwise. Andrea Smith (2005) argues that strategically framed reparations movements can contribute towards radical social transformation. While she is speaking from the American context, her argument is applicable to other settler societies as well: '[M]any of these demands [for reparations]...*strengthen* the demands of white supremacy. Those demands that simply call for individual payments for human rights abuses under slavery do not fundamentally challenge the economic structures that keep people of colour oppressed. In fact, they suggest that by simply paying a lump sum for the injustices it has perpetrated and continues to perpetrate, the U.S. can absolve itself of any responsibility to transform these institutionalized structures of white supremacy' (53; original emphasis).

Developing appropriate resistance strategies is therefore a significant concern necessitating further dialogue on coalition-building between Indigenous communities and communities of colour. Importantly, coalitions learning from the NSAHRC's example may wish to consider how such dialogue may begin and the barriers that may impede it.

Concluding Remarks

The findings presented here demonstrate that the process of working in coalition is complex and messy. The NSAHRC situated itself within anti-racism framework, yet also attempted to centralize Indigenous issues. Indigenous leadership was prioritized, and concrete strategies were developed to ensure the strength of this leadership. The NSAHRC also faced many challenges in its coalition work. There was clearly ambiguity around conceptualizing organizational priorities and concerns. Another challenge was around how to build shared agendas in the face of seemingly conflicting advocacy strategies. In short, the example of the NSAHRC raises critical questions and illustrates some of the contradictions and challenges inherent in coalition work.

NOTES

1 Interviews with NSAHRC members were conducted between May and July 2006. I also draw upon relevant project documents.

2 For example, see http://unitedagainstracism.ca. It is also worth noting that in Western Canada, there may be more Indigenous organizations organized around anti-racism than in Eastern Canada (thanks to Bonita Lawrence for sharing this insight in a personal conversation). This may be because policies of genocide came into effect later in the West than in the East (Lawrence, 2004: 19). As such, Indigenous peoples are, as a whole, more 'visible' in Western Canada than in Eastern Canada (ibid.).

3 This framing can also be challenged. As a subsequent section of this chapter will show, issues around framing were an ongoing point of contention in the NSAHRC. However, my goal here is primarily to show how the NSAHRC resisted mainstream interpretations of the Ahenakew incident.

4 Please refer to the Annual Report on the Operation of the Canadian Multiculturalism Act for details on current priority areas. http://www.cic.gc.ca/multi/rpt/index-eng.asp.

5 Community groups also use funding from other state departments, such as the Department of Justice, as well as arm's-length agencies such as the National Film Board , to carry out projects which may or may not be defined as anti-racist.

6 It is important to note that grassroots mobilizations – such as the campaign Justice for Jeffrey Reodica, a Filipino youth who was shot to death by Toronto Police – have continued to happen alongside the increased institutionalization of anti-racism, often with the support of more established community organizations.

7 Indigenous communities and communities of colour are criminalized and targeted by law enforcement, yet disproportionately experience racialized violence at the hands of the state, law enforcement, and other individuals (e.g., see Tator and Henry, 2006; Chan and Mirchandani, 2002).

8 Some community organizations have used anti-hate activism in more critical ways. For example, see the Council of Agencies Serving South Asians' 'Say No to Hate' project: http://www.cassa.on.ca.

9 According to the Alberta Law Foundation (1996), 'The criminal law in Canada is the responsibility of the federal government … In 1892, the Canadian Parliament passed a law called the Canadian Criminal Code. It was called a Code because it consolidated crimes and criminal law procedure into a single statute. It has been amended and added to many times over the last century.' http://www.law-faqs.org/nat/crimg-01.htm.

10 Some anti-racism organizers have framed their work around equity, rather than equality. Whereas equality suggests an end goal of making everyone 'equal,' the concept of equity is oriented around justice and human rights. The concept of equity can also be problematized; however, it is currently a useful concept for advocacy around race, gender, class, sexuality, and ability.

11 It is important to note that all former students who resided at a recognized Indian Residential School who were alive on 30 May 2005 will be eligible for the Common Experience Payment (CEP). Please refer to: http://www.ainc-inac.gc.ca/ai/rqpi/index-eng.asp.

12 'Loyalists,' according to the Canadian Genealogy Centre, 'refers to American colonists who remained loyal to the British Crown. Many of them served under the British during the American Revolution.' http://www.collectionscanada.ca/genealogy/022-909.003-e.html.

REFERENCES

Backhouse, Constance. 2005. 'Legal Discrimination against the Chinese in Canada: The Historical Framework.' In *Calling Power to Account: Law, Reparations, and the Chinese Canadian Head Tax*, 24–59. David Dyzenhaus and Mayo Moran. Eds. Toronto: University of Toronto Press.

Bolaria, B. Singh, and Li, Peter S. 1988. *Racial Oppression in Canada*. 2d ed. Toronto: Garamond Press.

Carrington, Bruce, and Bonnet, Alastair. 1997. 'The Other Canadian "Mosaic" – "Race" Equity Education in Ontario and British Columbia.' *Comparative Education, 33*(3): 411–31.

Chan, Wendy, and Mirchandani, Kiran. Eds. 2002. *Crimes of Colour: Racialization and the Criminal Justice System*. Peterborough, ON: Broadview Press.

Chinese Canadian National Council. 2006a. *Chinese Canadians Call On Prime Minister to Issue Full Parliamentary Apology*. Press Release. Retrieved 15 January 2007 from http://ccnc.ca/content/pr.php?entry=50.

– 2006 b. *Application Process Announced for Surviving Spouses of Chinese Head Tax Payers*. Press Release. Retrieved 15 January 2007 from http://ccnc.ca/content/pr.php?entry=92.

Clairmont, Donald H., and Magill, Denis W. 1999. *Africville: The Life and Death of a Canadian Black Community*. Toronto: McClelland and Stewart.

Das Gupta, Tania. 1999. 'The Politics of Multiculturalism: Immigrant Women and the Canadian State.' In *Scratching the Surface: Canadian Anti-Racist Feminist Thought*, 187–205. Enakshi Dua and Angela Robertson. Eds. Toronto: Women's Press.

Dei, George J. Sefa. 1996. *Anti-Racism Education: Theory and Practice*. Halifax: Fernwood Press.

Demont, John. 1998. 'Ottawa Says It's Sorry.' *Macleans. 19 January*, 32–3.

Diène, Doudou. 2004. *Report by the Special Rapporteur on Contemporary Forms of Racism, Racial Discrimination, Xenophobia and Related Intolerance: Mission to Canada*. Geneva: UN Office of the High Commissioner for Human Rights.

Dua, Enakshi. 1999. 'Canadian Anti-Racist Feminist Thought: Scratching the Surface of Racism.' In *Scratching the Surface: Canadian Anti-Racist Feminist Thought*, 7–34. Enakshi Dua and Angela Robertson. Eds. Toronto: Women's Press.

Dyzenhaus, David, and Moran, Mayo. Eds. 2005. *Calling Power to Account: Law, Reparations, and the Chinese Canadian Head Tax*. Toronto: University of Toronto Press.

Go, Amy. 1990. 'Chinese Canadian Women and the Effects of the Exclusion Act and the Head Tax.' *Fireweed*, 30 (spring): 20–2.

Go, Avvy. 2005. 'Litigating Justice.' In *Calling Power to Account: Law, Reparations, and the Chinese Canadian Head Tax*, 20–3. David Dyzenhaus and Mayo Moran. Eds. Toronto: University of Toronto Press.

Haig-Brown, Celia. 1988. *Resistance and Renewal: Surviving the Indian Residential School*. Vancouver: Arsenal Pulp Press.

Harney, Stefano. 1996. 'Anti-Racism, Ontario Style.' *Race and Class*, 37(3): 35–45.

Lawrence, Bonita. 2004. *'Real' Indians and Others: Mixed-Blood Urban Native Peoples and Indigenous Nationhood*. Lincoln: University of Nebraska Press.

Lawrence, Bonita, and Dua, Enakshi. 2005. 'Decolonizing Anti-Racism.' *Social Justice, 32*(4): 120–43.

Li, Peter S. 1994. *The Chinese in Canada*. 2d ed. Toronto: Oxford University Press.

Mawani, Renisa. 2004. 'Cleaning the Conscience of the People: Reading Head Tax Redress in a Multicultural Canada.' *Canadian Journal of Law and Society, 19*(2): 127–51.

McCurdy, Howard. 1995. 'Africville: Environmental Racism.' In *Faces of Environmental Racism: Confronting Issues of Global Justice*, 75–91. Laura Westra and Peter S. Wenz. Eds. Lanham, MD: Rowman and Littlefield.

Million, Dian. 2000. 'Telling Secrets: Sex, Power and Narratives in Indian Residential School Histories.' *Canadian Woman Studies 20*(2): 92–104.

Milloy, John. 1999. *A National Crime: The Canadian Government and the Residential School System – 1879 to 1986*. Winnipeg: University of Manitoba.

Monture-Angus, Patricia. 1999. *Journeying Forward: Dreaming First Nations Independence*. Halifax: Fernwood Publishing.

National Secretariat Against Hate and Racism in Canada (NSAHRC). 2004a. *Follow Up Action Plan: IBA/Quebec Native Women's Association 'Hate and Racism in Canada' Conference, 20–23 March 2004*. Retrieved 15 January 2007 from http://www.indigenousbar.ca/pdf/actionplanforsecretariat.pdf.

– 2004b. Meeting Minutes of 30 July 2004. Retrieved 15 January 2007 from http://www.indigenousbar.ca/pdf/IBA%20H&R%20Secretariat%20 FIRST%20MEETING%20july%2030%202004.pdf.

– 2004c. Meeting Minutes of 14 October 2004. Retrieved 15 January 2007 from http://www.indigenousbar.ca/pdf/NSHRC%2014-10-04.pdf.

– 2004d. *NSAHRC Terms of Reference*. Retrieved 15 January 15, 2007, from http://indigenousbar.ca/pdf/nshrctermsofreference.pdf

– 2005. Meeting Minutes of 6 March 2005. Retrieved 15 January 2007 from http://www.indigenousbar.ca/pdf/march6minutes.pdf.

Native Women's Association of Canada (NWAC). 1991. *Aboriginal Women, Self-Government, and the Canadian Charter of Rights and Freedoms in the Context of the 1991 'Canada Package' on Constitutional Reform*. Ottawa: Native Women's Association of Canada.

Office of the Prime Minister. 2006. 'Prime Minister Harper Offers Full Apology for the Chinese Head Tax.' Press release. 22 June.

Robertson, Angela. 1999. 'Continuing on the Ground: Anti-Racist Feminists Discuss Organizing,' In *Scratching the Surface: Canadian Anti-Racist Feminist Thought*, 309–29. Enakshi Dua and Angela Robertson. Eds. Toronto: Women's Press.

Royal Commission on Aboriginal Peoples. 1996. *Report of the Royal Commission on Aboriginal Peoples*. Ottawa: Department of Indian and Northern Affairs Canada.

Siemiatycki, Myer, et al. 2001. *Integrating Community Diversity in Toronto: On Whose Terms?* Toronto: Centre of Excellence for Research on Immigration and Settlement (CERIS).

Simpson, Leanne R. 2004. 'Anticolonial Strategies for the Recovery and Maintenance of Indigenous Knowledge.' *American Indian Quarterly, 28*(3/4): 373–84.

Smith, Andrea. 2006. 'Heteropatriarchy and the Three Pillars of White Supremacy.' In *Color of Violence: The INCITE! Anthology*, 65–73. Incite! Women of Color Against Violence. Ed. Cambridge, MA: South End Press.

Tator, Carol, and Henry, Frances. 2006. *Racial Profiling in Canada: Challenging the Myth of 'A Few Bad Apples.'* Toronto: University of Toronto Press.

Thobani, Sunera. 2007. *Exalted Subjects: Studies in the Making of Race and Nation in Canada.* Toronto: University of Toronto Press.

United Against Racism. 2005. *United Against Racism.* Retrieved 15 January 2007 from http://unitedagainstracism.ca.

United Nations Permanent Forum on Indigenous Issues. 2006. *United Nations Permanent Forum on Indigenous Issues.* Retrieved 15 January 2007 from http://www.un.org/esa/socdev/unpfii.

Wallis, Maria, et al. 1988. 'Defining the Issues on Our Terms: Gender, Race and State: Interviews with Racial Minority Women.' *Resources for Feminist Research,* 17(3): 43–8.

17 What New Relationship? Taking Responsibility for Justice and Sustainability in British Columbia

CAITLYN VERNON

> The relationship we seek will not blossom until you yourself are blossoming with the struggles and insights of the colonized. You have been held at gunpoint by the empire too? The fact gives you more depth for this task of understanding.
>
> – Chellis Glendinning, *Off the Map*

My story begins at an inner-city school in East Vancouver. To me, the daughter of first- and second-generation white immigrants to Canada, my Native friends seemed no more or less located in place than my Chinese, Pakistani, and Italian schoolmates or my own family. In retrospect, it seemed that we had all been transplanted there, disconnected from our history and our ancestors. I grew up knowing this place had once had huge Douglas fir trees and salmon streams, but not that I was walking on land shared by the Squamish, the Musqueam, and the Tsleil'waututh First Nations. Throughout my childhood, I was surrounded by communities struggling for peace and justice: for women, for workers, and for the environment. Working to end oppression, but not seeing with my young eyes that we ourselves were also oppressors. I didn't know that the apartheid system in South Africa that we protested against had been modelled after Canada's system of Indian reserves. And I didn't see that my family and I were benefiting from the actions of a colonial state that promoted settler[1] interests at the expense of Aboriginal peoples and the health of their land.

And now that I begin to see this, how can I be an ally with Aboriginal peoples? How do those of us in settler society, descendents of immigrants both old and new, stop oppressing First Nations? The wealth of British Columbia's settler society has in part been built by exploiting both the labour and the land of the many First Nations who call this province home. How do we stop exploiting the land that supports us all, in a way that reduces rather than exacerbates oppression and inequalities?

This chapter develops a theoretical framework for one mechanism through which these questions may be addressed: socially just and ecologically sustainable shared decision-making. I then use this framework to assess whether the 'New Relationship,' an agreement between the BC Liberal government and First Nations political alliances in BC, transforms colonial relationships or re-frames, and therefore perpetuates, unjust relations. Does the New Relationship reflect a transformation in how economic benefits are distributed, how decisions are made about the land, and how communities and ecosystems are sustained?

To answer these questions, I turned to contemporary and theoretical literature and also conducted a series of oral interviews.[2] While my focus is the relationship between First Nations' political alliances and the BC provincial government, my recommendations relate more broadly to how Aboriginal and non-Aboriginal peoples can together make decisions about the land in a way that reduces oppressions without exacerbating ecological unsustainabilities.

Theoretical Framework: Shared Decision-Making and Economic Throughput

In an attempt to resolve the social and ecological conflicts that have arisen as a result of resource management practices, the British Columbia provincial government initiated a variety of multi-stakeholder processes during the 1990s to enhance public involvement of both Aboriginal and non-Aboriginal peoples in land-use planning and resource management decision-making. While these initiatives in theory represented a step towards increasing public participation and have delivered some ecological and operational benefits, their implementation has been critiqued on a number of grounds, including: the extent to which participants are limited to an advisory capacity while government retains decision-making authority; the exclusion of controversial issues such as the annual allowable cut from deliberations; the ecological unsustainability of the decisions made; and the extent to which the processes effectively serve to legitimize existing land-use practices (Mascarenhas and Scarce, 2004; M'Gonigle, 2002; M'Gonigle et al., 2001).

The dual goals of ecological sustainability and social justice must underlie shared decision-making processes. Ecological sustainability (the long-term maintenance of ecological integrity in ecosystems around the world)[3] requires both a new economic paradigm that recognizes the ecological limits to growth, and a shift away from cultural constructions of the environment as separate from humans. Social justice must be situated within these ecological constraints, and is defined here as equal rights for all peoples, compensation for historical injustices, a re-allocation of decision-making authority, a reduction of the income gap, and an equitable distribution of benefits from resource management through a redistribution of wealth both within and between generations. Any discussion of resource management decision-making must consider both the *process* of who makes the decisions and how, and the *outcome* which depends not only on the process but also on the values of decision-makers and on overarching legal and economic structures.

The concept of economic throughput is central to determining what decision-making process would lead to outcomes that are both socially just and ecologically sustainable. Throughput is the linear flow of materials and energy from ecosystem sources such as mines, forests, and fisheries; through the human economy in production, transportation, consumption, and disposal; to end up in ecosystem sinks for waste such as oceans, dumps, and the atmosphere (Daly and Farley, 2004). Because throughput is linear, consumption involves the irreversible transformation of raw materials and energy into waste.

The concept of throughput highlights a fundamental contradiction inherent in neoclassical economics, which sees the ecosystem as a subset of an infinitely expanding economy and assumes that we can address ecological concerns through economic growth (see Figure 17.1). Contemporary Canadian political leaders from all parties repeatedly state that we can save the environment *and* have economic growth. But in our finite world, there are limits to what we can extract or dump back as waste before the global ecosystem loses its ability to recover from disturbance. When we recognize that the human economy must be constrained within ecological limitations, continuous economic growth (measured as growth in throughput) is no longer possible. Ecological economics presents an alternative model that recognizes the economy as embedded within a finite ecosystem (see Figure 17.2). We need not just become more efficient in our use of raw materials, but also more frugal, in order to decrease the supply of inputs required. Importantly, an end to growth does not imply an end to development per se, since development can be qualitative and measured as the ability to increase human well-being within a sustainable throughput.[4]

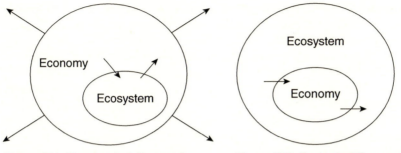

Figure 17.1 Neoclassical Economics   Figure 17.2 Ecological Economics

The implications of throughput for social justice are significant. The continuous growth model assumes that inequities will be addressed by allocating a larger share of the growing pie to First Nations; that is, as overall economic growth increases, First Nations will be able to increase their economic activity without settlers having to change or give anything up. But once we recognize the pie is finite, justice requires a *redistribution* of wealth. A sustainable scale of throughput requires the total amount of economic activity controlled by settler society to decrease, while concurrently providing an increase in economic opportunities for First Nations within a transition strategy towards a resource efficient economy that reduces everyone's dependence on unsustainable throughput.

Just and sustainable shared decision-making about land and resources requires both Aboriginal and non-Aboriginal decision-makers to have the *ability* to reduce the rate and amount of throughput. This ability depends on the autonomy of decision-makers to redefine progress in a way that privileges qualitative over quantitative development. This autonomy in turn depends on government policies and regulations, specifically regarding the balance of power between centralized governments and rural communities, both settler and First Nation. Within a system of centralized resource management, resources flow in one direction from rural to urban, while decisions are made in urban centres where consumption is the highest and where decision-makers are removed from the consequences of their decisions. Rural communities are excluded from decision-making and denied the political power to resist the liquidation of local resources and the accompanying socio-economic stress (M'Gonigle, 2002, Rees and Westra, 2003). A re-balancing of decision-making power between centralized governments and rural communities improves community stability, rural employment, and ecological sustainability. For example, rural communities could set the annual allowable cut for forestry in their regions at a level that maintains water quality and other non-timber forest values. Communities could choose to focus on qualitative development by enhancing the local circulation of goods and services and producing less for export.

Enabling a reduction in throughput requires a shift in who makes the decisions. But changing the institutional, regulatory, and economic environment to allow decision-makers the option to reduce throughput does not necessarily mean that they will choose to do so. For shared decision-making to reduce socio-economic inequities while sustaining ecosystems, both Aboriginal and non-Aboriginal decision-makers must also have the *desire* to reduce throughput. For this, they must first have a willingness to decrease overall levels of consumption, which in turn requires a reconceptualization of progress such that progress no longer equals economic growth. Second, choosing to reduce throughput requires an ecological citizenship in which we recognize that we have both *rights* to use the land as needed within sustainable limits, and *responsibilities* to ensure we are not depleting the ability of the resource to provide for future generations or other species. This means moving beyond seeing ourselves as separate from some external environment and instead as interconnected with the places in which we live. In the Haudenosaunee Thanksgiving Address, Jake Swamp (see Chapter 1, this volume) talks about the connection of all life, saying, 'For we are not better than a blade of grass or a leaf on a tree. We are all life forms. If nature goes down, we go down with it. Because we are only one part of that life form.'

Third, because unsustainable resource management practices are rooted in exploitative relations between settler society and First Nations, developing sustainable relations to the natural world requires addressing and resolving unjust colonial relations amongst humans.[5] This challenge is illuminated by Jake Swamp's words, that the hardest thing to overcome, so that everything we do works with the cycle of nature, is the prejudice and the anger that we have towards each other. To do so, he says, 'involves so much forgiveness, it involves so much humanity.' Finally, a reduction in throughput requires a transformation of the decision-making process: it is not enough to simply gather people around a table without establishing process mechanisms to respect and incorporate multiple forms of knowledge, values, and ways of participating, and seek to remove power imbalances that privilege some over others.[6]

Implementing these criteria for socially just and ecologically sustainable shared decision-making processes would signify a profound shift from how resource management decisions are currently made in British Columbia. Given the colonial context and the drive for continual economic growth, decision-making over BC's natural resources has historically neither enabled a reduction in throughput nor encouraged the desire to do so. The next section explores the ability of the New Relationship to transform resource management decision-making in BC.

The New Relationship: Transformative Change or More of the Same?

The Old Relationship

Two stories tell the history of British Columbia. The settler story is one of development, in which 'unused' land was put to better use and Native peoples were given the 'opportunity' to become 'civilized' (Harris, 2002). White reserve commissioners laid out the boundaries of Indian reserves, constraining Native access to land and opening up the country for sale. Forestry, fishing, and mining practices operated from the assumption that resources were inexhaustible and economic growth was limitless. Progress was equated with incorporating First Nations into the immigrant economy as producers and consumers.

The Aboriginal story is one of dispossession, in which their land was taken away and the little left to them was insufficient to live on (Alfred, 2005). The size and location of Indian reserves functioned to deny First Nations access to land and push them into the workforce (Harris, 2002). The impacts of colonialism, manifest in below average health, education, and employment statistics of First Nations in BC, 'are a direct result of the theft of their lands' (Alfred, 2005: 154). And yet, despite Indian reserves, the Indian Act, residential schools, racial discrimination, and drastic depopulation, First Nations have resisted assimilation and struggled to defend their rights and lands. To this day, First Nations across the province of British Columbia continue to assert their Aboriginal rights and title through legal challenges, treaty negotiations, and direct action.

Environmental exploitation that continues to threaten and endanger species and ecosystems underlies this story of dispossession. Corporate control and centralized decision-making of resource management has valued short-term profits above ecological integrity and has marginalized both Aboriginal and non-Aboriginal rural communities. In both fisheries and forestry, employment has decreased while the rate and amount of resource extraction has increased, leading to chronic socio-economic instability in rural resource communities while great wealth has accumulated in the hands of non-Aboriginal peoples.[7] As both the resources and the financial benefits are exported elsewhere, a struggle has arisen for increased local control over resources and for ecosystem-based management.

In short, denial of Aboriginal rights and title, socio-economic in-equalities, and ecological degradation are the legacy of colonial concep-tions of progress that continue to shape the present. It is in this context that the New Relationship has arisen as an attempt to rectify social in-justices and ecological concerns through more meaningful involvement of First Nations in natural resource management.

The Promise of New Relations

> We are all here to stay. We agree to a new government-to-government re-lationship based on respect, recognition and accommodation of Aboriginal title and rights. Our shared vision includes respect for our respective laws and responsibilities. Through this new relationship, we commit to recon-ciliation of Aboriginal and Crown titles and jurisdictions.

So begins the vision statement of 'The New Relationship,' an agreement between the province of British Columbia and the First Nations Leadership Council[8] (British Columbia, 2005a). The New Relationship intends to improve economic, social, and cultural opportunities for Aboriginal people, involve First Nations in natural resource management through shared decision-making about the land and resources, and share the benefits from resource-related activities so that First Nations can join in the economic development of BC. The New Relationship has been wide-ly lauded as a step towards significant change for First Nations, and there has been a sustained effort from both the Province and First Nations to work together and implement the agreement.

All of the individuals I interviewed agreed that a major impetus to develop the New Relationship arose from the desire by the provincial government, industry, and some First Nations to secure access to lands and resources for economic development. By 2005, overlapping Native land claims were threatening the political, economic, and social stabil-ity of BC by creating an uncertain business climate that caused a signifi-cant loss of investment, jobs, and wealth in the province (Council of Forest Industries, 2001; Rossiter and Wood, 2005). This uncertainty was compounded by the failure of the BC treaty process to reach any lasting agreements, rulings by the Supreme Court of Canada that government and industry were not adequately consulting First Nations,[9] the challenging of BC forestry agreements in the courts, and the increasing political mobilization of First Nations. Socio-economic disparities were deepening and the upcoming 2010 Olympics were putting pressure on the provincial government to improve its image regarding Aboriginal relations. It is in this context that the provincial government came to understand that it must deal more honourably with First Nations if economic development is to continue.

The political, economic, and legal pressures leading up to the New Relationship acted to shift the Province's stance away from its long-standing denial of Aboriginal rights and title and towards recognition. This shift has given hope to many First Nations. Indeed, many aspects of the New Relationship signal a transformation of relations between First Nations and settler society in BC that shifts the balance of power towards First Nations and begins to address historical injustices. At the outset, the provincial government entered into the New Relationship discussions in response to court decisions regarding consultation, but the First Nations Leadership Council managed to broaden the scope of the agreement. Areas of the provincial mandate that have been opened through this process include recognition of Aboriginal title, the commitment to address past injustices, and the emphasis on shared decision-making. The talk of revenue sharing, in recognition that the wealth generated from resource management in the province is largely taken out of First Nations' unceded traditional territories, is intended to provide increased economic opportunities for impoverished First Nations communities. One interviewee from the provincial government applauded the new 'climate of cooperation' that exists in these discussions. An Aboriginal interviewee emphasized the importance of having achieved a process that recognizes that First Nations still exist as governments. From the perspective of a non-profit organization working in solidarity with First Nations, another interviewee said that the New Relationship 'creates a mechanism for quite transformative law reform around issues like land-use planning, land protection, shared decision-making, and real benefit sharing.'

In contrast to previous attempts by the provincial government to erase colonial history from the official discourse, the New Relationship explicitly recognizes that 'the historical Aboriginal-Crown relationship in British Columbia has given rise to the present socio-economic disparity between First Nations and other British Columbians' (British

Columbia, 2005a), and sets out to close this gap. The BC Liberal government demonstrated its commitment to the New Relationship by quickly allocating $100 million for a New Relationship Trust Fund, to assist First Nation communities to enhance their capacity to participate in the process and in activities that arise from the New Relationship (British Columbia, 2006). Significantly, the provincial government has committed to review its approach to litigation, so that the Crown's legal defences will no longer be premised on the denial of First Nations as a people and Aboriginal title and rights (First Nations Leadership Council, 2006). Overall, the New Relationship represents a major shift on the part of the BC Liberal government.

One First Nations interviewee suggested that what was overcome in the New Relationship was 'the racism of the people in government and their supporters, to allow First Nations to be capitalists' also. Thus, under the New Relationship racial discrimination should no longer exclude First Nations from economic development projects. Revenue-sharing and shared decision-making are the proposed mechanisms for inclusion. Regarding shared decision-making the New Relationship states:

> We agree to establish processes and institutions for shared decision-making about the land and resources and for revenue and benefit sharing, recognizing, as has been determined in court decisions, that the right to Aboriginal title 'in its full form', including the inherent right for the community to make decisions as to the use of the land and therefore the right to have a political structure for making those decisions, is constitutionally guaranteed by Section 35. (British Columbia, 2005a)

An interviewee representing a First Nations community stated that after trying to get the provincial government to share management for so many years, the fact that the Premier is finally talking about shared decision-making is hugely significant. But can the shared decision-making as proposed in the New Relationship transform the way decisions are made about the land, the way economic benefits are distributed, or the way communities and ecosystems are sustained?

Is It a New Relationship?

All of the interviewees saw the possibilities for transformed relations arising from the New Relationship. However, as one First Nations person said, 'We've opened the door a crack, but I really think we need to kick it open.' Many interviewees questioned whether the agreement could move beyond good words to actually changing realities at the community level. Specifically, does the shared decision-making in the New Relationship enable a reduction in throughput or encourage decision-makers to choose to reduce throughput?

Shared decision-making under the New Relationship might enable a reduction in overall throughput if First Nations making resource management decisions in their territories choose to redefine development to occur within sustainable limits. This possibility is supported by the First Nations' vision, articulated in the New Relationship, of restoring habitats and ensuring responsible and sustainable resource use. However the many different interpretations of shared decision-making put into question the extent of power-sharing implied. Government officials downplay the significance of the term, insisting that there is a distinction between shared decision-making and 'joint decision-making,' or 'co-management' (Leyne, 2005). The government talks less about shared decision-making and more about its hopes that 'the New Relationship will find its home in jointly designed consultation and accommodation arrangements over lands and resources and social policy' (British Columbia, 2005b). A forest industry interviewee expressed that his vision for shared decision-making is multi-sectoral land-use planning with First Nation participation, where the provincial government continues to make the final decision. But an Aboriginal interviewee said that beyond consultation or participation in land-use planning, it is important for First Nations to have a say in statutory decisions such as setting the annual allowable cut. Thus, there are widely differing expectations regarding shared decision-making. The willingness of the Province to rebalance decision-making power with First Nations is as yet unclear, as is the possibility of reducing throughput.

For the most part, the New Relationship gives little indication that decision-makers will be encouraged to choose to reduce throughput. Only in the First Nations' goals is there any mention of taking responsibility for human actions within the natural world. Yet the rhetoric surrounding the New Relationship Trust Fund has focused on the capacity-building required for First Nations to participate in (unsustainable) government-led resource management and economic development. And in the high-level New Relationship discussions, occurring far from the resources and communities in question, there is little change to the process by which decisions get made, despite the inclusion of First Nations. One interviewee from a non-profit organization suggested that the Province is trying to redirect First Nations' resources away from oppositional activities into a dialogue that it can control and that provides some semblance of certainty in the meantime, saying that once the First Nation leadership gathers 'around the table talking … other forms of engagement stop because they don't have a lot of resources.' Meanwhile, development projects continue to deplete resources throughout the province without sufficient First Nations involvement or consultation.

Thus the New Relationship and the accompanying rhetoric give little encouragement to reduce throughput or redefine progress. More likely, the emphasis of the provincial government and some First Nations leaders on achieving certainty of access to land and resources for economic development, and the involvement of business interests in the New Relationship discussions, will serve to maintain a high rate of resource extraction without taking responsibility for the ecological impacts of human actions. While some First Nations and settlers voice opposition to this trajectory of development, many support the emphasis on economic growth.[10] As one First Nations interviewee put it, 'White people have realized that brown people can be just as good capitalists and rapers of the forest as anybody else.'

Indeed, the vision of Aboriginal citizenship harboured by BC's Liberal government 'turns squarely on an economic logic that identifies participation in regimes of capitalist accumulation as the ultimate sign of equality' (Rossiter and Wood, 2005: 364). As long as progress is equated with quantitative economic growth, decision-makers will not choose to reduce throughput.

Further, the talk in the New Relationship of distributing the benefits from future resource extraction does not consider redistribution of past or present wealth. Nor is there mention of reparations, and settler society is in no way required or requested to give anything up. The talk of 'closing the gap' is only about steps 'up' for First Nations and there is no discussion of steps 'down' that the rest of us need to make; and if there is no change in our levels of consumption, then there will be no decrease in throughput.

Overall, the basis of the New Relationship is conventional resource management but with greater First Nations involvement. The goal is economic assimilation, the same as it has been throughout BC's history. As one interviewee stated, to be truly transformative the New Relationship would have to be about more than just 'adding Indigenous people to the global economy and stirring.' Instead, the promotion of economic assimilation by the New Relationship represents a form of hegemonic persuasion.

Hegemony occurs when 'public consensus about social reality is created by the dominant class, whereby those in power persuade the majority to consent to decisions that are disempowering or not benefiting the majority' (marino, 1997: 105). Overall, the New Relationship appears to perpetuate the belief that economic development as typically defined (growth in material throughput) and resource management as typically practiced (ecologically unsustainable with decreasing jobs per biomass produced) is beneficial to all, when in fact the majority of the population as well as the natural world suffer while a small minority benefits. Those who are oppressed by this system consent to believe that these benefits will eventually reach everyone.

In this way, the New Relationship articulates the language of persuasion and consent that serves to maintain neoliberal economic dominance and ensure that no reduction in throughput is considered. The unquestioned goal of continued economic growth, manifested as the quest for economic certainty, is an example of 'common sense:' 'oppression so deeply embedded in a culture that it is assumed to be natural and inevitable' (marino, 1997:127). Willems-Braun (1996: 23) suggests that by not questioning the colonial geography of Indian reserves on which the BC economy is founded, the economy appears autonomous from colonial legacies and 'efforts to deal with the underdevelopment of Native communities have taken the form of "appending" or "incorporating" Native interests into an economy that ... is presumed to pre-exist, rather than to be built upon, Native marginalization.'

By conceding to some First Nations demands, or at least appearing to, the provincial government has diffused First Nations political mobilization while maintaining the benefits and privileges enjoyed by settler society. Comparing the $100 million allocated for the New Relationship Trust Fund to the billions of dollars spent on ecologically and culturally damaging industrial developments in BC, and the billions of dollars worth of resources that have been extracted from First Nations territories, Gerald Amos (2007) from the Haisla Nation notes: 'If money is the measure, then this government remains far more committed to the old relationships with industry, than to a new relationship with First Nations.' The New Relationship promotes an increase in development opportunities for First Nations as is necessary for social justice, but without the corresponding decrease in economic activity of settler society that a sustainable scale economy would require.

As Amos (2007) notes, 'the New Relationship needs to be about more than money – it must be about sharing leadership and responsibility for the health and survival of our People and the heath and survival of all Peoples with whom we share the earth's thin layer of atmosphere.' To be transformative, the New Relationship will need to implement shared decision-making that enables a reduction in throughput and encourages participants to take responsibility for their choices and actions as ecological citizens. This requires a truly new relationship: one that rebalances power, redistributes wealth and land, and reconceptualises progress to mean qualitative development. Transforming relations requires more than offering a few opportunities within a system that perpetuates injustice.

A Way Forward: Recommendations for a Transformative Relationship

Support for Aboriginal peoples must reflect upon, and act to change, the ways in which settler society is complicit in perpetuating colonial injustices. Settler privilege depends upon the dispossession of First Nations' land and the marginalization of First Nations from decision-making. Settler society is not monolithic and contains oppressive relations, for example, towards women, workers, and rural communities, but all settlers have benefited to varying degrees from the dispossession of First Nations and all must consider what will lead to more equitable relations. Further, because the oppression of First Nations enables, and is a consequence of, the exploitation of natural resources, redress of socio-economic injustices in the New Relationship must be made in conjunction with the goal of ecological sustainability.

Decreasing Consumption

Reducing material throughput is an ecological imperative that will come about either by intentional choice or inadvertently once we surpass the ability of an ecosystem to sustain itself. To maintain the human economy within ecological limits, natural resource decision-making under the New Relationship must focus on what to leave, not what to take.

Ecosystem-based management, which 'situates economic and political processes *within* the bounds of maintaining ecological integrity,' is one mechanism to constrain human exploitation of the natural world and limit the throughput to a sustainable level (M'Gonigle et al., 2001:

13, original emphasis; see also Allen, 2005). Ecosystem-based management bridges the dichotomy of conservation versus development, allowing the possibility of an intermediate path that recognizes humans as part of the ecosystem and focuses on managing human activities rather than managing ecosystems. The likelihood of ecosystem-based management and a reduction in throughput is increased by community-based management that brings decision-makers into closer contact with the implications of their decisions (M'Gonigle et al., 2001).

Ecosystem-based management must be accompanied by a transition strategy to redistribute the benefits of reduced throughput to poorer communities and thereby avoid 'eco-apartheid,' which is the maintenance of current uneven power relations and unequal levels of consumption (Rees and Westra, 2003). The burden of decreasing throughput must fall on those with wealth, to allow an increase in consumption (i.e., both qualitative *and* quantitative development) for impoverished First Nations communities. For this to occur within a sustainability framework, the total throughput of settler society must decrease: we must be willing to make do with less.

Shared Decision-Making

A truly new relationship includes a redistribution of land to First Nations.[11] On lands not returned, there must be a sharing of decision-making authority for the management of land and natural resources. A First Nations interviewee put it bluntly: 'Are they [the non-Aboriginal governments] prepared to recognize that they don't have absolute jurisdiction?'

Shared decision-making that rectifies socio-economic disparities while maintaining ecological integrity is not co-management as it has been implemented in BC, where the decision-making role is delegated and government retains the final say. Nor is it participatory planning processes that aim to increase public involvement in resource management decision-making. It is not consultation or accommodation of First Nations by government and industry, where First Nations are given short time frames to review predetermined plans. Nor is it innovative tenure arrangements, such as Aboriginal tenure or community forestry, where government sets the rate of harvest. Rather, the shared decision-making framework that must be adopted by the New Relationship is that of co-jurisdiction, where there is equal decision-making authority between First Nations and the non-Aboriginal government on a government-to-government basis.[12] For example, co-jurisdiction would mean that in its traditional territory a First Nation would have equal decision-making power with the non-Aboriginal government to set the rate of throughput such as the annual allowable cut. Co-jurisdictional shared decision-making requires settler governments to relinquish some of their decision-making authority. Further, to address both social inequalities *and* ecological limitations co-jurisdictional shared decision-making must allow the flexibility to reduce the rate and amount of material throughput through the economy, and must be structured and envisioned in such a way that decision-makers consider doing so.

Being an Ally

Being an ally means more than just offering our support to Aboriginal peoples' struggles – it means making changes in our own lives. Those of us who are settlers to British Columbia have directly or indirectly supported, and have benefited from, racist and genocidal government policies towards First Nations. Developing new relationships with Aboriginal peoples today means knowing the past and bearing witness to the present, apologizing for our shared histories and taking responsibility for our own complicity, offering compensation and working together to build new relations. Building new relationships means addressing the balance of power and challenging the privileges of settler society.

Developing a truly new relationship means recognizing that progress as we have traditionally defined it comes at a cost: our model of economic growth requires the exploitation of land and people. We need a new definition of progress that no longer naturalizes the exploitation of First Nations and the natural world as a necessary part of development. To stop exploiting the land that supports us all, in a way that reduces rather than exacerbates oppression of First Nations, we must reduce material throughput by implementing ecosystem-based management, constrain the consumption patterns of the wealthy, and redistribute the benefits of natural resource stewardship more equally among peoples both within and between nations, and between present and future generations. We must implement co-jurisdictional shared decision-making processes that re-balance power between First Nations and non-Aboriginal peoples, that give decision-makers the authority to set the level of material throughput, that reconceptualize progress, and that shift our understanding of our place in the natural world such that we take responsibilities for our actions and choose to limit the rate of throughput to a sustainable scale.

We can build this new relationship by forming alliances between environmental and Indigenous rights movements that understand interlocking oppressions, situate our analysis within ecological constraints, and frame our collective struggles accordingly. More generally, the responsibility lies with each of us in settler society; to be an ally with First Nations we must choose our actions based on the combined perspective of solidarity and ecological sustainability. As we journey into what Glendinning (2002:158) calls 'the uncharted territory that lies between empire and colonization,' as she recommends, we must humble ourselves, learn the stories of the oppressed and learn our own family histories, listen to others with respect, challenge our assumptions of entitlement, and learn to work together, to take responsibility for both justice and sustainability.

NOTES

1 I use the term 'settlers' to refer to all non-Aboriginal immigrants to British Columbia.

2 Observations are from research conducted for my Major Research Paper, Master of Environmental Studies, York University. In 2006 I conducted nine semi-structured interviews with representatives from the provincial government, forest industry, non-profit organizations, and First Nations individuals with community-level, political, and academic affiliations. The contemporary commentary that I reviewed included newspaper and magazine coverage, as well as press releases, promotional material, web and print publications, and other reports from the provincial government, the BC Treaty process, BC businesses, non-profit organizations, and First Nations organizations.

3 Ecological integrity is the diversity of components, functions, and structures, and the ability of an ecosystem to absorb and recover from disturbance (Allen, 2005).

4 Policy-makers use the total quantity of economic activity, the gross domestic product (GDP), to assess the welfare of Canadians under the assumption that economic growth leads to increased well-being, without accounting for the social and ecological costs involved. Yet 'GDP-based measures were never meant to be used as a measure of progress,' in particular because 'activities that degrade our quality of life, like crime, pollution, and addictive gambling, all make the economy grow' (Genuine Progress Index Atlantic, 2007, at www.gpiatlantic.org). Further, the GDP counts the depletion of natural resources as

an economic gain that is assumed to contribute to human welfare. The absurdity of the assumption that *all* economic activity improves human well-being and that unpaid activities have no bearing has led to the development of alternative indicators of progress and well-being. Some, such as the Genuine Progress Index (GPI), assign an economic value to unpaid volunteer and household work, environmental quality, population health, livelihood security, equity, free time, and educational attainment, in order to more accurately measure our societal well-being. To this end, the GPI counts sickness, crime, and pollution as costs not gains. Other measures of well-being are more qualitative, and avoid assigning monetary values to all aspects of life. For example, Kovel (2002) measures societal well-being by the extent to which communities have the autonomy to focus on maximizing use-value (the satisfaction of human needs, expressed qualitatively) in place of exchange-value (the exchangeability of a commodity, expressed only in quantitative terms and as money). Likewise, Mies and Bennholdt-Thomsen (1999) replace the goal of sustainability (so often used to mean sustainable growth, where growth implies increasing throughput) with a focus on subsistence, the indicators of which are independence, self-sufficiency, and self-reliance.

5 See, for example, Agyeman et al., 2003; Braun, 2002; Kovel, 2002; Rees and Westra, 2003.
6 See, for example, Guijt and Shah, 1998; Kapoor, 2001; Kothari, 2001.
7 See, for example, M'Gonigle et al., 2001.
8 The First Nations Leadership Council consists of the First Nations Summit, the Union of BC Indian Chiefs, and the BC Assembly of First Nations.
9 Haida Nation v. British Columbia and Weyerhaeuser (Nov. 2004); and Taku River Tlingit First Nation v. British Columbia (Nov. 2004).
10 See Alfred (2005) for a discussion of how a 'comprador class' of First Nations, cultivated by settler society, have adopted the economic model of settler society.
11 See Alfred, 2005; and Harris, 2002.
12 Clogg et al. (2004) recommend co-jurisdictional territorial land-use decision-making bodies as the appropriate mechanism for the implementation of ecosystem-based management.

REFERENCES

Agyeman, Julien, Robert D. Bullard, and Bob Evans. 2003. 'Joined-up Thinking: Bringing Together Sustainability, Environmental Justice and Equity.' In *Just Sustainabilities: Development in an Unequal World*, 1–18. Julien Agyeman, Robert D. Bullard, and Bob Evans. Eds. London: Earthscan Publications.

Alfred, Taiaiake. 2005. *Wasáse: Indigenous Pathways to Action and Freedom*. Peterborough, ON: Broadview Press.

Allen, Robert Prescott. 2005. *Review Report*. Coast Information Team. http://www.citbc.org.

Amos, Gerald. 2007. Speech at the First Nations Energy Summit. Vancouver. 2 April.

Braun, Bruce. 2002. *The Intemperate Rainforest: Nature, Culture, and Power on Canada's West Coast*. Minneapolis: University of Minnesota Press.

British Columbia. 2005a. 'The New Relationship.' Ministry of Aboriginal Relations and Reconciliation. http://www.gov.bc.ca/arr/popt/the_new_relationship.htm.

British Columbia. 2005b. Ministry of Aboriginal Relations and Reconciliation. [Speech by] Hon. Tom Christensen, minister of Aboriginal Relations and Reconciliation [to] BC Assembly of First Nations, 2nd BC Regional Chiefs Assembly, 18 October. Victoria, BC: Ministry of Aboriginal Relations and Reconciliation], 17p.pdf. Legislative Library of British Columbia.

British Columbia. 2006. '$100 Million Enables First Nations to Build Capacity.' Press release. 21 March. http://www.gov.bc.ca/arr/popt/the_new_relationship.htm.

Clogg, Jessica, George Hoberg, and Aran O'Carroll. 2004. *Policy and Institutional Analysis for Implementation of the Ecosystem-Based Management Framework*. Coast Information Team. http://www.citbc.org/pubpcit.html.

Council of Forest Industries. 2001. *Resolving Aboriginal Land Claims*. Position paper. Vancouver: Council of Forest Industries.

Daly, Herman E., and Joshua Farley. 2004. *Ecological Economics: Principles and Applications*. Washington, DC: Island Press.

First Nations Leadership Council. 2006. *Information Bulletin* 1(2) (March).

Glendinning, Chellis. 2002. *Off the Map: An Expedition Deep into Empire and the Global Economy*. Gabriola Island, BC: New Society Publishers.

Guijt, Irene, and Meera Kaul Shah. Eds. 1998. *The Myth of Community: Gender Issues in Participatory Development*. London: Intermediate Technology Publications.

Harris, Cole. 2002. *Making Native Space: Colonialism, Resistance, and Reserves in British Columbia*. Vancouver: UBC Press.

Kapoor, Ilan. 2001. 'Towards Participatory Environmental Management?' *Journal of Environmental Management*, 63: 269–79.

Kothari, Uma. 2001. 'Power, Knowledge and Social Control in Participatory Development.' In *Participation: The New Tyranny?* Bill Cooke and Uma Kothari. Eds. London: Zed Books.

Kovel, Joel. 2002. *The Enemy of Nature: The End of Capitalism or the End of the World?* Halifax: Fernwood Publishing.

Leyne, Les. 2005. 'A New Take on Aboriginal Concerns.' *Times Colonist Victoria*. 25 June, A10.

marino, dian. 1997. *Wild Garden: Art, Education, and the Culture of Resistance*. Toronto: Between the Lines.

Mascarenhas, Michael, and Rik Scarce. 2004. '"The Intention Was Good": Legitimacy, Consensus-Based Decision Making, and the Case of Forest Planning in British Columbia, Canada.' *Society and Natural Resources*, 17 (1).

M'Gonigle, R. Michael. 2002. 'Somewhere between Centre and Territory: Exploring a Nodal Site in the Struggle against Vertical Authority and Horizontal Flows.' In *A Political Space: Reading the Global through Clayoquot Sound*, 121–38. Warren Magnusson and Karena Shaw. Eds. Montreal: McGill-Queen's University Press.

M'Gonigle, R. Michael, Brian Egan, and Lisa Ambus (principal investigators), and Heather Mahony, David Boyd, and Brian Evans (co-investigators). 2001. *When There's a Way, There's a Will, Report 1: Developing Sustainability Through the Community Ecosystem Trust*. Victoria, BC: Eco-Research Chair of Environmental Law and Policy, University of Victoria.

Mies, Maria, and Veronika Bennholdt-Thomsen. 1999. *The Subsistence Perspective: Beyond the Globalized Economy*. London and New York: Zed Books.

Rees, William E., and Laura Westra. 2003. 'When Consumption Does Violence: Can There Be Sustainability and Environmental Justice in a Resource-limited World?' In *Just Sustainabilities: Development in an Unequal World*, 99–124. Justin Agyeman, Robert D. Bullard, and Bob Evans. Eds. London: Earthscan Publications.

Rossiter, David, and Patricia K. Wood. 2005. 'Fantastic Topographies: Neoliberal Responses to Aboriginal Land Claims in British Columbia.' *Canadian Geographer*, 49 (4): 352–66.

Willems-Braun, Bruce. 1996. 'Colonial Vestiges: Representing Forest Landscapes on Canada's West Coast.' *BC Studies*, 1(12) (winter): 5–39.

18 Re-Envisioning Collaborative Conservation through Indigenous Knowledges in Guyana

TANYA CHUNG TIAM FOOK

In the world's protected areas that overlap Indigenous territories, biodiversity conservation is not simply about the protection and sustainable management of environmental resources. Conservation also involves a dialectical relationship between peoples and their social-ecological environments that is historically grounded in specific knowledge forms, cultural articulations, and politico-ecological contexts (Chung Tiam Fook, 2006). Its discourse and policy have also become contested terrain in terms of how differentially positioned social groups choose to claim, define, and embody discourses and practices of wildlife conservation according to their respective world views and epistemic contexts. Yet, most of the empirical and case study literature on the tensions within conservation tends to emphasize functional issues such as use and control, particularly attributing conflicts – between conservationists and local communities, or between local communities and wildlife or ecosystems – to unsustainable uses and management practices by local communities. However, in light of the political and cultural issues underpinning wildlife and other resource conflicts, tensions appear to be more about disparities in power and access, and differences in each group's ideological and relational understandings of what land and animals mean (Raffan, 1993; Tsing, 2005). As such, collaborative conservation projects have become politicized sites where Indigenous material and sociopolitical struggles have become entangled with conservation initiatives (Tsing, 2005).

While contemporary conservationists who embrace the collaborative and community conservation narrative have professed to sharing deep ideological bonds with local communities, cases in Guyana (Colchester, 1997, 2004; LaRose, 2004), Brazil (Silvius, 2004), Africa (Adams, 2003), and Southeast Asia (Brosius, 2001; Tsing, 2005) indicate that differently situated social groups have diverged drastically when issues regarding land and resource rights, harvesting and use practices, management, and intellectual property entered the dialogue. Numerous Indigenous discourses (Merculieff, 2002; Tauli-Corpuz, 2003) pose a challenge to hegemonic and paternalistic forms of conservation policy and practice dictated by Western science, expertise, and capital. Imperative to Indigenous peoples in Guyana is that collaborative approaches do not just rhetorically acknowledge their resource rights and customary practices, but rather, embody them within conservation agendas and strategies defined by Indigenous peoples (Smith, 1999; LaRose, 2004).

Similarly, Adams and Mulligan (2003) challenge that while the more critical conservation discourses involve an analysis of hegemonic regimes within biodiversity conservation and development, such discourses are rarely sensitive to the specific needs and diversity of cosmologies from Indigenous and local societies. Inspired by Indigenous, postcolonial/decolonizing, and critical-theory discourses, this chapter will highlight strands of discourse that explore both the cultural politics of collaborative conservation and re-envisioning collaborative partnerships and knowledge-building between Indigenous peoples and conservation researchers. Based on a collaborative conservation partnership and community-led management initiatives in North Rupununi, Guyana,[1] this chapter explores the relational entanglements between Indigenous communities, conservation programs, and wildlife within the context of the Iwokrama Forest protected area and the partnership between the Iwokrama Centre for Rainforest Conservation and Development (hereafter referred to as the Iwokrama program), the North Rapununi District Development Board (NRDDB), and Makushi and mixed Indigenous communities of the region.[1]

I am particularly interested in how communities grapple with conservation's political and epistemic cultures while negotiating their own wildlife and forest management regimes based on a syncretism of modern and traditional frameworks. In some cases, collaborative partnerships present the opportunity for both groups to reach across the epistemic and cultural divide that separates them within the conservation domain. In particular, Indigenous people in Guyana have attempted to negotiate and transgress this divide through their appropriation of strategic aspects of the dominant conservation discourse, and through their active contributions to emergent, syncretized conservation frameworks. As such, re-envisioning requires a comprehensive study of the historical, social, and politico-ecological challenges and possibilities for building syncretic forms of locally grounded wildlife knowledge, research, and management within collaborative conservation and community-led regimes.

A Sense of Grounding within Indigenous and Conservation Worlds

My own sense of grounding within the discourses of this research is extremely important, for it has contoured the way that I interpret and articulate the diverse issues and perspectives inherent in approaches to collaborative conservation and cultural-ecological relationships within conservation practice. In terms of cultural worlds, I am a Canadian woman of multi-ethnic ancestry, including Guyanese-Amerindian/Chinese and Dutch. As an academic, conservationist, educator, and activist of such ancestry, I straddle the different paradigmatic and cultural worlds that I seek to better understand and bring into dialogue within my research and praxis. I am also conscious of my layered responsibilities to the Indigenous communities, conservationists, animals, and forests of Guyana. My location within the multiple worlds and discourses of my doctoral research is extremely important, for it has given texture to my world view and the epistemological assumptions framing my research study. Similar to Indigenous shamans (*Peaiamen*) in Guyana, some of whom can shapeshift into animals and other forms with the help of an animal spirit guardian, those of us who walk multiple paths and embrace multiple worlds are also shapeshifters. Thus, my grounding within the different discourses that I explore within this chapter also reflects the sense of purpose and responsibility that I feel towards these issues. In terms of including a brief understanding of the Indigenous perspectives from the North Rupununi context within the chapter, I have received permission from the North Rupununi communities to respectfully give voice to their unique knowledge, cultural practices, challenges, and relationships.

Guyana's Political, Economic, and Conservation Climate

Although shaped and nourished by diverse ecosystems of immense beauty and ecological significance, Guyana's diverse peoples have been historically locked into material, political, and social struggles that have created devastating impacts on both human communities and ecosystems, as well as on the relationship between them. The colonial period was a time of immense ecological disjuncture and transformation as Indigenous landscapes and plant and animal beings were uprooted, hybridized, or destroyed to give space for the transplantation of European varieties. Thus, at its essence, colonialism was both a biological and a cultural process in that its purveyors sought to dispossess, control, and transform Indigenous natures (landscapes, plant and animal beings), as well as Indigenous human bodies, cultures, and knowledges.

Like many developing countries of the global South, the post-independent nation state of Guyana inherited many of the political, economic, and cultural legacies of the colonial era – legacies that are constantly being reframed and reinforced through the current era of neoliberal economic development in Guyana. A clear example of neoliberal restructuring is the intensification of market-oriented conservation strategies within Guyana's interior, or, as Conservation International calls it, 'conservation as business' (Chapin, 2004). While Guyana's diverse ecosystems and animal and plant species have historically been under relatively little anthropogenic pressure due to low population densities, minimally invasive Indigenous ecological practices, and a minimal level of international development and investment, the 1980s marked a period of emergent competing, external interests over Guyana's interior resources. The penetration of global economic interests into Indigenous and peasant societies within Guyana have largely displaced many communities' subsistence and customary systems, thus exacerbating cleavages and impeding their capacity for long-term environmental sustainability (Schmink and Wood, 1987). It is no coincidence that the communities which have been most embedded and forced into dependency are also those with the deepest social dislocations, and whose territories have incurred the most environmental degradation (Bulkan and Bulkan, 2006). Colonial legacies, and the contemporary incursions by extractive industries, monocropping, bioprospecting, wildlife trade, and other external interests into Indigenous territories have not only systematically changed local livelihood patterns, but they have also reconfigured physical landscapes and interspecies relationships that have historically sustained and defined local societies. The Makushi and mixed Indigenous communities of the North Rupununi have situated ecological knowledge and customary systems based on social sanctions such as: specific periods; restrictions and boundaries for tree, wildlife, and non-timber forest product harvesting; areas of ancestral, cultural, spiritual, and material significance; consumption taboos for specific species; and shamanistic traditions. Such systems have traditionally controlled the access, harvesting, and use of forests, wetlands, and wildlife. However, political, economic, and socio-cultural shifts within the region have occurred rapidly and have begun to erode and supplant Indigenous knowledge and customary systems, thus exacerbating cleavages and impeding communities' capacity for self-reliance and long-term environmental sustainability (Schmink and Wood, 1987).

For more than a decade, Guyana has entered onto the international biodiversity conservation and development stage with its commitment to environmental development – particularly rainforest and wildlife research and conservation, environmental sustainability, and the intention to create the Guyana Protected Area System (GPAS). Funded by the Global Environmental Facility (GEF), the long-term goal of the GPAS project is mandated to 'ensure effective protection and sustainable management of representative ecosystems of Guyana through a national system of protected areas which is self-sustained, transparent, decentralized, and managed through partnerships' (Taylor and Griffiths, 2007). The most concrete and promising realization of this commitment has been the Iwokrama program and its partnership with the Makushi Indigenous communities and institutions of the North Rupununi to promote research and development of sustainable forest and wildlife management practices. In fact, the Iwokrama program (Iwokrama, 2006) attributes its significance as a national and global leader in tropical forest research and conservation to its unique collaborative partnership with the Indigenous-led North Rupununi District Development Board (NRDDB) and communities.

Indigenous Perspectives on Collaborative Conservation and Knowledge-Sharing

The argument has been made by numerous Indigenous and conservation researchers that in the current era of environmental politics and conservation management in protected areas such as the Iwokrama Forest, neither group can alone shoulder the onerous responsibilities of achieving local development, biodiversity conservation, and research

(Carlsson and Berkes, 2005; Langton, 2003; LaRose, 2004; Silvius et al, 2004; Wondolleck and Yaffee, 2000). While not without its challenges, the Iwokrama–NRDDB partnership appears to have been the most viable and flexible framework for Indigenous peoples in Guyana to co-manage the conservation process, as well as to assert their rights and interests regarding their knowledges, territorial claims, and customary practices. Imperative to Indigenous peoples in Guyana is that collaborative approaches do not just rhetorically acknowledge their resource rights, customary practices, and free, prior, and informed consent, but rather, embody them within conservation agendas and strategies defined by Indigenous peoples (Smith, 1999; LaRose, 2004). As such, the 1996 Iwokrama International Centre for Rainforest Conservation and Development Act (Iwokrama Act), and subsequent 2004 Memorandum of Understanding (MOU) between the Iwokrama program and the NRDDR, form the basis of the NRDDB-Iwokrama collaborative partnership. The Iwokrama Act and MOU legally recognize: a shared vision of sustainable use and management of the Iwokrama forest and related ecosystems of the region; Indigenous customary rights to exclusive use and management of the Iwokrama forest and its resources; valuing Indigenous knowledge and intellectual property rights, and implementation of equitable decision-making and benefit-sharing processes (Allicock, 2003; Iwokrama, 2006).

Indigenous environmental history narratives from Guyana and different eco-cultural contexts around the world represent intergenerational embodiments of individual and collective socio-ecological memory and knowledge which trace ecological change and social agency in the locality over time and space (Davidson-Hunt and Berkes, 2003). They help us understand the complexity and texture of human-nature and human-animal relationships as conditioned by processes of politico-ecological change. They also reveal the evolving strategies that human and non-human communities use to adapt to such change. For Indigenous communities in Guyana, struggles over the use and management of land and natural resources are simultaneously struggles for a sense of meaning and identity (Li, 1997).

As Pearkes (2002) writes of the Sinixt Nation's environmental history in the Upper Columbia Basin, narratives from the land form an anchor for each person's or community's sense of being and belonging, as well as forming a bridge between peoples, landscapes, and animals. The history, present, and future of the lands, waters, and wildlife of North Rupununi, Guyana, have been shaped by a reciprocal process that simultaneously naturalizes social relations among Indigenous and other peoples of the region, and socializes landscapes, plants, animals, and places through cultural relations between peoples and the natural environment. The dialectic of this relationship is one of mutual agency and transformation: agency of people in shaping and transforming natural landscapes, and agency of nature in shaping and transforming human history (Cronon, 1992). Environmental history narratives also reveal systematic transformation to habitats and peoples as a result of colonial and contemporary politico-economic processes. Such processes of disjuncture and change have changed local liveli-hood patterns; reconfigured physical landscapes and inter-species relationships; and reshaped Indigenous people's interior landscapes (Raffan, 1993). Consequently, people's internal knowledge and sense of place have been affected by an array of external and internal shifts. Thus, environmental histories demonstrate that Indigenous know-ledges and environmental praxis have developed through experiential engagement with shifting socio-ecological and power landscapes, that they embody cultural practices and institutions, and that they are dy-namic and adaptive to currents of change.

Graham Hingangaroa Smith (2000:210) posits that Indigenous peo-ples must 'name the world for ourselves.' As Indigenous peoples are agents in constructing and practising their knowledges, control over the usage of such knowledge and agenda-setting in matters that di-rectly impact them (such as environmental conservation) should reside directly with Indigenous communities. While their narratives and agency have been historically 'othered' and omitted from the dominant conservation discourse, Indigenous peoples in Guyana and other re-gions are becoming increasingly represented within national and inter-national conversations. The 1999 National Toshaos Conference in Guyana emphasized that protected areas should not only be estab-lished with free, prior, and informed consent by affected Indigenous communities, but, moreover, they should be owned or co-owned by communities as a way of recognizing their territorial and stewardship rights and protecting biodiversity (LaRose, 2004). Former spokesper-son for the Amerindian Peoples' Association, LaRose argues that Indigenous-directed protected areas, supported by conservation insti-tutions, are the only sensible solution, since Indigenous peoples 'have been protecting and managing our territories for centuries and have developed elaborate management systems that are dependent on the maintenance of our knowledges and cultures' (3).

Athough many conservation researchers and government authorities propound that Indigenous peoples are unequivocally opposed to conservation and environmental development objectives, most Indigenous activists clarify that what they are struggling against are hegemonic forms of conservation knowledge, policy, and practice that marginalize and undermine their rights and cultures as merely a 'transaction cost' (Brosius, 2004). Langton (2003) notably cautions that while many Indigenous peoples are open to reciprocally sharing their knowledges and practices within the context of collaborative approaches, conservation researchers must understand that such knowledges are part of the peoples' heritage and are not readily accessible or intended for mass consumption. The *National Strategy for the Conservation of Australia's Biological Diversity* (Langton, 2003: 89), Guyana's revised 2005 Amerindian Act and the Iwokrama Act similarly provision that: Indigenous peoples must be involved in any research and species recovery/conservation programs related to their territories; the collection and use of Indigenous knowledge is considered a privilege and should only be gathered and used with the free, prior, and informed consent of Indigenous peoples and to the direct benefit of local communities; there must be recognition of the continuation of Indigenous customary traditions and use practices; and Indigenous rights should be safeguarded in accordance with the 1993 *UN Convention on Biodiversity* and the 2007 *UN Declaration on the Rights of Indigenous Peoples*.

While spaces have opened up for Indigenous knowledges and narratives in positive and concrete ways, there is still a danger that when Indigenous discourses become mainstreamed and institutionalized by the dominant discourse, core knowledges, struggles, and beliefs will be supplanted and lost. In their interest to instrumentalize Indigenous knowledges, many conservationists, anthropologists, and policy-makers extract 'useful' fragments of these knowledges from complex historical, spiritual, and cultural contexts. When Indigenous knowledges are not addressed as potential tools for decolonization, their decontextualization by scientific and state researchers has been criticized by Simpson (2004) and by Smith (1999) as remaining within the framework of the neocolonial project. Odora-Hoppers (2002) and Bannerji (2003) further challenge that mainstream scientific constructions of Indigenous or local knowledges as depoliticized and dehistoricized systems of concepts and categories are neocolonial acts to silence and neutralize the historical and socio-cultural contexts that shape and reshape such knowledge forms.

Ubiquitous constructions of Indigenous knowledges have many times been misappropriated and re-narrated by conservation researchers, activists, and policy-makers for numerous political and strategic reasons that have arguably served their own interests and campaigns more than they have substantively contributed to strengthening Indigenous institutions (Brosius, 2001). Brosius argues that these are 'a way of constructing meta-narratives' by making 'land, non-human beings and people inviolable … by appealing to pre-existing categories of values they paradoxically genericize precisely the diversity that they are trying to advance' (309). Such attempts to appropriate Indigenous knowledges and make them complementary within dominant conservation and development frameworks do not equate with attempting to achieve a meaningful synthesis between the knowledge paradigms (Pottier et al., 2003).

Due to their different socio-economic and political positioning, Indigenous communities and conservationists each have particular forms of environmental knowledge and experience based on their situated perspectives and assumed truths, and are grounded in partial interests (Haraway, 1991). For both Indigenous and conservation communities, it is critically important to recognize the internal differentiation of power and control within and between their groups regarding who and what are included or omitted within their processes of producing and disseminating environmental research and management practices. Specifically, a meaningful critique of inequitable power relations, power-sharing, and the terms and agency of knowledge is required to meaningfully understand the nature, transformative potential, omissions, and consequences of such a synthesis (Odora Hoppers, 2002). It is of particular importance to Indigenous peoples that they have access to co-constructing conservation knowledge and practice grounded within their own ecological and cultural experiences and sense of memory and place, as the basis of meaningful environmental praxis.

Syncretizing Knowledge Forms in Conservation Partnerships

The knowledge that is dynamically constructed by an epistemic community embodies its ethical values and cultural assumptions about the nature of its realities (Rigney, 1999) and relationships with the environment that have been shaped and nurtured by particular historical and cultural contexts. Indigenous epistemology reverberates in the understanding that the beginning of knowledge is when one recognizes and understands that every being and every phenomenological event in the world is interconnected through relationships of shared agency and interdependency (Henderson, 2000). Substantively different from common non-Indigenous assumptions that Indigenous societies are naturalized beings or nature-oriented, many Indigenous peoples in Guyana and elsewhere understand themselves as being *nature-inclusive*. The human and natural worlds are thus perceived as interrelated and interconnected, and not as separate entities. Indigenous epistemology also refers to a people's ways of being present and aware in the world – of perceiving and constructing knowledge about their socio-ecological environment and cultural worlds through teachings and oral, symbolic, and ceremonial modes of communication (Gegeo, 2002).

In attempting to adapt and live in relationship with such change, Indigenous peoples in Guyana traditionally have forged alliances of shared responsibility and interconnection amongst all beings and ecological forces, where 'each person must decide to develop his or her potential by understanding their relationship to the earth. Any person who sets out on the journey to find his or her gifts will be aided by guardian spirits, guides, teachers and protectors along the way' (Henderson, 2000). Despite the diverse terrain of Indigenous knowledges emerging from different groups in different contexts, LaDuke (2005:127) reflects that 'there is a striking unity on the sacredness of ecological systems.'

As well, multiple truths and realities are embodied through cultural discourse. Deloria et al. (1999) further describe the principles of epistemological method from an Indigenous perspective as the methodological basis for gathering information about the natural world through reciprocal relationships between people, land, animal and plant beings that are based on responsible and respectful human actions. Cheney (2002) also links cultural expression to ethical practice through peoples' enactment of narratives relating humans, animal and plant beings, land, and the spiritual world. Since knowledge does not exist in any comprehensible terrain outside of human culture (Mentore, 2005), epistemology and knowledge forms must then be understood and interpreted through culture and cultural expression. As such, Indigenous ecological knowledges have developed throughout diverse cultural and bio-geographical contexts, and particularly reveal plurality and texture within their epistemology, articulation, and practice.

From my examination of the mainstream and critical discourses on collaborative conservation and Indigenous knowledges, the divide that exists between Indigenous and dominant conservation ontologies and knowledges appears incommensurable due to the disparities in power and interests that distance them. The differences between and among diverse Indigenous and dominant conservation knowledges can be organized along three axes (Agrawal, 1995): (1) *substantive* – differences in the content and characteristics of each paradigm; (2) *methodological and epistemological* – whereby each paradigm involves different methods in how it perceives and represents reality, and is shaped by different cultural assumptions and worlds of meaning, and (3) *contextual* – whereby each paradigm embodies the ecological, historical, and cultural contexts where it variously emerges. Although Indigenous and conservation knowledge forms are ontologically and strategically quite different, there are significant points of commonality in their goals for sustainability and their struggles against the incursion of extractive industries, developers, wildlife cartels, corrupt governments, and globally homogenizing forces in tropical forests such as those of Guyana.

Thus, despite the complex challenges, there are many Indigenous actors and conservation researchers who believe in and are striving towards collaborative conservation and integrated knowledge approaches. Since the cultural and political integrity of Indigenous communities in Guyana is integral to the sustainable use and governance of forests and wildlife populations, it is imperative that the locally grounded agencies, knowledges, and subjectivities of Indigenous peoples be at the centre of conservation research, education, and policy within their territories. Only then can 'alternative histories and alternative knowledges' (Smith, 1999) inspire alternative collaborative conservation partnerships. In his discussion of contact sites or spaces of synthesis between dominant and nativized religious systems within the Caribbean region, Taylor (2001) defines syncretism as a basis for communities with different systems to dynamically come together and generate a new system. It is important to understand that syncretism in this context does not refer to the assimilation or dissolution of one knowledge form or world view into that of the other. Rather, I use the term 'syncretism' here to embody the work of the Indigenous peoples and Iwokrama researchers in North Rupununi, Guyana, who are attempting to critically engage and synthesize their different world view and knowledge frameworks into sustainable and equitable wildlife conservation strategies.

Ethical Spaces for Collaboration through the Three-Legged Stool Metaphor

Collaborative conservation partnerships such as that between the Iwokrama program and NRDDB, and local people's encounters with animals, opens up the possibility for important sites of entanglement – what Cree scholar Ermine (2006) describes as ethical spaces for decolonizing, transforming, and promoting relationships and discursive spaces between Indigenous and non-Indigenous world views and knowledge forms. Ethical spaces are inherently political places where Indigenous peoples' agency and situated perspectives and practices are recognized in their ongoing negotiation and renegotiation of ecological knowledge vis-à-vis their encounters with and contestation of conservation, state, and commercial interests. The shifting complexity of knowledge-power relations (Foucault, 1980) is foundational to my examination of the socio-political interaction of Indigenous subjectivities, agencies, and environmental perspectives (as the subjugated knowledges) with dominant conservation perspectives. Particularly important is the potential for Indigenous societies, within the context of conservation partnerships and community-led initiatives, to resist marginalization within conservation sites by negotiating and transforming inherent power relations (Bhabha, in Kapoor, 2008; Foucault, 1980) in creative and syncretic ways. Thus, such spaces have the potential to become political and politically strategic (Kapoor, 2008) for Indigenous peoples and their allies to transgress the occlusion and dominance so often engendered within conservation discourses and projects. Spaces of overlap also entail opportunities for cross-fertilization of knowledges, experiences, and praxes that are articulated and embodied through cultural forms in both epistemic communities. Shiva (1993) writes that the diversity of ecological landscapes, animals, and plants is reproduced and conserved through the reproduction and conservation of cultural forms that celebrate a renewal of life as well as providing a format for constructing and practising knowledge.

Furthermore, an ethical space can potentially enable the capacity of Indigenous knowledges to construct new possibilities for collaborative and syncretic constructions of conservation knowledges and more equitable relationships. There are much broader definitions of what people understand – about wildlife, nature, knowledge, power and authority, ecological and cultural integrity, community, environmental conservation and management, discourse, and research – based on their specific social, environmental, and historical contexts. The cultural politics of nature and how it forms our engagement with ecosystems and human and nonhuman beings are both material and metaphorical. In his work on the politics of race and nature, Moore et al. (2003) discuss that natural landscapes are embodied by the diverse situated practices of gatherers, cultivators, hunters, pastoralists, slaves, colonists, explorers, labour migrants, and conservationists. Thus, the practices of such diverse social groups shape both the physical terrain, as well as their sense of identity and relationships with the natural world.

Many Indigenous societies around the world continue to use cooperation and consensus decision-making mechanisms as their central modes of negotiation and governance within their socio-political and ecological practices. Like many small communities of forest- and savannah-dwelling peoples, Makushi and other Indigenous peoples of the Rupununi region maintain egalitarian traditions around ecological and cultural activities and decision-making that are grounded in values of reciprocity and exchange; they 'emphasize simultaneously the autonomy of the individual and the importance of sharing between all members of the village or cluster of villages ... between humans and what we call "natures"' (Colchester et al., 2002: 22).

Cooperation, consensus, and partnership are often conceptualized by Indigenous peoples in Guyana through devices such as ceremony and metaphor because they have deep cultural meaning for communities and they effectively consolidate important processes and relationships (Mentore, 2005). Beverly Jacobs (2006) insists that the presence of ceremony within collaborative alliances embodies the sacred within relationships, particularly recognizing the spirit and intention of reciprocity and equality between Indigenous peoples and non-Indigenous actors. Cuomo (1998) describes metaphors as having normative implications in that they encourage peoples to perceive and engage with the natural world in ways dictated by their common understandings of what is symbolized. Yolngu elder, scholar, and educator Marika-Munungurrit of Australia (Kennett et al., 2004) explains how metaphors grounded in Indigenous knowledges can act as important symbolic vehicles to develop reconciliatory collaborative relationships in conservation initiated by Indigenous peoples.

The metaphor of the three-legged stool has been re-envisioned by Indigenous activist and Iwokrama program trustee Sydney Allicock (2003) to represent the struggle by the North Rupununi communities to sustainably control their lands, forest stewardship, and cultural practices through their collaboration with the Iwokrama program and the Guyanese government/private sector. The North Rupununi District Development Board in Guyana was created as an umbrella partnership structure directed by the Annai District and Village Council and village councils of the 16 North Rupununi communities, in collaboration with the Iwokrama program and the government of Guyana (although the partnership exists primarily with the Iwokrama program as the present government has been virtually absent at both operational and fiscal levels). The NRDDB independently monitors the Iwokrama program's activities, and, moreover, represents the rights, interests, and community development priorities of its constituent communities (Allicock, 2003). Another important NGO working alongside the NRDDB in its community development mandate is the Bina Hill Institute. This institute manages all of the region's educational and skills training initiatives within diverse thematic areas, including environmental management, conservation, and youth leadership.

The NRDDB-Iwokrama conservation partnership is unique in that it departs from the majority of collaborative approaches around the world, whereby the contours of knowledge, resource rights, and power in biodiversity conservation are very much dictated by Western science and capital. Thus far, the North Rupununi District Development Board communities maintain a meaningful, though critical, engagement with the Iwokrama program, and have ensured that Indigenous customary rights to exclusive use and management of the Iwokrama Forest and its resources are enshrined within the Iwokrama Act and the Memoranda-of-Understanding (Allicock, 2003). The Iwokrama Act mandates the predominantly Guyanese staff and researchers from the Iwokrama program to recognize and support capacity-building for community-led environmental management and conservation approaches, locally grounded ecological research, and collaboration through autonomous Indigenous community structures and village councils. After struggling for more transparent and democratic decision-making and collaborative processes in the formative years, the three-legged stool metaphor for collaborative conservation symbolizes the germination of a re-envisioned collaborative approach that has resulted in an increasingly community-led form of environmental governance. Such an approach has begun to address many of the issues and reforms for conservation and development identified by Indigenous peoples within Guyana (Colchester, 2006) and globally (First Peoples Worldwide, 2006), such as reclaiming knowledge, strengthening traditional institutions and local capacity, and recognizing rights and equitable benefit-sharing.

A catalytic element of these ground-breaking processes is that Guyana's Indigenous communities have become increasingly vocal and politically mobilized against the singular focus of governments and conservation institutions on creating protected areas and market-oriented conservation approaches that directly threaten both the environment and the survival of Guyana's Indigenous communities (Colchester, 1997; Colchester and MacKay 2004). Market-oriented conservation and joint business development strategies such as a sustainable low-impact logging initiative, a conservation concession, marketing-ecosystem service, and risk capital ventures to evaluate ecosystem services and ecotourism (Butler, 2008; Thomas, 2003) have particularly caused quite a cleavage between conservation institutions and Indigenous institutions and communities (Allicock, personal communication, 2007). While the Iwokrama-NRDDB collaborative partnership and management processes are still nascent and vulnerable to numerous external political, economic, and social pressures which can potentially threaten the ecological and cultural integrity of the region, Indigenous-led institutions such as the Amerindian Peoples Association, the North Rupununi District Development Board, and the Bina Hill Institute are struggling to ensure that Indigenous rights, knowledge, capacity, and leadership-building are formally recognized and remain on the agendas of political conservation and development interventions within the region (Colchester and MacKay, 2004; LaRose, 2004).

Re-Envisioning Collaborative Conservation through Younger Generations

In this chapter, I have explored how historically and culturally embedded perspectives and institutions, as well as modern conservation discourses and institutions have influenced Indigenous communities in defining their contemporary environmental knowledge, customary rights, management practices, and collaboration with the Iwokrama program. Rowan White (in LaDuke, 2005: 192) eloquently describes the symbolic significance of biodiversity within the context of Indigenous knowledges and ecological practice. In particular, diverse Indigenous varieties of plants in Guyana, such as cassava, not only carry immense value as food and medicine, but they also hold cultural, sacred, symbolic, and economic value and ecological memory for the communities who have conserved and used them for generations. The same is true of the forests, savannahs, and animals with which the Indigenous peoples of the North Rupununi have maintained close relationships despite the multiple challenges to their livelihoods and cultural worlds. Both the landscape and human societies are constantly in flux, and new changes require the seeds of memory and knowledge to also adapt and grow while retaining the foundations that continue to make them unique and viable. As with many Indigenous communities throughout the world, the passing of elder knowledge-keepers, the out-migration of youth, and the increasing politico-economic pressures which create social dislocation within communities mean that time and distance are quickly displacing and eroding those seeds of eco-logical memory and knowledge. However, when the younger generation of environmental leaders come along as new cultivators, the seeds can take root and flourish again.

Particularly inspiring are the younger generation, who are instrumental to NRDDB-Iwokrama conservation initiatives as environmental leaders (e.g., wildlife rangers, researchers, Wildlife Club members, and mentors). Engaged local youth are uniquely placed in their communities as recipi-ents and practitioners of situated, intergenerational knowledge and cus-tomary practice related to their environment and their oral histories. At the same time, they are learning modern conservation science and technology through their training and engagement with both the Iwokrama program and community-led environmental institutions. As such, the processes of nature-making and knowledge-making among local youth involve their ability to craft their own perceptions of nature, wildlife, environmental issues, and conservation based on a combination of traditional teachings, experiential knowledge, empirical and scientific teachings, intuitive and symbolic knowledge, and imagery.

In the North Rupununi. collaborative and community-led youth con-servation initiatives provide the possibility for Indigenous commun-ities to: (1) reclaim intergenerational knowledge, (2) syncretize Indigenous and scientific knowledge and frameworks, and (3) empower environ-mental agency. In cultivating their own understandings of identity, place, and social agency, youth are also able to strengthen and sustain a sense of active environmental responsibility and praxis within their communities. Furthermore, local environmental youth leadership dir-ectly contributes to broader processes of supporting and strengthening community-led, socio-environmental institutions, safeguarding the ecological and cultural integrity of the region, and enriching wildlife research and conservation within Guyana and internationally.

NOTE

1 The North Rupununi region is the traditional territory of the Makushi peoples, who are still the most prevalent Indigenous group in the region.

However, there are numerous villages which are mixed communities comprising Wapishana, Arawak, and Patemona people, as well as coastal Guyanese who have married into the communities. For the sake of inclusivity, I use the term 'Indigenous' throughout much of the chapter.

REFERENCES

Adams, William M., and David Hulme. 2001.'If Community Conservation Is the Answer in Africa, What Is the Question?' *Oryx,* 35(3): 193–200.

Adams, William, and Martin Mulligan. Eds. 2003. *Decolonizing Nature: Strategies for Conservation in a Post-Colonial Era.* London: Earthscan.

Agrawal, Arun. 1995. 'Dismantling the Divide between Indigenous and Scientific Knowledge.'*Development and Change,* 26(3): 413–39.

Allicock, Sydney. 2003. 'Developing Partnerships between the North Rupununi District Development Board and the Iwokrama International Centre Programme for Rainforest Conservation and Development.' Indigenous Rights in the Commonwealth Caribbean and Americas Regional Expert Meeting. Georgetown, Guyana.

Bannerji, Himmani. 2003. 'The Tradition of Sociology and the Sociology of Tradition.' *Qualitative Studies in Education,* 16(2): 157–73.

Berkes, Fikret. 2003. 'Rethinking Community-Based Conservation.' *Conservation Biology,* 18(3): 621–30.

Bhabha, H. 2008. *Postcolonial Politics of Development.* Kapoor, I. London: Routledge.

Brosius, J. Peter. 2001. 'Local Knowledges, Global Claims: On the Significance of Indigenous Ecologies in Sarawak, East Malaysia.' In *Indigenous Traditions and Ecology.* J.A. Grim. Ed. Cambridge, MA: Harvard University Press.

– 2004. 'Indigenous Peoples and Protected Areas at the World Parks Congress.' *Conservation Biology,* 20(3): 683–5.

– 2006. 'Common Ground between Anthropology and Conservation Biology.' *Conservation Biology,* 20(3): 683–5.

Bulkan, J., and A. Bulkan. 2006. 'These Forests Have Always Been Ours: Official and Amerindian Discourses on Guyana's Forest Estate.' In *Indigenous Resurgence in the Contemporary Caribbean: Amerindian Survival and Revival.* M. Forte. Ed. New York: Peter Lang.

Butler, R. 2008. 'Private Equity Firm Buys Rights to Ecosystem Services of Guyana Rainforest.' Mongabay.com. http://news.mongabay.com/2008/0327-iwokrama.html.

Carlsson, Lars, and Firket Berkes. 2005. 'Co-Management: Concepts and Methodological Implications.' *Journal of Environmental Management,* 75: 65–76.

Chapin, M. 2004. *A Challenge to Conservationists*. Washington, DC: Worldwatch Institute.

Cheney, Jim. 2002. 'The Moral Epistemology of First Nations Stories.' *Canadian Journal of Environmental Education: Telling Our Stories*, 7(2): 88–100.

Chung Tiam Fook, Tanya. 2002. 'Is WWF Transforming Its Conservation Approach? Analysis of WWF's Policy on Indigenous Peoples and Conservation from Rhetoric to Practice.' The Hague: Institute of Social Studies.

– 2006. 'Constructing Shared Meaning and Practice: An Amerindian Knowledge-Based Approach to Collaborative Conservation in Guyana.' *Society for Caribbean Studies*, 7.

Code, Lorraine. 2006. *Ecological Thinking: The Politics of Epistemic Location*. Oxford: Oxford University Press.

Colchester, Marcus. 1997. *Guyana: Fragile Frontier*. New York: Monthly Review Press.

– 2006. *Forest Peoples, Customary Use and State Forests: The Case for Reform*. Forest Peoples Programme. Paper for IASCP, Bali, 19-23 June 2006. Available at http://www.forestpeoples.org/documents/conservation/10c_overvies_jascp_jun06_engpdf.

Colchester, Marcus, and Fergus MacKay. 2004. *In Search of Middle Ground: Indigenous Peoples, Collective Representation and the Right to Free, Prior and Informed Consent*. 10th Conference of the International Association of the Study of Common Property. Oaxaca, Mexico: Forest Peoples Programme.

Colchester, Marcus, J. La Rose, and K. James. 2002. *Mining and Amerindians in Guyana*. Ottawa: North-South Institute.

Conklin, Beth A., and Laura R. Graham. 1995. 'The Shifting Middle Ground: Amazonian Indians and Eco-Politics.' *American Anthropologist*, 97(4): 695–710.

Cronon, W. 1992. 'A Place for Stories: Nature, History, and Narrative.' *Journal of American History*, 78(4): 1347–76.

Cuomo, Chris J. 1998. *Feminism and Ecological Communities: An Ethic of Flourishing*. London: Routledge.

Davidson-Hunt, I., and F. Berkes. 2003. 'Learning As You Journey: Anishinaabe Perception of Social-Ecological Environments and Adaptive Learning.' *Conservation Ecology*, 8(1): 5.

Deloria, Barbara, Kristen Foehner, and Samuel Scinta. Eds. 1999. *Spirit and Reason: The Vine Deloria, Jr. Reader*. Golden, CO: Fulcrum Publishing.

Ellen, Roy, Peter Parkes, and Alan Bicker. Eds. 2000. *Indigenous Environmental Knowledge and Its Transformations*. Amsterdam: Harwood Academic Publishers.

Ermine, Willie. 2006. 'Ethical Space: Transforming Relationships.' *Heritage Canada Traditions Discussion Papers*. Available at: http://pch.gc.ca/pc-chlorg/sectr/cp-ch/aa/rng-eng.cfm.

First Peoples Worldwide. 2006. *Indigenous Stewardship Program and Fund: Final Report*. Fredericksburg, VA: First Peoples Worldwide.

Foucault, Michel. 1980. *Power/Knowledge: Selected Interviews and Other Writings 1972–1977*. New York: Pantheon.

Gegeo, David W. 2002. 'Whose Knowledge? Epistemological Collisions in Solomon Islands Community Development.' *The Contemporary Pacific*, 14(2): 377–409.

Haraway, Donna. 1991. *Simians, Cyborgs, and Women: The Reinvention of Nature*. London: Free Association Books.

Henderson, James (Sa'ke'j) Youngblood. 2000. 'Postcolonial Ledger Drawing: Legal Reform.' In Marie Battiste. Ed. *Reclaiming Indigenous Voice and Vision*, 57–76. Vancouver: UBC Press.

Iwokrama. 2006. *Report 2006*. Georgetown, Guyana: Iwokrama Centre for Rainforest Conservation and Development.

Jacobs, Beverly. 2006. 'Panel Discussion on Aboriginal Women in Canada.' Toronto: Ontario Institute for Studies in Education, University of Toronto. 20 November.

Kapoor, I. 2008. *Postcolonial Politics of Development*. London: Routledge.

Kennett, R. 2004.'Indigenous Initiatives for Co-management of Miyapunu/Sea Turtle.' *Ecological Management and Restoration*, 5(3): 159–65.

LaDuke, Winona. 2005. *Recovering the Sacred: The Power of Naming and Reclaiming*. Cambridge, MA: South End Press.

LaRose, Jean. 2004. 'In Guyana, Indigenous Peoples Fight to Join Conservation Efforts.' *Cultural Survival Quarterly*, 28(1).

Langton, Marcia. 2003. 'The "Wild," the Market and the Native: Indigenous People Face New Forms of Global Colonization.' In *Decolonizing Nature: Strategies for Conservation in a Post-Colonial Era*, 79–107. William M. Adams and Martin Mulligan. Eds. London: Earthscan.

Lawrence, Bonita. 2004. *'Real' Indians and Others: Mixed-Blood Urban Native Peoples and Indigenous Nationhood*. Vancouver: UBC Press.

Li, T. 1997. 'Boundary Work: Response to Arun Agrawal's Communities in Conservation, Beyond Enchantment and Disenchantment.' Conservation Development Forum, University of Florida, Gainsville.

Mentore, George. 2005. *Of Passionate Curves and Desirable Cadences: Themes on Waiwai Social Being*. Lincoln: University of Nebraska Press.

Merculieff, L. 2002. 'Linking Traditional Knowledge and Wisdom to Ecosystem- Based Approaches in Research and Management.' In John R. Stepp et al. Eds. *Ethnobiology and Biocultural Diversity*. Athens: International Society of Ethnobiology.

Moore, D.S., J. Kosek, and A. Pandlan. Eds. 2003. *Race, Nature, and the Politics of Difference*. Durham, NC: Duke University Press.

Odora Hoppers, Catherine. Ed. 2002. *Indigenous Knowledge and the Integration of Knowledge Systems*. Claremont, South Africa: New Africa Books.

Pearkes, E.D. 2002. *The Geography of Memory*. Nelson, BC: Kutenai House Press.

Pottier, Johan, Alan Bicker, and Paul Sillitoe. Eds. 2003. *Negotiating Local Knowledge: Power and Identity in Local Development*. London: Pluto Press.

Raffan, J. 1993. 'The Experience of Place: Exploring Land as Teacher.' *Journal of Experiential Education*, 16(1): 39–45.

Rigney, Lester-Irabinna. 1999. 'Internationalisation of an Indigenous Anti-Colonial Cultural Critique of Research Methodologies: A Guide to Indigenist Research Methodology and Its Principles.' *Journal for Native American Studies*, 14(2): 109–21.

Schmink, M., and C.H. Wood. 1987. 'The Political Ecology of Amazonia.' In P. Little and M. Horowitz. Eds. *Lands at Risk in the Third World: Local Level Perspectives*, 38–54. Boulder, CO: Westview Press.

Shiva, Vandana. 1993. *Monocultures of the Mind: Perspectives on Biodiversity and Biotechnology*. Penang, Malaysia: Third World Network.

Silvius, Kristen. 2004. 'Bridging the Gap between Western Scientific and Traditional Indigenous Wildlife Management.' In *People in Nature: Wildlife Conservation in South and Central America*, 37–49. Kristen Silvius, Richard Bodmer, and José Fragoso. Eds. New York: Columbia University Press.

Simpson, Leanne R. 2004. 'Anticolonial Strategies for the Recovery and Maintenance of Indigenous Knowledge.' *American Indian Quarterly*, 28 (3 & 4): 373–84.

Smith, Graham. 2000. 'Protecting and Respecting Indigenous Knowledge.' In *Reclaiming Indigenous Voice and Vision*, 209–24. Marie Battiste. Ed. Vancouver: UBC Press.

Smith, Linda T. 1999. *Decolonizing Methodologies: Research and Indigenous Peoples*. London: Zed Books.

Strang, Veronica. 2004. 'Close Encounters of the Third World Kind: Indigenous Knowledge and Relations to Land.' In *Development and Local Knowledge*. Alan Bicker, Paul Sillitoe, and Johan Pottier. Eds. London: Routledge.

Tauli-Corpuz, Victoria. 2003. 'Biodiversity, Traditional Knowledge and Rights of Indigenous Peoples.' *IPRs Series No.5*. Penang, Malaysia: Third World Network.

Taylor, L., and T. Griffiths. 2007. *A Desk-Based Review of the Treatment of Indigenous Peoples and Social Issues in Large and Medium-Sized GEF Biodiversity Projects (2005–2006)*. Moreton-in-Marsh, UK: Forest Peoples Programme.

Taylor, Patrick. 2001. *Nation Dance*. Bloomington: Indiana University Press.

Thomas, R. et al. 2003. 'Small and Medium Forest Enterprise in Guyana.' Discussion paper. Georgetown: Guyana Forestry Commission and IIED.

Tsing, A.L. 2005. *Friction: An Ethnography of Global Connection*. Princeton, NJ: Princeton University Press.

White, R. 2005. *Recovering the Sacred: The Power of Naming and Reclaiming*. Winona LaDuke. Ed. Cambridge, MA: South End Press.

Wondolleck, Julia M., and Steven L. Yaffee. 2000. *Making Collaboration Work: Lessons from Innovation in Natural Resource Management*. Washington, DC: Island Press.

19 From Adversaries to Allies: Forging Respectful Alliances between Indigenous and Settler Peoples

ADAM BARKER

Introduction: The Problem of Hegemonic Alliances

To be an ally first requires recognition of the need for action in a real and present struggle: in this case, the struggle of Indigenous survival and resurgence against colonial and neo-colonial power, within Canada and globally. But after this recognition, it is no easy thing to be a Settler[1] person committed to acting as an Indigenous ally; combinations of active social and cultural pressures, passive understandings of 'normal,' and internal psychological and emotional barriers often create paralysis for Settlers attempting to act in de/anti-colonial ways. As a Settler who has been attempting to act as an ally for years, with varying degrees of success, I know these complexities all too well. It is a long way, physically and conceptually, from my origins in a white, middle-class suburb of Hamilton, Ontario, to focusing my life, academic and personal, on participating in social and political activism alongside Indigenous peoples and communities.

This is my attempt to put to theory my own experiences, successes, and failures in working towards acting as an ally to Indigenous struggles in Canada and beyond. I do not claim to have the answer to the question of how Settlers can move from Adversary to Ally in the struggles taking place in colonized areas, but I hope to be able to articulate my answers as part of a dialogue among Settlers as we collectively try to figure out our roles and protocols, strengths and weaknesses, and relationships among ourselves and with Indigenous peoples and communities. The framework in which I hope to situate this dialogue is twofold: first, I am inspired by Prudhonian federalism,[2] with an emphasis on personal responsibility and the prevention of domination;

and second, by an understanding of the Haudenosaunee Guswentha (Two Row) agreement, which calls for non-interference, but also relationship-building and dynamic alliance between Indigenous and Settler societies.[3] This exploration is predicated on several key points: first, that individual Settlers have the power to choose and change their level of colonial involvement (though the process is difficult and by no means free of opposition); second, that for a Settler to choose a decolonizing path requires unlearning much of what is taken for granted in contemporary Canadian society; and third, that what it means to be a decolonized Settler and act as a true ally remains an open and dynamic concept, which is not 'settled' now, and hopefully will never become 'settled.'

In *Wasáse: Indigenous Pathways of Action and Freedom*, Mohawk scholar Taiaiake Alfred (2005) comments on the phenomenon of Settler people seeking guidance from Indigenous peoples. His response is that it is the responsibility of Settler people to figure out for themselves what their course of action should be (235), reflective of a similar sentiment expressed in 1972 by Shuswap chief and founder of the National Indian Brotherhood, George Manuel (see Regan, 2006: 30). Alfred and Manuel, then, lay the primary responsibility for the 'how' of Settler involvement in Indigenous struggles at the feet of Settler people, both individually and collectively. Personal responsibility is a concept that I both agree with, and, from a historical perspective, find extremely problematic; Settler people, and Western society in general, have managed to 'solve' problems of oppression and tyranny in the past by developing newly oppressive, hierarchical structures. The Settlers who had utilized language of anti-oppression quickly became dictatorial when Indigenous action and intent did not meet up with unrecognized colonial ideals. This is ultimately a flaw in Western methods of political engagement – as Richard Day (2005: 80), an anarchist academic and activist, points out in his discussion of 'the hegemony of hegemony':

> Both liberalism and postmarxism, then, share a reliance upon a politics of demand, a politics oriented to improving existing institutions and everyday experiences by *appealing to the benevolence of hegemonic forces and/or by altering the relations between these forces*. But, as recent history has shown, these alterations never quite produce the kinds of 'emancipation effects' their proponents expect. The gains that are made (for some) only appear as such within the logic of the existing order, and often come at a high cost for others. (emphasis added)

So it stands: some Settlers attempting to act in alliance with Indigenous peoples have missed the contradiction between their goals and their actions, ultimately replicating the effects of colonization.

In order to generate long-term alliances, Settler people must work to understand why many attempted solutions to social problems caused by Settler political structures, social norms, and chosen lifestyles continue to fail, replicating hegemonic colonial harm. This approach inevitably points to continued colonial involvement among past and present Settler peoples and societies, and thus to decolonization as a response to colonialism. There is much discussion in the literature about the need for Indigenous peoples to 'decolonize,'[4] but there has traditionally been little recognition that Settler people can, and perhaps must, decolonize as well. Just as Indigenous peoples must defeat the legacy of prior colonization and the realities of current neocolonialism in order to achieve freedom, Settler people must do the same for themselves.[5]

The Colonist Who Refuses

A barrier to Settler involvement with Indigenous causes is detailed in Albert Memmi's (1965) identity construct of 'the colonist who refuses.' In *The Colonizer and the Colonized*, Memmi draws a distinction between colonials who actively, openly, and unashamedly engage in colonization, and those who refuse to participate (at least actively). His distinction is one based on intent, not on effect. The true colonial is the person who actively engages in colonial pursuits, inherently seeing hegemonic power and a homogenous society as important goals to pursue.[6] In the contemporary liberal state of Canada, this type of colonial is rare. Yet, colonialism is not over; Taiaiake Alfred and Cherokee scholar Jeff Corntassel (2005) identify with great clarity sites of ongoing colonialism, in Canada and elsewhere, including, 'a legal, political, and cultural discourse designed to serve an agenda of silent surrender to an inherently unjust relation at the roof of the colonial state' (598). The difference is that in the present context, the individual colonizer takes on a much more obfuscating attitude, presenting themselves as a 'friend,' an 'ally,' a 'concerned citizen' – they know that there is 'something' wrong – and it is these individuals that pose a subtle, shifting danger in their support of colonial regimes. In Memmi's words: 'Finally [the colonizer who refuses] realizes that everything may change. He invokes the end of colonization, but refuses to conceive that this revolution can result in the overthrow of his situation and himself. For it is too much to ask one's imagination to visualize one's own end, even if it be in order to be reborn another; especially if, like the colonizer, one can hardly evaluate such a rebirth' (40–1).

I suggest that the first step in becoming a decolonizing Settler is contesting against this colonial ignorance that allows Settlers to maintain thinly veiled power and privilege. As the Settler historian Paulette Regan (2006) notes, it is 'virtually impossible for us not to *know* [about the oppression of Indigenous peoples]. What we choose to deny is our complicity in perpetuating a colonial system that is rooted in violence and social injustice' (22; original emphasis). Indigenous peoples in Canada suffer from overwhelming levels of disease, starvation, alcoholism, and any other indicator that can track poverty, as well as racist treatment from individuals, courts, governments, and corporate interests. These issues are widely written about, and reported on, in scholarly circles as well as in popular media. However, colonial Settlers do not recognize or acknowledge their own roles in colonial practices that not only continue into the present, but pervade our own lives. I am often reminded of the words of Albert Speer (1970),[7] who declares that, 'had I only wanted to, I could have found out ... [B]eing in a position to know and nevertheless shunning knowledge creates direct responsibility for the consequences – from the very beginning' (19). To be in a position of privilege and power and not to question the source of that power and privilege indicates a deliberate choice of colonial action and intent. This, I assert, is one of the defining characteristics of a *colonial* Settler: the ability to access such knowledge, but the refusal to do so.

Memmi's (1965: 17) concept of the 'pyramid of petty tyrants' is a useful way of understanding why non-elites participate in imperialism and oppression. He notes how a member of colonial society is content to be oppressed as long as there is someone else upon whom they can exert power. For colonial Settlers behaving in this insidiously colonial manner, silently oppressing others through a refusal to question the systems and institutions which provide us with massive benefits, is considered simply normal. Alfred (2005: 109) notes that much of what is taken for granted in contemporary North American life is part of the larger colonial project:

The basic substance of the problem of colonialism is the belief in the superiority and universality of Euroamerican culture, especially the concepts of individual rights as the highest expression of human freedom, representative democracy as being the best guarantor of peace and order, and capitalism as the only means to achieve the satisfaction of human material needs.

It is this 'liberal dogma' that is the clearest and most present manifestation of Euroamerican arrogance, and it displays itself across the political spectrum and colonial class structure as racism, conservatism, and liberalism.

This normalization of colonialism for Settler people – even those who 'refuse' on the surface – both requires and relies upon the creation of colonial Settler 'myths' about our own history. Foundational to colonial Canadian Settler identity is the 'peacemaker myth.' Regan (2006: 11) notes:

> Canadians associate violence only with physical confrontation such as that which occurred during the Oka, Gustafsen Lake, Ipperwash Park and Burnt Church crises. We are disturbed by these violent conflicts because they call into question a core belief and tenet of the peacemaker myth: that our relationship with First Nations is built on non-violence. We congratulate ourselves on the fact that armed confrontation is still the exception in Canada, seeing this somehow as proof of the moral and cultural superiority we have demonstrated by willingly negotiating with Indigenous peoples over time.

Colonial Settlers become so entrenched in the 'idea' of themselves as benevolent peacemakers, that the terrible social conditions that affect Indigenous communities across Canada are honestly surprising and confusing; they cannot follow the logic to see that their own actions – for example, promoting resource extraction on Indigenous lands – leads to brutal consequences for Indigenous peoples. The embedded myths of colonial Settler society intentionally obscure the relationship between colonization and the person of the colonizer.

If Settler peoples are serious about becoming allies to Indigenous peoples, and serious about helping to solve the problems that Indigenous communities face in the present, they must first accept that these problems have definitive causes: as cliché as it sounds, there are no accidents. Further, we as Settler people are not immune to these problems, though our privilege tends to insulate us from the brunt of the effect of colonial action. For example, economic oppression which is a result of contemporary economic imperialism does disproportionately affect Indigenous peoples; however, Settler people who have come to occupy a lower stratus of the 'pyramid of petty tyrants' (which is to say have lower levels of imperial privilege) have begun to feel these effects. As imperial forces gain a more certain control of land, which political theorist James Tully (2000: 39) identifies as a main goal of colonization, new global imperialism begins to prioritize a different basis of power – a power base that rests on communications, technology, and the subtle manipulation of 'right' and 'wrong' to generate a decentred and deterritorialized imperial construct.[8] In this neo-imperialism, formerly essential colonizers, such as primary food producers like fishers, factory labourers, or those in the automotive industry, are no longer deemed essential, and so their privilege erodes.

From this it becomes clear that globalization, social oppression, and racism are connected to the wider imperial project. Rather than being based in separate, rigid, ideological, cultural, or economic concepts, these uses and abuses of power all serve the same overarching system(s). This awareness must be internalized by Settler peoples, or we can never hope to truly confront colonialism because we will always confront it with one hand while supporting it with the other. There can be no 'sacred cows' in Western society; rather, we must question literally everything we do, all of the assumptions which underpin our personal lives and larger societies, and the myths which inform our very identities. We must be prepared to face the fact that our comfortable lives, our 'privileges,' exist because we are useful to imperialism, and that being an ally and confronting imperialism requires us to risk our comforts and to confront the entire imperial system.

'What Should We Do?' – An Honest Question?

This brings us back to the question of what we Settlers should do if we wish to truly become allies. Asked frequently, and in many different settings, it is important to understand that, as an honest, engaged question, there is nothing wrong with it. However, if the question is a dishonest one, then it only serves to perpetuate all the negative aspects of colonial Settler society. Too often, this question is motivated by feelings of guilt or shame, generated when Settler people encounter the undeniable consequences of their lifestyles in the oppression of Indigenous peoples.[9] This indicates a concern for the problems evident in Settler society as a whole, but often a lack of willingness to sacrifice personally in order to solve the problems that have been presented. Here, the more direct question is actually, 'How do I restore comfort to myself?'

Two responses to this question are typical: the first is the empty apologizing in which Settler governments especially seem to revel. Witness the

1998 'apology' by then-minister of Indian Affairs Jane Stewart for residential schools abuses which only addressed overt sexual and physical abuse that occurred in the institutions.[10] At the time, and for several years following, there was no apology whatsoever for the fact that the schools were designed to carry out cultural genocide, had staggering mortality rates, or that the families of residential school survivors are still experiencing the generational effects of the abuses and the genocidal conditions found in the schools. The 'apology' was clearly not designed to deal with the effects of the schools, or to move towards real acknowledgement and restitution, but rather to deal with the obvious and undeniable parts of the residential school legacy that make Settler society feel guilty: extreme sexual and physical abuse of children. Further, these gestures of 'apology' are rarely combined with any kind of meaningful action on the part of the government to redress the serious wrongs they finally, and in such a limited way, choose to acknowledge.

The second response is what Corntassel (2006: 36) has called the 'Free Tibet syndrome.' In this instance, colonial Settlers engage with injustices, but only with those clearly perpetrated somewhere else, by someone else. This allows the release of pent-up guilt over opulent and privileged lifestyles through the contribution to 'some good end,' without actual personal sacrifice or discomfort. Further, involvement in such causes is often token – small donations, a bumper-sticker, standing at a rally outside of an embassy or legislative building, when convenient.[11] It is as if the pain that results from colonialism is commodified; the pain that results from being colonized and the pain that results from realizing that one is a colonizer are supposed to disappear because of donations that may or may not ever actually affect anyone's life. Meanwhile, practical actions that could be taken in the immediate social and political context of the colonial Settler's own life and location are ignored.

In order to ask the question honestly, Settler people must come to understand that colonization is motivated by an implicit individualism, functionally similar to selfishness: colonial Settler actions, even when not intended as such, can appear as greed for power and privilege, insulation from conflict or fear, and the freedom to completely ignore problematic 'others' as well as the effects of individual actions.[12] Decolonization, on any scale, cannot be motivated by an effort to maintain as much comfort or privilege as possible; given the nature of hierarchical oppression, confronting oppression requires that some individuals within the hierarchy will have to make significant sacrifices. Alfred (2005) highlights the need for means-ends consistency in Indigenous peoples' struggles for freedom: a violent revolution will lead to a violent society, an economic development solution to a competitive, capitalist society, and so on (52). For Settler peoples, a personal revolution based in self-preservation above all else will result in a selfish life. To ensure that this does not happen, Settler people who hope to become effective allies must move past the desire to re-establish comfort and ask the question, 'What do we do?' from a profoundly uncomfortable place. This place of profound discomfort, generated by an honest inquiry into the causes and effects of colonialism, and our individual responsibility for colonization, is what Regan (2006) has referred to as 'unsettling the Settler within.'

The fundamental premise of Regan's approach is that we as Settlers must learn to accept that being unsettled is not something to be avoided, but rather to be embraced and explored. We become unsettled when we are confronted with the inconsistencies of colonial logic, and the paradoxes of colonial ideals. As such, unsettling moments provide for Settler people a signpost that they are bumping up against one of the weak points of imperial existence: the internal inconsistencies that only continue to function because we overlook and tacitly accept them. An unsettled Settler person is in effect breaking free of what Regan identifies as the 'myths' of Settler existence; myths about freedom of choice and the individual, economic opportunity, democratic government, and the 'right' of Canada and America to exist (among others) are all part of the long roster of myths that Settlers must confront.

Of course, being unsettled does not necessarily mean that a Settler will (or must, or even should) begin a journey towards decolonization. However, free of the insulating effects of constructs which allow and encourage ignorance,[13] a Settler person makes a critical choice: to be openly colonial, or to reject colonialism and attempt to find a different way.[14] Some individuals will choose a colonial path, making the conscious decision to embrace domination, social stratification, and the pursuit and accumulation of power. This is not surprising, nor should these individuals be judged on moral grounds by those who pursue a decolonized path. What is truly at issue here is whether or not the colonial Settler is aware of their colonialism; if so, the decision must be respected, even as the results of it are actively fought on a social level.

The Settler who chooses a decolonizing existence must adjust to new and challenging realities. First, and most importantly, there must be an understanding that Settler people, including those who reject colonial society and culture, may continue to benefit from that society and culture on many levels. There must further be an understanding that, in order to restore a measure of balance to the inevitable power relationships and imbalances in society, Settler people must be willing to take the power that has been granted to them by virtue of their 'membership' in Settler society and put it at the disposal of those whose power has been violently co-opted or stolen. Richard Day (2005) cites the need for those working towards social change to engage in 'groundless solidarity and infinite responsibility,' working with other individuals and groups who share the same goal of confronting and defeating control, domination, and oppression (186–97). For the Settler person, this means working with the Indigenous peoples upon whose land and from whose resources Settler society has been built, and also requires that Settler people give up the often-seen need or desire for 'control' of groups or actions involved in confronting imperialism. This is the meaning of the term 'groundless': Settler people must be willing to assist Indigenous peoples, groups, and nations in the pursuit of their goals, regardless of whether or not these goals fit a Settler individual's pre-existing idea of what form the struggle should take.[15]

Radical Experimentation

What must settlers do in order to decolonize? What should be sacrificed? How are lifestyles changed appropriately? These are the questions that arise from an honest engagement with internalized, personal Settler colonialism. Even when the influences of colonial and imperial power are stripped away, there is no clear single alternative to contemporary Western society or to the dominant interpretation of a colonial world view which informs societal norms. For each individual, whole arrays of previously invalidated ways of knowing and being in the world become available. However, for the Settler person bounded by the goal of being an ally, concern for an ally and respect for the autonomy of that ally (core principles of both Prudhonian federalism and the Guswentha Two Row treaty) are principles too essential to alliance building to be ignored, and therefore give Settler people a place to start. However, just as Indigenous peoples come from diverse histories and cultures and face diverse contemporary challenges with many different desired outcomes, Settler people must not fall into the trap of attempting to distil one single world view, ethic, philosophy, policy, or plan of action.

Alfred quotes biblical scholar Donald Akenson in pointing out that 'There is no such thing as a nice monotheism ... the god of any other people is *traif* (non-kosher)' (Akenson, cited in Alfred, 2005: 108; original emphasis); any absolute truth incorporates an element of domination over those who disagree with that truth. In a general sense, as Hardt and Negri (2001) point out, contemporary Empire engages in juridical construction, which is to say the large-scale defining of right and wrong, moral and immoral, in order to engage in the bio-production of power which is used to 'directly structure and articulate territories and people' (31). While Hardt and Negri identify this as a problem specifically associated with oppressive power, Day (2005) demonstrates that the generation of 'absolutes' is also a phenomenon that has been internalized by many radical challenges to oppressive power, resulting in what Day calls the 'hegemony of hegemony' (80). Because oppression is now seen as being exercised not only through direct coercive tactics, but also through culture, socialization, economic pressure, and so on, confronting oppression can be characterized by Antonio Gramsci's concept of 'counter-hegemony.' Gramsci believed that 'a social group ... strives to 'dominate antagonistic groups, which it tends to "liquidate," or to subjugate perhaps even by armed force,' at the same time as it attempts to '"lead" kindred and allied groups' (Day, 2005: 7).

In Western societies, the historical result has been the adoption of the tactics of the oppressive establishment by rebels and radical groups. Power obtained by a particular group – for example, the Bolshevik revolutionaries in Russia – is used hegemonically to promote its own ends and to quash dissent; the result is, at best, infighting among radical groups who share otherwise-common complaints, and, at worst, the replacement of one type of oppression with another.[16] When Settler people choose to engage with their own colonial legacy, or with the neo-colonial nature of contemporary Settler societies, we must be careful to avoid developing a hegemonic counter to these forces. If our intent is to end colonial oppression, then we must always keep in mind that there must be a multitude of responses to oppression. These responses will differ depending on culture, personal experience, and goals, but also will differ over time and place, and in both proactive and reactive interaction with 'shapeshifting' colonial power (Alfred and Corntassel, 2005: 601). A tactic or response that works in the present may be useless tomorrow; as such, the principles not the tactic or perspective must remain central to the effort. It is my contention that Settlers must engage in radical experimentation, with a dual, self-reflective, and groundless affinity focus (Day, 2005).

Radical experimentation is the willingness to examine current colonial problems in both a broad and personal context, and to identify problems based on the exercise of imperial domination. Rather than simply 'reforming,' or using opportunities presented within the present system, radical experimentation directs us to seek out avenues of resistance, and to assert new, non-imperial forms that are not currently in practice and that may never have been tried before. The experimental nature of this endeavour is in the intent: every attempt at something new must be undertaken self-consciously and free from ego, so that if the attempt fails – which is a distinct possibility – the failure can be a source of learning for future experiments, increasing the possibility of success. Keeping in mind the concept of an 'experiment' is also crucial to prevent attempted solutions from taking on a life of their own and becoming 'institutionalized' in the Western sense, in the way the protests against state governments have now become expected and controllable. The goal is to prevent any particular tactic from becoming more important than the principles behind it, and thus becoming a site of weakness for imperial response that can bring a great deal of power to bear on techniques, groups, or formations that refuse to shift locale, whether conceptual or physical. This experiment must be conducted both internally and externally. Internally, Settlers must constantly confront the colonial legacy within their own psyches, and be aware that the decolonization process is never 'complete.' We are all subject to re-colonization if we let our guard down, and we should never be so arrogant as to assume that we have become somehow 'pure,' and transcended colonialism.

As Settlers attempt to decolonize, there is likely to be a shift or transmutation of values and principles. Sometimes this will involve the wholesale abandonment of some principles; at other times principles may broadly change meaning. The external component of radical experimentation stems from seeking out and building alliances based on these new understandings of principles, rather than simply strategic commonality or shared interests. This is consistent with the construct of the 'smith': 'Where the practice of the citizen is oriented to "staying on the road," as it were, and that of the nomad to destroying all roads, the smith is guided by an alchemical, metallurgical will to the "involuntary invention"... of new strategies and tactics. Rather than attempting to dominate by imposing all-encompassing norms, the smith seeks to innovate by tracking and exploiting opportunities in and around structures' (Day, 2005: 174).

The smith works with available materials and seeks constant improvement of both the community and the smithy in which they work. When circumstances dictate that a particular tool is no longer useful or needed, it is no longer produced, though the knowledge of the production remains. When a smith is no longer needed in a community, they move on to a community that has need, maintaining contact with previous home communities in case of future need. The concept of the smith is not a strategy for action, but rather a useful identity and set of principles. For a Settler, the life of a smith is flexible without being completely dislocated, and the smith produces work based on personally and communally perceived need rather than on orders received from 'above.' In short, the smith discards nothing except the assumption that anything is permanent, and humbly seeks to do the best they possibly can as circumstances shift; the smith gives of their own self, serving the requests of the people.

Conclusion – No Concrete Alternatives? No Models?

One of the frustrating implications of the decolonizing, unsettling, and, ultimately, respectful approach to becoming a Settler ally, which has been outlined here, is that there is no 'plan,' no universally applicable model, no clear set of friends and enemies. There is only a set of principles, and the individual commitment to follow those principles. This is largely alien to many of us raised in Settler society, exposed to the complications and controls of colonial power. However, it is necessary in order to escape the failures of past efforts to end the oppression of Indigenous peoples and transform Settler society. The vast majority of concrete alternatives that have been or are currently proposed rely upon those in power to 'fix' oppression. This is problematic because the conflicts that arise between Indigenous and Settler peoples are the result of the thoughts and attitudes within each and every person, within society collectively, and within aspects of Western culture that inform both individuals and society. This is to say that the problems currently faced by Indigenous peoples do not emanate simply from laws, structures of government, modes of economics, or philosophical views of relationships between humans and the rest of the earth, but from within us. Settler people accept and generate all of these systems and philosophies, and, as such, tacitly accept, support, and carry out colonization of Indigenous peoples primarily, but also of each other, and of every new generation of Settlers. No government or court can legislate how we think and feel; as such, relying upon these institutions to solve these problems abdicates responsibility for our individual and collective actions, and pours even the most well-intentioned energy into a bottomless pit. Even the most optimistic assessments of contemporary Western social institutions miss the crucial point: we are responsible for ourselves. The state, corporate power, and all other aspects of complex contemporary imperialism may influence Settler people, but Settlers are not destined to be colonial; at some level, conscious or unconscious, it is a choice.

Tully (1995) points out that, 'the unity of constitutional association consists in a centralized and uniform system of legal and political authority, or clear subordination of authorities' (83). This hierarchy demands unequal distribution of power in government, which is then reflected in all aspects of society – someone must govern, and someone must be governed. Individuals likewise participate in these systems in order to partake of the lower-level benefits available to collaborators – this is the contemporary 'pyramid of petty tyrants.' The lesson is clear: the power to change a society must be generated by the society itself; if it is imposed, it will be oppressive. And, if societal change is to be pursued seriously, the change must be fundamental. Rather than attempting to build new checks and balances, new government departments and economic development schemes, Settlers must start asking basic questions: who are we, what do we want our society to look like, and how do we wish to relate to the Indigenous peoples whose lands we live upon? In this scenario, an ally must accept that all potential solutions to the problems generated by imposed colonialism must be based in a clear and engaged understanding of principles – primarily, respect. Turner (2006: 49) provides an excellent definition of respect from the Haudenosaunee perspective that may inspire Settlers further. He notes:

> [I]n a political context, respecting another person's intrinsic value means that you recognize that they have the right to speak their mind and to choose for themselves how to act in the world. It follows that in principle, one cannot tell another what to do or how to behave … But respect functioned in a communal context; that is, individual respect was reciprocated. This form of reciprocity is what gave rise to freedom of speech and freedom of religion … The freedom of speech gave everyone the right to speak his or her mind, but it was embedded in the context that everyone else possessed the same right.

How this understanding of respect can be manifested in reality is hard to say, as it possibly calls into question fundamental legal and political principles of contemporary states, and definitely requires a paradigm shift in popular (colonial) understandings of individual rights, social responsibility, and basic conceptions of Indigenous 'integration' into Canada or America. In order to understand what needs to be done, decolonizing Settler people must first achieve an understanding of the meaning of respect, both in Western traditions and Indigenous traditions, and then experiment with manifestations of respect in relationships.

In the course of such efforts, some relationships will not turn out as expected or intended, and some plans may have to be scrapped and new ones undertaken. This must not be viewed as a reason to stop trying. So long as respect is the driving principle, mistakes are a source of useful information. There is no true failure when attempts to build a different world do not reach the lofty goals of those who plan them; there is only true failure if pursuit of those plans entails the abandonment of respect, or reliance upon control and domination, or an attempt to build harmful absolutes. Ultimately, to do nothing is itself failure; to risk oneself and become unsettled is a success in and of itself. There is no one way to be an ally, just as there is no one way to be colonial. There is not one single struggle against imperialism, and so there is no one single solution to these struggles. No one solution, that is, except to try.

NOTES

This chapter originally grew out of the presentation of an excerpt of my MA thesis at the Building Alliances Conference held at Trent University in November 2006. An earlier version was presented at the annual conference of the Western Social Sciences Association in April 2007. I would like to sincerely thank the participants in both conferences for their feedback. I would especially like to thank Taiaiake Alfred and Jeff Corntassel for their generous editing assistance, and Emma Battell Lowman for her support and guidance throughout.

1 The term 'Settler' refers, in general, to any non-Indigenous individual who is living on Indigenous lands and participating in contemporary Euro-American society. It is a term that attempts to break free of totalizing racial or ethnic signifiers such as 'white' or 'European,' while still recognizing the influence of race and heritage in identity construction and social privilege.

It is also designed to recognize that it is possible to be a Settler *without inherently being colonial in ideology and action*, as will be demonstrated in this chapter. I make no distinction between Settlers whose families arrived as colonists centuries ago, or immigrants to contemporary Settler states, such as Canada. I do exclude various groups from this definition; for example, some North Americans of African descent whose existence upon Indigenous lands and exposure to Settler society is itself predicated on imperialism and colonial actions. For a more complete discussion of the nature of the Settler identity, please see *Being Colonial* (Barker, 2006).

2 It is very difficult to define exactly what Prudhonian federalism 'looks like,' as it is necessarily context-specific and place-based. However, it is important to note that Prudhon (2005: 74) conceived of a 'federal system … contrary of hierarchy or administration and governmental centralization which characterizes, to an equal extent, democratic empires, constitutional monarchies, and unitary republics.'

3 Dale Turner (2006: 48) makes an important point in noting that, in addition to the well-known 'parallel rows' of the Guswentha, which signify a parallel partnership between allies, it is also 'crucial to point out … that there are three beads, representing peace, respect, and friendship, that bridge the two parallel rows.' As such, my theoretical framing is based on a concept of autonomy, but also of interconnectedness.

4 Please see Alfred (2005), and Linda Smith's (1999) *Decolonizing Methodologies* for two good examples among many.

5 As a grammatical note, I attempt to refer to Settlers in this chapter in a generalized or gender-neutral sense. I do not employ 'him/her' universally, as I reject this sort of strict dichotomy of sex or gender. More often, I use the pronouns 'they' or 'their' to represent individual Settlers; this is an intentional violation of grammatical rules in response to the lack of an appropriate neutral pronoun.

6 The basis of this homogenous society – nationalism, evangelical religious precepts, racial or ethnic 'purity,' or even strict political ideological demands (i.e., an insistence upon liberal capitalist democratic statehood) – is not important. The overall drive for homogenization that results is the key.

7 Albert Speer was a powerful member of the Nazi party in Germany during the Second World War, serving as the Minister for Armaments. He later repented his actions, pleaded guilty in Nuremburg, and served 20 years in Spandau Prison without attempts to appeal. His later memoirs are critical of imperialism in general, as well as his own actions and those of the Third Reich.

8 The nature of this 'decentered' and 'deterritorializing' imperialism is in dispute. While Hardt and Negri (2001: 35) rightly point out that imperial power

now seeks not just to control territory but to define the nature of society, Day (2005: 6) argues that this project does still have specific centres of power – state governments, international trade bodies, and capitalist elites – that can be identified and engaged with as 'struggles occur in an increasingly common context.' In some cases, such as that of Canada, where territory itself is still in question, the effect is one of generating a hybrid colonialism that simultaneously seeks to secure territory for the Canadian state, while constantly redefining reality for Canadian citizens, emphasizing colonial Settler 'myths' in order to maximize cooperation. This concept of hybrid colonialism is developed further in *Being Colonial* (Barker, 2006: 14–18).

9 At the National University of Ireland's Fifth Conference on Colonialism (Settler Colonialism), Haunani-Kay Trask (University of Hawai'i) asserted that there is a high level of this phenomenon in Hawai'i, a statement supported by Settler academics Eiko Kosasa (Leeward Community College) and Candace Fujikane (University of Hawai'i). From a panel presentation, 'Settler Colonialism in Hawai'i,' 27 June 2007, at the National University of Ireland, Galway.

10 The 'apology' has never actually been referred to officially as an apology, but rather as a 'statement of reconciliation' made as part of the *Gathering Strength* action plan that was announced on 7 January 1998, in direct response to the findings of the Royal Commission on Aboriginal Peoples. Please see *Gathering Strength* (1998) for the full text of the statement.

11 This is not to denigrate the efforts of Settler and other peoples who perceive and address connections between distant and local oppression, or the field of internationalism generally, which has long been a locus of Indigenous struggles. It is a comment, rather, on commodified activism.

12 I fully examine the existence of and rationale behind these colonial barriers to Settler decolonization in *Being Colonial* (Barker, 2006).

13 The complex, subtle, and overlapping systems and constructs which discourage critical inquiry are too numerous to fully describe here. However, as an example, Blackfoot philosopher Leroy Little Bear describes how Western focuses on individualism have generated a society of 'specialists': keepers of arcane knowledge in one narrow field, and disinterested in (or discouraged from seeking out) knowledge in other fields or commenting on matters not explicitly tied to their speciality. Please see Little Bear (2000: 75–85) for further investigation of this.

14 This is, of course, an oversimplification; the choice to be colonial or not is in no way dichotomous. There are many variations on and much 'grey area' in the general philosophy of decolonization. Personal experience,

spiritual and religious affiliations, family circumstances, and/or ethnic, gender, sexual, and class conditions can and do generate many different possibilities and problems. Further, we have no ability to predict the ways in which some 'established' institutions may be subverted, or the ways in which some methods of radical resistance and resurgence may themselves be co-opted. As such, it is impossible to comment on the full range of potential experience; however, this generalization is useful as an introduction to the possible range of decisions.

15 This has been a serious issue throughout the history of interactions between Indigenous groups and elements of Settler 'counterculture.' For example, the communist and post-Marxist socialist movements in the 1960s and 1970s attempted to draw direct parallels between their own ideology and Indigenous struggles for freedom, but remained unwilling to question their own ideologies even when they proved harmful to Indigenous interests.

16 While the founding of the Soviet Union is an obvious example of this, one could also look to the example of the American attempts to 'liberate' South American states through the use of the School of the Americas over the course of the twentieth century.

REFERENCES

Alfred, Taiaiake. 2005. *Wasáse: Indigenous Pathways of Action and Freedom*. Peterborough, ON: Broadview Press.

Alfred, Taiaiake, and Corntassel, Jeff. 2005. 'Being Indigenous.' *Government and Opposition*, 40 (4): 597–614.

Barker, Adam. 2006. 'Being Colonial: Colonial Mentalities in Canadian Settler Society and Political Theory.' Thesis submitted in partial fulfilment of requirements for the degree of Master of Arts, Indigenous Governance Program, University of Victoria, BC.

Campbell, Joseph. 1991. *The Power of Myth*. With Bill Moyers. Ed. Betty Sue Flowers. New York: Anchor Books.

Corntassel, Jeff. 2006. 'To Be Ungovernable.' *New Socialist*, 58 (September-October): 35–7.

Day, Richard. 2000. *Multiculturalism and the History of Canadian Diversity*. Toronto: University of Toronto Press.

– (2005). *Gramsci Is Dead: Anarchist Currents in the Newest Social Movements*. Toronto: Between the Lines.

Deloria, Vine. 1994. *God Is Red*. Golden, CO: Fulcrum Press.

Fields, Barbara J. 1990. 'Slavery, Race, and Ideology in the United States of America.' *New Left Review*, 181: 96–188.

Gathering Strength: Canada's Aboriginal Action Plan. (1997). Published under the authority of the Minister of Indian Affairs and Northern Development, Indian and Northern Affairs Canada. Last accessed 11 April 2006 from http://www.ainc-inac.gc.ca/gs/chg_e.html#reconciliation.

Hardt, Michael, and Negri, Antonio. 2001. *Empire*. Boston: Harvard University Press.

Hochschild, Adam. 1999. *King Leopold's Ghost*. New York: Mariner Books.

Little Bear, Leroy. 2000. 'Jagged World Views Colliding.' *Reclaiming Indigenous Voice and Vision*. Ed. Marie Battiste. Vancouver: UBC Press.

Memmi, Albert. 1965. *The Colonizer and the Colonized*. 1965. Boston: Beacon Press.

Pierce Erikson, Patricia. 1999. 'A-Whaling We Will Go: Encounters of Knowledge and Memory at the Makah Cultural and Research Centre.' *Cultural Anthropology*, 14, no. 4 (November): 556–83.

Prudhon, Pierre-Joseph. 2005. Excerpt from 'The Principle of Federation.' In *Anarchism – A Documentary History of Libertarian Ideas. Volume One: From Anarchy to Anarchism (300CE to 1939)*, 72–4. Robert Graham. Ed. 1863. Reprint. Montreal: Black Rose Books.

Regan, Paulette. 2006. *Unsettling the Settler Within: Canada's Peacemaker Myth, Reconciliation, and Transformative Pathways to Decolonization*. Dissertation submitted in fulfilment of requirements for the degree of Doctor of Philosophy, Indigenous Governance Program, University of Victoria, BC.

Smith, Linda. 1999. *Decolonizing Methodologies*. London: Zed Books.

Speer, Albert. 1970. *Inside the Third Reich: Memoirs by Albert Speer*. C. Winston. Trans. Toronto: Macmillan.

Tully, James. 1995. *Strange Multiplicity*. Oxford: Oxford University Press.

– 2000.'The Struggles of Indigenous Peoples for and of Freedom.' In *Political Theory and the Rights of Indigenous Peoples*, 36–59. Duncan Ivison, Paul Patten, and Will Sanders. Eds. Cambridge: Cambridge University Press.

Turner, Dale. 2006. *This Is Not a Peace Pipe*. Toronto: University of Toronto Press.

Willems-Braun, Bruce. 1997. 'Buried Epistemologies: The Politics of Nature in (Post) Colonial British Columbia.' *Annals of the Association of American Geographers*, 87, no. 1 (March): 3–31.

20 The Spirit of Relationships: What We Have Learned about Indigenous/Non-Indigenous Alliances and Coalitions

LYNNE DAVIS AND HEATHER YANIQUE SHPUNIARSKY

If you're going to do anything, then talk to us. Let's do it together, be-cause… our responsibility is not just for the [environmental] cause; our responsibility is for the generations to come. Everything is inter-related … Your agenda is so short and ours is so long …

– First Nations leader[1]

In a global world, Indigenous peoples may decide to work with social and environmental justice groups while defending their territories, as-serting their Aboriginal or Indigenous rights, or fighting against injus-tice. Coalitions and alliances may offer a stronger chance of achieving their goals by enlarging and strengthening the pool of political voices, resources, and energies. From the Inuit working on climate change issues in their homelands, to the Grand Council of the Cree who fought for decades to secure the *Declaration on the Rights of Indigenous Peoples* at the United Nations, to the Native Women's Association of Canada who want police action on missing or murdered Indigenous women, Indigenous peoples have worked in alliances and coalitions with non-Indigenous organizations and individuals. The struggles in Grassy Narrows (Da Silva, Chapter 3), West Coast First Nations homelands (Smith and Sterritt, Chapter 9), and the Ardoch Algonquin First Nation against uranium mining (Sherman, Chapter 8) are but three examples of alliances in this volume where a coalescence of interests brought people together. Alliances or coalitions may be initiated by Indigenous peoples; alterna-tively, social and environmental justice groups may approach Indigenous peoples to work together where they perceive shared objectives, or where they wish to express their solidarity.

Such relationships form within a larger context of ongoing colonization of Indigenous peoples in their homelands and in urban spaces. For decades, Indigenous leaders and scholars (e.g., Cardinal, 1969; Adams, 1989; Mercerdi and Turpel, 1994; Monture, 1999; Battiste, 2000; Alfred, 2005; Simpson, 2008) have been documenting the continuing colonization not only of lands, systems of governance, languages, spiritual practices, and identities, but also the mind itself through imposed systems of ideas and beliefs, a phenomenon that Battiste and Henderson (2000) call 'cognitive imperialism.' Such colonization is sustained not only by large structural forces such as legal regimes and schooling, but also through the discourses and practices of everyday life (Foucault, 1980; Said, 1979; Gramsci, 1971; Williams, 1973). The power relations conditioned by colonialism are at the same time pervasive but invisible to most Canadians. Such practices are, however, mobilized when Indigenous and non-Indigenous people enter into relationships such as alliances and coalitions.

Early anti-colonial authors such as Memmi (1965), Fanon (1991), and Freire (1970) have all elaborated analyses of colonization that have proven useful in understanding Indigenous and non-Indigenous relationships today: for example, the role of someone from the 'colonizer' group in the struggle of the 'colonized,' with all its layers of complexity. Such an analysis is very relevant to the two authors of this chapter, both of whom are non-Indigenous.

The Alliances Project was designed to examine the dynamics of such relationships,[2] drilling below the macro-forces that shape the colonial space within which Indigenous/non-Indigenous relationships function. Starting in 2004, three interview-based case studies were completed: the Coalition for a Public Inquiry into the Killing of Dudley George at Ipperwash; the Coastal First Nations' Turning Point Initiative; and a community study of a coastal First Nation. The latter two case studies have focused on First Nations' relationships with environmental groups on the West Coast of Canada. In addition, interviews were conducted with Indigenous and non-Indigenous leaders and activists who have long experience in working in alliances, coalitions, and partnerships. In each of these study components, individuals were asked why they chose to work together, what worked in the relationships, where the tensions were, what they learned from working together, and what advice they would give to others in entering into relationships. People were very forthcoming in sharing their experiences and they had lots of advice to offer to others. They did so with the hope that others could learn from their experiences so that stronger, more respectful relationships could be established.[3]

The initial findings of the Alliances research have been reported in Davis, O'Donnell, and Shpuniarsky (2007), an article which focuses on what we learned from examining the case study of the Coalition for a Public Inquiry into Ipperwash. Interviews were conducted with members and supporters of the Coalition, both Indigenous and non-Indigenous. In reading the interviews, three main themes were prominent, and we termed them: coalition as a microcosm of colonial relationships; coalition as a site of learning and transformation; and coalition as a site of pain. When the West Coast case studies were completed, the same themes were evident in the interviews with First Nations and environmental group leaders. And, again, the themes appeared in interviews with seasoned Indigenous and non-Indigenous leaders and activists.

Our purpose in this chapter is to elaborate upon these themes, which are far-reaching throughout the Alliances research.[4] In doing so, we will draw directly from what people shared about their experiences of working together, and also from the advice they offered to share with others. Their words reveal the architecture of complex social practices that produce shared meanings and understandings and that allow individuals to cross between social worlds. At the same time, we see that everyday social practices may undermine the possibility of mutual understanding, and instead construct boundaries that seem immutable.

1. Coalition as a Microcosm of Colonial Relationships

> We can create working relationships with these organizations, but we don't want to be controlled by them. Because I don't think anybody can tell us any better how to do the job than we already know. (First Nations leader)

Self-determination is a principle that Indigenous peoples insist upon in forming relationships with other parties. This is a value that is actively practised when Indigenous peoples interact with one another; it takes the form of non-interference in the business of other Nations. This principle reflects careful attention to power and control issues. Since Indigenous peoples continually face the imposition of laws, customs, and cultural beliefs by the Canadian state and Canadian society, many Indigenous people are highly attuned to social behaviours and ways of speaking that reflect paternalism. In the words of one First Nations leader: 'I can read in between the lines – being a residential school kid.

I know human behaviour pretty good. You don't have to go to school for that when you grow up with it. You could tell the intentions of people right off the bat.'

When Indigenous and non-Indigenous people come together in alliances and coalitions, paternalism may be mobilized, subtly or overtly. There are often breeches of Indigenous social codes of which many non-Indigenous people are simply not aware. As a result, the relationship can be marked by the same disregard of Indigenous values and traditions that characterize Indigenous/non-Indigenous relationships in the broader society. Despite the good intentions of the allies, colonial relationships can be reproduced. Everyone spoke about the importance of respect and trust as the foundation of building coalitions and alliances. In manifesting respect, relationships of power surface in such issues as control of the agenda and questions of voice. These are discussed below.

Respect and Trust

> The first meeting should be, let's get to know each other, and I think that would be really important ... get to know each other and always remember to respect one another. (Indigenous contributor)

Relationship-building is an ongoing process where respect and trust are built over time. Building personal relations of respect is a key to being able to work together successfully. Both Indigenous and non-Indigenous people emphasized the value of respect as the cornerstone of the relationships that they have built. One Indigenous contributor stated: 'You need to be respectful of each other; it doesn't matter who they are or where they come from ... It's not a one-sided deal all the time. It's got to work two ways.' A non-Indigenous participant stated: 'Sometimes, we're going to disagree because we're coming from different places, but if you don't at least respect where the other person comes from, you're going to have a lot of trouble.'

While there is wide agreement that respect is first and foremost in relationships, respect is something that has to be demonstrated in day-to-day interactions. It means following appropriate protocols when entering a community; participating in opening ceremonies and prayers at the beginning of a meeting; thanking and recognizing the Nation in whose territory a meeting takes place; remembering to provide an honorarium to an Elder who has been asked to participate in a meeting, if that is the local custom; and observing the cultural protocols of interaction that are considered respectful for those Nations who are meeting. To give just one example, from a non-Indigenous contributor: 'We just arranged that money be made available to First Nations people coming in for events, that they be supported in terms of their costs. So, we always did pay honorariums to traditional teachers as is appropriate [and], honorariums to drums or to anyone who was doing traditional teachings as part of what we had organized.'

Non-Indigenous people often make mistakes in interacting with Indigenous peoples. It takes time to learn appropriate protocols. As one non-Indigenous contributor commented: 'I think that part of the process of building alliances with Aboriginal people is that you have to open yourself to their ways. Not that you have to be in their ways all the time, but to be open to their ways. And to me it was incredibly enriching. I learned so much that ... I can't even put into words.'

There may be differences of opinion on how autonomously the solidarity group should operate. Partners in a relationship do not always agree, but they can still show respect.

In coalitions, trust is part of working towards a respectful relationship. Placed in the context of colonization, trust between Indigenous and non-Indigenous peoples is not always easy to achieve, as Dorothy Christian and Victoria Freeman remind us in the story of their evolving friendship (Chapter 23, this volume). Mistrust of non-Indigenous peoples is ever-present due to a long history of broken promises, racism, and lies. Even if the mistrust is not readily evident, it may take only one incident to bring these concerns to light. Both Indigenous and non-Indigenous participants stated that all parties should learn to recognize the historical lack of trust and work to overcome this together. As one Indigenous contributor stated: 'It's a very long road, because history has taught us that non-Aboriginal peoples are not to be trusted because they have broken promises.'

Honesty is an important component in building trust. As will be discussed below, this means being upfront about what each party has on their agenda. People need to be honest and clear about their motivations, and about the impetus involved in forming the relationship.

Control of the Agenda

Be open about your intentions. You always need to say, 'These are my intentions. This is what we're going out for.' But never, ever promise too much, like what you can give in return. That creates a lot of hurt in our community. (First Nations leader)

Both Indigenous and non-Indigenous people emphasized the importance of being open and honest about one's agenda from the start. Many non-Indigenous people come to work with Indigenous people with their own agenda in mind. But if relationships are going to be successful, the agenda of Indigenous people must have centrality. As one non-Indigenous contributor stated, 'We definitely learned early on to listen, and part of the respect for us was just to listen. And in doing that, we came up with, "Okay, control is their main issue," and then having the ability to implement things. Control over decision-making on the land, and then having the capacity/capital to be able to implement what it is that they want to do. Those are key fundamental issues for them.'

On the West Coast, Indigenous leaders noted that the narrow agenda of environmentalists presents challenges in working together. First Nations communities are active on many issues at once, and their holistic approach may elude the analysis of single-issue organizations: 'That's been one of the problems with forming strong relationships and coalitions and alliances with other parties,' said one First Nations leader. 'They're pretty much single issue in a short term, where ours are quite broad and involve issues from culture to economics to our heritage and land claims. So a lot of that time is eaten up by educating not only the proponent but also the parties involved in the process.'

Historically, Indigenous peoples have endured paternalistic relationships with Canadian governments: the Indian Act is still in force today, and continues to regulate the lives of First Nations peoples from cradle to grave. Colonization is tightly interwoven with paternalism. In some coalitions, non-Indigenous peoples may take actions without consulting their Indigenous partners. This may be easily rationalized because of experience, education, and class, but it is based on the insidious belief of racial superiority. This is very similar to actions taken by the government on behalf of Indigenous peoples without consulting them. Most Indigenous people that spoke to us acknowledged that having control over the agenda of a coalition was of utmost importance. Successful relationships tend to have an Indigenously driven agenda.

Voice

Who speaks, and whose voice has authority? This is also a very sensitive issue in coalitions and alliances. This has happened on the West Coast with environmental groups:

It was their assumption that they could speak for people that had no voices themselves, and I personally took great offence to that. But one of our top hereditary leaders said [to them], 'Don't ever assume that because we're a First Nation or we're Native that we don't have a voice of our own. Nobody speaks for First Nations. Nobody speaks for [our] people other than [our] people themselves. (First Nations leader)

The issue of voice is particularly potent in a field of power imbalances. In the wider society, it is quite evident that non-Indigenous voices are understood as the voices of authority. Within coalitions, when non-Indigenous people assume that they have the right to speak for their Indigenous partners, this acutely mirrors the wider society and echoes a historical experience in which Indigenous peoples were prevented from speaking for themselves. When this occurs in a coalition, it is a sign of disrespect and a reminder that control does not lie with Indigenous peoples. One Indigenous contributor stated: 'One of the biggest failings in some of the groups is that you get a person who figures they should have control over the whole thing ...'

And the following view from an Indigenous contributor illustrates well how colonialism and paternalism may be finely woven into the grain of daily interaction: 'What does it mean to work together in a good way? We're equal. I'm not trying to overpower you. I'm not trying to push my views. That is what the Church did to our people ... You begin to see that there are people who will come and tell you how to do it. They'll impose and they'll talk a lot. Talking a lot can be another way of taking over. And so you silence the other people. You begin to see that the person doesn't have as much value.' Coalitions have to be consistently aware of these tendencies. Successful partnerships are diligent in ensuring Indigenous peoples' voices are not only heard, but also guide the vision. Sometimes, Indigenous and non-Indigenous partners deal with potential tensions by entering into formal protocol agreements that outline mutual expectations with respect to communications, representation of an issue in the public domain, and dispute resolution.

2. Coalition as a Site of Learning and Transformation

One of the most striking aspects of building relationships is the significant learning that takes place for those involved, particularly non-Indigenous people. Most non-Indigenous participants in this research report that their experiences of encounter with Indigenous peoples, cultures, and traditions change their lives in profoundly important ways. Most of those interviewed spoke very movingly about their learning as a result of the relationships that were built and the experiences of being together.

A principal site of learning for many non-Indigenous participants is awakening to their own personal, family, and community histories. This foundation must be laid so that they can try to understand Indigenous histories and experiences:

> As part of the Christian community, we too have to own our share of the history of interaction between Aboriginal people and church in this country, and I think it was very important both that we owned it and recognized that there's a reconciling and a repairing of harm that we have to always be conscious of ... you never start from zero in your relationships from the church with Aboriginal people. (Non-Indigenous contributor)

Non-Indigenous peoples must also understand that they benefit daily from colonization, both past and present. Whether the heirs of early colonization or more recent immigration, Canadians depend upon the lands that the Canadian state has appropriated from Indigenous peoples; Canada's economy has been built through the cultivation of lands and the extraction of resources from Indigenous territories. Even the most basic of survival needs such as access to clean water has rested upon the displacement of Indigenous peoples from their traditional territories. Developing an awareness of these historic and contemporary realities is necessary in order to approach a relationship with Indigenous peoples honestly: 'People need to take responsibility for their own education,' one non-Indigenous contributor stated. 'People need to educate themselves about what territory they live in, what treaty it's covered under, and what treaty violation are they benefiting off of through the property they own, or whatever those issues are.'

Non-Indigenous people must not only become aware of their own histories, but also of the diversity of Indigenous nations and about the history of the formation of Canada. Understanding that each *First Nation* is very different, with a different history, and with different cultural protocols is fundamental to forming a respectful relationship. A non-Indigenous contributor put it this way: 'First of all, each First Nation is different. To use an analogy, you would not go into Sweden and say because I was in Portugal last month, Portugal and Sweden are both in Europe, therefore my appropriate behaviour and the motivations of those around me are the same here as they were in Portugal. You would be laughed out of the room. And yet we go from nation to nation as if they are all the same. So they're not, and you have to understand and respect the unique difference. The cultures are quite different.' Assuming that all First Nations are the same is to function under a potent and prevalent stereotype. One Indigenous contributor stated: 'When I worked at the park, I had someone come in and say, "Oh, are you a real honest-to-goodness Indian? Do you live in a tipi?"'

As the authors know from the experience of teaching in Indigenous Studies, non-Indigenous people are initially confused about language and terminology, particularly when it is appropriate to use such terms as 'Indigenous,' 'Indian,' 'Native,' 'First Nation,' 'Métis,' 'Inuit,' 'Indigenous,' or the name of a specific nation. This is particularly prevalent for individuals who have had little prior history of working with Indigenous peoples and who must learn to navigate a complex and shifting terrain of 'naming' that has deep power implications, depending upon the context.

Indigenous and non-Indigenous peoples who seek to build coalitions together must learn to establish a way of communicating across cultural differences. The way we choose to communicate with each other cannot be taken for granted and must be explored within the context of each relationship: 'Communication is very much needed in a way that everyone understands each other, so that we're all on the same page,' said one Indigenous contributor, '... because if we're not, then we'll end up doing things together thinking we're on the same page, but we're not. We're going to be running into each other and we're not going to be working together.'

Although there are definitely instances in the interviews where Indigenous peoples speak about their learning from alliance-building with non-Indigenous individuals and organizations, the more striking feature of the interviews is the fact that Indigenous peoples take on the role of teachers and mentors of non-Indigenous peoples. This can be a very time-consuming task, but it is one that Indigenous peoples may consider an important investment. As discussed in Davis, O'Donnell, and Shpuniarsky (2007), Indigenous spirituality is a very significant area of learning for non-Indigenous people, particularly in contexts where spiritual practices are openly shared. However, it is evident that Indigenous mentorship is wide-ranging and includes history, world views, values, and Indigenous knowledge, as in the example below:

That is how we got involved. We started by offering ... to join with them and participate in meetings, and we started by sharing in our culture and showing how we start off meetings with smudging, and then we started including our music, singing in opening ceremonies, and we've been involved since that time. (Indigenous contributor)

One of the things that I try to do at a regional level is try to get the environmental NGOs to come together ... as a group to have workshops around Indigenous issues so they can be educated more on a group basis. And it would be a matter of scale for us, that if we tried to go to every environmental NGO, that would be so time-consuming and expensive, so I thought that would be a good approach, bring them together and talk about our issues and why we're different, but also why we have a lot of things in common. (First Nations leader)

What I learned from Indigenous people and which I'm putting into practice now in what I'm doing, is ... that the decisions we make are for seven generations. (Non-Indigenous contributor)

Learning and transformation is a very prominent theme in the experience of coalition-building. People who may have been previously ignorant about Indigenous peoples, their diversity, and colonization, find they must become a quick study in order to continue a relationship successfully. Openness to embarking on a process of continuous learning is an important element in successful relationship-building.

3. Coalition as a Site of Pain

It's very hard learning how to do this kind of work. It's like jumping into cold water off the end of a pier when you don't know how to swim. It's hard building trust. It's very hard work to do. It's very painful work to do. You have to spend a lot of time. You have to really look at yourself. (Non-Indigenous contributor)

Working through something as intense and deep as colonization causes pain for both Indigenous and non-Indigenous peoples. During this process feelings can be hurt as people struggle with the concept and reality of colonization. As Indigenous peoples struggle to confront the pain of colonization in its many forms, non-Indigenous peoples struggle to look inward at their own role within colonization, and confront themselves.

Ignorance and Arrogance

Non-Indigenous people often manifest profound ignorance in relation to Indigenous history, spiritual practices, beliefs, world views, and knowledge. They do things and say things that are highly offensive, disrespectful, and cause hurt, often without realizing it. Dorothy Christian and Victoria Freeman document some of this dynamic in Chapter 23 of this volume. Sometimes, the dynamics are very subtle and unspoken, as shared by this Indigenous contributor: 'I have a hard time addressing a large group [of non-Indigenous people] ... I find that very difficult to do. I don't know why that is ... Sometimes I feel I am not heard ... "[I wonder] why are you asking me to come and talk if you are not going to hear, and you're not going to take [what I'm sharing]?"'

While hurt may occur in everyday interaction, it may also occur in more formal settings of alliance-building when non-Indigenous individuals are acting in their professional capacities, for example, as 'experts' such as scientists. As one First Nations leader explained, 'When I talked to some of the biologists and foresters and others who work for environmental groups, they've got a whole different idea of what happens within our traditional territories than we do. I mean, we understand because we live here; we were brought up here. And they have a learned understanding of what should be happening, but it doesn't always happen the way the books say it's supposed to.'

Here, the assumption of privilege is expressed in how outside experts respond to local traditional knowledge, which may be dismissed, minimized, or decontextualized. First Nations leaders talked about the arrogance of many environmentalists on the West Coast who simply do not understand that First Nations cultures are built on millennia of stewardship of local ecosystems, and that the people have intimate knowledge of their environments. This is but one example where paternalism and disrespect are the source of considerable pain and frustration.

Anger

One dimension of coalition-building that may surface in a relationship is anger. Colonization, carried out by white or non-Indigenous people, has caused much resentment in some Indigenous people. In a relationship, these feelings may surface, particularly when there is a misstep by the non-Indigenous person. Non-Indigenous people in a relationship with Indigenous people may become a focus for this rage. Participants in successful relationships are able to move past this difficult occurrence together.

In the words of Robyn Buyers, one of the leaders of the Coalition for a Public Inquiry into Ipperwash, '… as a white person, it's important to enter into alliances with Native people fully aware that you are the direct representative of a colonial history that has damaged or destroyed whole communities…' (Davis, O'Donnell, and Shpuniarsky, 2007). And, as a non-Indigenous environmental leader shared, reflecting back on the experiences of building relationships with First Nations: 'In those early days, some of those meetings were very ugly. Like the things that we would get called, and the things that would get blamed on us. What I learned is, all you can do is be compassionate and listen. No point in saying, but that's not me, but I don't feel that way … No. I am white, and this is what my people did. This is the truth.'

Mistakes

In many ways, these relationships can break new ground between Indigenous and non-Indigenous peoples, and there will be missteps. In most coalitions there are periods of adjustment as people get to know one another. In successful relationships, mistakes are dealt with in an open and honest fashion; no relationship is without its rocky patches. However, mistakes are opportunities to better understand each other and grow together. One non-Indigenous participant stated: 'We made mistakes …we all made mistakes. It was uncharted ground.'

Pain can be the teacher of some of the most important lessons. Despite the pain and the cultural missteps, most of the participants stated that the risk was worth it. Being vulnerable is one of the largest risks we take as humans, to let other people in and risk them hurting us. Once people are able to be vulnerable with one another, trust is built much more easily. Another non-Indigenous contributor shared: 'It really had the impact on me, realizing that there was no way to do that work and not be made that vulnerable … I think this [coalition] work was the first time I really worked with women who I just saw being vulnerable.'

Cultural misunderstandings, colonial encounters, miscommunications, and many other small interactions may result in pain. Individuals, both Indigenous and non-Indigenous, shared openly various moments of trauma and betrayal that they had experienced, and many such moments remain very fresh for those who have lived them.

Concluding Thoughts

Colonization is a looming presence in relationships between Indigenous and non-Indigenous peoples. Indeed, one of the most pressing reasons for forming relationships between Indigenous and non-Indigenous peoples is to combat current colonization and to try to deal with the many complex outcomes of past colonization. Colonization has many different faces, and these faces can show themselves in any relationship between Indigenous and non-Indigenous people, despite all precautions.

A very important part of colonization is perpetuating oppression. Most of the people we talked to said that when participants in a relationship are not aware, they will continue to live out various forms of colonization even if they maintain that this is not the case. This involves duplicating the unequal power relationships that exist between Indigenous and non-Indigenous peoples in the larger society in a coalition or alliance. In many cases, this can also happen when non-Indigenous peoples try to use Indigenous peoples to further their own agenda. The self-determination of Indigenous peoples is not respected, and decision-making power or control lies with the non-Indigenous partners in the relationship. Relationships such as these do not tend to be successful.

Then why form alliances and coalitions? There are certainly Indigenous leaders for whom alliances and coalitions with non-Indigenous people are peripheral or are to be avoided. They prefer to move forward on the basis of Nation-to-Nation relationships and deal with state actors directly. However, many of the people who shared their experiences, both Indigenous and non-Indigenous, have spent years thinking about what it means to work together. As researchers, we were struck by their candidness and by their genuine willingness to help others in building relationships based on respect, trust, and solidarity.

The findings of the Alliances research illustrate the complexity of creating alliances and coalitions. At the same time, those who were interviewed pointed to the opportunities that result from sharing resources, including social capital such as political influence, mobilization potential, and specific kinds of expertise (Davis, O'Donnell, and Shpuniarsky, 2007; Davis, 2008). On the West Coast, greater access to financial resources has also been a benefit to First Nations through their relationships with environmental groups (Davis, 2010). At times of crisis, when many alliances and coalitions form, people identify strategic advantages to working with together. As First Nations' territories become mapped by new glocalities (Drapeau, Chapter 14, this volume), the ability to reach across international state boundaries becomes crucial to undertaking strategic resistance such as market campaigns (e.g., Smith and Sterritt, Chapter 9). International mobilization with Indigenous peoples worldwide, as well as social and environmental justice organizations, can provide effective tools for advancing Indigenous goals, as illustrated by Benjamin, Preston, and Léger (Chapter 4).

The Alliances Project was initiated with a deep desire to help illuminate people's experiences of working together. We have learned that there is no simple recipe for respectful relationships, no 'best practices.' Relationship-building is an ongoing process that is fluid and constantly unfolding. It requires commitment, awareness, attention, and communication. There are 'ups' and 'downs,' but through it all, there are tremendous opportunities to work in solidarity and to make changes that will result in a more just world for present and future generations.

NOTES

1 In this chapter we use the word 'Indigenous,' except in quotes where we honour the words used by the person interviewed. We also use 'First Nation (s)' to refer to specific First Nations or First Nation communities or leaders.
2 The Alliances Project is a SSHRC-funded project under the Standard Grants program.
3 We extend heartfelt appreciation to the many Indigenous and non-Indigenous leaders, activists, and community members who contributed to the Alliances project by sharing their views and experiences. Their sharing was deep, profound, and moving. This analysis is based on what they shared.
4 It should be noted that the research to date has not addressed Métis and Inuit contexts, and we cannot comment on the extent to which these findings have applicability.

REFERENCES

Adams, Howard. 1989. *The Prison of Grass*. Rev. ed. Saskatoon, SK: Fifth House Publishers.
Alfred, Taiaiake. 2005. *Wasáse*. Peterborough, ON: Broadview Publishing.
Battiste, Marie. Ed. 2000. *Reclaiming Indigenous Voice and Vision*. Vancouver: UBC Press.

Battiste, Marie, and Henderson, James (Sa'ke'j). 2000. *Protecting Indigenous Knowledge and Heritage: A Global Challenge*. Saskatoon, SK: Purich.

Cardinal, Harold. 1969. *The Unjust Society*. Edmonton, AB: Hurtig.

Davis, Lynne. 2009. 'The High Stakes of Protecting Indigenous Homelands: Coastal First Nations' Turning Point Initiative and Environmental Groups on the B.C. West Coast.' *International Journal of Canadian Studies*, 39: 137–59.

– 2010. *Community Case Study*. The Alliances Project. Unpublished paper.

Davis, Lynne., O'Donnell, Vivian, and Shpuniarsky, Heather. 2007. 'Aboriginal-Social Justice Alliances: Understanding the Landscape of Relationships through the Coalition for a Public Inquiry into Ipperwash.' *International Journal of Canadian Studies*, 36 (1) (fall): 95–119.

Fanon, Franz. 1963. *The Wretched of the Earth*. New York: Grove Press.

Foucault, Michel. 1980. *Power/Knowledge: Selected Interviews and Other Writings 1972–1977*. New York: Pantheon Books.

Freire, Paulo. 1970. *Pedagogy of the Oppressed*. New York: Continuum Publishing.

Gramsci, Antonio. 1971. *Selections from Prison Notebooks*. Ed. and Trans. Quentin Hoare and Geoffrey Nowell Smith. New York: International Publishers.

Memmi, Albert. 1965. *The Colonizer and the Colonized*. Boston: Beacon Press.

Mercerdi, Ovide, and Turpel, Mary Ellen. *1994. In the Rapids: Navigating the Future of First Nations*. Toronto: Penguin.

Monture, Patricia. 1999. *Journeying Forward: Dreaming First Nations' Independence*. Halifax: Fernwood Books.

Said, Edward. 1979. *Orientalism*. New York: Vintage Press.

Simpson, Leanne. 2008. *Lighting the Eighth Fire*. Winnipeg, MB: Arbeiter Ring.

Smith, Linda Tuhiwai. 1999. *Decolonizing Methodologies: Research and Indigenous Peoples*. New York: Zed Books.

Williams, Raymond. 1973. 'Base and Superstructure in Marxist Cultural Theory.' *New Left Review*, 82 (December): 3–16.

PART 4

The Personal Is Political

'The Personal is Political' crystallizes a theme that runs throughout the writings of this whole volume. While many of the analyses in this text focus on Indigenous and non-Indigenous inter-group relations, it is individuals who interact, whatever the groups or institutions that stand behind them. Individuals are always historically, politically, and culturally inscribed actors that wear their social histories. As such, we express our beliefs and attitudes in multiple acts of speech and action in everyday social practices. In the Alliances research, Indigenous people who were interviewed often referred to specific non-Indigenous individuals whom they considered to be allies because they used their positions of authority and power to act in support of justice for Indigenous people.

In the matrices of power relations which are the context for social and environmental justice struggles, individuals engage with one another in ways that affect them at a deeply personal level. Their experiences become sites of learning, pain, and transformation (see Davis and Shpuniarsky, Chapter 20). The personal dimensions of this process lead people to excavate their social identities in order to make sense of their positioning within Indigenous/non-Indigenous relations. In theoretical explorations and reports of partnerships, texts are often silent on this plane of personal experience.

The authors in this section address the personal directly. Kevin FitzMaurice asks whether 'white people are obsolete,' and tries to untangle the complexities of being a white professor in Native Studies in the twenty-first century, while Marilyn Struthers reflects deeply on her action to stand up for her Nawash neighbours, thus preserving her own sense of dignity and community. Two chapters are written by Indigenous and non-Indigenous individuals whose friendship and collaboration have endured over time. Victoria Freeman and Dorothy Christian (Okanagan-Secwepemc) undertake a painful yet compassionate examination of their relationship, which has undergone periods of intense difficulty. Daystar/Rosalie Jones (Blackfeet) and Ned Bobkoff, as teachers of theatre and performance, explore their collaborations over many years of working together in different sites around the world. Their work foregrounds the special language of the performing arts in transcending the boundaries of cultural spaces that often seem impenetrable in other forms of communication. They represent hundreds of writers, performers, and artists who contribute to the advancement of Indigenous self-determination by using their creative work and public reputations.

These chapters speak to the complex dynamics of individuals directly confronting the possibilities and tensions that re/envisioning relationships entails. They do not shirk from hard questions about the terrain of relationships and their personal implications. They offer a wide range of perspectives, including examples of concrete moments when there are shared understandings, friendship, and solidarity. At the same time, they reveal clearly that personal relationships do not stand outside the shadow of colonization, which asserts itself again and again, conjoining the personal and the political.

21 Are White People Obsolete? Indigenous Knowledge and the Colonizing Ally in Canada

KEVIN FITZMAURICE

The question of white obsolescence arose as a first reaction to hearing a talk by Lynne Davis and Heather Shpuniarsky[1] in 2005 on their research findings into alliances between Aboriginal peoples and social and environmental justice groups. Briefly stated, their main findings pointed to the following key considerations when building successful alliances, namely the need for:

- respectful relationships,
- trust,
- taking time,
- acknowledging anger and the colonial legacy,
- understanding privilege and benefit,
- working through guilt,
- respecting difference,
- collaboration, and
- learning the history of Aboriginal/non-Aboriginal (or settler) relationships.

My second, more visceral response was a deepening sense of unease as I began to critically assess my own positioning as an ally. Was I, a white professor teaching and conducting research in the field of Native Studies, in fact an ally, or was my usefulness all used up? Had I, and perhaps my other remaining white colleagues, instead become obsolete?

Importantly, before proceeding further in the answering of these questions, I think it is helpful to initially clarify that throughout this chapter, my level of analysis remains primarily at the identities of Aboriginal and white. There are, of course, many sub-identities within these two groups, but I have chosen to look at the relationship from this more macro-perspective as a way of engaging with the possibilities of alliances across these particular positions of racial and colonial standing. Adhering instead to post-structural criticisms – which suggests that broad-based identities such as these deny internal multiplicity and lend themselves to stereotypes, and thus necessarily demand a further breaking apart into smaller, less dominant identities – is to negate both the claims to Aboriginality as something meaningful and real, and the recent efforts of 'Critical White Studies'[2] in challenging racism at this level.

Having said this, in addressing the question of white obsolescence there can be little doubt that the above findings of Davis and Shpuniarsky provide for a reasonable approach to fostering any good relationship, and that those concerning anger, the colonial legacy, privilege, and guilt are particularly poignant in terms of the common hazards that impede productive and respectful Aboriginal/non-Aboriginal relations. Nonetheless, I was unconvinced that the application of these findings was enough to have Aboriginal people look past the devastation of colonialism and agree to form new partnerships with non-Aboriginal people. Rather, I was left with a desire to work through the apparent disconnect between these larger political realities and the possibility of personal alliances. In other words, if the Canadian state persists in its efforts to both colonize and racialize[3] Aboriginal people, are not then its citizens, to varying degrees, active colonizers? And if so, can a colonizer also engage in an alliance with an Aboriginal person? Can one be both a colonizer politically and an ally personally?

My initial answer is an unqualified, 'No way!' It would seem reasonable to suggest that after more than 300 years of colonial oppression in North America, Aboriginal people have learned, and continue to learn, the many and invaluable lessons of colonial deception and oppression, and have lost the ability to trust non-Aboriginal society. By now, non-Aboriginal people must reasonably be, in the eyes of Aboriginal people, obsolete as potential allies, or well on their way to becoming so.

Although first reactions can be insightful, they are perhaps most useful as starting points for further considered reflection. To begin, it seems reasonable to presume that in a broad sense, the term 'ally' suggests a relationship across difference. In its basic form, to be an ally is to align oneself and to work cooperatively and collaboratively with a group other than one's own. However, within the context of the November 2006 Re/Envisioning Relationships Conference at Trent University and the chapters of this volume, the alliance being explored and discussed here is primarily one between Aboriginal and non-Aboriginal peoples, a relationship across not only difference, but differences in power and colonial standing. An ally of this sort, according to Anne Bishop's influential text, *On Becoming an Ally: Breaking the Cycle of Oppression in People,* is 'a member of an oppressor group that works to end that form of oppression which gives him or her privilege.'[4] Alliances of this kind, again according to Bishop, require a deep understanding of the ideological underpinnings of identity and difference, an awareness of the interrelated and mutually reinforcing relationships of oppression, and a recognition and accounting of one's own power and privilege in relation to others.[5]

I would further add, from the outset, that once having determined one's place, what we might call one's hierarchical positioning, in relation to a potential ally, and having found oneself to be of a greater privilege in terms of colonial, racial, class, gender, (and otherwise) standing, it is not enough to stop there. Meaningful alliances, in my experience, require a voluntary giving up of advantage as a coming together on the Other's terms. Within a colonial, Aboriginal/non-Aboriginal context, alliances are ideally constructed as partnerships with an equal sharing of decision-making power and functioning within a consensus-based, Aboriginal cultural framework. Attempting Aboriginal/non-Aboriginal alliances, therefore, requires a full consideration of the intersecting manifestations of power, race, and colonization. Becoming an ally within a colonial context is therefore no easy task.

Power as Colonial Force and Aboriginal Resistance

As the foundational factor to questions of race and colonialism, power can reasonably be thought of as synonymous with force and the ability, whether through the use of material or discursive strength, to influence the behaviour of others so as to effect their compliance with one's interests. Moreover, power can also be quite fluid and amorphous, and can often be found in unassuming places. Depending on a particular, situational context, a powerful and perhaps oppressive person might find himself in a vulnerable position in relation to someone otherwise perceived as marginal to larger societal power configurations.[6] Importantly, within Canada, Aboriginal people are not always in the position of oppressed victim. As power moves and changes across complex relationships, Aboriginal agency can either grow or diminish accordingly.

However, in spite of the potential fluidity of interpersonal (micro-) power relations, the more macro-political/power structures of colonialism continue to shape all interpersonal dynamics in favour of the colonizer. This colonial privileging is situated in conjunction with, and informed by, the ideology of race. Thus, despite the potential presence of Aboriginal agency in some relational instances, there remains, in Canada, a larger macro-reality of colonial and racial structures that function to create stable hierarchies of superior and inferior racialized identities and an abundance of corresponding sites of interpersonal oppression.[7]

Race and the Question of Whiteness

The colonial/racial flows of power are therefore a combination of unpredictable negotiations of interests and influence within a longstanding and stable architecture of inequality. They move in many directions within an overarching downward and oppressive pressure, the only relief from which can be found in the experience of whiteness. Importantly, to exclusively use the term 'white' is not to suggest that racialized, non-white/non-Aboriginal 'minority' immigrants do not benefit from the long legacy and current conditions of colonialism in Canada. They clearly do, and in so doing they participate and legitimize current Aboriginal/non-Aboriginal power relations. However, to be white in Canada is to be, at a macro/structural level, free of colonial/racial encumbrances; it is also to be the source of the downward push on all other non-whites. It is to be perceived as 'normal' and unmarked, always transforming oneself within a sea of others' conspicuous, fixed differences. In a very real way, it is to have a type of omniscient power to see without being seen and to speak as an individual beyond the constraints of culture, in clear contrast to the restricted members of parochial, ethnic identities.[8] Moreover, the power derived from one's whiteness in Canada tends to be jealously guarded. White people will almost always refuse their own racialization. To be recognized and named as white, to someone who only previously understood herself as an individual, is to experience a marked loss of power and the corresponding feelings of insecurity and discomfort.

It has been my experience that Aboriginal people understand whiteness and its powerful silence and invisibility. In resistance to its positioning as the default, normal experience of simply being human, Aboriginal people identify white people as such, with the implication that to be white is to be first and foremost an agent of colonization. For the Anishnaabe,[9] it is to be a *shahganash*, someone who does not understand the Aboriginal perspective of the world and fully believes him/herself to be superior to, and to know what is best for, Aboriginal people.

It is in these ways, as being both white and *shahganash*, that white people embody and reproduce most completely the colonial/racial structures of domination in Canada, and offer the most difficult challenge to the possibility of becoming an ally to Aboriginal people and the greatest potential for eventual, if not current, obsolescence.

The question of the 'white ally' is therefore the most difficult and challenging for me personally, offering the potential to reason myself out of my present positions of influence and power as a professor within a department of Native Studies. Ironically, however, such a thorough and compromising investigation might, if done well enough, satisfy Bishop's test of self-reflection and offer the potential for becoming a meaningful ally through an unveiling and checking of one's power and advantage. I remain unconvinced.

Counter-Racialization and the Making of a White Professor

In continuing to work through these issues, it is perhaps best to begin with the story of my own whiteness in relation to Aboriginal people. Essentially, I became a white person in 1990 as part of my first encounter with the chief and council of Cold Lake First Nation, who collectively referred to me as, 'Hey *munias!*' (translation from Cree: 'Hey whiteman!').[10] In those early years of reserve-based work with the First Nations Resource Council (from 1990 to 1995), I was also referred to as a 'white technician,' and there seemed to be an abundance of us working for Aboriginal leaders during this period. Previous to this, however, although my identity tended to change somewhat depending on geographic and situational contexts, I primarily understood myself as a singular person without a racial or ethnic group affiliation.

Nonetheless, with this newly imposed sense of collective whiteness and with the knowledge gleaned from bachelor degrees in political science and commerce, I worked at that time as a technical support person to the chiefs of Alberta. By 1995, I decided to leave my position as director of economic development within the council and pursue my interests in the politics of colonization in a more scholarly way at graduate school. Moreover, during those early days there seemed to be an accepted ethic among 'white technicians' that we were working for the betterment of Aboriginal people, and that we were to eventually 'work ourselves out of a job.' And so, after five years with the council, it was apparent that there were many recently qualified Aboriginal people that could excel at my former position. It therefore seemed like a good time to step aside and make room.

Following my interests, I entered graduate school in Canadian Studies, never anticipating that I would eventually continue on to complete a doctorate in Native Studies. Shortly after graduating, the Native Studies department at the University of Sudbury hired me, and I now teach classes in Criminal Justice, Family Law, and Native Politics and Theory. I now engage in a diversity of urban and First Nation community-based research projects, study and practice Indigenous knowledge, continue to read Western theory, and help Aboriginal and non-Aboriginal students along their university paths. This is what I have come to do now. I continue to support, in a variety of more specialized ways, the work of Aboriginal political leaders, and I continue to be white in the eyes of my Aboriginal friends and colleagues. I am, however, no longer referred to as a 'white technician,' and I am now very rarely referred to as a *munias* or *shahganash*. Within the larger academic context of identity politics and positioning, I have become a white, middle-class, able-bodied, straight, male professor. Although within the highly racialized circles of Native Studies, I am viewed most often by students and colleagues as a professor who is, first and foremost, white, and I have recently noticed that our numbers are shrinking.

All the way along this journey, my choice to continue to study and work within the Aboriginal sector or 'Indian country' has evoked a diversity of reactions from both Aboriginal and non-Aboriginal people. I have received a great deal of support from friends and mentors. As well, my choices have been met with confusion and resentment, and at times with much hostility and anger. Clearly, I am deeply implicated in, and benefit from, colonialism and racism in Canada. However, my entire educational and professional career has thus far been put towards the decolonization of Aboriginal/white relations. But am I a white ally? Can there really be such a thing within these persistent colonial/racial flows of power?

An Enduring Colonial Ideology and the 'Refuser Ally'

As I continue to work through this question of the 'white colonizing ally,' I need to now turn my focus to the phenomena of colonialism. To begin with, my reluctance to self-identify as an ally, and to question my own obsolescence and that of my white colleagues in Native Studies, stems from my earlier reading of Memmi's foundational text, *The Colonizer and the Colonized*, and, to some degree, Fanon's *The Wretched of the Earth*. In critically analysing the relational dynamics of colonization, Memmi first defines a colonizer as 'any European in a colony,' and goes on to identify three critical factors that are typical of such a person, namely: profit, privilege, and the usurpation of Indigenous land and political authority.[11]

The colonizer who accepts his role cannot help but acknowledge the dishonesty and corruption of his situation, and becomes caught in a tension of self-aggrandizement and Aboriginal debasement as he attempts to justify colonial usurpation to both himself and to the colonized.[12]

Divorced from the dominant reality, the colonized learn that they are inconsequential and inferior to the colonizer.[13] Under colonial regimes, resistance movements, when they occur, are severely repressed, leading the colonized to withdraw from participation in cultural and social responsibilities and to deficiencies in self-assurance and pride.[14]

Occasionally there are colonizers that 'refuse' the benefits of colonization, who recognize the colonial system as unjust, and who either withdraw from the conditions of privilege or remain to fight for change. Yet, although he can be compassionate, Memmi argues that he is ultimately 'detached from the struggle of the colonized.'[15] Moreover, the 'refuser' often does not make an effort to change his language or other tools of cultural domination. According to Memmi, a 'refuser' will always understand himself to be different and separate from the colonized, with the knowledge that there is little place for him in a liberated land; their freedom will never be his. And thus, unless he 'eliminates himself as a colonizer and returns to his mother country, he is politically ineffective; as long as he is in the colony, by virtue of his European ethnicity, he perpetuates the system and participates in its material advantages.'[16]

Memmi ultimately states that the colonized have two possible responses to the colonial system, assimilation or revolt. However, as Fanon suggests in *The Wretched of the Earth*,' assimilation is impossible within a colonial context as the colonizer will not fully allow it; you may work hard to become the same, but you will always be made to feel less than the colonizer.[17] By revolting, however, the colonized reject all colonizers, whether they be 'refusers' or colonialists. According to Memmi, revolt is the last stage in colonial alienation, and colonialism will not disappear until this stage is over.[18]

In Canada, Aboriginal people do revolt,[19] and their resistance, as Memmi suggests, is severely repressed. Importantly, it is not just some ethereal, distantly political idea of the state that colonizes, but Canadian citizens and their political representatives who usurp Native authority, and who profit, and who are privileged through the abuse of power and coercive force. We have created a colonizing state, and the state further creates us; and at the core of our belief in our two founding nations is fear.[20] It is the fear of being caught out in the profound lie of our legitimacy, and it leads to systemic denial and profound memory loss. As Memmi suggests, in writing Aboriginal people out of Canadian history, we have forgotten our treaties and the early contact period of alliance, trade, and goodwill, and we have forgotten that we are indeed foreigners to this land.

Moreover, it is colonial fear which has led to our creation of elaborate systems of legal and administrative control that shore up our power at the expense of Aboriginal people. As articulated within Section 91(24) of the country's foundational British North America Act of 1867, the Indian Act of 1876 and its subsequent amendments, and provincial laws that function (through Section 88 of the Indian Act) to complement federal laws, Aboriginal people have been pushed out of their once nation-to-nation treaty relations with the state and have become instead fully and completely regulated by an external power. Moreover, there currently exists an ever-expanding register of case law that functions to severely constrain Aboriginal rights discourses into limited understandings of usufructuary, ceremonial, and subsistence use of land and resources. And lastly, Aboriginal people are further controlled through governmental policy and procedure preferences that create unstable funding of Aboriginal agencies and cultivate dependency and great distrust.

It is this colonial fear that coalesces with whiteness to create a national idea of ourselves that inherently denigrates Aboriginal difference as it legitimates our dominance.[21] To be white in Canada is to be implicitly the same, and to be Aboriginal is to be different and therefore less than. White people, therefore, as an implicit function of being white in Canada, are unable to 'refuse' these deeply embedded structural and material advantages of colonial power and 'privilege.'

Whiteness is ultimately the cornerstone of a nationalist, racialized identity. It informs our collective sense of normalcy and becoming Canadian through the dehumanizing of others, simultaneously justifying our good work in managing, helping, and allying with Aboriginal people. And thus, the compassionate or 'refuser' white ally, who attempts to voluntarily give up power, remains caught within this ideological web of colonial privilege. To refuse as a white ally is to further mark one's power and privilege to make such a choice. It is my experience that Aboriginal people are often offended, and sometimes amused, by this type of savior/refuser racism. In a world of alliances and competing forces, most Aboriginal people would not knowingly choose to give up power; why would they?

Importantly, these expressions of state colonialism have a real impact on individual Canadians. When I think about Davis and Shpuniarsky's list of findings for successful alliances, above, I am left wondering about what coalition-builders call the 'turf war,' when interests are seen to be in competition. What happens when the white and the Aboriginal ally disagree?

This question of the 'turf war' over divergent interests competing within an overarching colonial/racial context reminds me of Henry Smith (name and situational context changed for anonymity). When I met Henry a few years ago, he was close to retirement from the federal public service where he had been a senior civil servant. In the course of his work, he had become aware of the difficulties in securing clean water in many remote First Nations communities across Canada. Given his level of seniority and influence, he was able to initiate partnerships with many federal and provincial ministries and had been able to secure several million dollars towards the initial phases of a clean water project. Once all the departments committed the money, he began to organize and sign construction contracts for the laying down of the infrastructure. Henry then initiated discussions with First Nations leaders in the northern area of a province to begin the project's implementation at the local level.

The Native leaders, although pleased with his efforts to raise the much-needed resources, informed him that they had a series of other priorities that would need to be addressed in conjunction with the development of the clean drinking water infrastructure, and that the money would also need to be used in a diversity of related ways. Henry recalled being disappointed at their hesitation, and insisted that clean drinking water was a top priority for their communities and that they should proceed with the existing plan, as the money was already earmarked for this particular purpose. To his great disappointment, the First Nations leaders insisted they knew what was best for their communities, and the project came to a standstill. In the end, the government's fiscal year drew to a close and the Federal Treasury Board eventually reclaimed the money.

Henry clearly had good intentions. He wanted to help those Aboriginal people in northern Canada by providing them with clean drinking water. His mistake was that he did not take the time to build trusting relationships with those he wanted to help. Henry did not respect First Nations leaders enough to ask them their opinion about what they, in fact, needed. And when challenged, he stood his ground in believing that he knew what was best for these communities. This is a clear case of colonial racism marked by an inability to let go of power and to recognize Aboriginal expertise in their own affairs and their ability to govern themselves. It is a failure to see Aboriginal people as anything but inferior, and to move past one's own paternalistic thinking.

Aboriginal people have often conveyed to me that it is for these reasons that they prefer to work among themselves and to build up their own power in relation to the state and its citizens. They prefer to use their own social service agencies, participate in their own political institutions, and hire their own faculty. There is much distrust and anger towards white people, and I feel this anger at almost every community meeting that I participate in. Within formal contexts, I am often perceived as representing the whiteness of the nation, and I am often the lightening rod for negative feelings.

Indigenous Knowledge and the Necessity of the Northern Direction

In contrast to Bishop's view of an ally as someone who, 'as a member of an oppressor group works to end that form of oppression which gives him or her privilege,'[22] Memmi draws a clear line of separation between the colonizer and the colonized, rejecting the possibility of a 'refuser' ally. According to Memmi, one cannot be both a colonizer and an ally. It is true, as Memmi would suggest, that I am different from Aboriginal people. I cannot claim to be Aboriginal and speak as an Aboriginal person, and it is always best that I do not initiate deprecating Aboriginal humour. As well, I am not permitted to lead Anishnaabe ceremony, and, although I may participate, I am not being trained to do so. Further, it seems even more correct to say, as Memmi would, that although I have actively challenged many aspects of colonization in Canada, Aboriginal nations are not my nations and their struggle for liberation and decolonization is not fully my struggle. It is also true that my very presence in Canada as a voter, taxpayer, and overall contributing citizen is premised upon a primary usurpation of Aboriginal authority. And thus it is a presence which functions to continually reproduce and legitimate the state at the expense of Aboriginal political and territorial sovereignty, while negating, in a significant way, Aboriginal and 'refuser' efforts at decolonization.

Although I am in general agreement with the Davis and Shpuniarsky findings discussed above, and I make every effort in my personal and professional relationships with Aboriginal people to be respectful, and to take the necessary time to establish trust while understanding my own power and privilege stemming from colonization, I am nonetheless suggesting that Memmi's lines of separation point to, in a compelling way, the impossibility of white, colonial alliances. According to this view, the only manner of genuinely relating to Aboriginal people as a white person is to fully acknowledge one's intrinsic, always/already complicity in the current racial and colonial project, and to simply step aside.

According to Memmi's view of colonizer/colonized incommensurability leads to some difficult questions, including those pertaining, in my case, to my relative worth as a white professor in Native Studies. What good am I doing, really, other than pursuing my own material and intellectual interests? Am I not taking the place of an Aboriginal person in pursuing theirs? These questions are even more troubling within the context of those occasional, hush-toned comments from Aboriginal people regarding senior white scholars who have 'gotten rich off the Indians.' Perhaps I am still privy to these remarks because I don't yet appear to be rich or senior.

Native Studies departments across Canada, to some degree, share Memmi's categorical view of colonization in that there is an expressed hiring preference for Aboriginal faculty and the incorporation of Indigenous knowledge and language into the curriculum. There is a desire for a clear and coherent sense of difference between what is Aboriginal and what is not. Nonetheless, it has been my experience that white professors, although a shrinking minority, continue to be hired on as Native Studies faculty. We currently teach a diversity of courses, and our research is informed by a variety of academic disciplines, although the younger white faculty tend to have a Native Studies, interdisciplinary background with grounding in Indigenous knowledge. And, although there appears to be some uncertainty as to our respectful place as teachers of Indigenous knowledge, this question is currently being negotiated as part of an overall ethic of inclusion, and reluctance to having white professors leave Native Studies departments completely.

It is this apparent desire to involve white faculty, albeit in an increasingly minor way, that is interesting, as it speaks to the uniquely Aboriginal, or, in my particular case, Anishnaabe approach to the question of autonomy and difference.[23] It is my understanding that Anishnaabe philosophy and spirituality privilege a more permeable sense of bounded difference that is associated with movement and interdependent relations, rather than the clear lines of coherent and stable separation suggested by Memmi. Rather, it is perhaps more appropriate in the Anishnaabe view to consider those complex, in-between spaces where

Aboriginal and white overlap, and where there may exist the possibility for colonizers and the colonized to relate in non-oppressive ways.

According to Anishnaabe tradition, white people are an integral part of the four colours of humanity. They are represented in the northern direction, and have been given their sacred gifts and offer their own, essential contributions to life. According to this view, Aboriginal people, although different from white people, are nonetheless in a sacred and essential relationship with them in which there are places of distinct and overlapping truths and where respect and care can hold this gift of diversity together. To paraphrase Elder Jim Dumont, it is a core value stemming from the Anishnaabe creation story that the Aboriginal self and the white Other are so inextricably intertwined that they are almost the same, connected by the spirit, and of the same mother, the Earth.[24] Moreover, it is a relationship that needs ongoing attention and care as it changes over time, in perpetuity.

It is in accordance with these traditions that, in spite of the great damages that have been, and continue to be, inflicted upon them, the Anishnaabe do not reject nor separate fully from white society. Rather, they continue to honour the sacred trust of the treaties while insisting on their political autonomy in relationship with the Crown. Moreover, they continue to negotiate peaceful, modern-day treaties and self-government agreements, fight in Canadian wars, and prefer a 'renewed relationship' and updated Royal Proclamation[25] to the all-or-nothing, Memmi-style revolt. Furthermore, it has been my experience that the Anishnaabe continue to share their knowledge with the hope of minimizing conflict and promoting balance, stability, and peaceful relations.

In his assessment of the 'limited refuser' as one who does not make the effort to change her language or other tools of cultural domination, Memmi perhaps did not appreciate the role of Indigenous knowledge, nor foresee the Native control of university departments where Aboriginal and non-Aboriginal faculty could instruct 'refuser' students in the language and practice of Indigenous knowledge at undergraduate, master's, and doctoral levels. It is through a studied engagement with Indigenous knowledge (theoretical training, building relationships with Elders, and ceremonial practice) that meaningful cultural learning, personal transformation, and decolonization become a real possibility. For the dedicated student, it is my view that Indigenous knowledge offers an alternative to the ideological confines and powerful hierarchies associated with colonization, whiteness, and their implicit foundation of inferior, racialized difference. Moreover, Indigenous knowledge suggests more than a world of coherent and separate identities based in fear and competing power. Rather, it offers the possibility of a theoretical, spiritual, and experiential understanding of interconnectivity, interdependence, and community within a view of power that is based in collectivity and spirit rather than being entirely about force.

Nonetheless, in response to the reality of colonization today, it has been my experience that Anishnaabe people do appreciate and recognize the need for defence through degrees of separation and the use of power as a force of resistance. Within this larger circumstance of colonial conflict, Indigenous knowledge, and Native Studies departments, there does appear, however, to be some remaining opportunities for a type of 'Indigenized white' ally as someone who is invited to enter into partnerships with Aboriginal people on their terms and within their own Aboriginal cultural contexts. Ultimately, however, the future of the white professor in Native Studies must be seen as precarious. In the Anishnaabe tradition, there is a sacred place for the white presence in the dynamic, interrelated relations of life. Moreover, there is still much scholarly work to be done towards decolonization and not enough Aboriginal scholars to do it, although this too is changing as an ever-increasing number of Aboriginal students complete graduate school.

It does, however, appear that the days of the 'white technician,' those most closely resembling Memmi's limited 'refuser,' are over. In spite of the persistence of poverty and related social problems in many First Nation and urban Aboriginal communities across Canada, employment and university-education levels for Aboriginal people are rising.[26] Moreover, there is a growing number of Aboriginal political and financial organizations and social service agencies, and recent studies further point to the emergence of a strong and growing Aboriginal middle class and intellectual elite in the urban centers.[27] Aboriginal political independence and autonomy is increasingly becoming a reality, and there is a noticeable decline in the number of 'white technicians' working in the service of Aboriginal leaders. In resistance to the power of Canadian colonization and racism, Native people can, and do, prefer to employ their own people in these roles.

Ultimately, then, in acknowledging the legacy and persistence of colonial and racial flows of oppressive power in Canada, and in response to the question of white obsolescence, it appears that Davis, Shpuniarsky, and Bishop are partially correct. Engaging in meaningful, non-oppressive alliances does require high degrees of respect and trust, as well as a deep understanding of the interrelated and often mutually reinforcing complexities of power, privilege, identity, and difference. It is also reasonable to suggest that it will take considerable amounts of time and energy in order to effectively move beyond stereotypical representations, learn about our colonial histories and current realities, and work through our negative tendencies towards white guilt and Aboriginal anger.

It is, however, only through a lifelong engagement with Indigenous peoples, their knowledges, and their spiritual practices that we may begin to transcend the powerful binaries of colonizer and colonized and the corresponding effects of colonization. In the end, it is this process of 'Indigenizing whiteness' that best provides for the possibility of meaningful alliances through the revealing, challenging, and the transgression of overarching and deeply embedded structures of colonial and racial ideology as a process of giving up colonial advantage through the coming together on the Other's terms. It is in this way that the question of white usefulness and obsolescence itself can give way to the possibilities of inclusion and contribution as members of Aboriginal/Allied communities.

NOTES

1 As a guest lecture in Native Studies 100 at Trent University.
2 The project of coming to understand and to name the social power of whiteness is a particular anti-racism strategy articulated as part of a growing body of knowledge on Critical White Studies. For more reading, see Dyer, *White*; Foster, 'Performing Whiteness'; Delgado and Stefancic, *Critical White Studies*.
3 I am using the term 'racialize' to denote the process of socially constructing racial hierarchies for the purpose of oppressing non-whites, and to acknowledge that the concept of race has long since been disregarded as a valid scientific category.
4 For more reading on the concept of allies, see Bishop, *Becoming an Ally*, 12.
5 Ibid., 42.
6 The idea that power is fluid and does not operate exclusively as large oppressive manifestations is largely attributed to Michel Foucault, and can be found in many of his writings. See Foucault , *Discipline and Punish; Nietzche, Geneology, and History*, and *The History of Sexuality*.
7 There is an extensive body of work on racism and power relations with regard to Aboriginal people in North America specifically. Some of the more prominent texts include Razack, *Looking White People in the Eye*; Stoler, *Race and the Education of Desire*; Churchill, *Fantasies of the Master Race*; Mackey,

House of Difference; Silman, *Enough Is Enough;* Battiste, *Reclaiming Indige-*
nous Voice and Vision; Montour-Angus, *Journeying Forward.*

8 For more reading, see Dyer, *White.*

9 Other Aboriginal groups have their own terms and specific meanings, although in my experience most are synonymous with the act of being a colonizer. The specific *shahganash* attributes of ignorance, sense of superiority,
and paternalism stem from interviews with Karyn Pugleise (APTN) and
Mary Larond (Anishnabek Nation) as cited in my 2005 research on Aboriginal-white relations as part of my doctoral dissertation.

10 I was hired to live and work with the Cold Lake First Nation and Driftpile
First Nation during the summers of 1991 to 1994 as part of the Ooskipuk-
wa, community-based research and development program run out of the
First Nations Resource Council in Edmonton, Alberta.

11 Memmi, *The Colonizer and the Colonized,* 9.

12 Ibid., 54.

13 Ibid., 106.

14 Ibid., 91.

15 Ibid., 19.

16 Ibid., 44.

17 Fanon, *Wretched of the Earth,* 158.

18 Memmi, *The Colonizer and the Colonized,* 127.

19 The more recent protests include: Stoney Point First Nations people and
Ipperwash Provincial Park (1995), the Mi'kmaq people in Quebec and
New Brunswick and their claim to Aboriginal fishing rights (1999), the
Secwepemc of BC protest against the Sun Peak Resort's development
(1998), and the ongoing Iroquois protest at Caledonia over a land title and
development dispute (2006).

20 According to Michael Thrasher, a Métis teacher of Anishinabi cultural traditions, the fear of the infinite is at the heart of finite understandings of the
Self and the foundation of all relationships, and therefore must be acknowledged and cared for in order to move towards a dynamic balance of peaceful relations.

21 For further reading on the creation of stereotypes of Aboriginal, inferior
difference please see Francis, *The Imaginary Indian;* and Berkhofer, *The*
White Man's Indian.

22 Bishop, *Becoming an Ally,* 12.

23 It is my experience that, although there are unique variations depending
on cultural group, the notion of dynamic interrelatedness is common to
many Aboriginal philosophies and spiritualities. I am, however, most familiar with this concept in relation to Anishnaabe teaching and practice.

24 Paraphrased from a discussion with Jim Dumont in March 2007 at the University of Sudbury.
25 Please see the 1996 Royal Commission on Aboriginal People for recommendation on a new Royal Proclamation that would set the terms of a renewed relationship; in Supply and Services Canada, *Report,* 4.
26 For more information on statistical data on social and economic developments in Aboriginal communities see Beavon, Maxim, and White, *Aboriginal Conditions.*
27 The emergence of an Aboriginal middle class was a key finding of the 2007 Ontario Federation of Friendship Centres' Urban Aboriginal Task Force Study (see FitzMaurice and McCaskill, 2007).

REFERENCES

Battiste, Marie. Ed. *Reclaiming Indigenous Voice and Vision.* Vancouver: UBC Press, 2000.

Berkhofer, Robert. *The White Man's Indian: Images of the American Indian from Columbus to the Present.* New York: Knopf, 1978.

Bishop, Anne. *Becoming an Ally: Breaking the Cycle of Oppression in People.* New York: Zed Books, 2002.

Churchill, Ward C. *Fantasies of the Master Race: Literature, Cinema, and the Colonization of American Indians.* San Francisco: City Lights Books, 1998.

Delgado, Richard, and Stefancic, Jean. Eds. *Critical White Studies: Looking Behind the Mirror.* Philadelphia: Temple University Press, 1997.

Dyer, Richard. *White.* New York: Routledge Press, 1997.

Fanon, Franz. *The Wretched of the Earth.* New York: Grove Press, 1963.

FitzMaurice, Kevin, and McCaskill, Don. Urban Aboriginal Task Force. Study in Ontario. Urban Aboriginal Task Force, Ontario Federation Centres, 2007. http://www.ofifc.org/ofifchome/page/index.htm.

Foster, Gwendolyn. *Performing Whiteness: Postmodern Re/constructions in the Cinema.* Albany: State University of New York Press, 2003.

Foucault, Michel. *The History of Sexuality.* New York: Vintage Books, 1990.

Discipline and Punish: The Birth of the Prison. First American edition. Translated from the French by Alan Sheridan. New York: Pantheon Books, 1977.

'Nietzche, Genealogy, and History.' In Paul Rabinow. Ed. *The Foucault Reader.* New York: Pantheon Books, 1984.

Francis, Daniel. *The Imaginary Indian: The Image of the Indian in Canadian Culture.* Vancouver: Arsenal Pulp Press, 1992.

Mackey, Eva. *The House of Difference: Cultural Politics and National Identity in Canada*. London and New York: Routledge, 1999.

Memmi, Albert. *The Colonizer and the Colonized*. Boston: Beacon Press, 1965.

Monture-Angus, Patricia. *Journeying Forward: Dreaming First Nations' Independence*. Halifax: Fernwood Publishing, 1999.

Razack, Sherene H. *Looking White People in the Eye: Gender, Race, and Culture in Courtrooms and Classrooms*. Toronto: University of Toronto Press, 1998.

Silman, Janet. Ed. *Enough Is Enough: Aboriginal Women Speak Out*. [The Tobique Women's Group.] Toronto: Toronto Women's Press, 1987.

Stoler, Laura. *Race and the Education of Desire: Foucault's History of Sexuality and the Colonial Order of Things*. Durham, NC: Duke University Press, 1995.

Supply and Services Canada. *Report of the Royal Commission on Aboriginal Peoples*. Vol. 5: *Renewal: A Twenty Year Commitment*. Ottawa: Canada Communications Group Publishing, 1996.

White, Jerry P., Maxim, Paul S., and Beavon, Dan. Eds. *Aboriginal Conditions: Research as a Foundation for Public Policy*. Vancouver: UBC Press, 2003.

22 Reflections on the Politics of Neighbourliness in Aboriginal/ White Alliance-Building from the Fishing Wars of 1995

MARILYN STRUTHERS

On Labour Day weekend in 1995, violence erupted in our little rural Ontario town of Owen Sound over rights to dwindling Great Lakes fish stock. While this weekend wasn't the beginning of the story, it was a turning point, the moment when a simmering conflict in our community reached the boil. Just two years earlier, priority fishing rights had been awarded to commercial fishers from Nawash First Nation in the 1993 Fairgrieve decision of the Ontario Provincial Supreme Court.[1] On the last Saturday of the summer, 1995, 100 white sports fishermen marched through the downtown, their destination the Nawash fish-seller's booth in the Farmer's Market.

These men were a cross-section of our community united by a love of fishing and the Bay. They were also angry, intent on demonstration. I and five or six others stood in front of the Nawash fish-seller's market table, inserting our equally white bodies between her and racial conflict. It was a moment of change in what before had always been a peaceful family and community space. The impact of the anglers' march that day was incendiary. Later in the weekend, two Native youths were severely stabbed in a brawl, and then the boats began to burn, and nets slashed from their moorings were set adrift in the Bay. The events launched our community's search for voice – for a middle way – between competing interests that appeared to be escalating out of control into racialized violence.

In 2005 I was invited to tell my part of this story to members of the Ipperwash Inquiry who had come to Nawash First Nation (FN) to explore systemic racism and to understand why the situation in our community had not escalated to more serious injury, as it had in Ipperwash that same fall. When my turn came to speak I found myself wanting to weep, despite the intervening years. On that day, as we put the very different threads of the story together, I began to see things I hadn't noticed before. The faces of the anglers in a W5 television clip reminded me that the men in the public protest in the market had, 20 years earlier, been an integral part of my life as a young bride in a new community: men I had danced with in the sportsmen's club dances, men my husband worked with, families I had cooked for in my home. It wasn't that I hadn't known this before, but there it was, tucked away in that part of one's mind that forgets things that are too painful to notice in the moment.

The following summer, more than a decade after the events, I was interviewed by a PhD student examining the conflict for its lessons for anti-racism work. I found myself weeping again. I had to ask myself why this story still had the power to evoke grief. Although it was tragic and exposed a hard-edged side of my community, it was long ago, and, fundamentally, it had affected others. Now, with an opportunity to write about this experience, I have finally begun to spin theory from tears, so many years later.

It is important to pay attention to where pain sits over time, because it is often the shift side of change. As white people in anti-racism work, we often focus on 'the other,' on the pain that white racism creates in First Nation's peoples, and disconnect from the hurt that it creates also in us. Suppression of feeling and the inevitable guilt of being part of something that is so damaging to another is not a powerful place from which to move mountains; fundamentally we have to learn to move the mountain of interracial conflict more productively, both in our communities and globally.

In this chapter I venture forth a little and expose what is for me a growing edge in my thinking. It is not very politically correct to examine the pain of white people caused by white racism, but in the women's circles where I travel in my organizing work, political correctness has seldom got us beyond conflict in the work of anti-racism. So I turn my thoughts now to what it is that sits under these recurrent tears, the story within the story, for what it might contribute to our thinking about white alliances with First Nations communities.

What we call the 'Fishing Wars' that hot summer of 1995 was the public manifestation of court-confirmed priority access to Great Lakes fisheries. As Nawash FN and neighbouring Saugeen FN fishers began to exercise that right, members of the Ontario Federation of Anglers and Hunters (OFAH) struggled to retain access to and control of the dwindling fish stock in the Great Lakes for recreational fishing. Organizers of one of the most important fishing derbies in Ontario, the local sportsman's club counted among its members, politicians, local government officials, and many others with influence on policy and decision-making in our little town and in the province. They had substantial investment not only in the economic benefit of the derby to our town, but also in years of volunteer work in fish stocking and spawning ground improvement.

Standing in front of the fish-seller that day, as an impromptu body shield, created a tectonic-order shift in my understanding of what it takes to hold peaceful relationship in community. The response to the events of the 'Fishing Wars' over the coming months was to create a small loosely knit new organization, the Neighbours of Nawash, as a foil to the sportsmen's club, to create a distinct and equally public voice in the community.

This story begins for me with a phone call: 'Come to the Market; the anglers are going to challenge the Nawash fish-seller.' Our community is little-town Ontario, a lovely networked community on the shores of Georgian Bay. We visit at our Market. When I go to the Market now, I go for one of Brigitte's pastries. An hour later, I have an armload of food, the latest gossip, and a dinner invitation. That's how it works. So when I agreed to go to the Market that Saturday, I was troubled, but in no way prepared to put my small body into the breach of conflict between this woman's right to participate in community commerce and the hundred or so men of importance in our community making a political challenge in such an intensely personal way.

In the scheme of things, it was a little like finding myself engaged in a war; I had no idea what was going on. I understood the dispute on the fisheries between the government and the First Nations from both my work and the press. But this kind of 'back garden terrorism' was new to our community. We also did not know that the Heritage Front, the notorious white supremacy group, had found fertile grounds in fishing conflicts. It was frightening, dislocating, and called for public response. Remaining silent and allowing this use of a public space, which had been long connected with food, family, and community, was to watch our way of life come under challenge and be fundamentally changed from what it was.

When the PhD student interviewed me for my memories of the summer, he asked why we had formed the Neighbours of Nawash. Like a good academic, he was looking for an ideological framework behind our actions: equity, anti-racism, peace-building. But it was none of these. Few in our community thought about race. A predominantly white Anglophone community, we had a black mayor and a prominent East Indian family that had given us a doctor, a crown attorney, and an accountant. There were also two Aboriginal communities with little engagement with the white community. It was, in retrospect, a bit of an age of innocence, and most of us were unprepared to act from a well-thought-out analysis of racism.

When we formed the Neighbours of Nawash as a small informal group of people prepared to speak in support of Nawash's right to fish, it was not from any strong sense of ideology or conviction about peace-building. Neither was it a strikeout for justice, nor about any ideal about being one's brother's keeper. It was, as I understand it now, an act of identity preservation. Fundamentally, it was about our own dignity and identity; it was not about the right for a First Nation's identity to coexist in our market, but for our own ability to be, as we understood ourselves.

The Neighbours of Nawash, as a public identity, could take up a public position. This produced ink on the page and money in the bank, quite literally, to represent our way of being and the peaceful, relational way of our town that we valued. Of course, we didn't know this at the time. It is only by sitting now, with what sits behind the tears, that I can catch hold of this painful reality so many years later. In the creation of this small organization, we named a white identity in relation to Nawash First Nation that was not a subsidiary of the Ontario Federation of Anglers and Hunters, but took up a distinctly different political space from the 100 men who represented our community so publicly on that day.

People still often confuse the name, using 'The Friends' as a short form, but being a neighbour carries a different politics of relationship. A neighbour is 'someone who lives in proximity.' Not necessarily your friend, certainly not family, but someone with whom you acknowledge a nodding relationship, a casual interest, the potential, perhaps, for something else. A neighbour is defined simply and explicitly by proximity. In our rural community, we understand and depend on neighbourliness. It is a good thing when the power is out and the snow is deep. When I am away, my neighbours trek across the concession road every day in the winter to check if my furnace is still running, because one bitterly cold February day, it wasn't. There are certain traditional obligations to being a 'neighbour.' Helpfulness, hot casseroles when there is death, support for a charity, visiting in hard times, and money in a public bank account if there is a survival threatening event: a barn burning, a major illness ... or a boat burning.

And so when the boats began to burn, we worked through the four banks in town to open a public account, meeting refusal after refusal. The banks feared the publicity, bags of smelling fish on their doorstep, stories in the press. We were surprised about this – and it seems now that we were just beginning to see the anatomy of systemic racism in the power relations of our community. The Royal Bank finally agreed to open the account, finding common ground with their new marketing strategy for banking services for First Nations. Community people began to deposit small amounts of money to support the fishers. They too were afraid, and some used pseudonyms: George N. Bay contributed, as did Mr. L. Huron. And we got ink. Front page coverage spun the alternative storyline about who we are as a community in relation to Nawash First Nation. In the pressure to maintain our own identity, as not anglers, we had of course begun the process of active differentiation, and had begun to generate the activities of care with which we needed to identify.

When the young Nawash men were stabbed, many of us did not recognize this event as part of the same story, and the press did not help us to do so. When one of our members saw the connection, she began to advocate and sit in the courtroom in our name. When the Mennonite Central Committee began to train community people as nonviolent witnesses who learn to stand in the midst of conflict as neutrals making public record, we signed up, using a traditional phone tree to reach into the community. When funding from a public funder for an Ontario-wide fisheries conference proposed by Nawash was blocked, we used public pressure to persuade. We began to learn about fishing science, and about our geography and community history from a First Nation's perspective, and in the process created some greater degree of relationship and access to the broader stories of biology, ecology, and entitlement. When we understood that Aboriginal science told a different and useful story about the fish in Georgian Bay, we realized that the sports fishermen and the Nawash fishers actually held common interest in the survival of fish species – and we eventually organized a civil and constructive public forum, with fishermen from both sides in dialogue about the survival of the fish.

Neighbours of Nawash was leaderless in a deliberate strategy to avoid repercussion to any one of us alone. There was never a formal membership; there was a phone tree, a network, and a connection point between our various interest communities; also a name and a temporary public vehicle. We didn't raise substantial funds, although the amount was respectable; we were never called upon to use our witnessing skills; and we have returned to our normal, side-by-side, neighborly relationships. Except perhaps for a little more visiting at the public events at Nawash First Nation, there is little left to mark this story. Still, more than a decade later, Neighbours of Nawash is understood in the Nawash community to be one of the reasons the violence didn't go further and didn't end in armed stand-off as it did in Ipperwash.

How does one evaluate a response to crisis, a strategy to change a world spinning out of control? Understanding of an anti-racism agenda is largely formed in Canada in sites and among people who are urban neighbours in communities of transience created by immigration, employment, and real-estate markets. What does the motivation of preserving dominant identity and neighbourliness have to offer those who would shift the mountain of racist sentiment in our communities?

Neighbours of Nawash did what it set out to do. It created a public vehicle that reflected the interests of those who had no role in the conflict, no stake in the anglers' cause, but who were also deeply affected by their actions and representation of our community. It created a clear message to Nawash First Nation that the behaviour of the sports fishermen was an aberration, not sanctioned or shared by all of us. That message was also available to the anglers, not through confrontation but as a reminder of the caring traditions of our community.

That day in the Market, the actions of the anglers brought diminishment, and that diminishment extended beyond the Aboriginal community to me and to the others who stood together in our community market as a human shield – where no such thing should ever have been needed. That betrayal brings the prickle of tears even now, but in the sadness of that diminishment it may be that we can also create learning of a more satisfying response when the power of racism begins to ignite in our communities.

Organizing for the preservation of self in the image of peacefulness, contentment, and community, which we so fortunately hold as normal in Canadian communities, both creates and strengthens the communities we desire. Unlike either guilt or moral certitude, it moves one to a deeply powerful position of protection of identity and a consciousness of what is good in the way we live. There is resilience in the relations of neighbourliness. Without the huge personal cost of confrontation or the strain of public conflict on more righteous grounds, neighbourliness simply addresses loss in a strategy of care. Further, neighbourliness is a sustainable strategy. Neighbours move forward into relationship in times of trouble, take up agency and respond, and then return to less intimate arrangements. They represent a latent capacity in community, that of strong motivation to respond to diminishment.

Yet the story here is still incomplete, evolving again through relationship. Some months after I first wrote this piece, a young friend from Wikwemikong, who is pursuing PhD studies in the politics of Aboriginal-white relations, challenged me to notice that while Neighbours of Nawash struggled with the identity politics of local race relations, we did not step into the broader arena of systemic racism that made a court challenge the only way for Nawash First Nation to claim inherently traditional rights to dwindling fish stock. The events in our community focused us on place-based strategies that emerged from the politics of our own relations of neighbourliness, but we see now that to have an effective anti-racism strategy, we must simultaneously hold our focus on the broader context of race relations within both place and politics. What do neighbours do about the structural inequities that produce localized conflict? As an organizing strategy, how does proximity limit or support the ability to act and affect change?

Extending the line of thinking set out in this chapter to effective strategy requires that responses based in local relationships extend also to relationships with regional and national organizations whose work impacts on broader political agendas. A turn in the direction of intervention raises interesting questions about opportunity. How do the larger organizations that toil in systemic and structural anti-racism strategy view and relate to local community-based organizing? How might the Mennonite Central Committee, the United Church, and the Canadian Auto Workers, who were all heavily engaged in the support of Nawash First Nation, have built greater relationship with the community organizing by Neighbours of Nawash, forging white-on-white alliances that might have more successfully linked place and politics to forge response to the broader issues that created disruption in Owen Sound? And what might we have learned from each other, respecting the 'expertise' of both locations in order to have had greater impact? These questions are an important stimulus for planning future action in the context of alliance-building.

Thank you to Rob Wimigwans for his thoughtful reflections on what has been written in this chapter. The credit of memory is also due to Linda Thomson, who played so large a part in both the actions and the thinking that shape this story that she would have co-authored this chapter, had she lived.

NOTE

1 In the Jones Nadijiwan decision, Judge Fairgrieve agreed with the Nawash FN argument that under Section 35(1) of the 1982 Constitution that they retained collective and treaty rights to fish for trade and commerce. Further, Judge Fairgrieve stated that the Ontario Ministry of Natural Resources had violated constitutional rights of Nawash through the use of a quota system, and that the Chippewas of Nawash were entitled to priority allocation of fish stock.

The History of a Friendship,
or Some Thoughts
on Becoming Allies

DOROTHY CHRISTIAN AND VICTORIA FREEMAN

This chapter consists of two separate commentaries which together reflect what we have learned about decolonization through almost 20 years
of friendship. We don't offer ourselves as exemplars of a perfect relationship – far from it, as you'll see. But we want to talk about how friendship
between Aboriginal and non-Aboriginal individuals can be a form of alliance, how it can build or deepen our commitment to work for social
change, and how powerful friendships can be in changing both parties
– actually helping people to decolonize at a personal level.

Dorothy Christian

If someone had told me 20 years ago that I would be consciously building alliances with non-Native settler peoples in Canada, I would have
laughed them out of the room. I am an Secwepemc/Syilx filmmaker in
Canada, and much of my work focuses on how the original peoples of
these lands relate to the settler governments. The question of who I am
in this country is consistently determined by how I relate to, or react to,
the settler cultures on my homelands.

In one of my productions for Vision TV, a Métis family has a tongue-
in-cheek look at how they select their various identities as they dress in
period costumes for a family photograph. They joke about a theme of
stereotypes and colonizers, and one daughter, Skeena Reece, a popular
Indigenous performance artist in Vancouver, made a profound statement: 'I'm just putting my issues on the table and some of them, a lot of
them have to do with being Indian, and that's pretty sad because if in
your life, your biggest kind of things that shaped who you are, are really negative, and from the outside, you haven't been able to explore who

you are from the inside ... so being an Indian takes up a lot of my time (laughs), and I want to free up some time so I can do some other things!' (Christian, 2000).

Skeena gives words to an indescribable obstacle I felt in reaching my full potential as a human being who happens to be 'an Indian woman' in Canada. Sadly, like Skeena, a large percentage of my time is taken up figuring out who I am on my own homelands. The paradox: this quest for identity is also what enables me to reach my full humanity. This chapter touches on my journey in taking my place on the land while reconciling my political relationship with the colonizers. On a personal level, a critical part of reaching an understanding evolved through a conscientious and conscious interaction with a thirteenth-generation North American, Victoria Freeman.

I have experienced disruptions that are familiar to many Indigenous families in Canada. My family members were forced into residential schools; my siblings and I were put into white foster homes during what is called the 1960s scoop;[1] and we have lived through poverty, alcoholism, childhood sexual abuse, and family suicides, all the debilitating social conditions that Statistics Canada reports on so regularly.

The tentacles of colonialism have touched every part of my life and have affected me in untold ways. Every rite of passage that is considered 'normal' in the stages of human development, that is, my childhood, adolescence, marriage, and giving birth, were all tainted by some aspect of the colonial relationship. An assimilation policy separated me from my brothers and sisters, which fractured our family structure. The Indian Act told me I was no longer an Indian when I married a man from the Mediterranean. The harshest and most painful experience was when I gave up my daughter for adoption because I was such a good little brown/white girl that I believed white people could do a better job of raising her. I wasted a lot of time spinning my wheels in a destructive anger.

As fate would have it, on 11 July 1990 I got a call at 4:00 a.m. and a voice said, 'The army has gone in.' Canada had mobilized its military against the Mohawks, who were under siege for 78 days while they protected their land rights. During this modern-day Indian War, the so-called Oka Crisis, I was able to use my rage by adapting my skills towards a good cause. I then had five short years to find healers to help me with my rage and post-traumatic stress syndrome, because there was another armed standoff within my own homelands, on Secwepemc territory at Gustafsen Lake in 1995. For the last 12 days of that resistance, I brought my communications skills to support the people who were upholding Aboriginal Rights and Title while I prayed they would not be massacred.

Both these Indian Wars strengthened my identity as an Indian woman. The line between the colonizer and the colonized was definitively drawn in the ground. The Indians had decided they were not going to give one inch more; too much had been given away already. I got stronger spiritually. But emotionally I had to find healthy ways to keep myself together, and intellectually I deconstructed many things. I started by taking apart the colonial policies and practices which wreaked havoc with me and my family. I needed to understand my relationship to these people who had chosen to settle on my homelands. And I needed to be a healthy and whole human being.

I have come to see these acts of war as the result of a hardened attitude of racism and a deep denial of colonial history by the settler cultures; otherwise, how could they turn their guns on the original people of Canada? How can they deny the existence of constitutionally protected Aboriginal Rights and Title and continue to use the old argument of how Aboriginal people stop progress and development when, in fact, their interest is motivated by monetary greed?

During the so-called Oka Crisis, Victoria was a valuable ally who opened inaccessible doors for me. She worked with me to raise consciousness at the global level about the Indigenous perspective on the land rights issues, and nationally she facilitated various things to educate Canadians on how unjust the actions of their government were to the Mohawks who were standing up for all the Indigenous peoples in Canada in terms of land rights.

Even though I knew Victoria was a political ally, she was still one of the 'occupiers of my land.' I tarred Victoria with the brush of being yet another 'do-gooder white woman' who wanted to 'fix things' for me. I remembered only too well those kinds of white women from the various churches I was forced to attend during my adolescence in the white foster homes. I realize now what angered me most was intuitively knowing that implicit in the actions or words of those 'do-gooder white people' was the assumption that I was not capable of taking care of myself.

Victoria and I come from opposite ends of the social and economic spectrums of the so-called multicultural mosaic of Canada. As an Indigenous woman, I grew up in very humble surroundings on a small reserve in the interior of British Columbia. Victoria is a 13th-generation North American settler from an upper-middle-class family that is part of the political elite in Canada. Embedded in our relationship are the power relations of the colonizer/colonized dichotomy which accentuate cultural, racial, economic, and class differences. We were the most unlikely characters to become political allies or to attempt to bring any kind of peaceful, coexisting relationship between Native and non-Native peoples in Canada.

In the ensuing years, Victoria gained some trust in the Aboriginal community and was a part of the Steering Committee of 'Beyond Survival: The Waking Dreamer Ends the Silence,' an international gathering of Indigenous artists, writers, and performers that I coordinated and fundraised for in 1993. She was the only white person on the all-Aboriginal Steering Committee. I was very grateful for her presence because she became my sounding board as I dealt with some of the complexities of Aboriginal politics.

In 1994 I moved back to my ancestral homelands and was contracted by the national multi-faith broadcaster, Vision TV, to produce mini-documentaries from an Indigenous perspective. In the meantime, Victoria published her book, *Distant Relations: How My Ancestors Colonized America* (Freeman, 2000), and I promoted her point of view on the newsmagazine program I worked for. At the same time, I filmed an impromptu dinner party at Victoria's home, of Native and non-Native intellectuals and activists discussing the Native/non-Native relationship in Canada. In 2000 that production was part of the submission that won a Gemini Award for Vision TV in the 'Best Talk/New Information' category.

In August 2003 Victoria and I were invited to Caux, Switzerland, by the Initiatives for Change organization, which hosted a week-long conference on 'Conflict Prevention through Human Security.' We addressed 700 people from all over the world. The presentations Victoria and I made changed the energy of the conference. We spoke to peoples on both sides of the colonial coin who were attempting to build peaceful relationships through a variety of projects; however, they had never discussed the very basics of their relationship as the colonizer or the colonized. It was the first time I was outside Canada co-presenting with 'one of the occupiers of my homelands,' where I was discussing my place as an Indigenous woman within the colonial state of Canada. I was working in the context of peace, rather than war.

This was the first time I had spent so much time with Victoria. We even had to share a room. This was a tenuous situation, because I have lived alone for many years and I have a tough time being with other people for any extended period of time. In most circumstances, I make sure I have 'alone' time to rejuvenate myself emotionally and spiritually. I do not want to offend anyone; however, my reality is that it is really hard work to be around white people, or it may be more accurate to say any peoples who are outside my cultural/spiritual psyche. By 'hard work' I mean that my mental/emotional/spiritual levels seem to reach a ceiling after four days, because I have to consistently think/feel/act with two mindsets: that of a Western-educated person and that of an Indigenous woman whose world view is diametrically opposed to Western thought. My already fragile situation was then exacerbated by a very profound experience.

I am not sure what happened during our presentation, I just know it was something very profound and very deep. Afterwards, my whole being wanted to curl up into a ball, so I escaped to our room in the castle with its auspicious history of peace-building. Although there was a heat wave in Europe that summer, I was shivering to the very depths of my being. I could not get enough blankets to warm me up. It felt like every cell in my body was being rearranged. All I wanted to do was sleep. At the same time, Victoria was busy arranging meetings for us to attend. She is good at networking, and very astute politically and socially. I am very direct in my manner of communicating, and that just does not work within the rules of engagement of high-level diplomacy.

Victoria dragged me out of bed to attend a significant luncheon with the group of young scholars who organized the conference. One of them asked me a direct question about being Indigenous in Canada, and before I had time to get my first word out, Victoria jumped in and answered for me. I was flabbergasted. I did not want to embarrass her publicly, so I kept quiet. Before the luncheon was over, she did it again! I wanted to slap her, but instead I internalized my anger and went back to our room and crawled back into bed.

The next day, another luncheon was arranged with people from the United Nations, and again Victoria dragged me out of bed. I told her to go alone but she insisted that I had to be there. After all, I was the Indian part of 'Understanding the Other!' By this time, I was getting really ticked at my companion on this alliance-building path, but I knew we had to take advantage of an audience we do not have access to in Canada.

Once we got back to our respective homes in Canada, I was at the hyper-boiling point in my anger at Victoria. We had the biggest fight of our friendship. We almost walked away from each other. One thing that Victoria Freeman and I have in our relationship is the ability to be brutally honest with each other, and neither one of us gives up very easily. But this time we almost walked away from each other. It took us six months to sort out our issues. It was a very painful time.

I do not know when the healing process started between us. We did not consciously say, 'We are now going to heal this relationship.' We were mindful of our interactions. We acknowledged the racism we consciously or unconsciously foisted on each other. We examined the stereotypes and distorted assumptions we had about each other.

In one of our many conversations, I asked Victoria, 'Can you love this land like I do? Can you love this Earth like I do?' I pose that same question to all settler peoples. My ancestral homelands are thought of as the 'Land of Milk and Honey' by many immigrant peoples. At what point do immigrant groups take responsibility for the land they have chosen to live on? At what point do they acknowledge that the original peoples of these lands are the landlords and they are the tenants?

When referring to my relationship with the colonizers of my land, many times I apply the metaphor of an abusive relationship; that is, as a 'colonized' person I am the assumed victim, and the colonial state, including the settlers, is the offender. In an abusive relationship, the offender controls the situation with a constant threat of violence that creates a situation where both parties 'walk on eggshells' around each other because at any given moment violence may erupt.

In the dysfunctional relationship between Indigenous peoples and the settler peoples of North America, there is an undefined 'walking on eggshells' that sits between us as a 'pregnant pause' or as a very LOUD silence. I believe this is founded in the fear that Indigenous peoples want the land back, that our suppressed rage compounded over centuries will explode at any given time on any given territory (e.g., Oka, Gustafsen Lake, Ipperwash).[2] Settlers know that the original peoples of Canada have a birthright to our lands and any benefits from its resources. I truly believe the denial of this entitlement and the lack of integrity that the settler governments have in the colonial relationship is at the core of this fear. Settler governments know they have assumed a privilege and an entitlement to these lands; yet at the same time they deny the privilege and entitlement of the Indigenous peoples. The original peoples of these lands are forced to spend thousands of dollars in litigation to prove their place on their homelands.

In an abusive relationship, when the victim becomes healthy and finally has the power to stand up and say, 'No more,' the offender is fearful because he knows the power has shifted and he may have to change, too.

In my healing process, I consulted an Elder about the history of abuse in our family. At the end of three hours, she told me a word in our language that is conceptual. It means, 'Making Your Heart Right with the Creator.' She emphasized that our only responsibility was to the Creator and to the life we carried within ourselves, that the first priority is to make things right with ourselves, then with the Creator, and finally with our abuser. If we maintain any vestiges of victimhood and point blame outwards, this is counter-productive to any change in the abusive relationship. The Elder taught me that the highest form of responsibility is to honour the life I carry, and, in doing so, I honour my humanity.

The work of another settler woman, Jessie Sutherland, principal of the 'Worldview Strategies' website and the author of *Worldview Skills: Transforming Conflict from the Inside Out,* played a role in my personal and political transformation. Jessie's work is thorough and her perspective is global. She presents the concept of reconciliation from various perspectives, which include the Indigenous world view: 'Genuine reconciliation involves a transition from systems of domination to relationships of mutuality. Consequently, genuine reconciliation also requires a parallel process of personal and political transformation.'[3]

In my transformation, I have applied what Sutherland identifies as 'transcend[ing] the victim-offender cycle,' which sets up a new framework of reference. I choose to be a sovereign, autonomous, and dignified Indigenous woman standing firmly on the land, just like my grandmother and great-grandmother did. I do not need to affirm my identity or my place on these lands 'in relation to' or 'in reaction' to the colonizers of these lands.

On a microcosmic level, my ally and dear friend Victoria Freeman co-creates a genuine reconciliation with me, which includes many ups and downs while relating in a very real way. She continues to decolonize the mindset of other settler peoples with me. We co-taught a course called, 'Can You Love the Land Like I do?' at the Interfaith Summer Institute at Simon Fraser University in August 2007. We continue to evolve and grow our colonizer/colonized relationship in our very distinct way!

However, on a macrocosmic level, the institutions and governments of the settler culture do not seem ready, willing, or able to decolonize themselves to reach a true reconciliation with the original peoples of these lands. It appears they are not prepared to 'make things right' with the Indigenous peoples of Canada, that they choose to 'maintain systems of domination' rather than seek 'relationships of mutuality' with the Indigenous peoples.

Victoria Freeman

The best relationships call out or even demand our best selves, and I think this is certainly true of my relationship with Dorothy.

Friendship between Aboriginal and non-Aboriginal people is certainly not all that is required for decolonization. There are entrenched, systemic issues of inequality, prejudice, violence, poverty, and theft of land that will take years of political action to address. But the relationship between our peoples does not exist only on a political level; it exists on every level, including the most personal. All of us are part of this relationship; all of us make it what it is. Working things through at a personal level can prepare and strengthen us for other kinds of more public work. The tricky part is to understand what in the personal is political or social in origin.

I have to start by talking about another relationship. Many years ago, I was working with a group of women of colour to organize a women's literary conference. I was a conscientious, white, middle-class woman with good intentions and some theoretical political understanding. I understood racism as something out there in society that I was busy fighting against. One day, one woman whom I had become friends with got terribly angry at me and accused me of racist behaviour. I could not understand how she could have interpreted my actions in this way, and at first vehemently denied her accusation. When I later asked her to help me understand her reaction, she would only respond: 'It's not my job to educate white women about racism!' This angered me in turn, because how was I supposed to make amends if I didn't even know what I'd done? My protestations only enraged her further and she cut off all communication with me. She did not speak to me for 10 years.

This incident challenged everything about me, my very understanding of who I was. No matter how much I tried to deny what my friend had said, or tell myself that she had misunderstood me, what I could not deny was the pain behind her rage. That someone I knew cared for me and who I cared for was so hurt and angered by my actions that she withdrew from our friendship broke through my denial of how racism and colonialism affected not only my society and my friend, but me, and led to the painful realization that in spite of my best intentions, I too was part of that awful dynamic.

The American educator William F. Pinar wrote, 'We are what we know. We are, however, also what we do not know. If what we know about ourselves – our history, our culture, our national identity – is deformed by absences, denials and incompleteness, then our identity – both as individuals and as Americans [or as Canadians] – is fragmented.'[4] What I didn't know was my own relationship to the history of colonization and racism in Canada, and how I had been shaped by it and continued to benefit from it. Furthermore, I had avoided knowing because I did not want to face the terrifying question of responsibility.

As I began to educate myself, I realized how racism or colonial relations could be embedded in the institutions and attitudes of a whole society, in the stories we told about our national history, in the attitudes that were passed on to me as a child. It was painful to see that even my family was part of this process. I came to accept that although I was now doing my best to decolonize my own thinking, occasionally I would probably unthinkingly do things or say things that still perpetuated these attitudes, but that I would still be a good person if I did my best to learn from these mistakes and make amends. I also came to see that I could not shake off my white privilege, no matter how hard I tried; I could not pretend I was not part of this system.

I was better prepared for working through such conflicts by the time Dorothy Christian became my friend and a colleague in promoting the work of Indigenous writers. I was intrigued by Dorothy but also nervous around her, because at the time she was often angry and confrontational with just about everybody, white or Indigenous. Although she unsettled me (which I sensed was perhaps a good thing), it seemed I could be useful to her just by listening. At this stage I was probably inordinately proud to have an Aboriginal friend, as if it proved I was an okay white person after all. But I learned a lot from our conversations: Dorothy opened a window onto Indigenous life in Canada. She talked to me about traumas in her family and community and her personal efforts to heal, as well as the difficult dynamics of various political struggles.

It soon became apparent that this was an unusual friendship. Dorothy said to me, 'Anything you want to know, just ask,' and she did answer unless the knowledge I sought was privileged information. Once, when Dorothy and the Okanagan writer Jeannette Armstrong were talking with me, I suddenly felt as if the wind had been knocked out of me, not by any aggression towards me, but simply from the power of a kind of truth I hadn't really known before. It made me aware of a deeper level of knowing than I had ever experienced, on what I might today call a spiritual level. I had been raised an atheist, and it was puzzling to me that my spiritual awakening came through Indigenous people. I felt a deep need to learn more, and wanted to explore these issues with Dorothy. I certainly began to appreciate and respect Native culture more, but at the same time Aboriginal people were starting to talk about the appropriation of their culture and spirituality, so I wasn't sure what was open to me and what was not.

During the Oka crisis in 1990, Dorothy provided support for both the Haudenosaunee negotiators and a solidarity Peace Run by the Syilx (Okanagan) people. I assisted her by getting information out to some international organizations, such as the World Council of Churches, and by setting up a conference call so that prominent Canadian writers could speak directly to the negotiators. Perhaps my most important role was simply being there for Dorothy as she went through the agony of that summer.

Then, in 1992–93, when we were both members of the organizing committee for Beyond Survival, a conference which brought together Indigenous writers, artists, and performers from around the world, our friendship went through a major crisis. We were walking through the woods near her home one day when we passed a sweat lodge she and her partner had made. A sweat lodge is a sacred place for purification, prayer, and contact with spirits; to Indigenous people every aspect of it has deep significance. I said something about hoping that we could be in a sweat together someday, and immediately our rapport dissolved. She turned to me angrily and said: 'Our spirituality is all we have left. Will you take even that?' Suddenly I was not Victoria, her friend, but just another exploiting, stealing white person, a colonizer. She said later that what galled her was my expectation that I could go into a sweat just by virtue of knowing her, without putting in the hard work to learn and be spiritually prepared. I remember responding angrily: 'Well, I didn't ask to be born here!' and the argument escalated.

What was different this time around was that I was less defensive and she was willing and able to work through this conflict with me. We managed to keep talking. Actually, I've heard her describe it as 'yelling and screaming,' but I don't remember it that way at all – though I believe that is how it felt to her, how difficult it was for her to confront me. Eventually, after several difficult months, we were able to hear each other. In fact, what happened was we reached a far deeper place of trust with each other, which enabled us to work together in a completely different way. We learned that personal and social healing starts from telling the truth, especially the difficult truth, and having that truth heard; that in going through a process like this together, we learn things about ourselves, each other, and our society that we wouldn't learn any other way.

That confrontation made me realize that I needed to know how and especially why my ancestors did what they did to Indigenous peoples, and what I had inherited from them. That led to seven years of research and the writing of my book, *Distant Relations: How My Ancestors Colonized North America*, as well as the public education work on Native-newcomer relations I have done since then. In the process, my relationships with First Nations people improved immeasurably, partly because I learned that most of what they said about our shared history was actually true. But another important change was that I let go of an amorphous guilt I had carried since I first realized that Indigenous people were the original people of this land. I saw that I was not responsible for what my ancestors had done, though I had inherited their legacy; that I was responsible only for what I did with that inheritance in the present. While I felt shame about that history, I also came to see that a lot of what I was feeling was not guilt or shame at all, but unacknowledged grief. I needed to mourn the devastation my people had wrought, all that pain and suffering and loss of life, the terrible waste of it all. Allowing myself to mourn freed me to act, because I was no longer afraid of uncovering that pain. Furthermore, my political commitment no longer came from a desire to 'help' First Nations people from some position of superiority, but from the need for all of us to decolonize, so that we can all live with integrity.

So many things came from working through this conflict. Together and with others we developed Turning Point: Native Peoples and Newcomers On-Line, a web site for dialogue and information-sharing (see Freeman, Chapter 10, this volume). Dorothy also made a video about my book and another on our relationship and intercultural dialogue.

Many years later, in August 2003, Dorothy and I went to Caux, Switzerland, to speak at an international conference on human security and conflict resolution. Our topic was 'Understanding the Other.' It was the first time we had ever shared a stage and spoken about our relationship. Something extraordinary happened that day when we spoke. This wasn't just our subjective perception, because others commented and wrote about it, too. People seemed to be very excited and very moved by our talk. I had challenged the Europeans in the audience to face the people they had colonized and to recognize the colonizer in themselves. That had an extraordinary effect, as if they had found a way to address this aspect of themselves and their history without hating themselves. Dorothy had talked about her struggle to move beyond hating white people to recognizing that both colonizer and colonized needed healing. This changed the focus of the conference from talking about the world's problems as something 'out there' to dealing with the colonial histories of the participants themselves.[5] Suddenly everyone was talking about colonialism, thinking about their own experience. There were people from Columbia, South Africa, India, and many other countries telling us 'your work is relevant to us,' which really surprised us, because we had only been thinking about our relationship in the context of Canada and Aboriginal/non-Aboriginal relations. I think when we spoke together we offered hope to people who had never witnessed a loving relationship between people on opposite sides of the colonizer/colonized binary.

From that incredible experience of deeply affecting other people simply by talking about our relationship, perhaps it was inevitable that immediately afterwards we would go through the biggest fight we had ever had, a conflict that reached into the deepest levels of our beings and almost resulted in our walking away from each other. There were several things I did at Caux that pushed Dorothy's buttons in ways that were very complex and challenging for me. First of all, there was her perception of how comfortable I was with my white privilege there among the hoi polloi of the UN, whereas she felt really alienated being among so many powerful white people. Worse, at a lunch we had been invited to, when someone asked about the situation of Indigenous people in Canada, I had apparently answered several questions that were directed at her, usurping her voice and speaking for her in the incredibly presumptuous and superior way that non-Aboriginal people often do. Unfortunately, I had absolutely no memory of doing this. Whatever I did was totally unconscious, which was very discouraging to me after all the years I'd spent trying to educate myself about racism. This raised a real dilemma for me; should I trust that her interpretation of my behaviour was correct, even though I had no memory of doing any of these things? In the end I decided to trust her on this, but it was very difficult to do so.

These issues became even more difficult for me when an interaction I had with someone else at the conference led Dorothy to believe I was abusing my power in relation to this person, who came from Africa. This was hugely triggering for her because of issues of abuse in her own life and her fear that my African friend did not recognize my colonizing behaviour. I did not share her interpretation of my actions, but I also found it hard to defend myself, first of all because she knew a lot more about abuse than I did, and, secondly, as I later realized, because of unconscious guilt I carried from early childhood experiences. This guilt had nothing to do with Aboriginal people, but arose from issues of exclusion, difference, and privilege in relation to my sister, who was born with Down's Syndrome. This is where relationships between our peoples can get so complicated – as all relationships can. But between Indigenous and non-Indigenous peoples, there is often already fear and mistrust, guilt and anger, a ready template of abuser and victim roles that can fuse with unconscious psychic wounds that we may already carry. Dorothy reinforced the critic in my mind that was already undermining my own perceptions of myself and my actions in the world – a dangerous mix.

The fact is that both of us carried elements of the abuser and the victim; to different degrees perhaps, but we both had wounds from the past that deeply affected how we interpreted each other's actions: we were both quick to attribute motives to each other's behaviour that fit into our own internal narratives. I was floored by her perceptions of my power, when I didn't feel nearly as powerful as she perceived me to be; at the same time, I was terrified by what felt like her hatred. I felt she was so angry at me that she wanted to and could annihilate me. This conflict upset us both so deeply we were unable to talk to each other for several months, and we nearly ended our relationship permanently. Each of us had to turn away from each other and take care of ourselves.

For me, then, a necessary development in our relationship was finding the courage to question her interpretations when she interpreted my behaviour solely in terms of the colonizer/colonized relationship, and attributed motives to me of wanting to colonize or wanting to be superior. At the same time I had to recognize that that was how our interaction made her feel, and that this might be the effect of my behaviour. I had to deeply question myself, but I also had to stop thinking that just because she's Aboriginal and I'm not, that she knows everything about these issues and I know nothing.

I had to say to her, 'You do not know my heart; you do not know all the reasons I do what I do. No one can know that.' I had to find a balance between listening to what she was saying about me and letting myself consider the possibility that she could see what I couldn't, at the same time honouring my own process and maintaining my sense of myself as my own person. I had to stop imputing motives to her behaviour, and focus instead on what was triggering my own issues.

It helped that Dorothy wrote at one point:

Remember, DON'T TAKE ANY OF THIS PERSONALLY – we are teachers for each other … I've always felt really good about our relationship in that I always felt we were working within a context of LOVE. That, no matter what – we would overcome it because of a DEEP LOVE we have for each other's humanity.

And I wrote to her:

If it is too hard, let's recognize that we have done our best and that the differences that come between us so horrendously sometimes are not really of our making, but are the products of our histories, our environments, what we were given to work with. If you say it is too hard, I will understand and still love you.

Somehow we got through that particular crisis. Dorothy and I are still loving friends, still working together on decolonization and reconciliation, still convinced of the importance of dialogue. We've reached an even deeper level of trust with each other. We know that we can question each other profoundly and survive. Did we resolve everything? We're not sure. But I believe that by confronting our history of oppression and colonialism together, and in learning from our responses to it and to each other, we are actively contributing to a healing that must take place between our peoples. It's hard to work through these kinds of interactions, to brave that maelstrom of anger, truth, and love, but I believe that it is very important that at least some of us try – as honestly and fearlessly as we can.

NOTES

1 During the 1960s scoop, 80 per cent of the children in my community were removed and put into white foster homes because my people supposedly were not good enough parents. Bear in mind that this wave of destruction was enforced after the colonial forces had already damaged any parenting skills of the generations before me through forced attendance at residential schools.

2 Canada mobilised its military against the Mohawks at the so-called Oka Crisis in 1990. One Sûreté du Québec officer was killed. In 1995 at Gustafsen Lake, in BC, the RCMP and Special Ops from Canada's military were mobilized against the Secwepemc peoples. No one was killed. In 1995, at Ipperwash, the Ontario Provincial Police mobilized their forces against unarmed Indigenous peoples who were reclaiming expropriated lands. A Native man, Dudley George, was killed.
3 See Sutherland, *Worldview Skills*, 23.
4 See Pinar, 'Notes on Understanding,' 60–70.
5 See Sutherland, 'Reconciliation,' 2,9.

REFERENCES

Christian, Dorothy. Segment Producer 'Indians & Who.' *Skylight Newsmagazine*. Dorothy Christian and Rita Deverell. Toronto: Broadcaster Vision TV, 2000.
– 'No Security for Indians in Canada When It Comes to Land.' Paper delivered at Conflict Prevention through Human Security Conference. Caux, Switzerland, 2003.
Freeman, Victoria. Distant Relations: *How My Ancestors Colonized North America*. Toronto: Mclelland and Steward, 2000.
– 'Understanding the Other.' Paper delivered at Conflict Prevention through Human Security Conference. Caux, Switzerland, 2003.
Pinar, William. 'Notes on Understanding Curriculum as a Racial Text.' In C. McCarthy and W. Crichlow. Eds. *Race, Identity and Representation in Education*. New York: Routledge, 1993.
Sutherland, Jessie. 'Reconciliation from the Inside Out: International Conference at Caux,' *Working Together*, Institute of Dispute Resolution newsletter, University of Victoria, 4 (winter) 2003.
– *Worldview Skills: Transforming Conflict from the Inside Out*. Vancouver: Worldview Strategies, 2005.

24 Cross-Cultural Collaborations: Friend or Foe? An Arts Interactive: Empowering the Individual within the Home Community and among Diverse Cultures

DAYSTAR/ROSALIE JONES AND NED BOBKOFF

As theatre and dance professionals who work individually for the most part, we have also worked in collaboration within mixed cultural groups both in the United States and abroad. As persons of differing cultural backgrounds ourselves, over the years we have become attuned to the cultural differences in others as a springboard to the highly creative atmosphere necessary in artistic work in the performing arts – theatre and dance. We have found that the process demands openness from everyone participating, an openness that allows for new discovery without sacrificing personal or cultural sensibilities. In the following pages we explore our experiences and insights, each in our own voice.

NED: We live in an age where cultural exchange and cultural divisions often go hand in hand. Witness the current events that represent the clash between cultures, events that dominate the news, our thinking, and our fears. Most importantly, the common bonds of humanity, so desperately needed in a fragmenting world, seem sorely tested in these times.

How do the performing arts cut across cultural boundaries and forge fresh relationships, through imaginative and transformational means? What are those time-honoured performance pursuits of doing, becoming, and revealing that work best cross-culturally? An answer often lies in small details that are singularly human and transformational.

I remember an incident that occurred at the College of Santa Fe where I was teaching 'Acting for the Camera.' The course was exploratory and incremental, since the equipment we had was new, and the work we did was observationally based. Students were given exercises where they spoke to the camera directly, and later did scenes in the studio, or outside where students blended interviews with external events. The point was to explore shifting realities and keep on track in front of or behind the camera, while all the time picking up the know-how as we went along.

A Navajo student would not work in front of the camera. It took me awhile to figure out why this was happening. I thought the reason he refused to stand in front of the camera might be the usual ones of unfamiliarity, shyness, stage fright, or some combination of these. But I also had a hunch that there was more here than met the eye. Did he feel that the camera, and more importantly the videotape, were capturing his spirit? When he asked me if his father could attend the class, I replied, 'Sure, why not?' When his father arrived and studied the situation, he became interested in the learning process involved in what we were doing. Afterwards we talked, and he gave his son permission to work behind the camera as a technician. The young man later became involved in videotape editing, and got to the point of interviewing another Indian student on camera. Eventually he stood in front of the camera and spoke about his experiences openly, with a great deal of charm. The other students were supportive of his efforts, and we all learned from him. We learned not to make immediate assumptions about why someone from a different cultural background might hesitate in a learning situation that is unfamiliar. Essential cultural beliefs sustain the integrity of communities and the uniqueness of an individual. Although the Navaho student may never have thought of himself as a teacher, he was, in a very real sense, both a student and a teacher. In my mind, students and teachers are often interchangeable.

Since the early nineties, I have worked with Daystar (Rosalie Jones), the artistic director of Daystar: Contemporary Dance-Drama of Indian America. We have worked independently, teaching and creating performances on our own, and we have worked together, throughout the United States, Canada, and abroad.

The Institute of American Indian Arts (IAIA)

DAYSTAR: There are differing personal, cultural, artistic, and educational 'perspectives' in both the facilitator and the participant. How do collaborators create the bridge of mutual understanding that is necessary for successful work in the arts? From our experiences, we have learned that one becomes the 'friend' when there is a willingness to truly see the other and consciously make an exchange: a give and take between individuals. And the exchange must be not only of professional/academic/artistic knowledge, but also of *cultural* knowledge. The 'foe' comes to the surface only as one gets in the way, refusing to allow this interchange between individuals and cultures. When the exchange is realized, personal and cultural understanding is achieved, and true, honest creativity can take hold.

In 1989 I was hired by IAIA (the Institute of American Indian Arts) in Santa Fe, to 'revitalize' their performing arts program, make it a 'Department,' and achieve accreditation for a two-year undergraduate degree. In the early 1990s Ned Bobkoff was hired at the IAIA to teach performance and creative writing courses, help establish an acting program, and coordinate the development of plays highlighting Native American concerns. It was also in 1990 that Congress passed the Native Graves Protection and Repatriation Act, which stated that human remains and objects found in Indian graves must be returned to their original owners (the tribes), thus reversing a century-old practice which made native human remains federal property.

Ned had started to write a play titled *Wild Water Running*, for use in the student acting class. The dramatic line of the play centres on a fictional incident concerning a Hispanic contractor hired to clear ground for a high-speed reactor in New Mexico. The contractor's men (both Hispanic and Native American) unearth not only low-grade radiation and laboratory materials from Los Alamos, but the bones of ancient Indigenous peoples as well. Enter the contractor's niece, a youthful but spiritually wounded Pueblo woman. The stage was set for a contemporary Antigone play: the confrontation of the niece and her uncle over the burial of relatives' remains, contrasted with the needs of the workers to maintain their jobs (see Figure 24.1).

NED: I approached acting students at the Institute of American Indian Arts with an outline and dialogue from *Wild Water Running*. I told them that I knew little or nothing of their cultural heritage. All I had was a concern over the issue, based on my own outrage over incidents in France, where anti-Semitic thugs were desecrating Jewish cemeteries. I felt completely over my head when it came to Pueblo tribal details and rituals, and the play was only a suggestion that the students could reject or work with as they saw fit. We read the play together. After a couple of sessions exploring and improvising around what I wrote, the students told me they wanted to work on it with me. The performers would fill me in on the accuracy of the cultural details.

We dove right into the work together. Episodes of humour and satire, developed by the students, also contributed to the overall collaborative

Figure 24.1 Nathan Romero (Santa Clara
Pueblo) working with mask for *Wild Water
Running* production, Institute of American
Indian Arts. 1990.

effort. I asked Daystar if she would choreograph the sequences in the
play that were necessary to ground the work in Indigenous tradition,
then expand on it with an eye on contrast and dramatic effect. As always
in theatre, work process expands theatricality, dictates the final result,
and adds to the dramatic impact. We staged the play at a local Santa Fe
performing arts centre to an invitation-only audience of parents and
Indigenous peoples. I learned yet another lesson about protocol and
goodwill: Do unto others as you would have them do unto you.

DAYSTAR: In 1995–96 Ned Bobkoff was hired as a lecturer in the
Theatre Arts program at the American University in Bulgaria, where he
taught theatre arts and playwriting to students from 12 Eastern
European nations. Ned and his students staged plays, folk tales
(Bulgarian and Korean), and mixed media events. I was invited as the

Figure 24.2 Daystar/Rosalie Jones congratulating two Bulgarian students (American University in Bulgaria) performing the Blackfeet Napi story 'The Origin of Death' at the American Embassy, Sofia, Bulgaria, 1996.

'Distinguished Visiting Lecturer' to speak about and present Native American dance and culture. Little did I know that Bulgaria has a well-placed romantic regard for the Native American, generated perhaps by a reminiscence of its own tribal past. I did the usual workshops, lectures, and master classes. A true cultural collaboration, however, was in the offing. Ned Bobkoff needed an end-of-semester dramatic work for his best students. I offered one of the stories of the trickster 'Napi' from the Blackfeet in my birth country. This was not one of the comic trickster stories, but one of the more profoundly serious of the Napi tales, 'The Origin of Death,' about death as the signature moment of human existence. The performance became a collaboration of the highest order. I danced Napi as the alter ego. Ned Bobkoff shaped the story into a play for the two main characters: Napi and his wife. The performance (see Figure 24.2) was delivered in the Bulgarian language, and eventually was presented at the American Embassy in Sofia, Bulgaria's capital. Napi had never travelled so far!

The summer of 1996 found us in Sliven, a town with a large Roma population, in a mountainous region of central Bulgaria. As a result of the American University experience, we were invited to create a 'new' work at the Sliven Summer Theatre and University, with well-trained, experienced Bulgarian actors and dancers. What 'new' work to do? Several possibilities were discussed, but the choice settled on was another Blackfeet story, 'Scarface' (called Piye in Blackfeet language). This story I had previously written, choreographed, and directed as a stage work to tour Montana for its Centennial in 1989. I knew it thoroughly because it is a cornerstone tradition of the larger and very sacred Medicine Lodge Ceremony of the Blackfeet people.

Certain portions of the story cycle had already found their way into print, oftentimes told by Blackfeet people themselves, to writers that they were well aware would publish it. This is not to say that any story can be brought to the stage, or reinterpreted into another medium, at random. Utilization of any cultural story should rightfully only be done after consulting with the proper cultural tribal authorities, whether that be elders, council members, or sanctioned tribal storytellers. I had already gone through that process.

The actors were, to say the least, intrigued by a story from the Native Americans. We cast the show, then went into rehearsal. Finally, costumes were found in the cavernous basement of the Sliven State Theatre (originally built and maintained by the Soviets while still in power). Each 'period' had a separate gigantic room with row upon row of possibilities: Greek, Medieval, Shakespearean, contemporary, what? We settled on interpreting the 'medicine woman' who gives Scarface a new handmade pair of moccasins for his journey as a blind 'seer,' complete with half-mask and tattered gown. A young, tall, sensitively alert young man became Scarface. Dancers became the townspeople who mock Scarface; the flying cranes who save him from destruction were choreographed by well-known Bulgarian choreographer Boyana Setchanova. Because of the journey element in the story, we decided to stage the work in the theatre lobby, which had three adjoining open rooms (one with a wondrous, sun-like sculpture) and a spiralling staircase for the blind 'seer.' The audience followed the action. Later, additional performances were developed with Bulgarian professional actors at the Varna International Theatre festival on the Black Sea.

The project successfully traversed a number of cultural and artistic hurdles. One hurdle was the language. I found that, rather than hinder the process, the time spent waiting to have what you just said translated from

English into Bulgarian, and the answer then given back from Bulgarian into English, gave everyone that all-too-precious element: *time*. We had *time* to look at each other and to register the reactions of each to the other. We had *time* to see eyes and read lips, gestures, and body language in that human method of communication that preceded speech.

Two young Bulgarian choreographers came knocking on our 'in-theatre' lodging rooms in Sliven, three days and nights in a row. Katia Ivanova Tenava and Snejina Teneva Petrova were co-directors of the aptly named Wild Women Folk Dancers of Biala. The final night, they came bearing flowers. That did it. We were literally whisked up a mountaintop to a little village called Biala. It would be the next summer before a creative project between us could be realized, thanks to a grant from ArtsLink, in New York City, which was especially interested in cultural exchange in the Balkans. Ned would videotape the project.

One of my fondest memories of that summer in Biala is of bells tinkling in early morning light. It was the sheep being herded past the house, on their way to the fields for the day. Each evening, they returned, still ringing bells, in the evening dusk. Those sheep held the clue to a traditional Biala story we would choreograph together. We set to work in the town theatre – small, badly in need of maintenance, but appreciated by all. The two Bulgarian choreographers, Katia and Snejina, wanted an artfully and culturally integrated approach to choreography, so that all three of us would jointly choreograph Bulgarian and Native American dance and stories in tandem. The Folk Company showed their dances, steps, and songs to me. I learned the Buglarian step series, and then set to teaching Native American Intertribal Dance. Eventually, the women's Shawl Dance and Swan Dance would be choreographed for the girls of the Folk Company. A particularly thrilling moment ensued during rehearsal: all three of us agreed to 'try' Bulgarian steps set to a traditional Native American powwow song. It was, to say the least, unheard of; hesitantly at first, but then with gusto, the lead male Bulgarian dancer realized that the tempo and rhythms were the same. We had found another inroad to bridging the cultural gap.

Katia and Snejina led me to the hill just outside of the village. Standing there was 'the tree' struck by a massive bolt of lighting, a sign from God that the people of Biala had transgressed an ancient rule of hunting: always let the first deer live; kill the second deer for food. The tally of the taboo was that deer would never come to Biala again; they would raise sheep for their livelihood. All of us gasped in recognition. I also knew a 'deer story' from the Americas, in which the bones of the deer

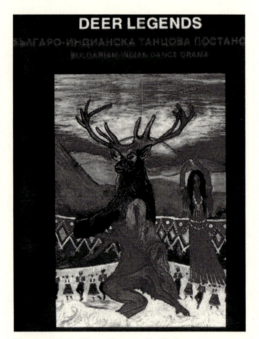

Figure 24.3 'Deer Legends: Bulgarian
Indian Dance-Drama' poster created by
the Samodivsko Bile – Biala (Wild Women
Folk Dancers of Biala), 1996.

taken in the hunt must be thrown into the water so that the Spirit of the
Deer can be released and reborn again, thus continuing to feed the
people. We would present 'Bones' and 'The Spirit of the Deer' in a cultural exchange in dance, song, music, and story, on the stage of a little
theatre on a mountaintop in Bulgaria (see Figure 24.3). Even the Peace
Corps representatives from Sliven showed up, but I will never forget
the bright eyes and expectant smiles of the grandmothers, grandfathers,
parents, friends, and relatives from the village, whose presence filled
the old theatre to the top of the balcony that afternoon.

The Turkish Experience

NED: In 1993–94 I was a guest director at the National *Konservatuvari*
for Music and the Performing Arts on the Yunis Emire campus of
Anadolu University in Eskishir, Turkey. Yunis Emire is a famous Turkish

Figure 24.4 Ned Bobkoff and Turkish theatrical assistant Erhan Tuna, with cast in rehearsal for *The Visit*, 1994.

folk poet, and the campus is located in Anatolia, the heart of Turkey, about halfway between Ankara, the capital, and Istanbul. The theatre students, ages ranging from 18 to 31, were among the most passionate, idealistic, and talented young performers I have ever worked with. Except for some basic everyday expressions, I didn't know a word of Turkish. When I arrived I immediately sat down with Erhan Tuna, a graduate student and my assistant director. We worked together on a translation of Friedrich Dirrenmatt's masterpiece, *The Visit* – a tragicomedy and a parable on the illusionistic and destructive nature of greed (see Figure 24.4). Working with performers without knowing their language provided unexpected opportunities to hit the target on cue. Cultural differences often give away to mutually shared expressions of behaviour, the visual cues and calculated rhythms of rehearsals, and the sense and sensibility of creative exchange. Erhan Tuna told me that I was usually in the range of one or two lines when I commented on a scene between the actors. *The Visit* later was invited to the Istanbul International Theatre Festival, at a theatre on the Asian side of the Bospherous, playing to a large, appreciative audience.

Figure 24.5 Performance of *Wolf: A Transformation*, at Yildiz Palace, Istanbul, 1994.

The International Theatre Institute had invited Daystar to perform at the Yildiz Palace Theatre in Istanbul. After a brief lecture, Daystar elected to dance her signature work: *Wolf: A Transformation* (see Figure 24.5). Using masks, upbeat Native American music, and intricately realized transformational states of being, *Wolf* is a highly theatrical comment on the unity of original man with the living creatures of this world. I was then asked to comment on my work with Daystar. As a third-generation American, I said to the audience that it was a privilege and honour to introduce the work of a First American. When people applauded, I turned back towards the stage to see if Daystar had appeared – I was to cue the music for the dance presentation. Refik Erduran, the director of the International Theatre Institute, told me that the audience was applauding my introductory remarks. I was stunned. Apparently the Turkish audience has a special sensitivity to cultural values, and they recognized these values when they heard them. Daystar's performance of the *Wolf* dance had captured the audience's hearts. Immediately afterward, we were treated to a memorable round of sightseeing and food tasting throughout Istanbul. The occasion marked a full measure of cross-cultural hospitality and friendship!

Figure 24.6 Students at Denison University (Ohio) demonstrating an Intertribal Women's Shawl Dance, 2004.

DAYSTAR: It is true that artistic expression, and teaching abilities no less, need an expressive vehicle. Without the vehicle, the spirit of the idea doesn't move. Over the years I developed a kind of 'method' for teaching Native American dance (via the culturally encompassing Intertribal Dance forms) to non-Natives as well. This process came full circle in a semester residency at Denison University in Granville, Ohio. Although it is still a rarity for a university dance curriculum to offer a single course in 'World Dance,' it is even rarer that in one university, a bona fide major or minor in World Dance would be certified. Such is the case at Denison University Dance Department, where I taught Native American Dance in the fall of 2004. There was not one Native person in my classes. However, these aspiring Western, mainstream dancers 'took to' the repetitive, aerobic, and oftentimes technical aspects of Native American Dance. I teach these dances as they have become standardized in the unique step patterns, body postures, floor patterns, and regalia of the Intertribal Dance forms now practised in the contemporary Powwow circuit. But here any similarities to Western 'modern dance' end abruptly. No one dancing Intertribal can dance only for technique, or only for 'show,' or only for self. If it is anything at all, Intertribal Dance is the expression of the collective culture of the community, in its regalia, in its protocols and etiquettes, in its songs, and in the spirit present when one dances.

Yes, those 30 dance majors and minors and elective students did learn to dance Intertribal. But they learned much more. Beyond the steps and the regalia (cultural term for dance apparel), they learned traditional singing, the instances in which one would dance or not dance, and why and why not, and what one dances about. They also learned the specific tribal culture from which a dance originated, where that nation is located geographically, what its history is now and has been in the past, and what it expects as a future. The etiquettes of dancers and dancing in Native communities take a lifetime to learn. In one semester, the teacher, facilitator, choreographer can only provide an entry way to learning. In turn, the student, recipient, dancer, performer can open his or her eyes to a new culture with earned confidence and appropriate respect.

The Denison University students finished the year with a performance of Intertribal Women's Shawl Dances (see Figure 24.6), the Men's Grass Dance, the spectacular and intricate Hoop Dance, the community Round Dance, as well as contemporary choreography based on Native storytelling. I have reason to believe that the experience was one they will remember for a lifetime. They had made a beginning in the learning and respecting of cultures from the inside out, from the body to the mind, and finally to the spirit, with respect for the dance forms, but, more importantly, with respect for the people from whom the dances originated. In short, dance frequently teaches what words cannot.

NED: Performance has something to do with learning from experience and using what you've learned to grow into someone you have never been before. It is not 'make believe,' a magic formula, a systematic collection of effects, a superimposition of behaviour, or a rigid, previously grounded concept. It is a process done by this person, in this time and place, with these means, and, at the same time, revealing someone we recognize. The experience of the 'someone we recognize' reveals our common bonds of humanity, and is at the heart of cross-cultural exchanges. It can happen in surprising incidents and unadulterated experiences, in any form – and it does – for better or worse.

In a time when political leaders are sorely tested, populations around the world see the performing arts, for the most part, as a frill, or a way of getting away from it all. Those of us who still have some power over how people will respond to what we do, know better. And that's the way it should be: No Audience Left Behind. We are all in the same boat.

DAYSTAR: Creative work always tests us in much the same way that life tests us. In the studio, however, we have that miraculous environment in which changes can be made to tell the story truthfully, to 'set the story straight' with insight and grace. To all who are timid, I say, 'Take the plunge!' You might see yourself reflected as on a mirrored surface, but diving beneath that surface begins to reveal realms of experience that may well transform your life and the lives of those around you. The creative process of the art of dance and theatre can empower us as individuals and as communities. That empowerment could transform our world if only we would drink from its deep waters.

Contributors

Adam Barker completed the MA in the Indigenous Governance Program at the University of Victoria, BC, with a focus on political theory. He is currently a PhD candidate in the Department of Geography, University of Leicester (UK). His academic research and social organizing with respect to Indigenous-Settler relations is concerned with conflicts and collaborations between Indigenous philosophies and anarchist and libertarian theories and the emerging field of anarcha-indigenism.

Deborah Barndt is a popular educator, community artist, and teacher of environmental studies at York University, Toronto. Since the 1970s, she has collaborated with various Indigenous groups in Peru, Nicaragua, Mexico, and Toronto. She is the author of numerous books on popular education, globalization, women, food, and social change.

Rick Cober Bauman is program director of the Mennonite Central Committee Ontario in Kitchener. He was the staff member for the MCC Ontario Aboriginal Neighbours Program during the years of the Nawash fishing rights struggle.

Craig Benjamin is the campaigner for the Human Rights of Indigenous Peoples at Amnesty International Canada. He has represented Amnesty International at many international meetings concerning the adoption of the *UN Declaration on the Rights of Indigenous Peoples*.

Ned Bobkoff is a theatre director, playwright, and teacher who has worked with performers from all walks of life and has taught in a variety of educational institutions, including those serving international and Indigenous student populations, such as the Institute of American Indian Arts in Santa Fe, the American University in Bulgaria, and the National *Konservaturari* in Turkey.

Dorothy Christian is of the Secwepemc Syilx Nations of the interior of British Columbia. She is a graduate student at the School of Communications at Simon Fraser University, Vancouver. Her research interests include Indigenous peoples, Indigenous film aesthetics, Fourth World Cinema, critical theory, cultural theory, cultural institutions/cultural policy, and visual ethnography. Her activism is primarily in Native/non-Native relations and the environment.

Samuel R. Cook is an associate professor in Virginia Tech's Department of Sociology, where he serves as director of American Indian Studies.

Judy Da Silva is Anishinabe from the Anishinabe Nation and a mother to five children. Judy lives in the small community of Grassy Narrows, located in northwestern Ontario, and has been part of an ongoing protest to protect her homeland, called Asubpeeschoseewagong. Her continuing goal is to share her experiences with people and to form positive alliances with others who want to protect the earth.

Lynne Davis is associate professor in Indigenous Studies at Trent University, Peterborough, Ontario. Her research interests are in Aboriginal education, sustainable communities, international Indigenous peoples, and alliances between Indigenous and non-Indigenous peoples. She is the principal investigator of the Alliances Project.

Thierry Drapeau is a PhD student in social and political thought at York University, Toronto. His research interests are in transnational social movements, everyday forms of resistance, and the history of labour internationalism.

Kevin FitzMaurice is an assistant professor in Native Studies at the University of Sudbury, Ontario. Kevin's research and teaching is grounded in an interdisciplinary, critical analysis of power relations that is further informed by a 'postcolonial dialogue' between Indigenous knowledge and Western post-structural theory. Over the last 17 years his research has taken many forms, including community-based, participatory, historical/archival, purely theoretical, and sociological;

and, as far as he can tell, he continues to be a useful Ally to Indigenous people in Ontario.

Tanya Chung Tiam Fook is a PhD candidate and course director in the Faculty of Environmental Studies at York University, Toronto. Her research interests are in collaborative conservation partnerships, Indigenous knowledge and environmental practice, wildlife ecology, human-animal relationships, Amazonian environmental history, political ecology, and environmental education.

Victoria Freeman is the author of *Distant Relations: How My Ancestors Colonized North America,* and the founder of Turning Point: Native Peoples and Newcomers On-Line (www.turning-point.ca). She is currently a doctoral candidate in history at the University of Toronto, writing her dissertation on the historical memory of the Indigenous and colonial past of Toronto. She was a member of the Re/Envisioning Relationships Conference organizing committee.

Gkisedtanamoogk (Wampanoag/Nipmuck) is adjunct faculty in the Native American Studies Department at the University of Maine. His interests include Wampanoag Spirituality, Wampanoag/Indigenous Theory and Law, Socio-political Development and Reform, and Cross-Cultural Relationships.

Beenash Jafri is a PhD candidate in Women's Studies at York University. Her research interests include the politics of identity, coalition-building and Indigenous solidarity, anti-racism organizing, decolonization, and critical research methodologies.

Daystar/Rosalie Jones (Pembina Chippewa) founded her company, Daystar: Contemporary Dance-Drama of Indian America, in 1980, and has recently become recognized as a pioneer of 'native modern dance' in the United States. Currently, she is teaching and implementing a curriculum in Indigenous Performance Studies at Trent University.

Tom Keefer is a PhD candidate in the Political Science Department of York University and an editor of the anti-capitalist journal *Upping the Anti*. He can be reached at tkeefer@yorku.ca.

Marie Léger has been working with Indigenous peoples, especially Indigenous women, for more than 15 years. She is the coordinator for the thematic work on the Rights of Indigenous Peoples at the Montreal-based International Centre for Human Rights and Democratic Development (Rights and Democracy). She holds a PhD in Sociology.

Lily Pol Neveu worked from 2003 to 2005 at Fort-Témiscamingue/Obadjiwan as an interpreter, which initiated her interest in Native issues. Holding a BA in Political Science from McGill University, Montreal, she recently completed a master's degree in political philosophy at Université Laval, Quebec City, where she worked on the issues of multiculturalism, Aboriginal studies, and the protection of the environment.

Jennifer Preston is the program coodinator of Aboriginal Affairs for the Canadian Friends Service Committee (Quakers). Her work in recent years has mainly focused on international Indigenous rights, and specifically on the *UN Declaration on the Rights of Indigenous Peoples*.

Laura Reinsborough holds a graduate degree in community arts and environmental education from the Faculty of Environmental Studies at York University. She works as a community arts facilitator for such cultural institutions as the Art Gallery of York University and the Art Gallery of Ontario.

Justin B. Richland is associate professor and vice chair of the Department of Criminology, Law and Society at the University of California, Irvine. His book, *Arguing with Tradition: The Language of Law in Hopi Tribal Court*, was published in 2008 by the University of Chicago Press.

Patricia Sekaquaptewa (Hopi) is executive director of the Nakwatsvewat Institute, a non-profit organization committed to furthering governance, justice, and education projects in Indian Country. She also currently serves as a justice pro tempore with the Hopi, Hualapai, and Little Traverse Bay Band tribal courts, and is a trained mediator. For the past six years, she served as director of the Native Nations Law and Policy Center and its Tribal Legal Development Clinic at the University of California, Los Angeles, and is currently a full-time lecturer in law at UCLA.

Paula Sherman is a Family Head on the Ka-Pishkawandemin Family Head Council of the Ardoch Algonquin First Nation. She is a faculty member in the Department of Indigenous Studies and is program director of the Indigenous Studies PhD program at Trent University. Her research interests include Indigenous histories and relationships.

Leanne Simpson is a leading Indigenous researcher, writer, educator, and activist. She is a citizen of the Nishnaabeg Nation, with roots in the Mississaugas of Alderville First Nation, and is the editor of *Lighting the Eighth Fire: The Liberation, Resurgence and Protection of Indigenous Nations*, (2008) and co-editor (with Kiera hadner) of *This Is An Honour Song* (2010), published by Arbeiter Ring Publishing.

Heather Yanique Shpuniarsky is completing her PhD in the Indigenous Studies program at Trent University. Her dissertation work focuses on the contemporary relationship between the Anishnaabeg and the Haudenosaunee. She worked with Lynne Davis as senior research associate on the Alliances Project between 2004 and 2006.

Merran Smith has been a key environmental leader in the campaign to protect Canada's Great Bear Rainforest, which culminated in agreements to protect five million acres of rainforest from logging, and commits to new sustainable logging practices in the region. Merran played a key role in uniting a divergent coalition – First Nations, logging companies, corporations, government, and environmentalists – and in raising $120 million for First Nations economic development. Merran is at the vanguard of a new environmentalism that actively promotes economic innovation and diversification as an integral component of environmental sustainability. She is now working on climate solutions.

Art Sterritt is from the Gitga'at First Nation and is executive director of the Coastal First Nations, an alliance of First Nations on British Columbia's North and Central Coast working to achieve economic and ecological sustainability. He has been involved in the areas of Aboriginal rights and title, self-government, and community economic development for more than 30 years. He is also an internationally known carver.

Marilyn Struthers has worked with civil society organizations and First Nations for more than 35 years, as an organizer, trainer, researcher, and, most recently, as a funder with a public foundation. She lives on the shores of Georgian Bay, Ontario.

Jake Swamp, a Mohawk Elder from Akwesasne and former sub-chief of the Wolf Clan of the Haudenosaunee (Iroquois) Confederacy, has a long history of active civil engagement. He has been a key figure in raising awareness of peace and environmental and cultural integrity, locally and around the world. He is the founder of the Tree of Peace Society.

Caitlyn Vernon is a Coastal Programs campaigner with Sierra Club BC, working in partnership with First Nations to support the implementation and monitoring of ecosystem-based management under the Great Bear Rainforest agreements. She holds a Master's in Environmental Studies from York University, where her research focused on the political ecology of natural resource management.

Rick Wallace holds a PhD in Conflict Resolution from the University of Bradford (UK), and is a community activist, mediator, and former international humanitarian worker. He is currently researching on issues of large-scale conflict, social change, and grassroots organizing in the context of relations of power and practices pertaining to Indigenous peoples and non-Indigenous peoples in Canada.

Karenne Wood (Monacan) directs the Virginia Indian Heritage Program at the Virginia Foundation for the Humanities in Charlottesville and is a doctoral candidate in anthropology at the University of Virginia. She works with Virginia tribal communities to educate the public about Indigenous history and cultures around the state.

William Woodworth *Raweno:kwas* is a member of the Six Nations of the Grand River community, the Mohawk Nation. He was a student of the great Iroqouian traditionalist, the late Jacob Ezra Thomas, from whom he received profound inspiration. He has a doctorate in Traditional Knowledge from the California Institute of Integral Studies, San Francisco. An architect by training and practice, he is executive director of the Beacon to the Ancestors Foundation in Toronto.

Index

Aboriginal appointments to Supreme Court, 262, 264

Aboriginal cultural traditions, 28, 60, 224, 249, 385; reclamation, 224

Aboriginal fishing rights, 49, 94, 368–9, 374; Bruce Peninsula, 91–108; opposition to, 49–50, 91, 96

Aboriginal middle class and intellectual elite, 3, 245, 361, 363

Aboriginal people. *See* Indigenous peoples

Aboriginal rights and title, 87,115, 217, 283 (*see also* Indigenous rights); BC First Nations assertion of, 281; denial of, 378; Great Bear, 138, 142; Omamawínini people, 115, 123

Aboriginal Rights Coalition Atlantic (ARCA), 48, 50–1

Aboriginal science, 372. *See also* Indigenous knowledge

Aboriginal traditional knowledge. *See* Indigenous knowledge

Aboriginal women. *See* women

academic contexts, 92, 94 (*see also* American Indian Studies (AIS); Indigenous Studies programs); colonial relationships in research, 171; decolonizing, 161–2, 166–7; Indigenous intellectuals and academics, 3, 245, 361, 363; privileging written texts over embodied ways of knowing, 169; Western academic culture, 245; white professors teaching Native Studies, 351, 355–6, 361, 363

African Canadian Coalition Against Racism, 260

Africville, 269

Alfred, Taiaiake, 3, 318–19, 322, 324; *Wasáse*, 317

Alliances Project, 4, 212, 335–47, 351

American Indian Studies (AIS), 46, 196–7 (*see also* Indigenous Studies programs; Native Studies); collaboration with Indigenous peoples, 196, 200; criticized as over-politicized, 203; financial challenges, 201–2; Indigenous knowledge in, 196–7, 201, 206; prioritizing tribal nation-building, 205; responsibility to Indigenous constituency, 197, 204–5; at Virginia Tech (*see* Virginia Tech)

respect, 143–4, 239, 329, 337–8, 341, 346, 359; global, 18; from Haudenosaunee perspective, 328

responsibility, 13–14, 20, 239, 285, 290; environmental, 310; personal, 316–17; pick up our responsibilities, 9

Royal Canadian Mounted Police (RCMP), 50, 217

Royal Commission on Aboriginal Peoples (RCAP), 3, 242–3, 267

Royal Proclamation, 362

Sachem (male representative of Clan), 45

sacred fire, 34, 76

Saugeen, 91; First Nation fishers, 93, 96, 368–9. *See also* 'Fishing Wars'

science: Aboriginal science, 372; experts, 344; independent science to inform decision-making, 137

'scorched earth' policies, 269

Secwepemc Watershed Committee (SWC), 216–17; armed standoff at Gustafsen Lake, 377; resistance against Sun Peaks Resort, 211, 213–28; transnationalism, 214, 224–6; trespassers on own land, 223; weakened by court injunctions, 219, 227

self-determination, 5, 44, 60–1, 184, 193, 237, 241–2, 336, 346; erosion of national unity, 239; ethical responsibility to support, 2

self-government, 237, 362

self-sufficiency, 70, 95

Settler people, 268, 317; benefiting from colonialism, 276, 290, 319, 323, 384; challenges to decolonize, 212, 316–17, 326; complicit in perpetuating colonial injustices, 288, 319; denial of colonial history, 94, 378; need to stop oppressing, 276; normalization of colonialism, 320; privilege, 261; power to choose level of colonial involvement, 317; refusal to question benefits, 319; 'unsettling the Settler within,' 323

'Seven Generations,' 24, 47

Shabot Obaadjiwan, 120–1, 124 (*see also* uranium exploration); deal with province and Frontenac Ventures, 127; participation in land claims process, 119

shapeshifters, 297; 'shapeshifting' colonial power, 325

Sharbot Lake, 55; protest marches, 120

Silver Covenant Chain agreements, 29, 36. *See also* treaties

Simpson, Leanne, 3, 172, 409

sistematicación, 173–4

Six Nations of the Grand River Territory, 26–7, 38, 87; Haldimand Proclamation, 77

Six Nations reclamation of Douglas Creek Estates, 78–80. *See also* Caledonia

Skwelkwek'welt Protection Centre (SPC), 214, 217, 226

Smith, Andrea, 265, 270

Smith, Graham Hingangaroa, 301

Smith, Linda Tuhiwai, 165, 167

Smoke, Dan, 6

social justice, 159, 212, 277–9, 281; groups, 4; issues, 92

social movements, 221; popular education and, 164; relationships with First Nations, 2, 4

Social Science and Humanities Research Council (SSHRC): limited